435

STORY OF AMERICAN PROTESTANTISM

" Blot out Britain and America from the map of the world, and you destroy all those great institutions which almost exclusively promise the world's renovation: but unite Britain and America in energetic and resolved co-operation for the world's salvation; and the world is saved."

Narrative of a Visit to the American Churches, by DR. ANDREW REED and DR. JAMES MATHESON, delegates from the Congregational Union of England and Wales (1836).

STORY OF AMERICAN PROTESTANTISM

BY

ANDREW LANDALE DRUMMOND

B.D., Ph.D. (Edin.); S.T.M. (Hartford Theol. Seminary, U.S.A.)

OLIVER AND BOYD

EDINBURGH: TWEEDDALE COURT
LONDON: 98 GREAT RUSSELL STREET, W.C.

1951

FIRST PUBLISHED 1949
REPRINTED 1951

PRINTED IN GREAT BRITAIN BY
ROBERT CUNNINGHAM AND SONS LTD., ALVA
FOR OLIVER AND BOYD LTD., EDINBURGH

DEDICATED TO AMERICAN FRIENDS
Representing Various Communions in the Church of Christ

WARREN S. ARCHIBALD, A.M. (Harvard), D.D., Second Parish in Hartford (Congregational, 1670)

KENNETH BECKWITH, B.D., and BETTY BECKWITH, Amherst, Mass. (Congregationalist)

W. RUSSEL BOWIE, D.D., Professor at Union Theological Seminary, New York; former Rector of Grace Church (Protestant Episcopal)

ROBERT W. BURNS, D.D., Peachtree Church, Atlanta, Georgia (Disciples of Christ)

ALFORD CARLETON, B.D., Principal of Aleppo College, Syria (Missionary of the "American Board ")

RUSSELL CLINCHY, L.H.D., First Parish in Hartford, Conn. (Congregational, 1635)

WILLIAM M. CRANE, PH.D. (Harvard), Richmond, Mass., Minister-at-large for Berkshire County, under whom I served as Home Missionary at Otis and New Boston (1929)

ELLIS H. DANA, B.R.E., Executive Vice-President, State of Wisconsin Council of Churches

HAROLD S. DAVIS, LL.B. (Harvard), Counsellor-at-law; Clerk (1920-1947) of the Old South Church, Boston (Congregationalist)

THOMAS P. HAIG, D.D., Somerville, New Jersey; ex-President of the General Council, Reformed Church in America (Dutch)

JOSEPH F. KING, PH.D. (Edin.), Oberlin, Ohio (Presbyterian)

FRED E. LUCHS, B.D. (German Reformed), Athens, Ohio

FRANCES LUIBRAND, M.A., Principal, The Dolsen School, Bay City, Mich. (Congregationalist)

ROBERT J. McCRACKEN, D.D., Riverside Church, New York (Baptist)

J. ROBERTSON PAUL, M.A. (Oxon.), Rhodes Scholar, my cousin; Session Clerk, First (Scots) Presbyterian Church, Charleston, S. Carolina

WALDEN PELL II, M.A. (Oxon), Rhodes Scholar, Headmaster, St. Andrew's School, Middletown, Delaware (Protestant Episcopal)

ROCKWELL H. POTTER, D.D., Dean-Emeritus, Hartford Theological Seminary (Congregational)

MRS. PLATO E. SHAW, New York (Methodist), whose late husband will be remembered as the author of *The Catholic Apostolic Church* (New York, 1946)

MR. AND MRS. WILL VAWTER, II, Benton Harbor, Michigan (Methodist)

ALMEDA C. VICKERY, B.D., S.T.M., Member of the Society of Mayflower Descendants, Minister of Religious Education at the Community Church, Glenbrook, Conn.

PREFACE

THE present book is an attempt to explain American Protestantism[1] in the light of its past. America is popularly supposed to be a breeding-ground for freak cults. Yet the weirder varieties of religious experience, apart from Mormonism and Christian Science, were mostly imported from Europe. "What are these in this great nation?" asked Henry Ward Beecher nearly a century ago. "They are little sections that step out of the line of the nation's march, live a little and die." Of the 256 denominations listed by the census, 200 compass only 3% of the total Church membership (2,000,000 out of 72,000,000). It is estimated that 90% of American Christians belong to seven big denominational families. The Roman Catholic communion is the largest, embracing about one-third of the total. According to numerical strength the Protestant Churches rank as follows. The Baptists, closely followed by the Methodists, easily lead. Then follow the Lutherans, Presbyterians and "Disciples". Last, but not least, come the Episcopalians and Congregationalists. It should be noted that the Oriental Churches as well as Protestant bodies are responsible for producing sub-divisions. The Orthodox are separated into racial Churches—Albanian, Bulgarian, Greek, Rumanian, Armenian; and there are "heretical" groups like the Assyrian Jacobites and Egyptian Copts. Dissentients from Rome are also to be found, such as the Polish National Church and the Old Catholic Church in America (Lithuanian and Polish).

The process of transplantation involves modification. It was the experience of European Churches to "suffer a sea-change into something rich and strange". Englishmen brought Anglicanism to Virginia and Puritanism to New England, just as Dutchmen brought the Reformed Church to New Amsterdam (New York) and Germans brought Lutheranism and Pietism to

[1] I use "Protestantism" as the most convenient term to cover Christian Churches that are neither Roman nor Greek (the Anglican Communion in the U.S. is "The Protestant Episcopal Church").

vi

Pennsylvania. Old names were retained, connotation was modified. This must be borne in mind by European explorers of the
American religious scene. They must be prepared for subtle, yet
real, differences produced in a new world with a different climate
(physical, mental, spiritual and ethical). The Anglican must not
expect to find the exact equivalent of the English Parish Church
in the United States. Erastian pride must not blind him to the
fact that his communion in the United States has no special
privilege, but is merely the most influential of the smaller denominations (the Anglo-Catholic will be mortified to find that it
is actually entitled " Protestant Episcopal "). The Methodist will
be surprised to find that his denomination has Bishops who wield
considerable authority even though they lack prelatic pomp and
circumstance. The Baptist has to adjust his perspective. In
England his " chapel " is a semi-private conventicle planted in
an environment that is often unfriendly to Dissent: in America
the same ultra-Protestant individualism flourishes, but the Baptist
Church in many States is the Church of the masses, and its
pronouncements and *mores* have a widespread influence on community life. The English Unitarian, reared in radicalism, will
discover that Boston, Mecca of American Unitarianism, is incorrigibly conservative. The Scotsman will not criticise American
Presbyterianism for want of Assembly pageantry, when he under-
stands that the *Ecclesia Scotica* is only one root of this, the largest
Presbyterian Church in the world. The Irish Presbyterian will
have to accustom himself to sights unfamiliar in Belfast—crosses
and chancels, robed choirs and processionals, read prayers and
responses. The Lutheran, accustomed to the State Church atmosphere of Scandinavia, will find his own liturgical tradition, but
will miss his Bishops, and may discover that his communion in
the United States is practically Presbyterian. The German
Lutheran, accustomed to a " go as you please " individualism in
theology, will find that his Church in America glories in creed-
bound Confessionalism. The English Congregationalist, for centuries the victim of social and ecclesiastical pressure, goes to New
England and encounters not only a more liberal theology but an
unsectarian *ethos*.

Dean Sperry of Harvard, in his discerning *Religion in America*,
notes as a fundamental characteristic the absence of an Established
Church. This was not so historically. Till the American Revolu-

tion, Anglicanism was established in the South, and the Dutch Church retained its privileges in New York. In New England the Congregationalists, thanks to their undeviating support of American Independence, retained state recognition till the early nineteenth century. The various colonies tended to be isolationist owing to government, religion and distance, till the middle of the eighteenth century. This "particularism" was largely surmounted by the Great Awakening, when Whitefield arrived from England. His Evangelical message fused a large section of American Protestants; and revivalism became the dominant pattern till Sankey and Moody, over a century later, repaid Whitefield's debt by their memorable mission to Great Britain.

Our historical quest will involve a basic study of the frontier which made Protestantism more "typically American" than when its early settlements hugged the Atlantic seaboard. What was the prevailing attitude to the Red Indian, the negro and the immigrant? How did the Foreign Mission movement arise in view of the clamant demands of Home Missions? In contrast to the individualism of the frontier were the growing social problems raised by industrialism in the East after the Civil War. The "Social Gospel" was interdenominational—like many other movements of the last half-century that gradually modified earlier attitudes to theology, preaching, liturgy, literature and art.

The "melting-pot" functions in things sacred as well as secular. The older attitude that the immigrant's only cultural objective was to assimilate the American way of life, has been revised. American Protestantism is no mere Anglo-Saxon product; it owes much to the Lutherans of Scandinavia and Germany, to the Dutch, Hungarian and German Reformed, and to Pietist communities from the Continent. It would appear that the influence of the major Continental Churches will eventually correct the inherited American tendency to individualism and stimulate a deeper recognition of the necessity of sound theology.

Among secular influences, the American climate has operated keenly in favour of what the Continental thinkers disparage as "American activism". André Siegfried said in 1927: "At times it seems as if the object of religion were no longer to kindle mysticism in the soul and spirit, but to enlist them and organise their energies. In this it is the most powerful lever for production that the world has ever known" (*America Comes of Age*). If

American thought in certain phases appears to us somewhat
superficial, we need to remember that the United States is still
a young nation; maturity will certainly come, it cannot be forced.
We in Great Britain have much to learn from our American
cousins in initiative, organisation and resourcefulness on the
Church's part, which are more needed than ever if apathy is to
be arrested and materialism routed. Now that the United States
is rapidly assuming world leadership, it is reassuring to know that
we have to deal with a country where the Christian tradition is
so strong and practical.[1] Apart from Marshall Aid, how many
British homes have benefited in recent years by food and clothing
parcels sent by Christian congregations all over the Union ? It is
important surely that British readers should come to a better
understanding of the place that Protestantism plays in American
life. History is one of the gateways to appreciation. To-day we
realise the importance of America in contemporary world affairs,
with an uncertain future in view. We may surely give a Christian
interpretation to Canning's famous dictum, voiced in 1826:

> I called the New World into existence
> to redress the balance of the Old.

A. L. DRUMMOND

Eadie Manse,
 Alva, Scotland,
  Reformation Day, 1948

---

[1] The U.S. is the largest Protestant nation in the world (44,000,000 members); it has the largest R.C. population (23,000,000 adherents); and it leads
in the number of practising Jews (4,600,000).

ACKNOWLEDGMENTS

I SHOULD like to record my indebtedness to Mr. W. R. Aitken, M.A., F.L.A., County Librarian, Clackmannanshire, for reading the proofs; and to Mr. G. F. Cunningham, B.A., Alva, for advice technical and literary. This book could not have been written without the indefatigable exertions of public librarians, ranging from Dunfermline to London, and from London to Aberystwith. I am indebted further to the Henderson Library (E.I.S.) and the Scottish National Library, Edinburgh, also to the Library of Congress, Washington.

I have to thank a multitude of friends for encouraging me to write this book. Most of them are in America, but I cannot forget Mr. W. Furness, Vice-master of Rossall School, who first interested me in American History. I gratefully recall the " Seminars " of Professor E. E. S. Johnson, at Hartford Theological Seminary in 1929. Memory enshrines many an enlightening discussion with American friends who include Dr. J. W. Buckham, of the Pacific School of Religion, Berkeley, Cal.; ex-President Palmer, of Chicago Theological Seminary; Miss Judith Welles, Ph.D., Wellesley College; and Dr. G. G. Atkins, whose interpretation of religion, literature and life has kindled my imagination ever since we first met in Palestine in 1926. To these I add the names of men who have contributed to Scottish-American understanding: President-Emeritus H. S. Coffin, of " Union "; Professor John Baillie; Rev. Howard Hageman, Newark, N.J.; Dr. Hutchison Cockburn; Rev. Erskine Blackburn, Aberdeen.

I desire to thank Dr. M. Spinka, Secretary of the American Church History Society, for bibliographical suggestions; also, the many writers whose works have been cited; may their readers increase! I would mention in particular Dr. Sweet, veteran in the vanguard of research; Professors Perry Miller and S. E. Morison, Harvard; Dr. W. E. Garrison, Chicago; Mr. Van Wyck Brooks, New York; Professor Latourette, of Yale; Dean Sperry of Harvard; and Dr. Lynn Hough.

A. L. D.

CONTENTS

Book I. COLONIAL GENESIS

Book II. UNIFICATION

Book III. SECTIONALISM

Book IV. THE FRONTIER AND THE FAITH

CONTENTS

BOOK I

COLONIAL GENESIS

CHAPTER I

THE SOUTHERN COLONIES

1. VIRGINIA

" The tobacco plant unfolding its broad leaves in the moist air and hot sun . . . gave a direction to economy that was big with fate."—BEARD

QUEEN ELIZABETH named Virginia in honour of herself. . . Misfortune overtook Raleigh's expedition, on Roanoke Island, but not before the first Indian convert (Manateo) and the first child born of English parents in America (Virginia Dare) were baptised, 13th and 20th August 1587.[1]

The first permanent British colony on the mainland of North America was founded on 13th May 1607, when 105 settlers landed at Jamestown (named after James I). A week later Chaplain Hunt administered the Lord's Supper beneath the shelter of a sail, the worshippers sitting on logs, a bar of wood nailed to two trees serving as pulpit. " This was our church till we built a homely thing like a barn." The Rev. Robert Hunt, who had been appointed after consultation with Archbishop Bancroft, was " a clergyman of persevering fortitude and modest worth ". He did not survive, however, for more than two years; his log-chapel and library were burnt, and he himself perished by pestilence or famine. Had he been spared, he would soon have worn himself out, trying to propagate the Christian religion (as the Charter of Virginia required) " to such people as yet live in darkness and miserable ignorance of the true knowledge of God ".

It looked as if the Virginian venture was to prove abortive like other Jacobean projects overseas. Captain John Smith was a seasoned navigator, but the Company that financed his colony knew nothing of America; they dreamed of quick profits and

[1] The first Church of England service on the Pacific coast was held in 1579 on the site of San Francisco for the crew of Drake's *Golden Hinde*. A stone cross in Golden Gate Park commemorates the event.

3

fabulous gold; indeed they threatened to treat the settlers as
" banished men " after the first year, unless they sent home
cargoes worth £2,000. Captain Smith warned the Company:
" Nothing is to be expected thence but by labour ". They had
sent him forty-eight gentlemen and only four carpenters: " I
entreat you send rather thirty husbandmen, gardeners, fishermen,
blacksmiths, masons, and diggers up of trees' roots."

The Company in London provided themselves with a new
Charter in 1609. There was a goodly roll of stock-holders, including merchants, clergy and peers. Lord De La Warr (Delaware)
was appointed Governor and the Chaplain was Master Richard
Bucke, recommended by the Bishop of London as " an able and
painful preacher ". Virginia received much publicity in English
pulpits. The Rev. William Crawshaw, preaching in the Temple
Church, made some telling points in connexion with the initial
promotion of right relations with the natives:

" If the planting of an English Church, if the conversion of the
Heathen, and the enlarging of the Kingdome of Jesus Christ, be not
inducement to bring them into this business, it is a pity they be in it
at all. . . Let us therefore cast aside all cogitations of profit, let us look
at better things. If we seeke first the Kingdome of God, all other things
shall be added unto us."

One wonders what investors thought of these exhortations.
Quick returns on their capital and Christian stewardship hardly
went together. Few of the intending settlers were qualified to
make Virginia " a colony of heaven " (*Phil.* 3.20, Moffatt's tr.).
They might " fall on their knees " on landing; later they would
probably " fall on the aborigines ". Captain Smith recognised
many of the types represented by a second batch of immigrants
who arrived in nine ships: " poor gentlemen, tradesmen, serving-
men, libertines and such like . . . men fitter to breed a riot rather
than found a colony."

By May 1610 only sixty colonists survived out of five hundred.
Dispirited and starving, they decided to abandon the settlement.
Before the retreating vessels left the James River, they were met
by the new Governor, Lord Delaware, and ordered to return.
The emaciated remnant fell on their knees before him and in
desperation prayed aloud. Reluctantly they returned to their abandoned huts. It was cold comfort that the Governor marched to
Church every Lord's Day, accompanied by red-cloaked halbar-
diers, " Counsell, Captaines, each in his place ".

Better times came in 1611 with the appointment of Sir Thomas Dale as " High Marshal of Virginia " and the Rev. Alexander Whitaker as "Apostle to Virginia ". Dale, by dint of " lawes divine, morall and martiall ", dealt firmly with the disorderly element that threatened " to be poyson " to the infant colony. Penalties were imposed for blasphemy, heresy and non-churchgoing, ranging from fines and whipping to the galleys and death. This code proved too draconian to be practical, and was repealed in 1619. The Virginia Company was largely Puritan, so its pamphlet claiming religion as " cheefe purpose of ye plantation " had a basis of reality as well as rhetoric. Sir Edwin Sandys, the treasurer, son of the Archbishop of York, was a believer in religious liberty; he was the " very loving friend " of Robinson, the Pilgrims' Pastor, and of so pronounced an Independent as William Brewster of Scrooby, also a member of the Company. Chaplain Whitaker was the son of the Regius Professor of Divinity in Cambridge, then a seed-plot of Puritanism. He left a north of England living to become the first country parson in Virginia. He sailed seventy miles up the James River; at a distant (and dangerous) spot he built a " faire framed house " and farmed his 100-acre glebe. The settlement of Henrico, where he ministered, had its suburb of Hope-in-Faith, defended by Fort Charity and Fort Patience. This Puritan nomenclature, so suggestive of the *Pilgrim's Progress*, was no mere formality. In 1613 there appeared in London a pamphlet entitled *Good Newes from Virginia* . . . from Alexander Whitaker, Minister in Henrico. This report to the Company was a sermon on the text, " Cast thy bread upon the waters ". Young men were " fittest for this country, and we have no need either of ceremonies or bad livers ". Writing later to a friend in London, he wondered why so few English ministers, " so hot against the Surplis and subscription, come hither where neither are spoken of ".

One of Whitaker's pleas was for Christians " to venture their persons hither, and . . . helpe these poore Indians ". Before his untimely death by drowning in the James River (1617), he was responsible for the conversion of Pocahontas, the Indian princess. The romantic story is well known and hardly needs re-telling. Pocahontas rescued Captain Smith from death, which resulted in a treaty between the English and her father, Powhatan. After Smith's departure the Indians became hostile again. Pocahontas was taken by High Marshal Dale as a hostage to his plantation;

B

there she was instructed in the Christian faith by Whitaker and baptised as Rebecca. She married John Rolfe (a pioneer in tobacco-export), who took her to England. There she met Captain Smith again and was received at Court; she died at Gravesend before returning with her husband to Virginia (1617). Her visit aroused considerable interest in the Indians. King James wrote to the Archbishops asking their assistance in raising funds for building schools and churches " for ye education of ye children of those Barbarians wch cannot but be to them [the colonists] a very great charge ". Dr. John King, Bishop of London, showed much interest in this fund. He was elected a member of the Council for Virginia. The spiritual jurisdiction of the Bishop of London over the Anglican Church in America seems to date back to this incident, though the question of authority is somewhat obscure.[1]

After the death of Lord Delaware (1619) an era of promise opened for Virginia. Sir Edwin Sandys, now the leading spirit in the Company was a moderate Puritan and a man of liberal views. This, of course, did not commend him to James I, who cried: " Choose the devil, if you will, but not Sir Edwin Sandys! " Largely through his advocacy active measures were taken to make the miserable settlement more attractive to intending colonists.

An elected House of Burgesses was instituted, consisting of two delegates from each plantation. " Young single women of blameless reputation " were to be dispatched to Virginia. Plans were made for increasing the number of tenants and for experimenting in the production of glass, silk and wines. The clergy were to be adequately paid in tobacco and corn. The Puritan complexion of the Company was revealed by laws to put down gaming and drunkenness, to restrict excess in apparel, and to enforce the observance of the Sabbath. These new ordinances attracted settlers from various motives, for in 1621 twenty vessels arrived with newcomers. The Company held a celebration service on 18th April 1622, and the sermon was afterwards printed—*Virginia's God be thanked.*

Little did the hearers of that sermon in London realise that just a month earlier, the Indians, no longer held in check by

---

[1] Failure to appoint Bishops during the Colonial era crippled Anglicanism in America. Confirmation could not be administered. Candidates for Orders had to cross the Atlantic; ordination was an expensive item. Archbishop Secker admitted that this was " without parallel in the Christian world " (see below, p. 137 f).

Powhatan, had massacred 347 whites on the Upper James River. The effects of this massacre were unfortunate for the natives; it drove a wedge between the races. The personal opinion of a Virginian chaplain seemed justified by events: " Till their Priests and Antients have their throats cut there is no hope to bring them to conversion." Attempts to educate, evangelise and uplift the Indians were abandoned for many years.

A worse blow fell on Virginia in 1624. The Company was dissolved and supreme control vested in the King. The alleged reason for this arbitrary decree was the failure of the Company to propagate the Christian faith and expand trade. The real reason was the refusal of the Company to appoint the King's creatures to key-posts, and thus further his desire to please their old enemy, Spain. A different type of Governor was sent to Virginia, ready to check both representative government and the moderate Puritanism of the colony. In 1641 Sir William Berkeley was " the man whom the king delighted to honour ". Appointed Governor by Charles I, he insisted on all settlers conforming to the Church of England. He was " a courtier very malignant towards the way of the New England Churches ". He expelled a Puritan deputation sent from Boston, not evidently strong in personnel, consisting of " those who might most likely be spared ". After many perils the New England reformers escaped from Virginia with their lives and one convert, Daniel Gookins:

> By Tompson's pains,[1]
> Christ and New England a dear Gookins gains.

Governor Berkeley offered a refuge to Prince Charles and his followers during the Civil War—the beginning of the legend fostered by romantic novelists that Virginians were all " loyal Cavaliers ", led by aristocratic " first families ". The appearance of a Parliamentary fleet in 1652 led to the collapse of Berkeley's régime and his retirement to his plantation. He returned to office at the Restoration, eager to demonstrate his filial fidelity to the text, " Kings shall be thy nursing fathers ". As the represen-

---

[1] Cotton Mather eulogised Tompson of Braintree, the leader, shipwrecked in Hell-gate:

> Upon a ledge of craggy rocks near stav'd
> His Bible in his bosom thrusting sav'd;
> The Bible, the best of cordial of his heart,
> " Come floods, come flames," cry'd he,
> " We'll never part."

tative of Charles II, he proved an adept in dictatorship. In 1671 he issued a glowing report on the prosperity of the province, concluding with the following remarks on the clergy of the 48 parishes: " But of all other commodities, so of this, the worst are sent us. But I thank God we have no free schools nor printing, and I hope we shall not have, these hundred years. For learning has brought disobedience and heresy into the world; and printing divulged them and libels against the government. God keep us from both."

The Virginia legislature was supposed to regulate Church affairs in general, while prominent laymen exercised local control. These Vestries, elective in origin, became self-perpetuating oligarchies after 1661. Sometimes they used their power to good purpose in refusing to accept the worst of the Governor's clerical nominees, but as a rule they reflected the selfish interests of the well-to-do. Dr. Truslow Adams has pointed out that in Virginian Anglicanism there was " a strong though unacknowledged undercurrent of Independency ". In 1681 the Rev. Morgan Godwyn wrote: " The Ministers are most miserably handled by these Plebeian Juntas, the vestries." The " hiring " and admission of clergymen was in their hands. In order to save money, they would often employ a lay-reader from year to year instead of inducting a rector officially for life. They were supposed to pay a uniform stipend of 16,000 lbs. of tobacco (1661) but prices varied as well as the soil from parish to parish. A succession of incompetent, dissolute parsons was imported to minister to a secularised Establishment (the communicants numbering only five per cent of the population).

At the close of the seventeenth century a pamphlet appeared with the title *Virginia's Cure*. The author had lived in the colony for many years, whither he had fled as a Loyalist during the Commonwealth. His cure for apathy and disorganisation was simple: " Send a Bishop out!"[1]

The Church of England sent out a " Commissary " who achieved much more than a Bishop could probably have accomplished, so far as one man could supervise lax clerics isolated by forest and river in far-ranging parishes (some of them 100 to 150 miles long). This Commissary was the Rev. James Blair, a Scotsman. At last a Bishop of London was prepared to implement the promise

---

[1] Dean Swift wrote to Governor Hunter in 1709: " All my hopes now terminate in being made Bishop of Virginia " (Campbell, *Hist. of Va.*, p. 377).

of his predecessor to take an active interest in the spiritual welfare of Virginia.

James Blair (1656-1743) was a graduate of Edinburgh, who became minister of Cranston under the Second Episcopacy. He might easily have continued all his days to divide the Word " with diligence, care and gravity " in that quiet Midlothian parish but for the tyrannical methods of Restoration prelacy. He was too independent to take the Test oath in 1681, but not independent enough to become a Covenanter. He resigned his living and went South. Influential friends procured him an introduction to the Bishop of London. Henry Compton (afterwards one of the " Seven Bishops in the Tower " who defied James II) saw in him just the kind of zealous missionary he wanted for such an " unimaginably discouraging " plantation as Virginia. Blair accepted the call and sailed in 1685, becoming minister of the most important charges in succession—Henrico, Jamestown and Williamsburg. His preaching was " plain, strong and especially practical for that time ". He was obviously marked out for promotion. Bishop Compton's belief in his protégé was borne out by his ability and zeal. He therefore appointed him his Commissary after he had only ministered four years in the colony. That meant that he was head of the Virginian Church, though he could neither confirm nor ordain.

The task of imposing discipline on a demoralised clergy was thankless. Yet the " Scots hireling ", like many of his countrymen, was firm, resolute and vigilant; even his enemies respected him— they had to, or else take the consequences. He suspended unsatisfactory clergy only as a last resort. He increased the number of ministers from 22 in 1696 to 40 in 1707, and by the time of his death in 1743 there were only two vacancies. He was convinced that the only means of ensuring a learned and pious ministry for the colony was to train Virginians in a college of their own.

In connexion with this proposal the legislature sent Blair to London in 1691 to obtain a Charter and funds. He interested the Archbishop of Canterbury and obtained royal approval for his new college, which was to be named " William and Mary " in compliment to the joint sovereigns. He did not, however, find the Attorney-general sympathetic when he presented the official order for the issue of a Charter. Seymour raised objections. " Virginians have souls as well as Englishmen," replied Blair.

" Souls, damn your souls!" retorted the Attorney-general, " Make
Tobacco!"   In spite of this setback the good Commissary eventually returned with a Charter, as " President ".   The design of
the new college was entrusted to Wren and cost £3,089; it was
completed in 1693 and rebuilt after a fire in 1705. A mere grammar
school in its beginnings, the College of William and Mary was
functioning effectively by 1729, with a faculty of six professors
who were graduates of English and Scots universities; Indians
were admitted and at one time there were as many as 70 in residence. For two centuries this seat of learning has set its mark
on Virginia; no less than three Presidents of the United States
were among her alumni. The British visitor will find it worth
while to visit Williamsburg, the college town. He will be able to
make his own conclusions anent the founder's claim that the new
academy was " not altogether unlike Chelsea Hospital ". He will
be intrigued to find that the entire town, colonial capital of Virginia since 1699, has been restored to its original aspect. Indeed,
it has been so meticulously restored that if James Blair were to
return he would feel quite at home in antique taverns, barber's
shops stocked with wigs (all modern improvements surreptitiously
in the background). He would find Bruton parish church much
as he left it, complete with canopied pulpit, box pews and the desk
where the clerk would " line out " the metrical psalms much as
in the Scotland of his youth.

The sight of the Governor's official pew would remind him of
his fierce quarrels with Sir Edmund Andros, who considered him
a formidable rival. It is a commentary on official stupidity that
Andros, dictator of New England under James II, should not
merely have been unpunished but actually commissioned by the
" Glorious Revolution " government to repeat his tyranny in Virginia (1692-8). Commissary Blair was the only man capable of
standing up to Andros; he certainly did so and procured his recall
to London and the termination of his career in America. There
could be no doubt of Blair's driving power. It enabled him to get
the better of other tyrannical governors besides Andros. One of
these was Alexander Spotswood, a veteran of Blenheim, who considered that the main blessings of Virginia were " peace and tranquillity, under a due obedience to the royal authority and a
gentlemanly conformity to the Church of England ".

Professor Wertenbaker has found that only three families in

Virginia " derived from English houses of historic note " and three more sprang from the " minor gentry ".[1] Nevertheless, the farmers and planters of the " tidewater " region blossomed into an aristocracy as they prospered. They built themselves mansions and imported English luxuries; ships from Bristol and London sailed right up to their riverside lawns. There was much closer intercourse between the South and the mother-country than between England and New England.[2] Rich colonials would send their sons " home " to be educated, or would import tutors (Thackeray's picture of *The Virginians* is authentic;[3] he actually visited " the Old Dominion "). During the earlier eighteenth century, " indentured servants " were more characteristic of Virginia than negro slaves. These were white men, whose status was semi-servile for a period of five or seven years. Some indentured servants paid for their passage by binding themselves to work on the land; others were " kidnapped " by " spirits " in English ports; and there were unfortunates who had got on the wrong side of the law. A certain number of these bondmen, when released, became successful farmers in the hilly interior, where they could make a fresh start, in a more democratic environment. A large proportion, however, never rose above the status of " poor whites "; their position deteriorated as negroes increased; plantations were self-sufficient, and there were few towns to support tradesmen. At the beginning of the eighteenth century over sixty per cent of the Virginians owned neither slaves nor indentured servants. The rise of land values, however, and the consolidation of vast entailed estates, changed all that. " Tidewater Virginia " became an aristocratic preserve; only in the central part of the colony had the independent white man a chance of achieving success and self-respect. A time was coming when the Great Awakening would give new hope to the backwoods " Qu'hoes ", but till then the " Tuckahoe " gentlemen controlled Church and State.

James Blair had done his best to enforce Church order in Virginia, but sound discipline and education cannot create spiritual life. A " Commissary " was a poor substitute for a Bishop; the mere fact that he was not a native of the province was against him; few Virginians of good family " went in for the Church ", and few

[1] *Virginia under the Stuarts*, 1607-88 (1914).
[2] May Stanard, *Colonial Virginia: Its People and Customs* (1917).
[3] Mary Johnston romanticised Virginia in her novels, *By Order of the Company* and *The Old Dominion*.

candidates could afford to travel to England for ordination. The
mother Church, instead of sending young, eager clergy, exported
men " who left their country for their country's good ". In
Thackeray's classic words: " Noblemen's hangers-on, insolvent
parsons who had quarrelled with justice or the bailiff, brought
their soiled cassocks into the colony in the hopes of finding a
living there."

One of the few achievements that may be credited to Colonial
Virginia is its Church Architecture. Great mansions like Westover,
Shirley and Drayton Hall had their less pretentious, but pleasing
ecclesiastical equivalents.[1] As early as 1632 St. Luke's was built
in Isle of Wight County. A brick sanctuary of " survival " Jacobean Gothic, it would remind worshippers of a typical English
parish church, complete with square tower, buttressed and
traceried windows. Abandoned after two centuries (1832) St.
Luke's was restored in 1888. It stands in a pine forest clearing,
for like many sanctuaries of the South it is sequestered. A number
of cruciform churches were erected during the early eighteenth
century. Carefully designed, often quite costly, they reflect the
quiet, intimate reverence that used to characterise English country
churches before the Gothic Revivalists laid hands on them. Here
are shapely pulpits with carved sounding-boards, well-propor-
tioned altar-pieces engraved with creed and commandments, small
transept galleries with panelled fronts, box pews with armorial
bearings and barrel-vaulted ceilings in plaster, the white interior
providing a cool background for the furniture. The style is
classic, flavoured with curious Gothic and Jacobean reminiscences.
One of the best preserved examples is Christ's Church, Lancaster
County, built in 1732 by " King " Carter, an opulent planter who
insisted on the worshippers standing until he entered for divine
service; the church is approached by a three-mile avenue of cedars.
One of the last churches to be erected before the American Revolution was in Truro parish (1769), where George Washington was a
vestryman. By that time, however, the Great Awakening had
swept Virginia, leaving the Establishment high and dry. Revival,
however, came at length. In the early nineteenth century Bishop
Meade[2] did so much to renew the spiritual life of the Virginian
Church that a modern historian, a Congregationalist, has described

[1] R. A. Lancaster, *Historic Virginia Houses and Churches* (Philadelphia, 1915).
[2] Author of *Old Churches, Ministers and Families of Virginia* (Philadelphia,
1857).

it as " offering perhaps the most agreeably mellow form of religion in the American scene ".[1]

2. MARYLAND AND THE CAROLINAS

Between Pennsylvania and Virginia is wedged the small state of Maryland, settled in 1634 by the enterprise of George Calvert, first Lord Baltimore, after whom the capital was named a century later. The founder resembled William Penn and Roger Williams in welcoming colonists on the basis of freedom of worship. He differed from them in being neither statesman nor prophet. No Quaker or Baptist was he, but a Roman Catholic. He can hardly be claimed as a doctrinaire Apostle of religious liberty, yet he acted directly counter to Papal policy. He may be defined as an adroit politician, fired with a dash of idealism, and endowed with the adventurous instincts of an Elizabethan. Prominent in promoting the New England and Virginia Companies under James I, Calvert invested in a colony in Newfoundland, the soil and climate being quaintly represented to him as " genial ". After nine years of experiment, he was glad to cut his losses (£30,000), and sailed to Virginia, where he offered to " plant and dwell among them " (1629). Having recently become a Romanist, he was unable to take the oath renouncing Popery, even in the " mitigated " form he himself proposed. Charles I had already given him estates in Ireland with the title of Lord Baltimore. With the lavish hand of a Stuart, his Sacred Majesty granted him what a Maryland historian has called " the most ample privileges ever conferred by an English sovereign ".

After the death of Lord Baltimore in 1632, his son Cecil decided to initiate the American enterprise. This tactful Englishman was well aware of the pitfalls that awaited colonisation conducted by a convert to Catholicism, who had absolute authority as Proprietor. Would any Protestant believe in his sincerity ? His own co-religionists were not a migratory class. In any case, to confine the enterprise to Roman Catholics would be asking for trouble and courting disaster. He would be " all things to all men " in order that his venture might succeed. He therefore welcomed " all liege subjects of the King ". No offence was to be given to Protestants,

[1] Dr. Russell Bowie, former Rector of St. Paul's, Richmond, Va., characterises the Church in Virginia as " definitely Evangelical, broad in sympathy, and generally simple in ritual ; ministers of other communions are frequently invited to Episcopal pulpits."

and all " Acts of the Romane Catholique Religion " were to be
observed " as privately as possible ". Two Jesuits joined the ship
inconspicuously as the company of 300 emigrants passed the Isle
of Wight; they were subsequently so successful in making converts that it was deemed politic to replace them by secular priests.

The Proprietor and his agents were sensible enough to avoid
the economic mistakes that ruined early colonisation in Virginia.
Friendly relations were established with the Indians at the outset,
and the first year's tobacco was grown in fields purchased from
the red men. In 1638 the second Lord Baltimore surrendered his
sole right to initiate legislation, and an elected Assembly was
instituted. Puritan settlers from Massachusetts and Virginia were
made welcome. The activities of the Jesuits were controlled. A
Catholic was actually fined 500 lbs. of tobacco for engaging in
religious controversy, the sum to be ear-marked for the support of
the first Protestant minister to arrive. A Protestant Governor was
even appointed by the Proprietor. Governor Stone was instructed
to pass a Toleration Act through the provincial Assembly. This
law provided freedom of worship for all except non-Trinitarians
(1649). Heavy penalties were to be inflicted on all who " in a
reproachful manner " called anyone a " Heretic, Idolater, Jesuited
Papist, Anabaptist, Antinomian, Roundhead, etc."

Unfortunately, Stone's Catholic deputy, in his absence, proclaimed Prince Charles as King during the Civil War. In England
the Commonwealth authorities were alarmed. A parliamentary
commission took over the administration of Maryland and confined
the benefits of the Toleration Act to Puritans. Cromwell, however,
far in advance of his fellow-Puritans as an advocate of toleration,
refused to admit this unjust discrimination and restored the
Baltimore régime (1657).

In 1688 there was some delay in proclaiming William and Mary
as King and Queen, owing to the Proprietor's absence on a frontier
dispute with William Penn. Protestant agitators took advantage
of the embarrassing situation; they seized power and the Crown
intervened. In 1692 the new royal Governor proclaimed the
annexation of Maryland, without depriving the Baltimores of the
actual ownership of the soil. An *Act for the Establishment of the
Protestant Religion* was rushed through the legislature. To the
official coterie, *that*, of course, meant the Church of England. Till
the arrival of some Irish at the end of the century, there were only

2,000 Catholic communicants and eight priests. The Protestants certainly numbered three-quarters of the population, but only a minority were Anglicans. As in the other American colonies the " Glorious Revolution " made the position of dissenters rather worse than under the Stuarts. A typical Colonial Governor was Sir Francis Nicholson of Maryland. Profane, arbitrary and conceited, he considered that religion could best be served by enhancing the privileges of the Church of England and making life as difficult as possible for all beyond her pale. Anti-Catholic legislation (1691) prohibited priests from hearing confession, celebrating the sacraments and ministering to the dying; services could only be held in private houses; laymen were refused permission to have their children educated by co-religionists, within or without the province. Roman Catholics were disfranchised in 1715; governing rights were only restored to the fourth Lord Baltimore on his conversion to Protestantism.

The historian of the American Colonies, H. C. Lodge, considered that the Anglican Establishment in Maryland " was perhaps as contemptible an ecclesiastical organisation as history can show ", demonstrating " all the vices of the Virginian Church, without one of its safeguards or redeeming qualities ".[1] It was felt that something must be done to reform, or at least restrain, the worthless clergy supplied by England. Dr. Bray was appointed by Compton, Bishop of London, to do for Maryland what the Rev. James Blair was doing for Virginia. Thomas Bray (1656-1730), a graduate of All Souls, Oxford, was a country parson in Warwickshire when he was selected as Commissary in 1696. On arrival he found that clerical demoralisation had not been exaggerated. He visited each of the sixteen parsons at his own expense, provided them with books from England, and took active measures against those who proved recalcitrant. The application of discipline by an outsider not only raised sympathy for erring clerics but incensed Governor Nicholson, who considered that church affairs was *his* sphere. Bray's action was ill-advised in ordering every minister in the colony to use the Anglican Prayer Book; it at once antagonised the majority of the people, who did not belong to the Church of England. Hearing that his high-handed policy was being criticised in Parliament, the Commissary hastened home. The disapproval

[1] Paradoxically, Maryland had ferocious anti-blasphemy laws (1692-1820). Boring through the tongue was the punishment for a first conviction, branding for a second conviction and death for the third.

of the Attorney-general forced him to modify his plan for Maryland. Nevertheless his amended scheme provided for an Anglican
Establishment; Quakers and other dissenters were to be allowed
bare toleration according to the English Act of 1689, but this
limited benefit was not extended to Roman Catholics. The irony
of it! " Maryland, which had been founded for the sake of religious freedom by the toil and treasure of Roman Catholics, was
now open to all who called themselves Christians save Roman
Catholics " (Professor W. W. Sweet).

During this controversy Dr. Bray published a *Memorial upon
the State of Religion in America*. This pamphlet sought to interest
the public in a scheme to enlist active ministers for the colonies.
The " refuse of the clergy in England would not do for American
missionaries ". The call for forty young men " of a missionary
spirit " resulted in the formation of " The Society for the Propagation of the Gospel in Foreign Parts ".[1] Dr. Bray attended the
first meeting of the " S.P.G." in 1701. He never returned to
America, but achieved far better results through his missionary
influence than by his personal exertions. The subscription list
was headed by the Archbishop of Canterbury, to whom candidates
had to report. The new missionaries were to be circumspect in
their personal lives, to avoid controversy, to preach plainly, to
explain and administer the Sacraments, to distribute the Society's
tracts and to undertake personal evangelism. They were to be
allowed £50 a year and £10 for outfit. They were also encouraged
to keep up their scholarship through book-grants; libraries were
established for their benefit in seaports where they were likely to
be detained by adverse winds.

In 1702 the Society's representatives, the Revs. George Keith
and Patrick Gordon surveyed the field of future operations from
Boston to Charleston; it was a strenuous two years. Keith was an
ex-Quaker who knew America well (see below, p. 30 f). His *Journal
from New Hampshire to Caratuck* (London, 1706) gives a vivid
account of his travels; he had all the virtues of a proselyte. Thank-
ing a former associate for saving his life, he offered to be the means
of saving his soul. " George, save thine own soul, for I have no
need of thy help." " John, I will pray for thy conversion." John
had the last word: " The prayers of the wicked are an abomination."

Between 1702 and the achievement of American Independence

[1] C. F. Pascoe, *Two Hundred Years of the S.P.G.* (1901).

over 300 missionaries were sent out by the Society. They were
men of a very different calibre from the lazy incumbents of Virginia and Maryland. Their devotion and heroism deserve all
praise. They were the "working clergy" who planted new
churches, fostered decaying congregations and kept in touch with
scattered Church people. It was the task of the S.P.G. to extend
a network of organisation along the Atlantic coast-line. Before
they commenced operations, the Church of England owned only
one church in New England (King's Chapel, Boston), one in New
York, none in New Jersey and only a handful in Pennsylvania.
The S.P.G. missionaries were zealous but sectarian. However did
they expect that a tone of arrogance and official patronage would
win the affections of "dissenters" to the Mother-Church ? Admitting this superiority-complex, we cannot withhold appreciation
for their missionary endeavour; but for them the Church of
England would hardly have existed outside the colonial capitals,
with the exception of Virginia, which possessed a regular establishment. Their work in the Carolinas was noteworthy during the
early eighteenth century.

The early history of North Carolina is strewn with the wreck of
abortive enterprises, like the Huguenot colony at Beaufort (1562).
Permanent colonisation came late and proved to be a slow process.
It will be remembered that Charles II discharged his debt to
William Penn by giving him the vast tracts of Pennsylvania. He
was as lavish in his grant of the Carolinas to his courtiers—Albemarle, Clarendon and Shaftesbury. Shaftesbury entrusted John
Locke with the task of drafting a written constitution. This " blue
print " proved quite unworkable, as the representatives of the
Proprietors soon discovered on arrival in 1670. Feudal ideas were
utterly irrelevant in a colony sparsely populated by merchant
adventurers from New England (interested in the coasting trade),
insolvent debtors, and settlers from Barbados seeking a less torrid
climate. Vain attempts to impose " seigniories, baronies and precincts " were abandoned by 1693 and royal authority replaced
that of the Proprietors in 1729. Locke's constitution, however,
provided for religious toleration, as we might expect from such
a philosopher.

Here was an " open door " for a sect persecuted by Puritan and
Anglican alike—the Quakers. George Fox visited the infant colony
in 1672 and was received by Governor Carteret and his wife

" lovingly ". The chief secretary of the province was " convinced " by Fox's earnest preaching. The seed fell on good ground. Many a " precious meeting " was held and the " sacrament of silence " harmonised with the solitude of the surroundings. One of the Proprietors (or " Landgraves "), John Archdale, influenced by Fox, gave the Friends every encouragement. Appointed Governor in 1695, he " mixed his forces in the Council—High Churchmen, Low Churchmen, Dissenters. Archdale established friendly relations with the Spanish Catholics of Florida, protected the Indians, insisted on kindness to shipwrecked mariners, and regulated the liquor traffic. The Carolinas attracted immigrants from England and merited Archdale's claim—an " American Canaan ". He was a pioneer also in securing citizenship for the Huguenots and other foreigners none too popular with British colonists. When the Quaker Governor returned to England, the Carolinian public presented him a testimonial: " By your wisdom, patience and labour you have laid a firm foundation for a most glorious superstructure."

John Archdale was as unfortunate in his successors as that other pioneer of toleration, Lord Baltimore; the Quakers of North Carolina suffered, like the Catholics of Maryland. For a quarter of a century the Friends had been the only organised Christian community in the colony. The arrival of the first Anglican clergyman in 1700 was a signal for a campaign to " establish " the Church of England. This attempt was foiled, for over half the Assembly was Quaker, and they were supported by the Proprietors. However, by an Act of Parliament (1704) all office-holders were required to take the oath of allegiance to Queen Anne. The Quakers accordingly were excluded and a Church of England minority took control. A " Vestry Act " disfranchised all non-Anglicans. The Quakers took no part in a small rising against the new régime led by exasperated dissenters (some of whom had left Virginia for conscience' sake). The Church of England minority consolidated their privileged position in 1711, and the Quakers, who had laid the foundations of North Carolina's institutions and ideals, remained without civic rights till the American Revolution.

South Carolina, divided by a wilderness from North Carolina, started its separate existence in 1688. Some years earlier " operators " in England sought fat dividends in a land of promise between the Ashley and Cooper Rivers, where Charleston now stands. Glowing circulars promised English immigrants that, in addition to temporal prosperity, they would have the ecclesiastical advantage of belonging to " the only true and orthodox church ". Dissenters were promised freedom of worship; one company came from Somerset under Joseph Blake, the brother of Cromwell's illustrious admiral. Dutch Calvinists, dissatisfied by the English régime in New York, went south, as did Baptists persecuted by New England Congregationalists. Covenanters and Huguenots fled from their persecutors. Indeed, it has been said of South Carolina that the greatest names in her history are generally either French or Scotch. At an early date the Quakers made many converts, not from the churches but from the unchurched, who were deeply impressed by their simple, earnest faith and brotherly attitude. English officialism, however, was singularly blind to the need of treating with respect this richly varied pattern of religious experience. Their one idea was to leave no stone unturned till the Church of England was " Established "; beyond that, religion did not interest them. In 1704 the Whig majority of the House of Lords intervened to prevent a Test Act from being imposed by which members of the legislature would be compelled to take the Sacrament according to the Anglican rite. Yet in 1711 the clergy of this Church had their way, although they were a mere handful.

To-day, the British traveller will find in Charleston a survival of the old, Colonial South—shaded streets, pillared porticoes, dignified mansions set in charming gardens. The churches of St. Michael and St. Philip look just as if they had been transplanted from the narrow lanes of London to an environment of palmettoes, magnolias and azaleas. Their decorous worshippers are the descendants of the old families who held sway when the Church of England was Established. The descendants of the exiles have still their appointed habitation—the Old Scots Kirk, the Huguenot " temple ", and a number of Lutheran places of worship. If, however, we leave historic towns like Charleston, we will find that we are in the land of the Methodist and Baptist.[1] The Great Awakening swept over the South and almost obliterated the old ecclesiastical landmarks of Colonial times. The Quakers are no longer numerous. The Church of England, by its lack of elasticity

[1] In South Carolina in 1906 out of 655,000 communicants, the Baptists led with 341,000, followed by the Methodists with 249,000. There is a tremendous drop to the " also ran "—Presbyterians, 35,000; Lutherans, 12,000; Episcopalians, 8,000. In the Southern States generally this proportion is fairly general.

its inability to adapt itself to a new continent, lost a great opportunity.

3. GEORGIA

The southernmost coast colony, Georgia, originated as an experiment in the " Social Gospel ". The founder, General Oglethorpe, " prosecuted philanthropy in the spirit of a paladin," said Austin Dobson, " rejoicing in the obstacles, the encounters, the nights *sub Jove frigido* " (*A Paladin of Philanthropy*). In response to his invitation to people of all creeds, a ship arrived there in 1736, bearing a Moravian bishop and two youths afterwards famous. Charles Wesley came as Governor's secretary, while his brother John was to be Anglican chaplain and Indian evangelist.[1] On landing, they were met by August Spangenberg, the Moravian pastor. " Do you know Jesus Christ ? " asked Spangenberg. " I know he is the Saviour of the world," replied John Wesley. " True," observed the pastor, " but do you know that He has saved you ? " It was only after his return to England that he was " taught the way of the Lord more perfectly ". Had his conversion occurred in Georgia, his work would surely have borne fruit, as it did afterwards wherever he preached. As it was, John Wesley behaved like a fool, imposing High Church discipline and practices on a frontier community that (apart from the Moravians) hardly knew the elements of the Christian faith. Georgia was indeed a hard school for a young clergyman whose knowledge of the world was confined to Oxford. He got into trouble with the law by excommunicating a girl who had jilted him.[2] His career in Savannah was closed and he sailed for England.

When he arrived at Deal, he heard that a ship in harbour was about to sail for the very colony that he had quitted. A member of the " Holy Club " in his Oxford days was actually on board. Instead of trying to meet George Whitefield, he sent him a brief note advising him to return home. Wesley gave this advice after casting lots, to discover the divine will. Whitefield was naturally " somewhat surprised ", but decided to continue his voyage: " I knew that my call was to Georgia . . . and could not justly go from the soldiers committed to my charge." At first it seemed as if Wesley's case was to be repeated—the failure of zeal without know-

[1] C. E. Vulliamy, *John Wesley*, Ch. 5 (London 1931).
[2] For a fair, well-told account of the episode, see Marie Oemler's novel, *The Holy Lover*.

ledge of human nature. The " boy evangelist " had made a stir in London, but merely excited the smiles of the soldiers bound for Georgia. To one of their officers he announced that he was going to have prayers with them daily. " I think we may," was the reply, " when we have nothing else to do!" The first Sunday," nothing was to be seen but cards, and little heard but blasphemy ". Stormy weather, however, gave Whitefield the opportunity of demonstrating his faith as well as his devotion to the sick. By the time the *Whitaker* reached Savannah (May 1738) the young preacher had won all hearts; he was surrounded by eager, enthusiastic hearers; and this was the best preparation for the ministry that awaited him across the Atlantic.

The soldiers had been sent with the object of building up British resistance in the South against attacks on the part of the Spaniards, who then possessed Florida (their capital, St. Augustine, is now the oldest city in the present United States). Georgia was to be a buffer-settlement to protect South Carolina. That was its political *raison d'etre*. General Oglethorpe, founder of Georgia, had served with distinction under Prince Eugene against the Turks. His strategy, however, in America was a philanthropist's rather than a General's. It was his aim to found a new colony predominantly British, with room for the distressed of any nationality. To this end he approached various groups—Moravians, Mennonites, Vaudois, and Jews, to give Georgia a good moral and economic start.[1] Poor Highlanders were welcomed. Several hundred Protestants from Salzburg, given eight days notice to quit by the Prince Archbishop, gladly accepted Oglethorpe's invitation. An old print represents a Salzburger declaring: " I set my staff forward in God's name, and wander cheerfully in a strange land. Though I must forsake house and home, the Lord is with us on our way." A Christian nucleus was badly needed, for " the best people are not to be looked for in new colonies " (Southey).

Governor Oglethorpe's aim was also to provide for the undischarged debtors who languished under the most appalling conditions in English jails. As an M.P. he called for an enquiry in

[1] Had New Englanders been drawn to the South, they might have made a valuable contribution. A group of them founded Midway Church, near Savannah (*c.* 1753). For more than a century this congregation flourished, giving Georgia four Governors and the World Church 100 ministers and missionaries.

C

1729. It was obvious that the debtors were a motley crowd. Some of them were the victims of circumstance; they might succeed in a new environment as farmers, mechanics and labourers. Others " left their country for their country's good " without " making good " overseas. There were lazy, cunning, brutal men, as well as loose, noisy and mischievous women among the beneficiaries. They were not fitted for the hard life of the frontier, but their economic and moral welfare was safeguarded effectually, judged by eighteenth-century standards.

A Charter was issued by Parliament in 1732, appointing Trustees furnished with £10,000 to launch the enterprise (apparently the only government subsidy ever granted by Britain to an American colony). The sale of rum was prohibited in Georgia. Slavery was forbidden, not altogether on humanitarian grounds, but because the Trustees did not want to create a province filled with blacks, the precarious property of a few, " impairing the independence of poor white settlers ". Georgia, named in honour of George II, was to be run purely for the benefit of the colonists: a strange innovation in Walpole's England, when " every man had his price ".

James Edward Oglethorpe was one of the most remarkable men of the eighteenth century. His interests were literary as well as activist. He was the friend of Goldsmith, Burke and Boswell; had Boswell written his life (as he would have liked to) he would have had materials for a biography almost as interesting as Dr. Johnson's. Oglethorpe, unfortunately, was not permitted to complete his work in Georgia. His family traditions being Jacobite, suspicion was aroused on his return to England, especially after the '45. Without justification, the government refused to trust such a capable soldier. Ignored and excluded from public life, he was not even consulted many years later when British differences with the American colonies widened into estrangement. In religious matters his counsel would have been particularly helpful. A loyal Anglican and founder of a colony, he had worked in concert with Christians of various communions, whom he refused to brand as mere " dissenters ". He would have done his best to make the government of George III realise that the fear of English bishops being imposed on America had a good deal to do with colonial unrest. Unfortunately the services of this " Imperial Idealist ", as a recent biographer, Mr. A. A. Ettinger, has justly called him,

were not required. " I have a new admirer," wrote Hannah More
in 1784; " it is the famous General Oglethorpe. He is ninety years
old; the finest figure you ever saw. He perfectly realises all my
ideas of Nestor. His literature is great, his knowledge of the
world extensive, and his faculties as bright as ever."

Oglethorpe was the moving spirit of the Georgia venture. He
landed with the first colonists in 1733, closely supervised their
settlement and planned Savannah with its broad streets and
spacious squares. When Whitefield arrived five years later, he
found a ready collaborator. The new chaplain, unlike Wesley,
blended " social service " with the Gospel. He spent money contributed in England on colonial outfits for his new parishioners;
£300 was laid out in shoes, breeches, stockings, dresses, etc., for
men, women and children. These donations of course attracted
the people, while Wesley's ritual and asceticism had repelled them.
Whitefield thus secured a ready hearing. One of his favourite
projects was an orphanage to encourage settlers to come out to
Georgia, " assured their children will be provided for after their
decease ". He sailed to England and returned with a grant from
the Trustees, furnishing a site and support for " Bethesda ". In
1740 the new institution, " America's oldest charity ", was built
on an impressive scale, a ten-mile avenue connecting it with
Savannah. Whitefield also thought of a college, but when the
Archbishop of Canterbury insisted on an Anglican foundation,
the promoter replied that " it should be on a broad bottom and
no other ".

In one respect Whitefield was out of touch with the best humanitarian thought of his time, led by the Quakers. Aware of the evils
of slavery, he made no attempt to use his superb gifts to secure
its limitation or amelioration. " Georgia never can nor will be a
flourishing province," he asserted, " without negroes." Naturally
this was popular doctrine with most colonists whose aim was
material self-betterment. The Salzburg refugees wrote home to
Germany for advice. They were gratified to hear from their religious guides: " If you take slaves in faith and with the intent of
conducting them to Christ, the action will not be sin, but may
prove a benediction." Eventually the Trustees allowed slavery
under pressure, as they had been badgered till they permitted rum.
It was some consolation for the coloured people to be assured that
they were " already freemen of the heavenly Jerusalem ". When

slavery was legalised in 1750 Whitefield purchased a plantation at Bethesda—did not servitude facilitate conversion ? The Trustees, weary of their thankless task, gave up the Charter in 1752. Georgia then became a royal province like the Carolinas. Material prosperity was built on a basis of involuntary human toil, and the colonists were quite reluctant to give up the British connexion in 1776.

Whittier wrote of Whitefield in " The Preacher ":

> Alas for the preacher's cherished schemes . . .
> Of all his labours not trace remains
> Save the bondman lifting his hands in chains.
> The woof he wove in the righteous warp
> Of freedom-loving Oglethorpe,
> Clothes with curses the goodly land . . .
> And a century's lapse reveals once more
> The slave-ship stealing to Georgia's shore.

Whittier's impassioned humanitarianism carried him rather too far. He failed to realise that Whitefield was a man of the earlier eighteenth century, not the nineteenth. There were few Christian leaders who denounced slavery except among the Quakers. Yet Whitefield might have heard echoes of their voices in his own heart. He had a blind spot in his moral vision. " It seems a thousand pities," says his biographer, Dr. A. D. Belden, " that he did not see his way clear, like Wesley, to take the Abolitionist attitude towards slavery, for if, with his unique power of public persuasion, he had linked this clear duty to the converted state of the soul, he might have antedated the work of Wilberforce and Woolman, and made a bitter civil war in America unnecessary."

CHAPTER II

THE MIDDLE COLONIES

1. PENNSYLVANIA

"The unity of Christians never did, nor ever will, nor ever can stand in uniformity of thought or opinion, but in Christian love only."

THOMAS STORY, 1737.

THE Puritan persecution of the Quakers in New England has been illustrated by the following letter said to have been sent by Cotton Mather to "the aged and beloved John Higginson":

"There be now at sea a shipp (for our friend Elias Holcroft of London did advise me by the last packet it would be some time in August) called *Welcome*, which has aboard it a hundred or more heretics and malignants called Quakers, with William Penn, the scamp, at the head of them. The General Court has accordingly given secret orders to Master Malachi Hazett of the brig *Porpoise* to waylay said *Welcome* . . . and make captives of the Penn and his ungodly crew, so that the Lord may be glorified and not mocked on the soil of this new country with the heathen worshipps of these people. Much spoil may be made by selling the whole lot to Barbadoes, where slaves fetch good prices in rumme and sugar and we shall not only do the Lord great service . . . but shall make good gayne, for his ministers and people."

Here was another damning indictment against the "Puritan Priest" who signed himself "Yours in bonds of Christ". As late as July 1936 the English *Congregational Quarterly* printed it, with caustic comment on the kind of "Christianity" it implied. Yet this precious epistle couched in Cotton Mather's characteristic style has been traced to its source—a mischievous provincial journalist,[1] who enjoyed fabricating anti-Puritan propaganda. Historians are indebted to the *Readers' Digest* for giving publicity to the fact that the hoax has been already exposed.

Nevertheless, Massachusetts was guilty of needless cruelty to the Friends. When Ann Austin and Mary Fisher arrived at

---

[1] James F. Shunk, editor of the *Argus*, Easton, Pennsylvania (1870).

Boston[1] in 1656, Deputy-governor Bellingham " sent officers aboard and searched their trunks and took away . . . about 100 books . . . the said books were burned in the market place by the hangman ". The women were imprisoned on shore, deprived of pen, ink and paper, and their window boarded up. After being stripped and examined to see if they were witches, they were kept in jail for five weeks under cruel conditions and finally sent back to Barbados. Two days after they left, a ship arrived from London with eight more Quakers; the captain was forced to take them back to England. Savage laws were hastily devised and rigorously applied. A Quaker named Wenlock Christison was about to be hung on Boston common for returning to the colony after banishment when a " King's Missive " arrived from Charles II; he and twenty-seven co-religionists were set at liberty.[2] Henceforth, Quakers subject to the death-penalty were to be sent to England. This, however, did not prevent the magistrates of Massachusetts from inflicting savage penalties short of death up till 1677. Even women were " stripped naked from the middle up, tied to a cart's tail, and whipped through the town and from thence " to the next town and until they were conveyed out of " our jurisdiction ". In Longfellow's " New England Tragedy ", *John Endicott*, we find the authentic atmosphere. Quakers were accused of interrupting services, claiming to be filled with the Holy Spirit, "which, as your Calvin says, surpasses reason ". They attack " preaching for hire ". Pastor Norton is incensed; need they quake like Daniel, wail like dragons and mourn like owls ? " Ye verify the adage that Satan is God's ape! Away with them! " To the godly Puritans such antics as women dressing in sackcloth, " prophesying " during public worship with grease-smeared faces and broken bottles, or emulating the Hebrew prophets by appearing in the streets literally " as a naked sign " . . . were nothing less than devilish. Actually they were the result of hysteria reacting to high-pressure persecution. That hysteria was not confined to Quakers was revealed by the case of Ann Austin and Mary Fisher. As George Bishop said to the magistrates of Boston in 1660: " Two women arriving in your harbour so shook ye, to the everlasting shame . . . of your established order, as if a formidable army had invaded your borders."

---

[1] From Barbados—it is difficult to-day to visualise the West Indies as a scene of Quaker activity.

[2] See Whittier's dramatic use of this incident in his poem, *The King's Missive*.

During the Commonwealth George Fox visited Maryland, Rhode Island, the Carolinas and other tolerant colonies. Quakers became numerous along the Atlantic coast. They were influential enough to modify the public policy of the above plantations; by 1672 the Governor, Deputy-governor and magistrates of Rhode Island were Friends, and the colony passed largely under their control. Three years later, under Governor Coddington, this plantation refused to join the other New England provinces in preparing for a defensive war against the Indians; consequently the towns of Providence and Warwick were burned by the insurgent natives. The " passive principle " was later to prove an obstacle to the continuation of Quaker rule in Pennsylvania.

A new field for Quaker enterprise was opened in 1664 after New Amsterdam became New York. The Duke of York granted the territory south of the river Hudson, New Jersey, to his friends Sir John Berkeley and Sir George Carteret. These new proprietors welcomed settlers of all denominations, and Quakers moved into the Raritan Valley (1674). Berkeley disposed of his rights to two Friends, who obtained a Charter for West Jersey in 1675. Carteret's heirs sold East Jersey to a land company, in which Quakers had a controlling interest, William Penn being one of the trustees. Thus the way was paved for the " Holy Experiment " in the more extensive territory south of the Jerseys.

The story of William Penn has often been told;[1] it is an important chapter in American history and need not be re-told in detail. We think of the shy, meditative youth drawn to the persecuted Friends, despite his father's ire and all that it entailed. After the Admiral's death, the young idealist was faced with the problem of extracting a debt of £16,000 from the Merry Monarch. Penn knew the art of the courtier as well as the psychology of evangelism. It was a master-stroke to persuade Charles II to settle the debt (a considerable sum in those days) by transferring to him vast tracts of woodland, appropriately named " Sylvania ", his majesty insisting on the prefix " Penn-". Subject to appeals to Parliament, the proprietor was given considerable authority which he decided to share with an elected assembly of freeholders. " Let the people think they govern, and they will be governed." His " Frame of Government " blended paternalism and democracy.

[1] The film, *Penn of Pennsylvania*, dealt with his earlier life and neglected the opportunity of dramatising " the Holy Experiment ".

In one of his early letters, he wrote: " I propose . . . to leave myself and successors no power of doing mischief, that the will of one may not hinder the good of an whole country."

The new constitution was to be " an example to the nation ", but the founder was a business man as well as a philanthropist. To the large investor Penn offered 5,000 acre lots at £100 each, with 50 acres added for every " indentured servant " transported to work the land (he took to heart the foolish precedent of those who supplied Virginia with a superfluity of " gentlemen "). To the small man he offered a 100-acre holding at 40s. provided he would " seat " his family in Pennsylvania. His system of an annual quitrent was afterwards to sow trouble between proprietor and tenants. Penn's aim was to attract farmers who wanted modest homesteads rather than rich men who sought to imitate the planters of Virginia or the lordly " patroons " of the Hudson Valley. Economic policy and religious principles merged. English landlords would not be able to adapt themselves to the hard task of making the wilderness blossom like the rose—even though the soil and climate were far more genial than in New England. Nor would English landlords be likely to be drawn, as a class, to Quakerism; the Restoration had made them stiff Anglicans.

The Founder of Pennsylvania did not attempt to make his province a one-sect colony like New England; he knew that he could not muster enough Quakers to carry out the idea effectively in such a vast territory. He therefore guaranteed freedom of worship. He did more; he advertised it. Penn had a flair for publicity that has subsequently become an American characteristic. He was an adept at " selling " his ideas. Not content with Anglo-Saxon immigrants, he toured the Continent, offering a new home to hard-working peasants and artisans who were persecuted by Romanist or Lutheran governments. He accepted the idea of America as a " melting-pot ". Indeed, he was ready to welcome even Catholics and Jews provided they were willing to tolerate the opinions of others. His creed was a minimum—belief in God the Creator. There was nothing insular in William Penn. He found time to turn from his colossal American venture to suggest the necessity of a Parliament of Europe; each state was to retain internal sovereignty only, " and if this be called a lessening of their power, it must be only because the great fish can no longer eat up the little ones". He foreshadowed the "United Nations" of to-day.

Penn's racial reconciliation was far in advance of his age. The aborigines were backward " children of God ", not savages to be exterminated or exploited; they and the white men " must live in harmony as long as the Sun gave Light ". His Treaty with the Red Indians was not so unique as Benjamin West's famous picture suggests. Allowing for romantic exaggeration, the fact remains that the Indians were loyal to the Great White Chief and his successors for seventy years, as long as the administration adhered to the spirit of the Treaty.

In 1682 Penn reached America in the *Welcome*. He soon demonstrated his fitness to carry out his " Holy Experiment ". Less individualistic than the early Quakers, he showed a true " community sense " in his enlightened plan for Philadelphia. Under his leadership English and Welsh Quakers flourished as farmers. They were not " of the world "; but " in the world " they proved useful, productive citizens. The " inner light " imparted poise to personality and dignity to labour. " There is a charm as of apostolic simplicity and beauty," said Dr. Leonard W. Bacon, " in their unassuming hierarchy of weekly, monthly, and yearly meetings, which realises the type of the primitive church represented in the *Didaché*."

By 1700 no less than forty meeting houses had been erected, ranging in size from a room to a large hall. The eighteenth-century examples form an attractive feature of the Pennsylvanian landscape, bowered by ancient trees and surrounded by the nameless graves of the forefathers. Built of stone, brick or timber according to local material, they are the product of devoted craftsmanship. Doggedly domestic in appearance, they make no concessions to popular ideas of an " ecclesiastical edifice ". Gables, shutters and doors (sometimes graced with plain Doric pilasters) are painted white. The interior is austere with whitewash and hard benches, though here and there gallery-fronts and partitions are pleasantly panelled. Women sit to the left and men to the right of a central passage, facing the elders' dais, which is furnished with a long curved sounding-board over their heads. Through these old-world sanctuaries, little changed, still flows the healing sacrament of silent worship.[1]

Penn's troubles were largely due to long periods of absence in

[1] For excellent photographs see P. B. Wallace, *Colonial Churches and Meeting Houses—Pennsylvania, etc.* (New York, 1931).

England. The reasons were manifold—the necessity of clearing himself from compromising relations with James II, boundary disputes with neighbouring provinces, the management of his estates in England, and the unwillingness of his family to bury themselves in Pennsylvania; not least was his failure to appoint the right men as his deputies. Such " Hurries and Perplexities " did not help the " Holy Experiment ".

As people of different sects and languages streamed into Pennsylvania, an anti-Quaker party crystallised in the provincial Assembly. In three respects the Friends were in a weak position. They were pledged to a Puritanical way of life, yet they could not apply this code to a mixed population; it was different in New England where the people were homogeneous and the magistrates were not afraid of punishing any who questioned their authority. In the second place, the Quakers were humane in their attitude towards other races, seeking to prohibit the sale of rum to Indians and to prevent the worst abuses of negro slavery; yet their ideals could not be enforced against selfish men whose one object was gain. Finally, the Quakers had a western frontier to defend against savage Indians, leagued with French Canadians who would not listen to conciliation talk; yet these Friends were prevented by their religion from organising an army. Their position in England was quite different (assuming legal toleration); *there* they were a sheltered society protected by the State; but how could they, as a Church-State in Pennsylvania, offer protection to those who settled within their borders ? *Quis custodes custodiet ?* This difficulty no doubt accounted for the provision in Penn's Charter that reserved to the British Parliament the right to tax Pennsylvania, whereas in the other American colonies finance was left to the provincial legislature. If the Quakers were not prepared to defend the colony, someone else must do so. The people of Pennsylvania, on the outbreak of the Seven Years War (1756), felt that they could not afford to take further risks; they therefore accepted the voluntary withdrawal of the Quakers from political leadership.

One article in the Charter gave the British Government the right to send out an Anglican clergymen, should twenty freemen desire it. This would have occurred sooner or later in the natural course of events. From the Friends' point of view, this dreaded visitation was worse, because it came partly as the result of a split. George Keith, who had undergone persecution for the cause of a prominent Friend in Pennsylvania,[1] turned against his leader and accused him of being a Deist. This charge was unjustified, but he was right in pointing out that Quaker organisation was inadequate for such a scattered community; " the candle needed a candlestick ". He therefore founded the " Christian Quakers ", which was regarded as schism by the London Yearly Meeting. It was not long before Keith came to the conclusion that only the Church of England could provide a " candlestick " capable of holding the flame of faith. He was accordingly ordained by the Bishop of London and returned to America in 1702 as a missionary of the ultra-orthodox Society for the Propagation of the Gospel.

A more serious blow was the apostasy of Penn's sons and their return to Anglican allegiance. This put the Church of England on a semi-official footing, so far as Philadelphia was concerned; Christ Church attracted people of standing and education (even Franklin became a pew-holder). After the death of William Penn in 1718, the Friends continued to lose ground. He had warned them (in vain) to " have a care of cumber ". Industry and frugality in farming and business had made many of them prosperous, and some of them rich.[2] A quiet worldliness gradually overlaid the old fervour. A spirit-born movement declined into a family tradition. Here is a striking instance of the proverb, " Religion gave birth to wealth, and was devoured by her own offspring".

" Birthright membership " reduced the Society from a fellowship of believers to a corporation organised on a family basis, irrespective of that " change of heart " once deemed essential. Penn's spiritual descendants isolated themselves from a world which he had sought to conquer, marking themselves off from their fellow-citizens by their external manners and customs. Dominant cliques " excluded from meeting " those who married out of the ancestral sect or differed from them in trivial matters. The gift of utterance failed. Many meetings were held on the First Day in absolute silence. The Bible, which had nourished the early friends, ceased to hold the central place; there was a definite decline in Scripture-reading, the most frequent excuses being objection to " fixed times " and the danger of formality

[1] A fellow-Aberdonian, Barclay of Ury, was appointed Governor of E. Jersey, on the strength of his famous *Apology* for Quakerism.

[2] Successful Friends, turning to the world, have been satirised in American literature. Fenimore Cooper, brought up as a Friend, has depicted some interesting Quaker types, e.g., Judge Temple in *The Pioneers* (1823) and Natty Bumppo in *The Pathfinder* (1840).

unless one was " inwardly moved ". Christian education was
neglected and young people were apt to grow up Friends by tradition rather than by conviction. " The soil was therefore prepared
for the introduction of almost any new opinions that might be
plausibly presented."

In the early nineteenth century Elias Hicks of Long Island found
ready hearers when he preached that the genuine Quaker way called
simply for readiness to follow " the light within " in the service of
God and man. Jesus was only superior to the rest of men because
he had a greater task to perform. At the great Yearly Meeting in
Philadelphia, Hicks announced: " The blood of Christ—why, my
friends, the actual blood of Christ itself is no more effectual than
the blood of bulls and goats—not a bit more." This outburst was
greeted with heated protest; it provoked the " Hicksite " schism
that divided the Friends in 1827 and still divides. Logan Pearsall
Smith, descended from an old Philadelphia family, but personally
dissociated from the Friends, has confessed: " Even now, when
I meet in London Philadelphians of Hicksite blood, I seem to
know them at once, by instinct, by a kind of subtly mingled sense
of theological and social repugnance, which I find it extremely
difficult to overcome."[1] This odd antipathy is doubtless explained
by the fact that Hicks was a man of elementary education, who
rejected the decorum taken for granted by the polite merchants of
Philadelphia; he lived in Long Island (near New York, but its
rural antithesis) and grew up in the same simple environment as
Walt Whitman; both appealed to democratic sentiment. The
orthodox Quakers, who regarded Hicksites as radicals and Unitarians, were directly influenced by well-to-do English Friends
like J. J. Gurney, who visited America with the full endorsement
of the London Yearly Meeting (1837). This section was definitely
Evangelical, seeking to recover for the Friends the full doctrine
of substitutionary atonement. The " general sense " of Quaker
testimony, however, deprecates emphasis on doctrinal schemes
which " run out into notions ". Litigation accentuated bitterness
between Hicksites and orthodox Friends. The latter, however,
fared better than the Trinitarians of Massachusetts (p. 187 f); they
secured most of the Philadelphia property, while the former had
to be content with the country meeting houses of Pennsylvania.

In the East, the Friends have attracted a number of adherents

[1] *Unforgotten Years*, p. 31 f. (Boston, 1939).

from other denominations, tired of sermons and singing, or drawn by sympathy with Quaker convictions of non-resistance in war-time. In the Middle West their " accommodation " to churchly ways (hymns, prayers and " hireling ministry ") has failed to produce positive results; in Indiana an actual decline of member-ship has been registered. The Quakers have held their own wherever they have been faithful to their essential historic testi-mony, without losing touch with modern ways of living and thinking. In the South, where Quakers were once numerous (par-ticularly the Carolinas) they have declined. The slavery issue made life difficult for them, and the present racial tension and rigid Evangelicalism prevailing south of the Mason and Dixon line makes the spiritual climate of the South uncongenial.

The entire membership of the Friends (orthodox, Hicksite and other branches) does not exceed 100,000, compared to 30,000 at the close of the Colonial era. Its influence has been out of all proportion to its numbers. Even during the dead eighteenth cen-tury, known as " the middle age of Quakerism ", the " fruit of the spirit " was being produced in tolerance (far in advance of the age) and constructive citizenship. Quaker character became pro-verbial for probity. These men brought the " inner light " to bear on business (they were the first to place a definite price on goods offered in shops). The New Testament rather than the Law of England or the Mosaic code, inspired the Pennsylvanian penal system, which was highly commended in Europe as humane and genuinely reformative. Philadelphia was laid out as " a green country town, which will never be burnt, and always wholesome " —a garden city. The streets were lined with trees, each quarter of the town was to have its open space of eight acres, with public buildings set at focal points and a pleasant promenade along the river front. The Friends surely learned the art of living together in Philadelphia, " city of brotherly love ". Visitors discovered that " the Holy Experiment " was not a complete failure.

As young Jean-Jacques Rousseau left the city of Calvin in search of freedom, so an apprentice named Benjamin Franklin cast off the dust of the city of Cotton Mather. In his fascinating *Auto-biography* he has revealed his personality. Seeking an ampler air and better opportunities than Boston offered, he sold his *Pilgrim's Progress* and invested in " better books " (all useful). In 1723 Franklin arrived in Philadelphia in rags, a dollar in his pocket,

It was the " First Day ", so finding a meeting house open, he entered and went to sleep during the soothing silence of Quaker worship. He soon found employment as a printer, spent eighteen months in London to gain experience, and returned to America to make a name for himself. This " father of all Yankees " (as Carlyle named him) was too commercial in outlook to be completely " Quakerised ", but the humanity and public spirit of the Friends undoubtedly tempered his acquisitive, prudential morality. To his favourite sister he wrote: " There are some things in your New England doctrine which I do not agree with; but I do not therefore condemn them, or desire to shake your belief . . ." (quite Emersonian in sentiment). Franklin supported the Scots-Irish element in their determination to defend Pennsylvania, but he was too enlightened for these dour Presbyterians. He was a pioneer in applying religion to citizenship, and deserves to be remembered for more than the self-regarding maxims of *Poor Richard's Almanack*. He initiated one public enterprise after another—fire-brigades, postal services, street-lighting, circulating libraries and hospitals. He sometimes forgot that " the soul of all improvement is improvement of soul ", but gave American religion its strong bent towards philanthropy (with " uplift "). In 1775 he was President of the Philadelphia Society for the emancipation of slaves.

Quaker Quietism had declared against slavery early in the eighteenth century. From 1743 onwards John Woolman travelled from meeting to meeting, testifying against it as sin.[1] Slavery was rooted out of the Society of Friends, while in other denominations voluntary emancipation remained merely the pious opinion of individuals. The pamphlets of Anthony Bénézet (1713-84), the son of a Huguenot exile, were widely read in England and roused Clarkson against this social crime. In course of time the corporate conscience of the Quakers, exercised through their Quarterly Meetings, declared not merely against the slave trade but against the keeping of slaves. A series of resolutions between 1758 and 1775 finally excluded slave-holders from the fellowship of Friends. Example counted for more than precept. J. H. St. John de Crèvecœur, a Frenchman, in his charming *Letters from an American Farmer* (1782, in *Everyman* ed.), compares the Quakers

---

[1] His *Journal* is a Christian classic. Lamb, Coleridge and Crabb Robinson drew attention to the fact that a man of poor education should have commended New Testament religion so attractively. See Dr. Smellie's ed. (London, 1898).

favourably with other denominations, for sincere application of
the Gospel. He cites a clergyman at George-Town who urged
his planters from the pulpit to treat their slaves with " the benig-
nity of Christianity " rather than with their customary severity.
" Sir," said one of his hearers, " we pay you a genteel salary to
read to us the liturgy, but we do not want you to teach us what we
are to do with our blacks." The clergyman, he tells us, " found it
prudent to withhold any further admonition." Crèvecœur is apt
to idealise the new " American " civilisation that he saw coming
into being, but his picture of Pennsylvania, where men of all
creeds lived peacefully together, is worth quoting:

" Let us suppose you and I to be travelling; we observe that in this
house, to the right, lives a Catholic, who . . . believes in transubstantiation;
he raises wheat, he has a large family, hale and robust; his belief offends
nobody. About one mile farther on the same road, his next neighbour
may be a good honest plodding German Lutheran, who addresses himself to the same God . . . and believes in consubstantiation; by so doing
he scandalises nobody; he also works in his fields, clears swamps, etc.
What has the world to do with his Lutheran principles ? Next again
lives a Low Dutchman, who implicitly believes the rules laid down by
the Synod of Dort. He conceives no other idea of a clergyman than that
of a hired man; if he does his work well he will pay him the stipulated
sum; if not he will dismiss him, and do without his sermons . . . But
notwithstanding this coarse idea, you will find his house and farm to be
the neatest in all the country."

William Penn was a complete contrast to the New Englanders
who were set on building up a homogeneous Anglo-Saxon community. Not only did he welcome Welsh farmers with the promise
of land, self-government, and the unrestricted use of their own
language. He visited Holland and Germany from 1671 onwards,
with a view to attracting colonists. This invitation assumed practical shape when a Pietist lawyer, Francis Pastorius, organised the
Frankfurt Land Company, which purchased 25,000 acres in Pennsylvania. He led the first contingent across the Atlantic in 1683
and founded Germantown, now a pleasant suburb of Philadelphia.
Whittier, feeling that history had neglected these pioneers, while
the *Mayflower* had become a familiar epic, did ample justice to
Pastorius and his followers in *The Pennsylvania Pilgrim*—a poem
which distils perfectly the aroma of German mysticism and the
woodland charm of Pennsylvania.

The various groups of sectarian settlers came mostly from the
lower Rhine; many of them were descended directly from the six-

teenth-century Anabaptists, but they had long abandoned the revolutionary projects of their ancestors; they were akin to the Quakers, trusting in " the unresistible might of meekness ". These Mennonites belonged to the Baptist family, but intense persecution had accentuated their peculiarities and produced even more eccentric offshoots such as the Dunkers and the Amish. These groups are intensely pacifist. They practise immersion, foot-washing, the kiss of peace (strictly between the same sex) and observe sumptuary laws of Mosaic preciseness. " Be not conformed to this world." Women wear a " devotional head-covering " at worship, and men, black felt hats of Hebraic style. The razor is used with reluctance, beards being trimmed in conformity with Leviticus, 21.5. Mennonites have a morbid fear of worldliness, abstaining from amusements, public life, mixed marriages, household decoration and " fashions ". The " Amish " (founded by Jacob Amen in Switzerland in the seventeenth century) go so far as to banish buttons in favour of hooks and eyes (which would have supplied Carlyle with an extra chapter for *Sartor*). The ban is placed on trade unions, the Y.M.C.A., life insurance—even suspenders, telephones, bicycles and hymnbooks with notes. Such legalistic taboos provide capital illustrations of Harnack's " sanctifying power of blind custom ".

Not content with " keeping themselves to themselves " in farm communities, some of these sectarians have obeyed to the letter the apostolic precept, " Come out and be separate ". The valleys of Pennsylvania used to resemble the ravines of North Africa in the early Christian centuries, for they were honeycombed with lonely hermitages. The old-world cloisters for " brothers " and " sisters " can still be seen at Ephrata.[1] It is surprising to find such Catholic features reproduced among ultra-Protestant groups. To this day the Mennonite and similar communities preserve their uncouth German dialect and picturesque seventeenth-century customs. They form the hard core of the " Pennsylvania Dutch " (*Deutsch*) population, which for two centuries has lain, as it were, encysted in the body of the surrounding people.[2]

Franklin estimated that in the middle of the eighteenth century at least one-third of the colonists were of German extraction,

[1] For selections from the quaint *Chronicon Ephratense* see P. G. Mode, *Source Book for American Church History*, pp. 173-7.
[2] See illustrated art. by E. C. Stauffer, *Nat. Geographical Magazine* (July 1941).

another third being Quaker. When Louis XIV laid waste the Palatinate in 1688, it was feared that the exodus of Calvinists, speeded by Romish persecution, would depopulate the Rhine valley. Pennsylvania was their goal. In 1690 some 30,000 of these " displaced persons " assembled at a huge transit-camp near London. The English public helped to alleviate the sufferings of these " Poor Palatines ". Lutheran immigrants were also desperately poor. Many of them were cruelly exploited by shipping agents; unable to pay all their fare, they found themselves put up for auction on arrival and sold as " indentured servants ". These " redemptioners " were as sheep without a shepherd, and increased rapidly. In 1741 Count Zinzendorf, the Moravian leader, arrived in Philadelphia. He hastened to Bethlehem, where the foundations of various institutions (charitable, educational and missionary) had already been laid. There were about 20,000 German Lutherans who needed the Gospel. Their few existing congregations were near Philadelphia. Pastors and schoolmasters were often drunken and immoral adventurers. Zinzendorf was invited to preach in the principal Lutheran church. Germans of all denominations flocked to hear his simple, fervid Gospel. He proposed that they should all worship together, whatever their sect, in a fellowship to be called " the Congregation of God in the Spirit " (Eph. 2.22).

Then beat the drum ecclesiastic. The Pietist Lutherans of Halle had been haggling over the details of a scheme to supply their fellow-countrymen in America with religious ordinances; hearing that they had been forestalled, they suddenly reversed their co-operative attitude and decided to send out their own apostle. This was Heinrich Melchior Muhlenberg, a native of Hanover, on whom Francke had pressed the claims of his countrymen in America. Muhlenberg arrived in 1742 with providential promptness, to the surprise of Philadelphia. Zinzendorf gracefully retired from the field, " being satisfied if only Christ were preached ". The disciples of Francke and Spener, by refusing to share burdens, were impelled to shoulder a mighty responsibility.

No better apostle could have been chosen than young Muhlenberg. He was robust, friendly, with undoubted gifts of leadership. His apprenticeship under Francke at Halle had laid the foundations of a Pietism that was much better balanced than that of the emotional Zinzendorf. He kept well in touch with Halle and sent

D

home detailed accounts of his work. Extracts from his letters and diaries were published in Germany, to keep alive public interest. These " Halle Reports " are the chief sources for study of his methods of evangelisation.[1] His motto was *Ecclesia Plantanda*, " the Church must be planted ". He served a parish at Trappe, Pennsylvania, from 1742 till his death in 1787 (this quaint old Augustus Church is still preserved, one of the shrines of American Lutheranism). From Trappe Muhlenberg's energy radiated in all directions. Like Wesley, he was always on the move, planning, building, and smoothing out squabbles. In 1748 only ten congregations were represented in the Synod. By 1771 these had increased to seventy in Pennsylvania alone; by 1787, 75,000 out of 110,000 Germans in the province were Lutherans.

Muhlenberg found it a hard task to overcome parochialism, to get people " to understand the connexion and interest of the whole ". Fortunately he was able to preach in English, German and Dutch. He looked ahead with confidence, seeing hope and not frustration in the linguistic and racial differences of those who acknowledged the Augsburg Confession. " A twisted cord of many threads will not break." As the century passed it became obvious that the resources of Halle Pietism were not equal to the tremendous task of building an American Church. Muhlenberg, however, had fostered self-government from the beginning. There could naturally be no question of any German State Church having compulsory jurisdiction over any Lutheran in America, corresponding to the authority of the Church of England over Colonial Anglicanism. Lord Acton's generalisation that " Lutheranism required to be sustained by the civil power " certainly did not hold good in America. From the early eighteenth century American Lutheranism had built into a broader framework conciliar principles borrowed from the free Lutheran congregations of London. It was largely due to Muhlenberg " the Patriarch " that by the time of the American Revolution, Lutheranism had achieved a free, synodical constitution, thus completing Luther's ideals which were arrested at the Reformation by the necessity of regarding the German princes as *summi episcopi* or " nursing fathers ".[2]

[1] *The Journal of Muhlenberg*, Vol. I (Philadelphia, 1942) gives a realistic view of an unpromising situation.

[2] R. Fortenbaugh, *The Development of the Synodical Polity of the Lutheran Church in America* (Philadelphia, 1926).

Muhlenberg co-operated gladly with the Protestant Churches of America, particularly with the struggling German Reformed, which was outgrowing its feebleness under the leadership of Michael Schlatter, a Swiss pastor (c. 1746). Lutherans and Reformed spoke the same language and used simple liturgical forms that differed mainly in details; e.g. in the Lord's Prayer, some said *Vater unser* and others *unser Vater*. The impoverished people of the Rhineland and Hesse were in no position to support their Reformed brethren in Pennsylvania. Much of the burden was borne by the *Classis* of Amsterdam. Schlatter circularised an appeal for £20,000 in Great Britain; but German pride was hurt by the idea of churches and schools being built by foreign funds. Alarmists feared that a plot was being engineered to undermine German language and institutions. So vocal were the protests that Schlatter resigned the leadership of the Reformed Church.

In 1743 the *Classis* of Amsterdam transmitted a proposal of the Netherlands synods to the Presbyterian Synod of Philadelphia. In view of similarity of doctrine and polity, might not the Dutch and German Reformed join with the Presbyterians in America ? The needs of a new world justified this step, but linguistic and national jealousies forbade it. In the American Lutheran Church Muhlenberg made the mistake of weeding out men of Moravian sympathies, with the following result: after his death many Lutheran congregations sank into a state of apathetic rationalism, while Moravians were apt to become a clique of sentimentalists. The one side needed radiant zeal and brotherly fellowship: the other needed the ballasting weight of historic doctrine and order. Unfortunately for the future of America, " the head and the heart felt no need of each other ".

2. NEW YORK

In 1609 an Englishman named Henry Hudson, in search for the north-west passage to China, sailed up " the River of Mountains " in a Dutch East India ship, the *Half-moon*. Posts were established on the banks of the Hudson, but for some years the Dutch showed themselves more interested in a lucrative fur-trade than in colonisation. By 1623 a Dutch West India Company, secure in commercial monopoly, established the New Netherlands. Five years later the village of Manhattan, now numbering about 270 souls, welcomed their first pastor, Jonas Michaelius, from

Holland. With the assistance of governor Minuit and the Company's store-keeper, as elders, he proceeded to organise the Reformed Church. Subsequent governors like Van Twiller and Kieft were incompetent and corrupt. All that the latter did for religion was to undertake the erection of a stone church, when reproached by a visitor who spoke of the New Englanders' building as good meeting houses as they could afford, after providing their own houses. Kieft thought that a social occasion afforded the best opportunity. The marriage of the step-daughter of the pastor, "Domine" Everardus Bogardus (1642) was utilised for gathering subscriptions. As the wine circulated, "all with light heads subscribed largely, competing with one another; and although some well repented it when they came to their senses, they were compelled to pay". Thus the first church of New Amsterdam was erected in inauspicious, inebriating circumstances. Domine Bogardus withstood Governor Kieft's misgovernment and insisted on referring their differences to the authorities in Amsterdam. The case, however, was called to a higher court, for the ship on which they sailed was wrecked before reaching the Netherlands. Deadly lethargy again prevailed in the Colonial Church.

The Dutch authorities, discouraged by the prospect of New Amsterdam remaining a mere trading-post, sought to stimulate colonisation by granting estates to men of means who would undertake to bring out fifty able-bodied colonists. The most notable of these "patroons" was Killian van Rensselaer, an Amsterdam jeweller, who settled up the Hudson near the site of Albany (the future capital of the State of New York). This magnate built a church in his manor and imported a pastor named John van Mekelenberg. This Domine "Megapolensis" was a man of much better character than most of the Dutch clergy. He tolerated Lutherans, Mennonites and Roman Catholics. He learned the Mohawk tongue and became one of the first Indian missionaries.

The position of the New Netherlands, however, was economically and politically bad on the arrival of the last Dutch governor, Peter Stuyvesant, in 1647. Stuyvesant's energy restored trade. To prospective settlers from New England he promised "liberty of conscience according to the custom and manner of Holland". Lutherans and Quakers were not so fortunate in obtaining toleration, although there was plenty of scope for competitors, the Dutch Reformed staff consisting (after thirty years) of four ministers and one schoolmaster. The West India Company at Amsterdam disagreed with the Governor's policy; they wanted good colonists, whether orthodox or heterodox. Stuyvesant's capture of " New Sweden ", however, in 1655, was a feather in his cap and the honourable surrender involved liberty of worship for the Lutherans there.

Gustavus Adolphus had thought of a Swedish colony in America. After his death during the Thirty Years War, Chancellor Oxenstierna managed to secure a foothold on the banks of the Delaware in spite of Dutch opposition (1637). A fort was built on the site of the modern city of Wilmington. Pastor Campanius preached here to red men as well as white, some forty years before Penn's ministry of racial reconciliation. There is something pathetic about this little colony of 700 souls, cut off from their native land, yet clinging to the Swedish language and the Lutheran liturgy of their forebears. The community is commemorated by two venerable churches still in use: " Old Swedes ", Wilmington, Delaware (1698) and " Gloria Dei ", Philadelphia (1700). These congregations were eventually absorbed by the Church of England, after a period of Dutch rule. The Swedish colony, with its three counties, was swallowed up in Pennsylvania, but regained identity as the province of Delaware (1711).

The Dutch capture of New Sweden (1655) was but the prelude to the loss of their own colony; New Amsterdam surrendered to the British and was re-named after the Duke of York (1664). The " Rip-van-Winkle " spirit of the Hudson Valley, afterwards satirised by Washington Irving, continued to characterise the town of New York. Even a century of British rule left its external aspect almost untouched—brick houses with crow-stepped gables facing the street, " stoops " at each door where bovine burghers sat of an evening with their *vrouws*, taverns that recalled Teniers, well-banked canals and gardens bright with tulips. The Dutch Church was characteristically torpid, so long as the English made no difficulties about the ecclesiastical terms—free exercise of their solemn, austere worship, and payment of pastors' stipends. The Reformed Church was at its lowest ebb. The roll of six clergy was reduced to three, supposed to look after a population of 10,000 dispersed in three towns and thirty villages. The *Classis* of Amsterdam were responsible throughout the period of British rule for the supply of ministers. They neglected their task shamefully, and it would have been no surprise if the Royal Governor had pushed aside the feeble Dutch Establishment. Nevertheless, the Restoration Governors observed the treaty stipulations[1] and offered toleration to all sects. New Englanders, seeking relief from the Puritan theocracy, found refuge in New York; Quakers and Anabaptists found the administration less oppressive than in most other colonies; and after the Revocation of the Edict of Nantes a stream of Huguenots flowed in from France (their memory is still preserved in suburban place-names like New Rochelle). There was some anxiety when James II sent out a Roman Catholic named Dongan; yet he proved one of the best Restoration Governors. He had orders to proclaim absolute toleration for " differing Opinions . . . provided they give no disturbance to ye public peace, nor do molest others in ye free Exercise of their Religion ".

The Revolution of 1688 marked no advance in religious freedom. Governor Sloughter announced toleration for all save Papists, but he was instructed to carry out the provisions of the Test Act of 1673, obliging office-bearers to take the Sacrament according to the Anglican rite. This seemed to indicate the Establishment of the Church of England. The Governor's next act was to secure the passage of the *Ministry Act*, providing for the " proper maintenance of a minister in every town where there were forty families or more". This law applied to the city of New York and the neighbouring counties of Richmond, Westchester and Queen's (1691-3). English Governors interpreted the Act as the Establishment of the Church of England,[2] while a strong party in the provincial legislature considered that it permitted the settlement of any Protestant minister acceptable to the local community. The colony was cosmopolitan. In 1695 an Anglican military chaplain stationed in New York reported that only 90 families adhered to the English Church, while the corresponding figures were:

[1] They used their influence to promote Dutch ordinations in the colony instead of sending pastors across the Atlantic, like the Anglican clergy seeking " Orders " in the homeland. By the middle of the eighteenth century Dutch ordinations took place on American soil, with a local *Coetus*, subject to the *Classis* of Amsterdam.

[2] Churches founded by " Dissenters " sometimes got into the hands of " Churchmen ". Thus, Rev. J. Bartow wrote (1702): " My Lord Cornbury requested me to preach at Eastchester; accordingly I went (though some there had given out threatening words. . .). Their Presbyterian minister, Mr. Morgan, had begun service in the meeting-house, to which I went straight way . . . in the afternoon I was permitted to perform the Church of England service; Mr. Morgan being present, and neither he nor the people seemed dissatisfied . . . and they desired me to come oftener." Imperceptibly, the parish became Episcopal.

Huguenots, 260; Dutch Reformed, 1,754; Dutch Lutheran, 45; English Dissenters, 1,365. A Bishop would be useful in shepherding wandering sheep into the Episcopal fold, but meanwhile a beginning might be made by building walls. In 1695 a charter was given to Trinity Church. The vestry, representing the citizens at large, elected the Rev. William Vesey. As he was a Congregationalist, the Governor refused to endorse his nomination. The candidate proved pliable, agreed to go to England and returned in all the glory of "Orders". He had the zeal of an apostate, and his defection was one of the hardest knocks sustained by the non-Anglican majority. Moreover, all the arts of persuasion were brought to bear on the Huguenot congregations, e.g. New Rochelle, so that they might gracefully conform to the official cult. So uneasy were the Dutch that they felt impelled to secure a Charter for the Reformed Church, in guarantee of its property and privileges. They seemed to care for little else, for in 1696 Domine Selyns announced complacently, "Our number is now complete " (meaning that there were now four ministers for the whole province). It is not surprising that the Dutch Church remained one of the least of the tribes of Israel, and, but for the Great Awakening under Whitefield, might have died out altogether.

A test case affecting the claims of the English Church in New York arrested public attention in 1706. A young Presbyterian minister, Francis Makemie, passing through New York, was invited by the Congregationalists to preach and was offered the use of the Dutch Church. His companion, John Hampton, officiated at Newtown, Long Island. Lord Cornbury, the royal Governor, had them both arrested for holding forth at a "conventicle ". The charge against Hampton was not pressed, but Makemie was accused of being "a Jack-of-all-trades, doctor, merchant, attorney, preacher, and—worst of all—a disturber of governments". He was defended by three able lawyers who had no difficulty in proving that he had complied with the English Toleration Act by procuring a licence to preach in Barbados. David Jameson maintained: "We have no Established Church here; we have liberty of conscience by an Act of Assembly made in William and Mary's reign. This province is made up chiefly of Dissenters and persons not of English birth." Makemie himself declared: "If your Lordship require it, we will give security for our behaviour; but to give bond not to preach . . . if invited by the people, we neither can nor dare do it." Cornbury roared: "Then you must go to the gaol!" Makemie won his case, but had to pay £83 in costs. He published at Boston his *Narrative of a New and Unusual Imprisonment of Two Presbyterian Ministers*, which had some effect in securing the tyrant's recall. An Anglican cleric named Urquhart, in a letter to the S.P.G., described Lord Cornbury " as a true nursing father to our infancy here ". Not all the " Churchmen " of New York were so subservient. The Rev. Thoroughgood Moor, rector of Trinity, was actually imprisoned because he rebuked this Governor for his dissolute life.

The year of Makemie's trial marked the beginnings of organised Presbyterianism in America; in 1706 he founded the first Presbytery at Philadelphia. Born in Donegal of Scots parents in 1658, he made his way to Glasgow University, and after completing his studies for the Ministry was licensed by the Irish Presbytery of Laggan. It was at a meeting of this Presbytery that he heard a letter read, describing the religious destitution of Presbyterianism on the eastern shore of Maryland; the writer, curiously enough, was an Anglican, Colonel Stevens. Young Makemie responded to this urgent call to " come over and help us ". He crossed the Atlantic in 1683 and visited isolated Presbyterian settlers down the coast from New England to the Carolinas. Cotton Mather welcomed him to Boston, although New England was already committed to the " Congregational Way ". New Jersey, however, was a province where there was room for Presbyterianism; the first regularly constituted congregation was formed at Freehold in 1692, and there the first recorded Presbyterian ordination was solemnised. A monument now marks the site of the kirk.

Makemie visited England in 1691 and again in 1704. He also corresponded with various ministers and synods of the Church of Scotland; effective response was evoked through Principal Stirling of Glasgow University, a public-spirited promoter of American missions. An appeal for men and money was also made to the liberal-minded and wealthy Presbytery of Dublin. Most support came from Ulster. The Presbyterians of Northern Ireland were numerous but poor. They were persecuted by the Anglican Establishment, while their trade and manufactures were artificially discouraged by the English Government. Under these circumstances it is not surprising that the tide of emigration rose steadily from about 1713 till 1730-40; by that time more than half the

Presbyterian population of Ulster (one million) had moved to America. There they realised the freedom that the Battle of the Boyne had failed to guarantee at home—equality with Protestant Episcopalians. The original Presbytery of Philadelphia contained two Ulstermen, two Scots and three New Englanders. This ratio, however, was not maintained. New Englanders usually accepted Presbyterianism on crossing the Hudson, but they were certainly not Presbyterians by temperament. The Scots element was not so prominent after the Revolution of 1688 had ended the persecution of the Covenanters. The Scots-Irish, on the other hand, came in their thousands, bringing with them a belligerent brand of hard-shell Presbyterianism that accounts for the strong conservative tradition in the American Church.

Ulstermen came in large groups, sometimes landowners with their tenants, more often congregations with their ministers. A number of them settled in Virginia and Maryland, but conditions were more favourable in the " middle colonies " of New Jersey and Pennsylvania, where there was no Anglican Establishment. William Penn offered substantial inducements to these settlers, but James Logan, his secretary, termed them " bold and indigent strangers ". They soon prospered ; their enthusiasm and energy blended love of freedom and religious zeal that set its mark on these provinces. The Scots-Irish brought with them a unifying religion in marked contrast to the variety of beliefs and practices that characterised the German Pietist immigrants. Their dominating, determined temper is well illustrated by the recorded prayer of an elder: " Grant, Lord, that I may be right, for Thou knowest I am hard to turn."

Dr. Makemie, the father of American Presbyterianism, died in 1708. By 1716 the single Presbytery which he founded had blossomed into the Synod of Philadelphia, with four presbyteries that stretched from Long Island near New York to Snow Hill, Maryland, with outposts in Virginia. There were only seventeen ministers as yet, but the organisation was ready to cope with the fresh influx of new life that was destined to flow from revival as well as immigration. The Presbyteries had to deal with numerous applications for " supply of sermon " and for ordination. It was not always easy to maintain the high Presbyterian standard of an educated ministry in view of the pressing need for evangelism. Yet the Presbytery of Philadelphia made good precedent in the

case of David Evan, " a lay person ", who had been preaching to
the Welshmen of the Great Valley. They criticised him for taking
too much on himself; he " had done very ill " (1710). He must
" lay aside all business for a twelve month and apply himself
closely to study " under the supervision of two ministers. Evan
submitted to this discipline, was examined annually by the Presbytery, and finally ordained in 1715.

A time was coming when rapid growth and revival would impel
men to the Ministry who claimed that conversion and ability to
preach the Gospel were the only essential qualifications. In the
early eighteenth century the problem was one of doctrine rather
than of discipline. It was no longer safe to take for granted the
orthodoxy of incoming ministers from the old country. Irish
Presbyterianism had been split by the Arian controversy and
latitudinarian ideas had appeared in the Church of Scotland. The
Scots and Irish element in American Presbyterianism were determined to prevent the intrusion of " many pernicious and dangerous
corruptions in doctrine, which have grown so much in vogue, such
as Arminianism, Socinianism, Deism, etc." A creedless church
was no church, and hitherto American Presbyterianism had been
guided by tradition rather than thirled to an official Confession.

The Congregationalists who had crossed the Hudson from New
England and settled extensively in New York and New Jersey
usually affiliated with Presbyterian churches. Calvinistic as they
were, their tradition was more flexible; they did not like the idea
of creed-subscription, and found themselves more in sympathy
with the Presbyterians of London and Dublin in this respect.

Reconciliation was effected by the *Adopting Act* of 1729.
American Presbyterianism adopted the Westminster Standards
" as being, in all the essential articles good forms of sound words ".
The Confession, Directory of Worship and Catechisms were to
be observed " as near as circumstances will allow and Christian
prudence direct ". The Presbytery was to determine how this
was to be applied. There was inevitable friction between the
stricter, confessional party (mainly Scots-Irish) and those who
claimed more latitude (mainly New Englanders), in view of the
needs of a new and vast continent. Should Presbyterianism be
exported and stereotyped exactly as it was in the Church of Scotland? Or should it be reasonably elastic, with power to expand and
become definitely American ?

CHAPTER III

THE NEW ENGLAND WAY

Religion stands on tip-toe in our land
Readie to passe to the *American* strand.
. . . Then shall Religion to America flee:
They have their times of Gospel, ev'n as we.

GEORGE HERBERT: The Church Militant.

1. SIFTED SEED-CORN

IT IS A PITY to condense the epic of New England's founders, when they can tell us their own story in moving and graphic words. Any good general history of the United States will present the settlement of this region in proper perspective, avoiding panegyric and undue disparagement. The pioneers were not all saints and heroes: nor were they men impelled solely by economic motives, who sailed under the colours of Christianity merely by way of propaganda. The truth lies between the two extremes. British readers will not understand the great migration unless they grasp the fact that there was a distinct difference between the small band of Separatists who founded Plymouth in 1620 and the larger Puritan company that colonised Massachusetts Bay in 1629. The name " Pilgrim Fathers " was not coined till 1799, and up till the middle of the nineteenth century was applied indiscriminately to all the founders of New England. Historians now restrict the title to the pioneers of 1620, their successors being known as " the Puritans ".[1]

---

[1] See Geo. F. Willison's chapter, "Apotheosis", *Saints and Strangers* (Heinemann, London, 1946). The evolution of this New England " mythos " is traced to " The Old Colony Club ", founded by young men of old family at Plymouth (1769). Several of these fled to England at the Revolution. Chandler Robbins, in a Memorial Sermon (1793) quoted " They knew they were pilgrimes ", and so happily named them. After 1840 the " First Comers " became " The Pilgrims ", and Plymouth, a mere county seat since 1692, became a place of pilgrimage for all good Americans, its Rock the fetish of a cult. The " Pilgrims " first appeared on the stage in Croswell's *A New World Planted* (1802). Pageantry culminated in the Tercentenary (1920).

It is a strange irony that has transformed the timber of the *Mayflower* into the family trees of ambitious Americans anxious to prove their distinguished ancestry. Those who sailed in 1620 were definitely plebeian in origin. Two-thirds consisted of men who wanted a new start—social misfits unable to make a living or at odds with the law. They were not " Saints " but " Strangers ", hailing mostly from London and the south-east. They found regimentation irksome, especially in the new world. What had they in common with the " Saints "—the tradesmen, mechanics and farmers of strenuously sectarian convictions ?

The settlers' leader, William Brewster, lived in the small manor of Scrooby, situated in an obscure part of East Anglia, near Gainsborough. His followers were humble folk who outdid the Puritans in their radical demand for a new order in Church and State. These " come-outers " were determined to fashion for themselves a true Christian community on the New Testament model, " without tarrying for any ". To conservatives, they were revolutionaries. To men of the world, they were Pharisees— " come not near, for I am holier than thou." To the orthodox Puritans who sought to bring the Church of England nearer the Genevan ideal, they were extremists who discredited the Calvinist cause—" Brownists ", etc. They were " Separatists ", to be sure, but hardly fanatics. Their conception of the " gathered Church " as a close spiritual fellowship is well suggested by lines written a century later by Watts:

> We are a garden wall'd around,
> Chosen and made peculiar ground;
> A little spot enclosed by grace
> Out of this world's wild wilderness.

After severe persecution, the Scrooby nucleus joined other English exiles in Leyden, where the tolerant Dutch allowed them to form a congregation (1608). Life at Leyden was less idyllic than the " Separatists " expected. They fell out among themselves on minute points of doctrine and order. They purged the Church of the incurable and incorrigible " when no other means would serve; which seldom came to pass ". As foreigners they were ill at ease, even in a Reformed land. They did not consider that the Dutch were strict enough in observing the Sabbath. As " displaced persons ", they were dissatisfied with their unpromising economic condition. They were faced with the prospect of their young people being assimilated by the Dutch community. Twelve years in Holland did not reconcile them to exile. Elder Brewster and Pastor Robinson felt that a fresh beginning was essential. To England the congregation could not return; that meant Newgate or " the Clink ". What about a New England, across the Atlantic, where they would be free to build a Bible Commonwealth for themselves ? They might well have expressed their aim in the memorable words of William Stoughton: " God hath sifted a nation, that He might send sifted seed-corn into this wilderness " (1669).

Sir Edwin Sandys, Puritan treasurer of the Virginia Company, granted the Pilgrims permission to settle in " the northern parts of Virginia ". It was surely an act of God's providence, that His free winds landed the exiles, not in a colony where they would subsequently have been persecuted again by Anglicans, but in a land where they would be free from further interference. In the autumn of 1620 the weary Pilgrims landed on the desolate shores of Cape Cod, Massachusetts (11th November—a *dies mirabilis* in our own times). The immigrants had no legal right to settle where they did, but in true Independent fashion they made a solemn compact in the cabin of the *Mayflower*, " in the presence of God and of one another, covenanting and combining themselves into a civil body politic ". They " joined themselves in the fellowship of the Gospel, to walk in all His ways, made known, or to be made known . . . whatever it should cost them, the Lord assisting them." Bradford adds with touching simplicity: " And that it cost them something, this ensuing history will declare."

William Bradford, like John Knox, was the chief actor in his own history. The Pilgrim leader made it his aim " to begine at ye very roote " and " take up his parable in a plaine style, with a singular regard for ye simple truth in all things ". The manuscript of his *Plimouth Plantation* passed from Bradford's descendants to " The New England Library ". Deposited in the tower of the historic South Church, Boston, it disappeared during the American Revolution. It is believed that it was taken to England by Hutchison, the last royal Governor of Massachusetts. It was eventually discovered in the Bishop of London's Library at Fulham Palace. The clue to the lost history consisted of certain quotations from a manuscript cited by Bishop Samuel Wilberforce of Oxford, in his *History of the American Episcopal Church* (1844).

American historians, conscious for some time of a " missing link "
in the Pilgrim saga, tracked these quotations to their source.
Bradford's " History " was at last printed in 1856. The *Mayflower*
men and women now appeared in three dimensions as " real
humans ". Too late, unfortunately—by the time Bradford's narrative was read by the descendants of the Pilgrim Fathers, Longfellow and Whittier had already romanticised the " Puritans ",
and this popular tradition dies hard. Representations were made
that the historic document should be returned to the United
States, but Victorian prelates were none too friendly to " dissenters " even as far distant as New England. Bishop Creighton,
himself an historian and a Churchman of good will, finally returned
the precious manuscript to the Commonwealth of Massachusetts,
after it had been reproduced in photographic facsimile (1897).
The romance of the *Plimouth Plantation* was completed.

The landing of the Pilgrims marked the beginning of democracy
in Church and State. No royal governor inaugurated the " Plantation " by solemnly proclaiming the authority of King James I.
No ordained minister accompanied the Pilgrims and dedicated
their house of worship; for nine years Elder Brewster " divided
the Word ". Pastor Robinson, who had ministered to the Pilgrim
congregation at Leyden, did not sail in the *Mayflower*. He
intended to cross the Atlantic later with reinforcements, but died
in Holland in 1626. The loss of this distinguished divine, a
graduate of Cambridge, deprived the colonists of far-sighted, sane
and inspired leadership. Even Robert Baillie, Scots opponent of
the sectaries, praised him as " the most learned, polished and
modest spirit that ever separated from the Church of England ".
He was well aware that the Pilgrims needed a double portion of
prophetic spirit. The Christian enterprise to which they had
dedicated their lives demanded a larger measure of mutual understanding, charity, breadth and brotherhood. His farewell message
on the growing revelation of Divine truth resounds through the
centuries:

" We are now ere long to part asunder, and the Lord knoweth whether
I shall live to see your faces again. But whether the Lord hath appointed
it or not, I charge you before God, to follow me no further than I have
followed Christ . . . I bewail the condition of the reformed churches who
are come to a period in religion . . . The Lutherans cannot be drawn to
go beyond what Luther saw. And the Calvinists, as you see, stick where
Calvin left them . . . Luther and Calvin were precious shining lights in

their times, yet God did not reveal his whole will to them . . . I am very
confident that the Lord hath more truth and light yet to break forth out
of His Holy Word."

The Pilgrims had much need of this inspiring message. The
Mayflower was as crammed as Noah's ark. Of 102 souls who
embarked, nearly half were dead after four months. The survivors
were in peril from cold, starvation and false brethren sent as spies.
They were also in debt to a London Merchant Company who
advanced £7,000. expecting profits from pioneers battling with
nature on a barren shore; by a superhuman effort they bought
themselves free by annual instalments of £1,800. Plymouth Rock
was a fitting symbol of adversity; but after the first grim winter
an Indian chief, Massosoet, kindly showed them what sort of
crops the poor soil could produce. After the first harvest (1621)
the Pilgrims gathered for worship, followed by a dinner of corn,
pumpkin and wild turkey, the Indians joining them in the open
air. This has become an American folk legend—a justification
for autumnal family reunions. For many a year " Thanksgiving
Day " was a festival peculiar to New England, celebrated all the
more gladly when Christmas was banned. Since the American
Revolution and particularly since the Civil War, Thanksgiving
has been observed throughout the United States on the last
Thursday in November, church service being followed by family
dinner.[1] The Episcopalians recognised this Pilgrim festival in
1789, the Roman Catholics following suit a century later. The
Pilgrims are also honoured by " Forefathers' Day ", now observed
on 21st December.

After ten years Plymouth Plantation consisted of 300 inhabitants, which increased to 2,500 only by 1643. " Let not the
smallness of our beginnings make the work seem despicable,"
wrote Nathaniel Morton in *New England's Memorial*, " but let
the greater praise be rendered unto God who hath effected great
things by small means." How did the " sifted seed-corn " prosper,
planted in a wilderness infested by Indians ? The Colonists
imported English institutions (civil marriage seems to have been
the only thing borrowed from Holland). They had little time for
constitution-mongering. Constant vigilance was the condition of
survival. As in Nehemiah's day, " every one with one hand

[1] The author had the interesting experience of reading from an American
pulpit a Thanksgiving Proclamation, " By his Excellency the Governor ", concluding with the words, " God save the Commonwealth of Massachusetts ".

wrought in the work, and with the other held a weapon." A
Dutch merchant of New Amsterdam gave the following description of their worship in 1627:

" Upon the hill they have made a large square meeting house, with a
flat roof . . . upon which they have cannons. The lower part they use
for their church. They assemble by beat of drum, each with his musket
in front of the Captain's door [Miles Standish]; they have their cloaks
on, and place themselves in order, three abreast, and are led by a sergeant.
Behind comes the Governor [William Bradford] in a long robe; beside
him, on the right hand, comes the preacher [Elder Brewster] with his
cloak on, and on the left the captain, with his side arms and a small cane
in his hand; and so they march in good order, and each sets his arms
down near him."

.   .   .   .

Nine years after the arrival of the *Mayflower* at Plymouth, a
fresh influx of English immigrants reached Salem, in Massachusetts Bay. These were the Puritans, who found the yoke of
Archbishop Laud and Charles I intolerable. They claimed to have
separated, not from the Church of England, but from its corruptions and ceremonies. They were a cross-section of English life,
and therefore more representative than the Pilgrims—squires, merchants, university graduates, yeomen, tradesmen and labourers.
The promoters had procured a Charter for their " Massachusetts
Bay Company ", and those who did not intend to go to America
withdrew from the corporation. Thus there were no absentee
stockholders in England, clamouring for dividends; and the
governing body was firmly set on American soil.

The leaders belonged to the sturdy stock that gave the motherland her Hampdens, Pyms and Cromwells. There was John
Winthrop of Groton Manor, Suffolk—an attractive personality,
man of affairs and man of culture; through the seasoned wisdom
of this Puritan aristocrat, the Bay Colony weathered many a storm.
Frequently elected Governor till his death in 1649, Winthrop
safeguarded the interests of Massachusetts against threatened
Parliamentary interference. In 1643 he was successful in federating the " United Colonies of New England ". His *Journal*
traces the history of the Bay Colony from its genesis. Winthrop's
style is less picturesque than Bradford's, but his narrative is worth
reading (not published till 1790). Cotton Mather, in his *Magnalia*,
pays filial tribute to the founding father:

" Let Greece boast of her patient Lycurgus. Let Rome tell of her devout Numa. . . Our New England shall boast of her *Winthrop*, a law-giver as patient as Lycurgus and as devout as Numa; a governor in whom the excellences of Christianity made a most improving addition unto the virtues, wherein even without *those* he would have made a *parallel* for the great men of Greece, or of Rome, which the pen of a Plutarch has eternalised."

Another founder of the Bay Colony was Thomas Dudley, who belonged to the elder branch of the Leicester family (associated with the names of Lady Jane Grey and Queen Elizabeth). There was no lover's gaiety in Thomas Dudley, who bore Northampton-shire flint in his soul. He was the over-rigid type of Puritan, merciless to any opinion that deviated a hair's breadth from orthodox Calvinism. At his death the following quatrain of his own composition was found in his pockets; it neatly sums up his intolerance:

> Let men of God in courts and churches watch
> O'er such as do a Toleration hatch,
> Lest that ill egg bring forth a cockatrice
> To poison all with heresy and vice.

The promoters of the Massachusetts Bay Company did not see eye to eye when it came to the persecution of heretics; but they were knit together by common religious convictions, and were men of affairs, in a position to obtain capital. One of the pivotal persons behind the enterprise was " Master " John White, rector of Dorchester, who had already gained experience through floating a " Company of Adventurers " to establish trading posts on the New England coast. White was a moderate Puritan. He now aimed at providing a permanent basis for the fishing industry, a colony for the unemployed, and a refuge from Laudian tyranny. Publicity agents extolled the climate of New England, which was more temperate than that of Virginia, though the soil was poorer. A contemporary ballad shows how ordinary folk were persuaded to " come along for the truth's sake " as well as for self-betterment, with comradeship as an incentive.

> Our compeny we feare not—
> There goes my Cosen Hanna—
> And Ruben doe perswade to goe,
> His sister, fair Susannah. . .
> And Ralph Cobler too with us will goe,
> For he regards his soule;
> And the weaver, honest Symon,
> With Prudence, Jacob's daughter.

E

In reply to tendencious theorists, special pleaders for "the economic interpretation of history", Professor S. E. Morison of Harvard answers the question: *Were the settlers of Massachusetts Bay Puritans* ?[1] He has no difficulty in proving that though the trade in fish and furs was lucrative, and poor folk were attracted by the offer of a fresh start in life, most of the Colonists left their English homes with religious motives uppermost.[2] The religious zeal of the ministers, merchants and magistrates who headed the expedition doubtless outran that of the rank-and-file; but the initial phase of the Bay Plantation did not involve the dragooning of a non-Puritan majority by a fanatical oligarchy. We catch the note of enthusiasm in Captain Edward Johnson's *Wonder-working Providence in New England*, published in London.

"Oh yes! Oh yes! Oh yes! All you the peopel of Christ that are here Oppressed, Imprisoned and scurrilously derided, gather yourselves together, your wives and your little ones, and answer to your several names as you shall be shipped to . . . the Westerne world. Could Caesar so suddenly fetch over fresh forces from Europe to Asia, Pompy to foyle ? How much more shall Christ call over this 900 leagues Ocean such instruments as you . . . Know this is the place where the Lord will create a new Heaven, and a new Earth in new Churches, and a new Common-wealth together."

The ships that reached Massachusetts Bay in 1629-30 represented a cross-section of English society, with the significant exception of "the lords spiritual and temporal". The ministers, landowners, merchants and professional men in control of this exodus had no intention of departing unnecessarily from the stratified structure of English society, but they had few doctrinaires among them who sought to transplant feudal ideas, as in Virginia. The "elect", it was freely admitted, belonged to all stations of life. The majority of the colonists accepted the Puritan pattern of life to which they were accustomed in England. On the other hand, the immigrants did not all realise that they were "in for" a rigorous, "totalitarian" régime, involved by the very programme of a Church-State modelled on the Old Testament.

The leaders of the expedition had no intention of abjuring the Church of England. They merely sought to purify it from the

---

[1] *Builders of the Bay Colony*, Appendix (Boston, 1930).
[2] Cotton consulted his friend John Dod, of Fawley, Northants., whether he should leave England or not. Dod replied: "That the removing of a Minister was like the draining of a Fish-pond; the good Fish will follow the Water, but Eels, and other Baggage Fish, will stick in the Mud."

abuses of prelacy and ritual, although they were not sure what to put in its place. After Land's End passed out of sight, the Rev. Francis Higginson called his children and fellow-passengers to the stern and exclaimed: " We will not say, as the Separatists were wont to say at their leaving of England, ' Farewell England! farewell Babylon! farewell Rome! ' but we will say, ' Farewell dear England! Farewell the Church of England, and all the Christian friends there! We do not go to New England as separatists from the Church of England, though we cannot but peacefully separate from the corruptions in it; but we go to practise the positive part of church reformation and propagate the gospel in America.' "

What was the prospect of cordial relations between the Separatists of New Plymouth and Puritan Anglicans of Salem ? The former, in Cotton Mather's words, were " few and poor ", the latter " numerous and prosperous ", including " gentlemen of ancient family and great merchants ". Apart from theology, there were social causes calculated to produce chilly isolation. It was human need that evoked latent brotherliness. There was widespread illness in the new Bay Colony, and the only available physician was Dr. Fuller, a deacon in the Plymouth church. Governor Endicott wrote to Governor Bradford in connexion with this call of mercy, using healing contact as a bridge of fellowship. " Right Worthy Sir: It is a thing not usual that servants of one Master and of the same household should be strangers. I assure you I desire it not." There is no record of Governor Endicott's discussion with Deacon Fuller. The latter evidently took to heart Pastor Robinson's advice " rather to study union than division ". They probably discussed among other matters the covenant-basis of the local " gathered church ", the value of free fellowship as opposed to outward constraint, and the disadvantages of affiliation with a National Church three thousand miles away. The good doctor was as effective in administering propaganda as in dispensing pills. Endicott realised that the difference between the Pilgrim Separatists and the Church of England Puritans was merely academic in the wilderness.

The Plymouth principles prevailed to a surprising degree. The Puritan congregation of Salem signed a Covenant reminiscent of the Pilgrims' Compact. They actually " ordained " Higginson as " teacher " and Skelton as " pastor " (20th July 1629), although both had already been regularly ordained in the Church of England. A minority of the Puritans, led by John and Samuel Brown, influential members of the Council at Salem, clung to fragments of the familiar Prayer Book. Governor Endicott informed them that " New England was no place for such as they ", and shipped them home—a high-handed action that disturbed the Massachusetts Company in England, who were to some extent " conformable Puritans " (like John White of Dorchester). Furthermore, the " church " was " gathered " in Separatist style, at Wollaston, Dedham and other settlements. The Rev. Thomas Hooker carefully registered such precedents, with this comment: " The Church, in *totum essentiale*, is and may be before officers." Independency was a reality in New England from the beginning; and for a time Presbyterianism faded into the background like Episcopacy. Robert Baillie, the Scottish critic of New England, was sometimes wide of the mark in his strictures, but was well-informed when he remarked that " Plymouth did incontinent leaven all the vicinity ". Their " way " did " hold out so much liberty to the people, that made it very suitable and lovely to a multitude who had lately stepped out of the Episcopall thraldom in England, to the free aire of a new Worlde." Here was the democratic element stirring in New England.[1] Long repressed, it eventually triumphed.

The Puritans prospered, however, more than the Pilgrims. The Bay Colony increased its population to 20,000 in ten years. " Plymouth Plantation ", on the other hand, marked time; when it was finally merged with Massachusetts (1691) it had no more than 7,000 inhabitants. It was the Puritans, not the Pilgrims, who were destined to give the " New England Way " its characteristic contours.

In May 1631 the " General Court " or legislature of Massachusetts took the significant step of limiting the franchise to members of the new Puritan Church. This marked the beginnings of theocracy and the checking of democratic tendencies. One would expect that this might have disposed a large number of people not in sympathy with the ideal of a " Bible Commonwealth " to conform outwardly. But as Dr. Truslow Adams has noted, " even under strong social and political temptation, three-

[1] Cotton Mather, no democrat, expressed the gratitude of the second Puritan generation to the Pilgrims—" those beloved old planters who laid the foundations of a remarkable country ".

quarters of the population, though probably largely Puritan in sentiment and belief, persistently refused to ally themselves with the New England type of Puritan Church."[1] Frustrated, they agitated for the extension of the franchise. The pastors controlled the government, as the admission of communicants was in their hands, and the way was not made easy for intending members.[2]

" I honoured a faithful minister in my heart," declared Governor Winthrop, " and could have kissed his feet." What was proclaimed from the pulpit was not long in being promulgated as legislation. On the basis of English law arose a legal fabric that owed much to the Old Testament. Heavy penalties were provided against blasphemy, heresy, profanation of the Lord's day and the " reviling of magistrates ". On the other hand, it must be allowed that this draconian code was milder than the law of England, in that the death penalty was prescribed for a score of crimes, instead of for three score.

At an early stage the expedient of public taxation for the support of religion was introduced (it was soon found that voluntary subscriptions were inadequate). The English precedent of tithes and "parson's freehold" indicated the extension of the " Establishment " principle. This was one of the few respects in which the structure of the English Church was to some extent copied. Settlers who dared to use the Prayer Book were disciplined, and if recalcitrant, were shipped back to England. Appeals to English courts were refused when " Remonstrants " like Maverick and Vassall growled: " This captious government will bring us all to nought ". One of these critics was Robert Child, the best educated New Englander, an M.D. of Padua and a colonist of scientific outlook. Child eventually found his way to London, but Cromwell's deadly blow at Parliament (" Pride's Purge ") prevented the " Remonstrant " attempt to secure the establishment of Presbyterianism in New England.[3] The theocracy made it clear that they were prepared to allow no such freedom as most

[1] J. Truslow Adams, *The Founding of New England*, p. 144 (Boston, 1921). Admission to Communion was somewhat of an ordeal. In the remote Highlands of Scotland, even to-day, the high standard of holiness demanded by public opinion deters many people from joining the Church, who attend it regularly.

[2] In 1647 non-communicants were allowed the right of citizenship in the towns of Massachusetts (the unit of local government).

[3] Edward Winslow had been sent to England to thwart their schemes. In reply to *New England Jonas cast up at London*, he issued an equally spicy pamphlet, *New England's Salamander discovered*.

Protestant sects enjoyed at home under the Commonwealth.[1]
" 'Tis Satan's policy," said the Rev. Thomas Shepard of Harvard,
" to plead for an indefinite and boundless toleration." The leaders
of the Bay Colony were as bigoted as Archbishop Laud. William
Blackstone, one of the " old planters " (original settlers) confessed
that the " Lord-Bishops " had merely been exchanged for that
of the " Lord-Brethren ". As regards democracy, the Massachusetts Oligarchy agreed with Laud. Governor Winthrop could
find no warrant for it in Scripture. " Among nations it has allways
been accounted the meanest of all forms of government "; to
allow it would be "a manifest breach of the Fifth Commandment".
John Cotton did not consider democracy as " a fit government
for either church or commonwealth ". His idea was " a theocracy
as near as might be to that which was the glory of Israel, the
peculiar people ".

Cotton was the " un-mitred pope of a pope-hating people ".[2]
He arrived in the Bay Colony four years after its foundation, to
find that the important town of Trimountain had been re-named
Boston in his honour. A victim of Laud's tyranny, he left behind
him the memory of a noble ministry in the great church of St.
Botolph, Boston, whose " stump " is still a lovely landmark of
Lincolnshire.[3] As " teacher " of the First Church in Boston,
Massachusetts, he exercised an even greater influence. " Whatever he delivered in the pulpit," said a contemporary annalist,
" was soon put into an order of court . . . or set up as a practice in
the church." According to his grandson, Cotton Mather, " many
believed God would not suffer Mr Cotton to err." An ardent
student, he was accustomed to call twelve hours " a scholar's
day ". He was well read in the Fathers and Schoolmen, but in
old age he loved " to sweeten his mouth with a piece of Calvin
before he went to sleep ". This " walking library " knew men as
well as books—shrewdness blended with humility. " I'll go and
put a trick on old Cotton," said a roysterer to his companions.
Creeping up to the aged divine, he whispered: " Cotton, thou
art an old fool." To which he replied: " I confess I am so: the
Lord make both thee and me wiser than we are." Dr. Benjamin

[1] As late as 1642 only 3 out of 120 London ministers were suspected of
Independency. In 1644 there were only 54 Anabaptist congregations in England, and not more than 80,000 Independents out of a population of 4,000,000.
[2] Judith B. Welles, *John Cotton* (1584-1652), *Churchman and Theologian*
(Ph.D. Thesis, Edinburgh University, 1948).
[3] A. M. Cook, *Boston goes to Massachusetts* (Boston, Eng., 1945).

Woodbridge, the first graduate of Harvard, compared him to Moses (with emphasis on literary productivity!):

> He had been bred and born upon the mount.
> A living, breathing Bible; tables, where
> Both covenants at large engraven were;
> Gospel and law in's heart had each its column,
> His head an index to the sacred volume.
> His very name a title-page; and next,
> His life a commentary on the text.
> O what a monument of glorious worth,
> When in a new edition he comes forth,
> Without erratas, may we think he'll be,
> In leaves and covers of eternity!

Cotton, like many Puritan ministers, was a Cambridge graduate.[1] He was therefore gratified at the decision to build a new Cambridge near Boston (1638). The same year the college got its name through John Harvard, a New England minister, who bequeathed £780 and 300 books to furnish " a school of the prophets ". It was not long before the " New Nests " were filled with scholars. Harvard very nearly procured a distinguished European educationalist as President in 1642. Can we imagine so advanced a thinker as Amos Comenius seeing eye to eye with the Boston theocrats ? But this was not to be, as Cotton Mather explains: " The solicitations of the Swedish Ambassador diverting another way, that incomparable Moravian became not an American " (*Magnalia*, II, iv, 10).

Harvard was one of " New England's first-fruits ". The first college in America, it set its mark on the Puritanism of the New World.[2] Its gates are appropriately inscribed with this moving quotation from a contemporary letter:

AFTER GOD HAD CARRIED US SAFE TO NEW-ENGLAND, AND WEE HAD BUILDED OUR HOUSES, PROVIDED NECESSARIES FOR OUR LIVELI-HOOD, REAR'D CONVENIENT PLACES FOR GODS WORSHIP, AND SETTLED THE CIVILL GOVERNMENT; ONE OF THE NEXT THINGS WE LONGED FOR, AND LOOKED AFTER WAS TO ADVANCE LEARNING, AND PERPETUATE IT TO POSTERITY; DREADING TO LEAVE AN ILLITERATE MINISTRY TO THE CHURCHES, WHEN OUR PRESENT MINISTERS SHALL LIE IN THE DUST.

[1] He was a Fellow of Emmanuel—a college that above all contributed ministers to New England. Queen Elizabeth asked Sir W. Mildmay: " So, Sir Walter, you have erected a Puritan foundation ? "—" No, madam . . . but I have set an acorn which, when it becomes an oak, God knows what will be the fruit thereof."

[2] In 1696, 76 out of 87 Massachusetts ministers were Harvard men, also 31 out of 35 in Connecticut.

Massachusetts has the credit of providing for public education two centuries before it was seriously contemplated in England. The " Old Deluder " Law of 1647 (so called because it was Satan's " chief project to keep men from the Scriptures ") enacted: that every township with fifty householders was to procure a school-master to teach the elements to all children either at public expense or at moderate charge to the parents; townships with over one hundred families were to set up a " Latin " or grammar school to prepare pupils for Harvard. " Indoctrination " was the mainspring of this educational system. Infants were nourished on John Cotton's *Spiritual Milk for Babes, Drawn out of the Breasts of Both Testaments, for . . . Boston Babes in either England* (1646). The famous *New-England Primer* did not appear till 1688, but expressed the ideals of the founders without any concessions to refinement. It was an ABC in rhyme, compact of common sense and relentless dogma, illustrated by crude sketches that ranged from " Adam's Fall " to Zacchaeus " climbing a tree, his Lord to see ". Till 1768 " the Pope or Man of Sin " was pictured as bugbear on the front page. At a much later date, the cross, so universally used as a symbol by the modern descendants of the Puritans, was still anathema. For one hundred and fifty years this Primer was the basis of New England education.

The same year that the " Old Deluder " Law was promulgated, there appeared one of the first books for adults, written by Nathaniel Ward, minister at Ipswich, Mass. It bore the arresting title:

THE SIMPLE COBLER OF AGGAVVAM IN AMERICA

Willing to help 'mend his native country lamentably tattered, both in the upper-leather and sole, with all the honest stitches he can take. And as willing never to bee paid for his work . . . I pray, Gentlemen, keep your purses.

By Theodore de la Guard. London 1647
(reprinted 1713, 1843)

The " Cobler " is anything but simple. Not even the most learned could follow his precious jargon. He garlanded the thorns of scholastic divinity with Elizabethan conceits. He invented new words in almost every sentence, lamenting the appearance of " nugiperous gentledames " even in Boston, so " surcingled " as to follow the " nudiusterian " fashion of the Court; " if I see any of them accidentally, I cannot cleanse my phansie of them for a moneth after." Ward's critics dismissed him as " a Pedantick ", but he merely carried to absurdity tricks of academic wit, then popular in English literary circles. He possessed one faculty rare among the Puritans—a sense of humour. His very prejudices endear him to the tolerant modern reader:

> The world is full of care,
> Much like unto a bubble;
> Women and care, and care and women,
> And women and care and trouble.

No one could read the " Simple Cobler " and conclude that the author had been transplanted straight from an English Puritan rectory to a New England parsonage. Nathaniel Ward had spent ten years as a London lawyer, and then travelled on the Continent, armed with introductions to the most eminent people. He had dandled Prince Rupert on his knee in princely Heidelberg; in the same city David Paraeus, the leading Calvinist Professor of Germany, persuaded him to enter the ministry. His first charge was at Elbing, East Prussia, where he was chaplain to the Eastland Company (whose Deputy Governor was Theophilus Eaton, organiser of the Massachusetts Bay Company). He was well acquainted with the Continent before the Thirty Years War. He learned much of Calvinistic orthodoxy and the Counter-Reformation, but this did not teach him toleration—nor did his experience of Laud broaden his theology. As positive as a Jesuit, he made a " black list " of " pernicious hereticks . . . making a hell above ground "

" Some [sects] are playing like young Spaniels questing at every bird that rises . . . others are at a dead stand, not knowing what to doe or say; and are therefore called Seekers . . . they never Moored their Anchors well in the firme soile of Heaven [but] are weather-waft up and down with every eddy-wind of every new doctrine. The good Spirit of God doth not usually tie up the Helm, and suffer passengers to Heaven to ride a drift . . ." (Morison, ibid., Ch. VII).

The " Cobler " announced: " He that is willing to tolerate any discrepant way of religion, besides his own, unless it be in matters merely indifferent, either doubts of his own, or is not sincere in it." Indeed, he will presently " hang God's Bible at the Devil's girdle ". Ward considers that his wide experience entitles him to be God's spokesman: " I dare take upon me, to be a Herauld of New-England." His comments on the new country are worth

noting. " We have a strong weaknesse in New-England that when
wee are speaking, we know not how to conclude: wee make many
ends before we make an end: the fault is in the Climate; we cannot
helpe it. . ." Here is an American characteristic, early noted—
the tendency to orate, stimulated by the invigorating air of a new
continent to over-confidence in onself ! Ward did not evidently
find the cultural climate of New England to his liking. He returned
to England fiery and breathless, to find himself a celebrity. In
1648 he subsided into the tranquillity of a country parish, and
died four years later during the Commonwealth. He considered
himself a " beacon ", but the " burning and shining light " who
was most effective in illuminating New England was John Cotton.

Cotton had not Ward's wit, but he was certainly an ecclesiastical
statesmen. It was his consistent aim to mould the New England
Zion after the model of Calvin's holy commonwealth. To this
end, he was instrumental in convening the " Cambridge Synod "
in 1646, seventeen years after the great Puritan migration. Massachusetts, Plymouth, New Haven and Connecticut sent representatives " to discuss, dispute, and clear up, by the word of God
such questions of church government and discipline as they shall
think mette ". The Westminster Confession was accepted " for
substance of doctrine ".[1] The really knotty problems were those
of polity. How was the rigid separatism of the Pilgrims and the
staunch independency of the Puritans to be reconciled with the
Presbyterian system,[2] which was the logical concomitant of Calvinism in Scotland and other Reformed lands ? Cotton argued
that " the way in which we walk doth not differ in substance from
that which Mr. Cartwright pleaded in England ".[3] He did not go
so far as to recommend the formal adoption of Presbyterianism,
though some of his brethren were strong for it. On the other hand
he was successful in preventing the adoption of the word " Independent ", which was coming into use in England. New England
preferred " Congregational ",[4] which suggested local autonomy

[1] See Perry E. Miller, *Orthodoxy in Massachusetts*, 1630-50 (Harvard, 1933).
[2] To Robert Baillie, the Scottish Presbyterian champion, who had attacked
New England as a breeding-place of heresy in his *Dissuasive from the Errours
of the Time*, Cotton replied in *The Way of the Congregational Churches Cleared*
(1648).
[3] Cotton's *Keyes to the Kingdom of Heaven* and *Way of the Churches in
New-England* (London, 1644-45).
[4] Professor Powicke has traced the term " Congregational " to Henry Jacob
(d. 1624), who followed the Pilgrims to N.E. " Independent " was still a new
name in 1643, used in England for 200 years till displaced by " Congregational ".

with neighbouring churches linked by fellowship in local groups. As the late Mr. Bernard Manning put it: Presbyterianism is the centralised way of organising the Reformed Church, Congregationalism is its decentralised form.

The " Cambridge Platform " (1648) is a notable milestone in " the New England Way ".[1] It declared that the federated colonies were spiritually independent of European Churches. It outlined an ecclesiastical system of checks and balances. It indicated practical appreciation of Paul's phrase, " the care of all the churches ", by requiring each flock to secure the approbation of neighbouring congregations for Ordinations, etc. The liberty of the elders[2] was to be kept within due limits by " the liberty of the brethren ". Winthrop was not alone in opposing the principle that ministers' stipends should be raised by taxation. Nevertheless this was enforced, and the legislature was charged with the duty of seeing that the " towns " (rural and urban) made adequate provision for religious ordinances. Such in substance was the Cambridge Platform. If it did not quite succeed in making all concerned " agree sweetly together ", it was generally applied in New England as a standard till about 1780, and was followed at a respectful distance for many years after. It suggested a working compromise between Congregationalism and Presbyterianism, which was eventually applied in the " Plan of Union " (p. 251 f). Massachusetts preferred the decentralised form and Connecticut became "Presbygational" (p. 250f). The fact that New England already suffered from " ecclesiastical discipline " worked against the extension of the " conciliar principle ". The gradual growth of democratic ideas favoured the original feature of the Pilgrims—congregational autonomy. The very word " synod " became suspect; two hundred years elapsed between the Cambridge Synod (1646) and the next comprehensive council, the Albany Convention of 1852.

Associated with John Cotton as co-moderator of the Cambridge Synod was Thomas Hooker. Pastor Hooker had no sympathy with the ministers and magistrates who wanted the " Standing Order " to embody the ideals of oligarchy. He did not agree with

---

[1] Williston Walker, *The Creeds and Platforms of Congregationalism* (New York, 1893).
[2] A pamphlet of 1725 considers the elder as " no more than a human creature ". The deacon assimilated his waning powers but became a stock figure, much caricatured, like the Scots elder.

Governor Winthrop's maxim that "the best part is always the least, and of that best part the wiser part is always the lesser". His comrade, Samuel Stone, had no use for a Congregationalism that was just "a speaking Aristocracy in the face of a silent Democracy". So the sturdy freemen of Newtowne (Cambridge) marched through the forests towards that noble river, the Connecticut (1636). At Hartford (named after Hertford, Stone's birthplace) Hooker founded a new commonwealth on the basis that the foundation of authority is the free consent of the people. Other congregations migrated from Massachusetts (e.g. Dorchester, Watertown) and co-operated with Hartford to form a federation of free towns. Here was democracy in Church and State, at a safe distance from the Boston theocrats. In 1639 the "Fundamental Orders of Connecticut" formulated "the first written constitution known to history, that created a government". It contained no allusion to "our gracious king" or any authority outwith Connecticut; it provided for the election of Governor and legislature by what was practically manhood suffrage, irrespective of church membership; and it achieved a remarkable stability. Fiske went so far as to claim that "it marked the beginnings of American democracy, of which Thomas Hooker deserves more than any other man to be called the father."

The theocratic tradition, however, was planted at New Haven, in the south of the modern State of Connecticut. This colony was founded in 1637 by the Rev. John Davenport, a London vicar, one of Laud's victims, who had gone first of all to Boston ("My arm shall reach him even there!" declared the Archbishop). Accompanied by his wealthy parishioner and boyhood friend, Theophilus Eaton, Davenport founded a Bible Commonwealth on authoritarian lines. He adopted a Code compiled by his friend, John Cotton, which proved too rigorous for even the Bay Colony. Some of the New Haven pioneers, attracted from Massachusetts mainly by land hunger, discovered that their daily lives were uncomfortably controlled by a draconian code (*Moses his Judicialls*). This was a parallel to the Scots Act of 1667 making the eighteenth chapter of *Leviticus* statute law. What did this mean for New Haven? Trial by jury was rejected, for instance, as unknown to Scripture. Other English improvements on the Mosaic code were excised. Each town was governed by ecclesiastical officers, the seven "pillars of the church". The clergy were omnipotent.

New Haven, however, was particularly obnoxious to Charles II, for the people sheltered two regicide judges, Whalley and Goffe, who had condemned his father to death. The royal detectives vainly tracked these regicides up and down the woodland paths of the little Puritan Commonwealth. However, Charles II secured his revenge; New Haven was dissolved and absorbed by Connecticut in 1664, but to some extent set its stamp on the larger colony.

Every New England schoolboy has heard of the " blue laws " of Connecticut. During the American War of Independence an Anglican Loyalist, who had fled from New England, made mischief by pouring ridicule on Puritanical rigour. The *General History of Connecticut* by the Rev. Samuel Peters (London 1781) was long supposed to be mere burlesque; Southern orators made use of it as ammunition against " Yankee bigotry " during the Civil War. Making due allowance for wilful exaggeration, it has been ascertained that out of forty-five " blue laws " enumerated by Parson Peters, fully three-quarters existed in some form in the Puritan colonies,[1] e.g., the imposition of the death penalty for adultery, also for " concealing or entertaining Quakers or other blasphemous heretics ". In view of the scant provision for women's rights in the seventeenth century, it is surprising to read: " a wife shall be good evidence against her husband." In Massachusetts, married people had to live together or be imprisoned. The Rev. Stephen Bachelor, of Lynn, when nearly ninety, married a third wife; matrimonial trouble was followed by a Court order for the arrest of the couple unless willing to " lyve together as man and wife " (1650). This resourceful octogenarian escaped the clutches of the law and re-married; after six years his disconsolate New England wife petitioned the General Court for divorce. On the other hand, a Captain Kimble, on returning from a three-years' voyage, greeted his wife with a kiss: he soon found himself put in the stocks (" bilbowes ") for two hours, for " publicque " osculation on the Sabbath was a " lewd and unseemly " act! Even tolerant Rhode Island and Pennsylvania retained the time-honoured English punishments of pillory, ducking-stool and whipping at the cart's tail. New Englanders made the punishment fit the crime by forcing offenders to display explanatory labels or letters on their clothing; the free-lance preacher would be placarded as a " Wanton Gospeller ", while others would be compelled to go

[1] W. F. Prince, *The Report of the American Historical Association* (1898).

about bearing " T " for thief, " D " for drunkard or " A " for
adulterer (hence the title of Hawthorne's novel, *The Scarlet
Letter*).[1] Perhaps the quaintest and most uncomfortable punishment was that inflicted on a woman for blaming an elder; she was
forced to go about with a cleft stick affixed to her tongue!

As a compensation for draconian codes and " blue laws " the
Puritans solaced themselves with good liquor—ale, rum,[2] spirits
and imported wines. Smoking also was allowed, though men were
liable to arrest " for drinking tobacco on the heighway ". Unfortunately the suppression of innocent amusements in favour of
totalitarian religion caused a considerable amount of unhealthy
repression, which found pathological expression in drunkenness
and sexual irregularity. This discipline, overdone even from a
seventeenth-century point of view, was the collective expression
of a group-mind attempting to put into practice a high spiritual
and ethical ideal. There is much in Lowell's saying: " Puritanism,
believing itself quick with the seed of religious liberty, laid, without
knowing it, the egg of democracy."

2. " WITH FLAME OF FREEDOM IN THEIR SOULS "

Felicia Hemans' rhetorical tribute to the Pilgrim Fathers, as
pioneers of the freedom of faith, is certainly not true of New
England Puritanism as a whole.[3] The founders of the Bay Colony
outdid Laud in their utter lack of tolerance towards any who
deviated from their doctrines and discipline. The Cambridge
Synod of 1638 catalogued no less than 82 opinions—" some
erroneous, others blasphemous and all unsafe ". No Anglican
dared practise his liturgical worship. Quakers and Baptists, being
Dissenters in both England and New England, were in a position
even more unfortunate. Massachusetts was no land of freedom
for them; conformity or exile were the only alternatives to
scourging, branding and mutilation. Quakers, even women, were
flogged from town to town as " vagrants " (cp. p. 25 f). Baptists

---

[1] As late as 1847 deserters from the British army were branded with an
indelible " D ".
[2] Particularly in demand at funerals, along with gifts to mourners of rings,
scarfs and gloves. As in Scotland, no prayers were offered.
[3] This sentimental English versifier received a greengrocer's parcel, wrapped
in a Boston newspaper. Fascinated by reading therein an account of Forefathers'
Day (1824), she was inspired by the Muse to write a poem. No wonder historians questioned her accuracy; she never visited America, but her verse is
still quoted (*Landing of the Pilgrim Fathers*).

also suffered. To both sects the gates of freedom were mercifully open—in Rhode Island, Maryland, and later, Pennsylvania.

In Parliament questions were asked about the penalties imposed in Massachusetts for denying infant baptism. Edward Winslow assured the right honourable gentlemen that the law would be " gently executed "—which was exemplified by the whipping of " one Painter, for refusing to let his child be baptised ". Painter actually declared that " God had assisted him in his ordeal ". Persecution awakened public sympathy, and converts were made by the Baptists, mainly among humble folk. A startling defection occurred in 1650. President Dunster, who had raised Harvard from a grammar school to a college, announced his conversion to Baptist tenets. This was as startling in the seventeenth century as conversion to Communism in the twentieth—for the " Anabaptists " had " levelling " tendencies.[1] A Baptist President of Harvard *then* would have been as unthinkable as a Baptist President of a Roman Catholic college to-day. It was not till 1718 that the immersionist faith ceased to be a *religio illicita* in Massachusetts, when Cotton Mather preached at a Baptist ordination on " Good Men United ". Conciliation, however, did not increase the number of Baptist churches by 1730 to more than six in New England, outside Rhode Island.

One of the Massachusetts theocrats, Nathaniel Ward, expressed the majority view when he announced: " All Familists, Antinomians and other Enthusiasts shall have free liberty to keep away from us." This was not rhetoric, but for many years constituted the standing orders of the Bay Colony. According to Cotton Mather, " the *first rebel* among the divine *church-order* established in the wilderness " was Roger Williams.[2] Williams was a Londoner, born in 1603, the son of a " merchant taylor ". After graduating at Cambridge, he became a tutor in the house of Sir William Masham, M.P., where he was in touch with

[1] Prof. Morison of Harvard thinks that the College treated Dunster " with a consideration that no other dissenter enjoyed . . . he was never banished from Massachusetts " (ibid. p. 214 ff.)

[2] Robert Baillie, Scots Presbyterian stalwart, admitted that " only they in New England are more strict than we, or any church, to suppress, by the power of the magistrate, to banishment . . . even to death, or perpetual slavery." Samuel Gorton, " sometime a famous citizen here for piety ", was sentenced to slavery, with ten followers, for rejecting the ministry of the Word and sacraments. " They lie in irons, though gentlemen; and out of their prison in Boston write to the admiral here, to deal with the parliament for their deliverance " (Baillie's *Letters*, II, 17, 18).

Puritanism. He attended a meeting of the Massachusetts Bay Company in 1629 and met John Cotton and Thomas Hooker. Laud's agents got on his track and he sailed for New England the following year. He was welcomed as a most promising young man and preached at Salem and Plymouth with acceptance. The authorities at Boston, however, were not long in hearing of his " windy fancies ", his " rockie strength " concealed by a genial manner, pledged to " disturbant doctrines ". John Cotton was sadly disappointed in his young protégé. He was charged with holding (a) " that we have not our land by patent from the king, but that the natives are the chief owners of it "; (b) " that the civil magistrate's power extends only to the bodies, and goods, and outward state of men ". What did this imply ? That the colonists had taken the Indians' land by force, not by legitimate sale—which was robbery. In the second place, he argued against compulsory tithes, taxes, and church attendance; all religious persuasions ought to be on an equal footing. It was obvious that here was no true-blue Puritan, but a separatist whose religious ideas were tinged with a subversive levelling tendency.

In July 1635 Roger Williams was summoned before the legislature or " General Court " of Massachusetts, charged with " erroneous and dangerous opinions ". His call to the church of Salem was "judged a great contempt of authority ". Time was given for him to adjust relationships with Salem, but he proved to be a born controversialist unwilling to meet his opponents half way. At the October meeting of the General Court, he was given six weeks notice to quit their jurisdiction. On account of his bad health he was given permission to remain at Salem till the spring, provided he kept silent and did nothing " to draw others to his opinion ". Roger Williams was not a man to be muzzled. Secretly warned that the authorities had decided to send him back to England, he determined to escape. Invalid as he was, he stepped out into a January blizzard and entered the forest with a sundial and pocket compass. For fourteen weeks he wandered through a " howling wilderness ", without knowing what " bread or bed did mean ". Fortunately he fell in with friendly Indians. In April 1636 his family were able to join him. Crossing the Seekonk River they were greeted by natives on the Rhode Island shore: " What cheer ? " (the spot is duly marked by the " What cheer " monument). In June Williams settled near a spring on the slopes of a pleasant hillside, to which he gave the name of Providence, in remembrance of having been guided by God through all his troubles. He bought land from the Indians, learned their " rockie speech ", and sat in their filthy wigwams, talking to them about the Gospel. As an Apostle of Christian conciliation, Roger Williams forestalled William Penn. He fought against slavery (Indian and negro), he secured for white " indentured servants " a weekly day of rest, and he championed the elementary rights of women. Nor should we forget that he heaped coals of fire on the heads of his opponents at Boston, for he induced the Narragansets to ally themselves with the Bay colonists when they were menaced by the Pequot Indians. The Puritans had cast out a prophet; they had good cause to call him " a dear fellow ".

The new " plantation " was designed by Williams to " shelter persons distressed by conscience ". He was soon joined by refugees of varying views. A compact was then drawn up, whereby the subscribers agreed to the incorporation of a township, with authority over all inhabitants—" but only in civil things ". Thus the separation of Church and State was achieved on a diminutive scale. The founder of the infant community was its " nursing-father "; anxiously he watched over the slow growth of Rhode Island. He visited England in 1643 to procure a Charter—a constitution declared " democratical ". In 1652 he had to undertake the long voyage again as the privileges of the colony were menaced; it was some consolation to have the opportunity of making friends with Milton and Cromwell. Providentially, he left his travelling companion, John Clarke, in England. Clarke stayed on till the Restoration and obtained a new and generous charter from Charles II in 1663. The Stuarts (with the exception of James II) were more open-handed towards the American colonies than the Hanoverians. Rhode Island was left alone, to work out its own salvation. "More ideas that have become national", remarked the historian Bancroft, " emanated from this little colony than from any other."

Roger Williams, like other extreme separatists, was drawn to logical Baptist individualism. He was re-baptised along with a dozen others, and was instrumental in forming what was probably the first Baptist Church in America. He did not go so far as to require immersion and therefore would hardly qualify as an ortho-dox Baptist founder. In later life he preferred to call himself a

F

" Seeker "; like Emerson, he was too independent to submit to the restrictions of any sect. Even then, he failed to attain Cromwell's beatitude, " happy seeker, happy finder ! " Professor Sweet doubts whether he was " as emancipated from ecclesiastical tradition as he professed ". He had actually scruples at one time about the validity of a ministry depending on the apostolic succession of presbyters, and therefore did not assume the office of pastor. Afterwards he grew so pessimistic about the corruption of all branches of the Church that he concluded: " There could be no recovery out of that Apostasy till Christ shall send forth new apostles to plant churches anew." Had he been born two centuries later, he would have called Edward Irving brother and perhaps become a " pillar ", " prophet " or " apostle " of the " Catholic Apostolic Church ".

Roger Williams was tolerant in the sense of allowing absolute freedom of conscience without any sectarian tests for voting or holding office. He welcomed persecuted Quakers and encouraged Jews to build the first American Synagogue. That did not prevent him from being a hard-hitting controversialist. We smile nowadays at his pamphleteering recklessness, but his opponents were able to look after themselves. He hunted the Quakers with a wordy tirade, *George Fox Digg'd out of his Burrows*. The " Fox " retaliated with *A New England Fire-brand Quenched*. More significant was his controversy with John Cotton, the Massachusetts theocrat. During his visit to England (1643) he saw a pamphlet by Cotton defending imprisonment for erroneous opinions in religion. He replied by publishing *The Bloudy Tenent of Persecution*. This provoked from Cotton *The Bloudy Tenent washed and made white in the blood of the Lamb* (1647). Williams had the last word in his *Bloudy Tenent yet more Bloudy* (1652). Cotton compared him to a whirling windmill.[1] Opinionative, erratic and unstable he certainly was; but in the perspective of history his antics pass, his true testimony abides.

Roger Williams, controversialist, declared that there ought to be " permission of the most Paganish, Jewish, Turkish or anti-Christian consciences and worships ". Enforced uniformity bred hypocrisy as well as persecution; external conformity degraded

[1] Although Cotton did not come well out of this controversy, he smuggled an ethical element into his theology, which mitigated its rigour. " A Calvinist is our Cotton," claimed eulogists, but he had less to say of hell and damnation than his contemporaries.

religion in spirit and in truth. " Persecutors seldom plead Christ,
but Moses." The historical importance of Williams depends, not
on his theology, but on the fact that he founded a little commonwealth where a secular compact excluded theological tests. In
the arid, scholastic wilderness of the seventeenth century a foun-
tain was opened and in this oasis men learned to appreciate the
blessings of " soul-freedom ".

Among those who sought in Rhode Island " God's free air
and better things " were eccentric sects similar to those that
spawned· in England during the Commonwealth. These were
mostly Antinomian in tendency,[1] minimising ethics, while some
were " Familists ", emphasising their own " revelations ", in
opposition to historic Christianity. Mingled with much human
clay there was a mystical strain, destined to attract attention in
Emerson's time. In a hell-haunted age, Samuel Gorton, the
" Familist ", struck out a luminous phrase that revealed him as
a Universalist born prematurely: " There is no heaven but in the
hearts of men; no hell but in the mind " (uttered in 1637, not
1837 or 1937).

The most attractive of these " Come-outers " was Mrs. Anne
Hutchinson. " Like Roger Williams or worse ", groaned the
Boston ministers as they saw the crowds forsake their meeting
houses to frequent her lectures.

" Come along with me," said one of her proselytes; " I'le bring you
to a Woman that preaches better Gospell than any of your blackcoates
that have been at the Ninneversity, a Woman of another kinde of spirit,
who hath had many Revelations of things to come; and for my part,
saith hee, I had rather hear such a one that speakes from the meere
motion of the spirit, without any study at all, than any of your learned
Scollers, although they may be fuller of Scripture."

This accomplished gentlewoman was kindly and helpful, as well
as magnetic. Cotton could not help liking her—she and her husband
had been among his admirers in Boston, Lincolnshire.[2] In Boston,
Mass., she embarrassed her friends. Sir Harry Vane, afterwards
a champion of freedom in England, sheltered her from clerical
critics, but after his departure, her condemnation was a foregone

[1] See Charles Francis Adams, *Three Episodes in Massachusetts History*
(Boston, 1896). Brilliant though acid in tone.
[2] Her "ready wit and bold spirit " reminded historically-minded critics of
the Montanist prophetesses in the early Christian centuries. Her husband was
" a man of very mild temper and weak parts, and wholly guided by his wife."

conclusion.[1] Thomas Welde described her as " The American Jezebel ".[2]

Mrs. Hutchinson was a pioneer feminist, born out of due season. She really belongs to the era of Margaret Fuller, only she was the last person to " accept the Universe " (like that redoubtable Transcendentalist and "blue-stocking"). She organised women's clubs at a time when the weaker sex languished in legal bondage. She was a forerunner of the lady doctor. Her " competent wit and voluble tongue " made her a " non-such among the people ". She even criticised the ministers' sermons—no wonder they were astounded at her " antics ". She was an utter contrast to the godly Puritan dames; they therefore pronounced her to be " a woman not fit for our society ". She had a considerable following in Boston, even among the men, but in course of time the theocrats had their way. She was put in custody and subjected to " third degree " treatment. " Divers of the elders resorted to her." Her utterance was reduced to raving; and thus she was convicted of heresy and " delivered up to Satan ". The Boston authorities would have agreed with Lowell's " Parson Wilbur " that " the Church had more trouble with one *she*resiarch than with twenty *he*resiarchs, and that the men's *conscia recti*, or certainty of being right, was nothing to the women's ".[3]

Mrs. Hutchinson's heresy consisted in criticising the Old Testament legalism that was so characteristic of the Massachusetts Church-State. Her prophetic protest found a ready response in the hearts of those who hungered for freedom of the mind and spirit.[4] Undeterred when the theocracy discharged such heavy ordnance as " antinomian " and " enthusiast ", the keenest "Come-outers " accompanied Mrs. Hutchinson to exile in Rhode Island (1638). Five years later she was killed in an Indian rising[5]—" an

---

[1] Winthrop replied to Vane's protest: " That's a matter of conscience, sir; your conscience you must keep or it must be kept for you."

[2] Author of *Rise, Reign and Ruin of Antimonians, etc.* (1st ed., p. 31, 1644).

[3] In the *Biglow Papers* the Rev. Homer Wilbur, A.M., of the First Parish of Jaalam, is disturbed by the " wild notions " of Miss Parthenia Almira Fitz (1844).

[4] Asked how she recognised what was revealed to her to be of the Spirit, she asked a counter-question: " How did Abraham know that . . . God bid him offer his son ? " Deputy-Governor: " By an immediate voice." Mrs. H.: " *So to me by an immediate revelation.*" D.-G.: " How! an immediate revelation ? " Mrs. H.: " By the voice of His own Spirit in my soul."

[5] She settled at Eastchester (now a New York suburb) and was massacred there (1643). A tablet marks the spot. On her land a meeting house was built (1665), which afterwards became St. Paul's, an " historical Episcopal shrine " (see below, p. 155 n).

act of God ", said her enemies in Boston. Others lamented the
passing of " a burning and a shining light ".

Mrs. Hutchinson, like Emerson, claimed " direct inspiration ",
thus incurring the charge of being an " enthusiast ". She proclaimed the supremacy of the " inner light " over the written word
(final, authoritative and inerrant). She was not actually a Quaker,
but her inner attitude was akin to theirs. Many a hunted Friend
found refuge in Rhode Island. The settlement became a " Cave
of Adullam " for Baptists persecuted by the Boston theocracy.
In 1651 three Baptists had the temerity to cross the border of
Massachusetts to visit a co-religionist at Lynn. While a service
was being held in the house of William Witter, the Rhode Island
strangers—Clarke, Crandall and Holmes—were arrested; the first
two were heavily fined, the third imprisoned for several months
and publicly flogged.[1] " It was grievous," said the spectators,
" to watch the executioner seize Obadiah Holmes, striking with
all his strength with a three-corded whip, yea, spitting on his
hands three times! " This treatment was quite as savage as that
meted out to English Dissenters by the squirearchy of the Restoration.[2] Such intolerance drove a wedge of isolation between brother
Congregationalists more estranging than the Atlantic. By about
1680 the English Independents had moved on to a full acceptance of Roger Williams' great doctrine; the New England
Independents " stuck ", to use John Robinson's phrase, where
their fathers had left them. They forgot that " the Lord hath
more truth and light yet to break forth from his holy word ".

In spite of the " soul-freedom " offered by Rhode Island, it did
not attract many immigrants from England. One might have
thought that its political advantages would have appealed to lovers
of liberty in the old country. After 1691 it shared the distinction,
with Connecticut, of being the only American colonies allowed to
elect their own Governor. There was no royal representative to
draw sycophants to a miniature Court, no attempt to interfere
with the legislature, no alien officialism, no " sect of the
Herodians ".

Massachusetts complained that Rhode Island was " a recep-

[1] When in England on business, Clarke gave a candid account of the proceedings in *Ill News from New England* (1652).
[2] Sir George Downing, cousin of the younger Winthrop, writing of the
English attitude to Massachusetts, referred to that " law of banishing for
conscience, which makes us stinke everywhere ".

tacle of all sorts of riff-raff people,[1] nothing more than a *latrina* ". This is the jargon of ecclesiastical vituperation rather than the language of plain sense. The innocuous sectaries who found the plantation a welcome " Cave of Adullam " were too heterogeneous to learn the art of living together. Political and religious individualism was carried to extreme lengths. The government was almost shorn of power by the legislature, which migrated from county to county till 1854.[2] These conditions did not make for progress or prosperity. Toleration was a blessing, but it did not have the " drive " adequate to build churches, schools and public works. Rhode Island remained " the least of the tribes of Israel ". Shifting, unstable coteries were incapable of producing the homogeneous communities characteristic of Massachusetts and Connecticut. Sixty years after the foundation of Providence there was no adequate house of worship in the town; and at the end of Rhode Island's first century there were less than a dozen churches of any denomination, " and these mostly in a very feeble state ". Only in the second half of the eighteenth century did the Great Awakening summon from torpor the land of Roger Williams.

3. THE PURITAN OUTLOOK

Edward Johnson, in his *Wonder-Working Providence in New England* (1654), declared: " The Lord Christ intends to achieve greater matters by this little handfull than the world is aware of."

For over half a century the " Wilderness Zion " was practically an independent republic. " We came hither," said Cotton Mather, " because we would have our posterity settled under the full and pure *dispensation* of the Gospel; defended by *rulers that shall be of ourselves* " (*Magnalia Christi Americana*, 1702). From the landing of the Puritans in 1629 till the interference of James II in 1686, Massachusetts was a law unto itself.[3] Anglicans, Baptists,

---

[1] The historian Hutchison, last royal Governor of Massachusetts, considered that the Bay Colony " from the beginning endeavoured to preserve two distinct ranks, gentry and commonalty ".

[2] In the early twentieth century, the city of Providence, containing half the population, was represented by one Senator out of 38 and by 25 Representatives out of 100 in the State Legislature. Till 1888 the foreign-born (then a third of the population, and mostly Romanists) were disfranchised.

[3] No freedom from privation and loneliness. Cotton Mather admitted that ladies of culture could not stand it. Isaac Johnson's wife came to an early grave. Her husband " tried to live without her, liked it not, and dyed ".

Quakers "and other sectaries " were punished by Congregationalists, who themselves had been penalised for their beliefs in
England. Once the Puritans had founded their ideal commonwealth in New England, they were as determined as Archbishop
Laud to enforce uniformity of creed and worship. Increase Mather
spoke for the theocracy when he denounced " the hideous clamour
for liberty of conscience ". Individualists like Roger Williams and
Anne Hutchison had " free liberty to keep away " and find refuge
in such a " Cave of Adullam " as Rhode Island. Good theocrats
like John Davenport hived off with their congregations to outposts
in Connecticut. In course of time, settlers began to move westwards on their own, seeking more fertile land The " Reformed
Synod " of Massachusetts (1680) complained about this tendency
to " forsake Ordinances and live like heathen, only so they might
have Elbow-room enough ".

If the theocracy was afraid of losing control, the people in their
scattered settlements were afraid of " infernal powers ". Forest,
mountain and desert were swarming with evil spirits and Indians.
The French were in league with them, making their way stealthily
southwards from Quebec by frontier trails (there was a real danger
of a Catholic French Empire arising in the Mississippi Valley);
and in the South West the vast domains of enfeebled Spain were
ripening for annexation by the stronger Latin power.

Fear bred fanaticism. One of the most popular New England
books was Wigglesworth's *Day of Doom* (1662). This is one of
the ghastliest poems every written, a sadistic picture of hell,
reminiscent of Dante at his worst. Its horror was enhanced by its
jog-trot metre, which extended to no less than 224 stanzas. It is
surprising to learn that its 1,800 lines were memorised for pleasure,
not only for the punishment of schoolboys. " It was the solace of
every fireside," said Lowell, " the flicker of the pine-knot by
which it was conned perhaps adding a livelier relish to its pre-
monition of eternal combustion." The *Day of Doom* was popularly
considered to be only second in inspiration to the Bible. Most
people to-day would assent to Louis Untermeyer's[1] definition—
" a sort of belated and brutalised Talmud ".

Michael Wigglesworth was born in England in 1631 and reached
America in his seventh year. He was not therefore old enough to

---

[1] See his excellent, annotated anthology, *American Poetry from the beginning
to Walt Whitman* (Cape, 1932).

enter into the cultural inheritance of the old country; he was the first of the second generation of New Englanders, who had no Cambridge education to mitigate their creed and consequently became provincial and tough-minded.[1] The fact that Wigglesworth was a physician as well as a minister, did not induce him to relent. He introduced unbaptised infants thus:

> You sinners are, and such a share
> as sinners may expect,
> Such you shall have; for I do save
> None but mine own Elect.
>
> Yet to compare your sin with theirs
> who lived a longer time,
> I do confess yours is much less,
> though every sin's a crime.
>
> The glorious King thus answering,
> They cease, and plead no longer;
> Their consciences must needs confess,
> His reasons are the stronger.
>
> A crime it is, therefore in bliss
> You may not hope to dwell;
> But unto you I shall allow
> The easiest room in hell.

" The easiest room in hell "—what a concession! Milton's *Paradise Lost* appeared in 1667, yet the New Englanders actually preferred the *Day of Doom*. A best seller, it ran to fourteen editions before 1828, was reprinted in 1867 and in 1929.

Nathaniel Hawthorne, the novelist, claimed to be liberated from the web of Calvinistic fatalism, yet he remained rooted in the dead but unforgotten past, when the mystery of iniquity haunted the New England mind like a recurring nightmare. The hereditary Puritan trait of introspection influenced Hawthorne to isolate an individual act from its setting and to universalise it.[2] Thus his fancy brooded over the " Scarlet Letter " that Hester had to wear; the Unpardonable Sin committed by Ethan Brand; the mysterious Black Veil worn by a certain minister till his dying day; the Red Cross that Endicott dramatically slashed out of the New England flag and the Maypole that he cut down at Merry Mount. Sym-

---

[1] A financial crisis near the end of the seventeenth century was attributed by Cotton Mather to the toleration of an Episcopal Chapel in Boston: the Governor and Council solemnly wrote to England, stating that the disaster was due to God, who had " spit in our faces ".

[2] Cp. Ll. Morris, *The Rebellious Puritan—Portrait of Mr. Hawthorne* (New York, 1927).

bolism and allegory were carried so far that the author lost touch with reality; his characters are mostly shadowy figures, whether moral failures or thwarted idealists. We can appreciate these *Twice-told Tales* as literature and yet feel dissatisfied with his portrayal of New England's heroic history. He was much less prudish than most of his early Victorian contemporaries. What was wrong was this: his ideas were too few and overworked. We see the Puritans through a mist when we read Hawthorne's novels; they are vague, shadowy, almost fantastic. We miss the substantial Puritan world that is revealed in Samuel Sewall's *Diary*.

This Diary is a storehouse of New England life and character. It has not, of course, the wit of Pepys' (its humour is unconscious), but instead of being confined to ten years, it ranges from 1675 to 1729. Thanks to Mark Van Doren, it can be read in an abridged edition (*American Bookshelf* series, 1927). Sewall provides for us the usual Puritan allusions to lightnings, comets and eclipses, with theological and moral implications. Yet this kindly, earnest judge is amusing in his matter-of-factness, and human withal. He trembles for the ark of the covenant, spends Christmas Day arranging the coffins in the family vault—" an awful yet pleasing Treat ".[1] He retains the traditional Puritan antipathy to Christmas, observing in 1685: " Shops open as usual: some people observe ye day but are vexed I believe that ye body of ye People profane it, and blessed be God no authority yet to compel them to keep it." A little earlier he notes: " Mr. Randolph and his new wife set in Mr. Joycliffe's pue [in the South meeting house]; and Mrs. Randolph is observed to make a curtsy at Mr. Willard's naming Jesus, even in prayer-Time." Judge Sewall is concerned for his soul—also for his digestion. He jumps from his meditation on Habakkuk on hearing the guns salute the new Governor.

He visited England in 1695, and was broad-minded enough to attend the Established Church: " I am a lover of musick to a fault, yet I was uneasy there; and the justling out of the Psalms by the boisterous organ . . . can never be justified by the great master of Religious Ceremonies " (Sewall's *Letters*, I, 155). The

---

[1] Coffins were apt to obsess the Puritan mind. Over 150 years later, the students of Andover were directed to support themselves by manufacturing coffins—which would also serve as a salutary theme for moralisation. Mrs. Harriet Beecher Stowe (wife of a professor) moved into this abandoned coffin workshop, which she made her home under the name of " The Stone Cabin ".

judge turns easily from moralising to matrimony. Describing his
courtship of a widow, Madam Winthrop, he records: " Offer'd
me no Wine that I remember. I rose at 11 o'clock, saying that I
would put on my coat. She offer'd not to help me. I pray'd her
that Juno might light me home, she opened the shutters, and said
twas pretty light abroad; Juno was weary and gone to bed. So I
came home by star-light as I could." The spirit of the good judge
is finely interpreted by Whittier in his poem, *The Prophecy of
Samuel Sewall*, 1697.

Thanks to the Society for the Preservation of Old-Time New
England and the *New England Quarterly*, we are able to correct
the over-sombre picture of the Puritans, popularised by Hawthorne
and kept alive by magazine illustrators. The men did not invari-
ably dress in black nor the women in mouse-grey. If the poorer
people wore less colourful attire than the gentlefolk, the reason
was partly " sumptuary legislation " that standardised costume
according to social station. Men like John Hull of Boston, the
goldsmith, not merely enjoyed beautiful articles for life, but made
them.[1] In spite of the discomforts and discouragements of frontier
life, Mistress Anne Bradstreet (died 1672) kept alight the sacred
flame of poesy; she was a practical mystic, like her nineteenth-century successor, Emily Dickinson. Her London publisher acclaimed
her in 1650 as " The Tenth Muse, lately sprung up in America ".
John Norton once said that if Virgil could only have heard the
seraphic poems of Anne Bradstreet, he would have thrown his
heathen doggerel into the fire! Such absurd compliments are
eagerly quoted by modern Puritan-baiters, who conveniently ignore
the fact that New England, cut off from the continuous impact of
European culture, inevitably became provincial.

Up till 1856, the historians of New England were mostly of the
" filio-pietistic school "; some of them might be justly termed
" ancestor-worshippers ".[2] In that year Peter Oliver published
The Puritan Commonwealth, which he compared to " a dreary
waste overhung by a wintry sky ". His successors, Brook Adams
and Charles Francis Adams, scorned the " theologico-glacial era "
and held up the theocracy to execration. Dr. G. E. Ellis replied
in a candid, dispassionate apology (*The Puritan Age*, 1888). More

---

[1] S. E. Morison, op. cit., Ch. V.
[2] J. G. Palfrey's *History of New England* (5 vols., 1858-90) was apologetic,
but is of lasting value for reference.

recently social historians like T. J. Wertenbaker[1] have attributed
Puritan zeal to economic motives. Literary men with a bias against
Puritanism, like Charles Angoff[2] and Vernon Parrington[3], have
quoted the hell-fire passages and ignored what did not fit in with
their preconceptions. In view of results yielded by the patient
research of scholars for the last thirty years, there is no excuse for
judging historic Puritanism by the activities of the " Anti-Saloon
League " or the Methodist " Board of Temperance, Prohibition
and Public Morals ". The New England Fathers did their utmost,
amidst the most discouraging circumstances, to preserve the goodly
heritage of learning which they had brought across the Atlantic.
Their hard exterior often revealed an unsuspected tender-hearted-
ness, exemplified by such a sentence as this from Thomas Hooker:
" I know that there is wilde love and joy enough in this world, as
there is wild Thyme and other herbes, but we would have garden
love and garden joy of God's own planting."

Perry Miller and Thomas Johnson have done ample justice to
the New England forefathers by letting them speak for themselves
in *The Puritans* (London, 1939), a noble anthology. An intro-
ductory chapter corrects mistakes that persist as to their views,
e.g., their unqualified animosity to the arts. Then follows a series
of representative extracts, illustrating their views on the State,
ethics, education, literature, science and social customs. These
Puritans had their limitations, but there is no justification for
applying to them the fashionable theory of Weber and Tawney
that Calvinism released the business man from restrictions of
profiteering imposed by the medieval Church. The principle of
" just price " was consistently maintained: " A man may not ask
any more for his commodity than his selling price, as Ephron to
Abraham, the land is worth thus much." The New England mind
was much cramped by its dogmatic setting and pioneering background, but by no means was it lacking in historic perspective.

St. Thomas Aquinas' *Summa Theologiae* was known in New
England; Governor Winthrop quoted from it at length in his
discourse on arbitrary government; and his educated readers would
appreciate his quotation, for was not the *Summa* among the
recommended books at Emmanuel, that nursery of Puritans in

[1] *The Puritan Oligarchy* (1947). As a Virginian, the Professor resents New
England's claim to have blazed the trail of freedom and progress.
[2] *A Literary History of the American People*, Vol. I (New York, 1931).
[3] *Main Currents in American Thought*, Vol. I (New York, 1927).

old Cambridge ? Indeed, the Puritans were much more familiar
with " Catholic " literature generally than their emancipated successors. They read the Fathers, the Schoolmen and the authorities
of the Counter-Reformation. Cotton Mather could think of no
compliment higher than to compare John Norton, the unflinching
Puritan, to the great writers of pre-Reformation Christendom.

ON JOHN NORTON

The schoolmen's *Doctors*, whomsoe'er they call,
Subtil, seraphick, or *angelical*;
Dull souls! their tapers burnt exceeding dim;
They might to *school* again, to learn of him.

Lombard must out of date; we now profess
Norton the *master of the sentences*;
Scotus, a *dunce* to him; should we compare
Aquinas here, none to be named are.

Of a more *heavenly* strain his notions were;
More pure, sublime, scholastical, and clear.
More like th' Apostles Paul and John, I wist,
Was this our *orthodox* evangelist.

(*Magnalia I*, p. 297, 1853 ed.)

Between 1620 and 1640 no less than 26,000 Englishmen had
crossed the Atlantic to find a new home—a great migration which
the more ardent likened to Israel's exodus from Egyptian bondage.
When Puritanism triumphed in England, New England received no
further influx. When Puritanism was repressed at the Restoration,
not even persecution stimulated a new wave of colonisation. This
cannot be entirely explained by the assertion that New England
Puritanism was too rigid for ex-Cromwellian zealots. The settlers
of 1620-40 multiplied on their own soil, with scarcely any infusion
of fresh blood till after the American Revolution, and little inclination to strike westwards across the Hudson River—the Jordan of
their " new Canaan ". If the land was poor, it was peopled with
good yeoman stock; there were few " redemptioners " as in Virginia (indentured white servants who bound themselves for a
stated period in order to pay their passage); few " kidnapped "
shiploads found their way to New England, to become the pro-
genitors of " white trash "; finally, the few negro slaves that were
kept worked as domestics. Manual labour was honoured, as was
scholarship. There was no unbridgeable chasm between rich and
poor.

John Fiske has noted: " There is not a county in England of which the population is more purely English . . . than New England at the end of the eighteenth century." More than ninety-eight per cent. could trace their origin to England, particularly East Anglia. By 1890 the original 26,000 increased to some fifteen millions: at least a quarter of the population of the United States had sprung from New England stock.

The English visitor to New England finds it refreshing to note resemblances in names, traditions and institutions that have " suffered a sea-change ". The village green, the parish, the parson and his parsonage, the sexton, even the squire (till Emerson's time) remind us of the affection with which the Puritans tried to reproduce the familiar English scene. The basis of New England's culture, however, was Calvinist granite; as in Scotland, there was a solid foundation in the Westminster Confession and Shorter Catechism. Mr Van Wyck Brooks, in his *Flowering of New England*, has reminded us of this affinity: " The bitter climate, the hard soil, the Calvinism yielding to more gracious forms of faith, the common schools, the thrifty farmer-folk, the coast line with its ports and sailors' customs, the abundant lakes and mountains, all suggested the land of Sir Walter Scott."

In New England the unit of local government was " the town " (*anglice* parish), whether rural or urban. This was indeed a compact area compared to the extensive counties of New York and the South, with their large estates, scattered throughout a vast region with poor communications. Although class distinctions were by no means non-existent in New England, they did not run as deep as in other colonies. The local community met (as in Saxon days) in a " town meeting " (*moot*) to transact business of all kinds. On the Lord's Day they assembled for worship in the same " meeting house ", which belonged to the community.[1] The dual use of one building, located in the very centre of the village, symbolised the unity of citizenship and church membership. At a time when the cities of Europe were becoming congested, a more open type was foreshadowed in New England. A happy marriage of town and country was intimated by the proximity of the streets to the river

---

[1] Cotton Mather, " Puritan Priest ", expressed public opinion when he " found no just ground in Scripture for applying such a trope as *church* to a house for public assembly ". Medieval churches were not exclusively reserved for worship, as Addy reminds us in his *Evolution of the English House* (4th ed., 1933).

and elm-shaded common. " The generation which planned these villages," says Professor S. E. Morison, " seemed incapable of making anything ugly; if their laying-out was unconscious, the more to the credit of their instinct; for it was done in harmony with the contours of valley and slope, the curve of stream and shore.　Crude settlements contained the seeds of sound development.[1]　Timber was abundant.　Instead of making unsightly " log cabins " like later frontiersmen, the colonists built seemly " frame" houses, like those still surviving in East Anglia.[2]　When a community became too unwieldy to socialise and assimilate its members, the more active citizens would · hive off and form a new village.

The meeting house, at the centre of every village, was " rear'd in ye fear of ye Lord and of ye Indians ".　It was decorated only with the grinning heads of wolves, brought in by bounty-seekers and " nayl'd to the Walls to give notis thereof ".　Without were the stocks and whipping-post; within, the stool of repentance.

After the first half-century of colonisation, a superior type of meeting house became common.　It was almost square, with a pyramidical roof crowned by a turret, containing a bell which replaced the primitive " beat of drum or sounding shell ".　Light was admitted by two rows of small diamond-paned windows (later sashed).　When galleries were added, so were dormers.　Inside, the walls were unplastered.　The bare rafters were profusely hung with spiders' webs, and frequented by swallows who flew in and out of the open bell-cote.　The oaken cross-beams were useful for storing gun-powder kegs, as no fires were allowed.　Sometimes, on crowded occasions " ye sprightly lads sat on ye beams over ye heads of ye congregation ".　When a new fabric was completed, controversy was occasioned by the " dignifying of the meeting house ".　This was the assignment of sittings on a " points " system—age, office, social status and military service.　The sexes were severely separated; children were relegated to the galleries. Inevitably segregation broke down.　Wives urged their husbands to build them " pues " that afforded some comfort from the cold. High family enclosures appeared along the walls and soon invaded the central area; these afforded greater " ease in Zion " and

---

[1] Lewis Mumford, *The Culture of Cities*, p. 140 f. (London, 1938).
[2] M. S. Briggs, *The Homes of the Pilgrim Fathers in England and America* (Oxford, 1932).

became a symbol of social prestige according to location.[1] The pulpit ceased to be a " scaffold " (in John Cotton's significant phrase); it became " the throne of the Word of God ", a lofty two-decker. The sounding-board ceased to be an uncouth menace to the preacher (often infested by bats). It gave the pulpit dignity, for it was decorated with panelling and furnished with cushions, curtains, balls and fringes.

Not many houses of worship survive with all these features intact, but there is an interesting example at Hingham, on the outskirts of Boston. This " Old Ship meeting house " (1681) is the oldest place of worship in the United States in continuous use, the name denoting its shape and construction, which recall an overturned hull. The exposed timber roof (for long hidden by a plaster ceiling) has recently been restored and is a marvellous piece of carpentry, surprising the visitor by its genuine Gothic spirit.

" Raring a meeting house " was a community effort, like building a medieval church. Everyone helped to raise the heavy " frame " (and latterly the steeple). Considerable quantities of rum, beer and cider were provided at public expense; only after two centuries did community-opinion veer round to East Hartford's innovation—" Ample supply of crackers, cheese and lemonade, but no rum!" (1835). Spirituous refreshment was considered a necessity during the Colonial era; not even brimstone preaching could generate sufficient warmth. In Judge Sewall's *Diary* we read: " Bread frozen at Lord's table " (15th January 1716). Only gradually were little foot-warmers tolerated. During the interval " between services " the worshippers would enjoy a well-earned lunch.[2] In course of time it would be consumed in a special " Sabba' Day " house nearby, where they could gather round a welcome fire. This was the humble harbinger of the well-equipped American " parish house " of to-day.

The Sabbath was a social event, bringing scattered neighbours together, the sermon providing material for knotty, metaphysical

[1] Thus, despite the public character of the meeting house, the pew became a " property-symbol ": thrifty non-residents might even let their pews and use the proceeds to support another church.

[2] Amusing incidents are recorded. A dog, enticed by milk on the pulpit stair, approached under cover of the " long prayer ". Lapping, he got his head caught in the pitcher and ran up and down the passages in desperation. The minister, shocked by laughter, opened his eyes—and laughed too! Public worship was adjourned till the afternoon. An old autobiography speaks of " diversions " being frequent: " The duller the sermon, the more likely it was that some accident would be done to help to pass the time."

discussion during the week. Taverners were required to " cleer
their houses of all persons able to go to meeting ". The minister
was a purveyor of news as well as herald of the Good News. One
preacher is said to have turned the hour-glass, anticipating his
hearers' thirst for the Word: " I know you are good fellows—
stay and take another *glass*! " The young did not usually share
this zeal. They were apt to go to sleep, and had to be kept awake
by a " tithing-man " who would prod the boys with a knob at
one end of his wand and tickle the girls with a feather attached to
the other end. Children were examined when they got home on
the contents of the discourse (as in Scotland)—hence the useful
little flaps for note-taking still to be found occasionally in the
pews of unspoilt meeting houses. Catechising was a home-rite
reserved for Sunday evening—the *Shorter Cathecism* or such alternatives as Cotton's *Milk for Babes*. At last the long day of " rest "
drew to its close. " When five stars could be seen, the Sabbath
was at an end ",[1] though the stricter sort criticised the innocuous
" street-walking " of pent-up youth. One minister (a bachelor)
refused to baptise infants " so irreverent as to be born on the
Sabbath ". Another preacher was cured of similar scruples by
having twins born to him on the Lord's Day.

Baptism was administered at public worship, although there
were no funeral services, and marriages were conducted by
magistrates (the clerk reading the banns on Sabbath). Before the
" long " prayer a string of notes was read, in which individuals
requested the prayers of the people for particular ends, such as
recovery from illness. Exposition of a Scripture portion[2] preceded
the sermon; only " advanced " congregations like Brattle Street,
Boston, tolerated Bible reading without comment (1700), stig-
matised as " dumb-reading ".   At the close of the service the
faithful came forward and presented their offerings to the deacons.
Whereupon the people dispersed according to the " dignity " of
their status. Whittier's picture of a typical New England congregation is authentic:

> In the goodly house of worship, where in order due and fit,
> As by public vote directed, classed and ranked the people sit;

[1] W. S. Davis' *Gilman of Redford* (Macmillan, 1927) gives us the authentic
atmosphere of 1770. When the usual gun boomed, " Uncle Eleazer literally
jumped from his chair. ' Sun-down!—Sabbath's over! ' he exclaimed spryly.
' We can talk secular. Well Peleg, if you've brought those papers I'll consider
the Barbados venture. You're to find the ship and I'm to find the rum . . .' "
[2] Only gradually did the King James Version oust the " Geneva Bible ".

Mistress first and goodwife after, clerkly squire before the clown,
From the brave coat, lace embroidered, to the gray frock shading down.

The Lord's Supper was dispensed once a month, the Church members remaining after the ordinary service—" a great deal less in number than those that goe away ", Lechford noted. The minister and elders sat at a small table in front of the pulpit, the people remaining in their seats. Communion did not mean so much to the worshippers as the thin-sown " Occasions " of Scotland, when kirks were crowded with folk from neighbouring parishes. Preaching was the real New England sacrament.

Babette May Levy has corrected traditional misconceptions in her *Preaching in the First Half Century of New England History* (Hartford, Conn., 1945). The earlier preachers did not overdo damnation, like some of their successors. John Cotton used to preach in lyrical vein about the heart of Christ resembling a hearth, " whereon the fire of his love towards us burneth continually ". Thomas Shepard, of new Cambridge, was a gentle mystic[1] in spite of his theocratic intolerance. Here is a passage from Shepard overlooked by anthologists of devotional literature:

" As 'tis with Woman when the fullnesse of the Husband's love is seen, it knits the heart invincibly to him, and makes her do anything for him; so here. And as we say of Trees, if the Tree begins to wither and dye, the only way is . . . water the root. Love is the next root of all grace. Love Christ, and you will never be weary of doing for Christ; love Him and He will love you."

Thomas Hooker, founder of Hartford, delighted in homely imagery. He exhorted his hearers to make room for Christ by sweeping their hearts; " cleanse every sinke, brush downe every cobweb . . . and when thou hast swept every corner of the house, doe not leave the dust behind the doore, for that is a slut's trick ". This plain style was a characteristic of early New England preachers. One of them compares sin to contagion : " A man catcheth cold on his feet, it fils the head with distempers . . . or suppose the stomack to be somewhat annoyed through ill dyet or ill digestion, what then ? It strikes up to the head presently; you cannot annoy the feet, ancles or middle Parts, but the head will feel both." Preachers spoke to the condition of their auditors, frequently resorting to human imagery, such as the relationship

[1] Shepard was much read by the Covenanters, and again in nineteenth-century Scotland. Dr. Alexander Whyte edited his *Spiritual Experience and Experimental Preaching* (Edinburgh, 1912).

G

between bridegroom and bride, parent and child. If they quoted
the classics, they did so tersely, and avoided " humane testimonies " in deference to the Bible, contenting themselves with
" as the poet says " or " as the heathen writer says ". Considering
their abhorrence for the play-house, it is surprising to find them
fond of such metaphors as " slipping off the stage " of life,
" taking off their masks " (well aware that " hypocrite " comes
from the Greek for actor!); Augustine's lofty phrase gripped them:
Theatrum mundus, spectator Deus.

> To see three things was holy Austin's wish,
> Rome in her flower, Christ Jesus in the Flesh.
> And Paul i' the pulpit; Lately men might see,
> Two first, and more, in Hooker's ministry.

Some New England sermons were " lively, searching and
awakening " but not all. The preachers were usually too long.[1]
The Rev. Samuel Whiting (1597-1679) was no exception, in
preaching for an hour and a half. So drowsy were his hearers,
he used to tell them that they looked like " stacks of straw "; on
one occasion, he left the pulpit " to feed his fowls "—he would
be back when they had finished sleeping! These preachers do
not seem to have considered the alternative, shorter sermons.
The public demanded " beaten oyl " (Exodus, 27.20). They
would not tolerate read sermons, yet expected careful preparation
and free delivery. Consequently, there was much repetition,
" hydra-heads " serving as necessary aids to over-worked memory.
In printed form these sermons were usually scholastic, liberally
seasoned with quotations (Greek, Latin and Hebrew). Commonly,
as Dr. Whyte complained of Shepard, they were in " execrable
English ". This is accounted for by the fact that they were often
printed from the notes of hearers, without the author's corrections
and sometimes without his permission. The first New England
sermon to be printed was delivered by a Pilgrim who was neither
a minister, nor a university man, but a wool-carder by trade.[2]
Many " solid men " and " useful men " followed his " plain
style "; nevertheless they must have been as boring as Higginson:

> Thousands of sermons did he preach
> Not to Please Ears, but Hearts to reach.

[1] Their rough-cast prose sometimes flowers with a felicitous phrase, e.g.,
" Time is a little river which runs into Eternity," " God is the journey's end
of all a man's labours and life and travels." The oases, however, were too few
and the arid stretches too wearisome.
[2] Elder Cushman's Discourse, in *The Pilgrim Fathers* (Everyman's Lib.).

Even among the first generation, there had been signs of degeneration among congregations. Shepard, preaching in the 1630's and 40's, complained about families being late for meeting, young people coming with merely marriage in mind: " Oh how many men are there that become quite sermon-proof now-adays! Are not men blockish, dull, senseless [at meeting] . . . whereas elsewhere, O how lively and spirited they are! " It did not seem to occur to preachers that frequent and tedious services may make men " gospel-hardened ";[1] one can have too much of a good thing. As the seventeenth century drew to a close, hearers dared to criticise pulpiteers; gone were the days when a man could be brought before the Quarterly Court for saying, " he had as Leave to heare a dogg Barke, as to heare Mr. Cobbett preach." Doubtless it was the lessened popularity of the clergy that partly motivated Cotton Mather to over-praise the earlier lights of the theocracy. Consider his eulogy of Urian Oakes:

" As a *Preacher*, he was an Orpheus, that would have drawn the very *Stones* to discipline; had *Austin* been here, he might have seen *Paul in the pulpit*: indeed, he was, as one said, *An uncomfortable Preacher*: Why ? he drove us to Despair, namely, *Of seeing such another*."

To counter growing indifference, the clergy cultivated a more ornate style. Thus President Hoare of Harvard, in a funeral discourse compared the things of this life to " a boat to waft us over the water, which can doe us no further service when we come on shore, as our cloathes that we put on in the morning and off at night " (*The Sting of Death and Death Unstung*, Boston, 1680). The English literary style of Tillotson was followed (at a respectful distance). By the early eighteenth century written discourses, taboo among the early Puritans, became " extremely fashionable ". Many of these sermon MSS. have been preserved, noting date and list of churches where preached. The pages, which usually measure $7 \times 4\frac{1}{2}$ inches, are stitched into booklets, but the writing is apt to be minute and closely spaced.

One seventeenth-century divine, Samuel Whiting, was bold enough to wish for the Episcopal service, so that frequent change

---

[1] Under the theocracy, Baptists and other dissenters were sometimes forced to attend the official meeting house. Naturally they were recalcitrant. Gorton, the " Familist ", describes these sermons as " meat to be digested, but only by the heart or stomacke of an ostrich " (*Simplicitie's Defence*, p. 57). Constables would reply that such objections were " nothing to them ".

of posture would keep his listeners awake.[1] Not even in the eighteenth century were written prayers tolerated, but preachers would sometimes jot down their "heads". The Rev. Thomas Clapp, who graduated at Harvard in 1725, left a "Scheme of Prayer" covering six pages, divided into five heads, with 240 sub-divisions; it must have contained a complete body of divinity. The later Puritans owed much to Isaac Watts in psalmody, but seldom applied his concise directions for prayer:

> Call upon God, adore, confess.
> Petition, plead, and then declare you are the Lord's.
> Give thanks and bless,
> And let Amen conclude the prayer.

Passing from prayer to praise, we think of the Pilgrim Fathers raising their austere metrical psalms on the barren strand at Plymouth. Longfellow was quite correct in the *Courtship of Miles Standish* (1859) when he pictured John Alden's visit to Priscilla:

> Open wide on her lap lay the well-worn psalm-book of Ainsworth,
> Printed in Amsterdam, the words and the music together,
> Rough-hewn, angular notes, like stones in the walls of a churchyard,
> Darkened and overhung by the running vine of the branches.

Ainsworth was a typical Jacobean Separatist, so his Psalter (1612) was not acceptable to the Anglican Puritans who swarmed across the Atlantic after 1630. They determined to make their own version, keeping closer to the Hebrew original than other renderings. The editors, like Sternhold and Hopkins, "had drunk more of Jordan than of Helicon"; they were "sons of Zion", not "of Greece". Was poetry sacrificed to literal accuracy? They dismissed the objection: "God's Altar needs not our polishings". In 1640 Massachusetts Bay received the promised home-grown version, which bore the proud title, *The Bay Psalm Book*.[2] It was printed by Stephen Daye at Cambridge, where Harvard College had just been planted. Critics expressed the opinion that the typography was as villainous as the versification, but after all, it was the first book printed in British North America. Out of 1,700 copies, only about a dozen survive (one in the

---

[1] They sang sitting and prayed standing. So long were the prayers that the "Standing Order" (the Congregational Establishment) was jocosely explained as the product of this posture.

[2] For metrical psalmody, see Henry Wilder Foote, *Three Centuries of American Hymnody* (Harvard, 1940).

Bodleian). It was not till the ninth edition appeared in 1690 that notes were provided—the first (surviving) book with music to be printed by Englishmen across the Atlantic. Only about a dozen tunes were known—old favourites like *Litchfield, Windsor, Low Dutch, Martyrs, York*. There was little progress in congregational singing after half a century, even in Boston, where Judge Sewall led the praise for twenty-four years. He tells us: " I set York tune and the congregation went out of it into St. David's in the very second going over. . . I set Windsor tune, they ran over into Oxford, do what I would." The gallery being in the habit of " carrying irresistibly " his own choice into something else, the good Judge took this as " an intimation for me to resign the Praecentor's Place to a better Voice ". If such unsatisfactory conditions persisted even in the historic Old South Church, what must they have been like elsewhere ? Apart from the uncouth versification and the lack of musical ability, the reading of each line by the precentor before it was sung (an English Puritan practice introduced into Scotland and still surviving in parts of the Highlands) produced ludicrous distortions such as:

> The Lord will come and he will not
> Keep silence, but speak out.

Cotton Mather took comfort in the fact that New England Praise was " recommend'd by Strangers as generally not worse than what it was in many other parts of the world ". In spite of this faint eulogy, the *Bay Psalm Book* became New England's standard Psalter, displacing the Ainsworth version used by the Pilgrims at Plymouth, and spreading south as far as Philadelphia. By the close of the eighteenth century fifty editions were called for. Despite the superiority of the *Scottish Psalter* of 1650, the *Bay Psalm Book* was actually reprinted in Scotland between 1732 and 1769.

In the first half of the eighteenth century many booklets were published in New England on " The Art of Singing by Note ", and young people found recreation as well as edification in singing schools. There were, to be sure, objectors who argued: " If we begin to *sing* by rule, the next thing will be to *pray* by rule and *preach* by rule, and then comes popery." In spite of this prejudice public opinion became enlightened enough to insist that precentors who " deaconed " the singing should cease " reading the line ".

This encouraged the promoters of better praise to break down one-man leadership. One congregation after another voted to allocate " three seats in the back gallery for those who inclined to sit together for the purpose of singing "; sometimes it was stipulated that they were to be personally responsible for any expense in the adaptation of sittings! At all events, the choir came modestly into being as the century passed its zenith. They were not satisfied, however, with these concessions. They would smuggle into their loft a " pitch-pipe ", an innocent-looking little instrument for regulating the singing. The die-hards denounced this as " the thin end of the wedge ", and so it was—for musical instruments in weird variety began to appear in meeting houses as well as in Episcopal churches. To be sure, John Cotton had allowed " the private use of Instruments ".[1] But even a century after his time most of the ministers and deacons of New England would have said " Amen! " to the conviction voiced by Sir Edward Deering in the Long Parliament: " One groan in the spirit is worth the diapason of all the church music in the world."

In recent years the tolerance of the Pilgrims has often been praised, over against the intolerance of the Puritans. This holds good of persecution in its more odious forms, but hardly of religious practices involving ceremonial or celebration. Plymouth was in agreement with the Bay Colony wherever any attempt was made to use the Prayer Book or observe the Christian Year. A number of settlers arrived at Plymouth by the *Fortune* in time for Christmas. Requested by Governor Bradford to work in the fields as usual, they " excused themselves and said it went against their consciences to work on that day ". At noon, the authorities found them in the street pitching the bar, playing stool ball and other games of Old England. Bradford " took away their implements and told them it was against his conscience that they should play and others should worke. If they made the keeping [of Christmas] mater of devotion, let them kepe their houses but ther should be no gaming or revelling in the streets. Since which time nothing hath been attempted that way, at least openly."

The Pilgrims had much more trouble with Thomas Morton, " of Clifford's Inn, Gent.", who settled within the jurisdiction of Plymouth. Morton was an Anglican " more addicted to the feasts than the fasts of the Church ". He not only celebrated Christmas

[1] *Singing of Psalms a Gospel Ordinance* (1647).

openly in 1627. He named his settlement Merry Mount, " as if this jollity would have lasted always ". On May-Day he boldly erected a Maypole, indulging with boon companions and Indians in Old English frolics. " The said Morton became lord of Misrule, and maintained, as it were, a school of Atheisme." When the Pilgrims arrived on the scene, they beheld the revellers inspired by abundant liquor, " frisking like so many fairies or furies ", and reviving " the beasley practicses of the madd Bacchinalians " (Bradford). The sober Pilgrims surveyed these goings-on with unconcealed disapproval. The maypole they termed " an Idoll . . . threatening to make it a woeful mount and not a merry mount". Governor Endicott of Salem,[1] the very personification of zealous austerity, added his usual condiment of unconscious humour by rebuking these " worshippers of the goddess Flora "; whereupon he re-named the accursed place " Mount Dagon ", and cut down the maypole. The serious offence that lay behind this rustic festivity was the fact that Morton made a practice of selling fire-arms as well as fire-water to the Indians. This "pestilent fellow " was sent home to England and his house demolished, " lest it be a roost for such unclean birds ". Yet " mine host of Ma-re Mount " kept on " returning to his old nest in the Massachusetts ", though heavily fined and repeatedly " laid in Irons to the decaying of his Limbs ". He eventually died at York, Maine, a broken-hearted old man, pathetically " content to drink water ".

When Morton was in England in 1637 he published his *New England Canaan*,[2] in which he ridiculed the " precisians " to the delight of Archbishop Laud and his friends. Gilbert and Sullivan could have made a delightful light opera out of his adventures. Here was an appropriate Cavalier and Roundhead interlude for 1066 *and All That*. As a matter of fact he did provide material for fiction—Hawthorne's *Maypole of Merry Mount* (1836) and Motley's *Merry Mount* (1849). Charles Francis Adams elucidates the incident in his *Three Episodes of Massachusetts History* (Boston, 1896).

Thomas Morton was an agent of Sir Ferdinando Gorges, an Elizabethan adventurer, who was instrumental in procuring a patent for the Plymouth Company. Sir Ferdinando was in touch

[1] His lineal descendant, Mary Crowninshield Endicott, married Joseph Chamberlain (1892), who battled long with the Tories, successors of the Cavaliers.
[2] Reprinted by The Prince Society (Boston, 1883).

with the Puritan peers for business reasons, but had no sympathy
with that party—especially when they questioned his right to take
possession of vast tracts in Maine, granted him by the King.
Aided and abetted by " ye archbishop of Counterberies " (Laud),
he intrigued against Edward Winslow, the Plymouth envoy,[1]
who was thrown into jail.

Another agent of Sir Ferdinando Gorges was that picturesque
cavalier, Sir Christopher Gardiner, Knight of the Sepulchre (somewhat " whited ").[2] He arrived with a comely young woman, his
" cousin ". " She (after the Italian manner) ", explains Bradford,
" was his concubine." A modern apologist considers that Sir
Christopher was " unfitted for the quiet pleasures of domestic
life ". One can understand that, for word reached New England
that he had two wives in London, one calling for his conversion,
the other for his destruction! In 1631 the Bay Colony ordered his
return to England along with other prisoners on the good ship
Lyon. He escaped, fled to the Indians, was recaptured, imprisoned
in Boston and set free. The following year found him in London,
joining in the intrigues against the Massachusetts Charter. The
Bay Colony was accused of separating from the Church of England
and threatening to cast off allegiance to the Crown.

Another adventurer, John Mason, was granted extensive
domains in New Hampshire, like Sir Ferdinando Gorges in Maine.
The aim of these men was to set up as " Counts Palatine " or
" Lords Proprietor " on semi-feudal lines, establish the Church
of England, and promote institutions to the liking of themselves
and their royal master. This small band were unable to hold their
own against the Puritan colonists; the expansionist policy of
Massachusetts prevailed; attempts to emulate the aristocratic
system of the South were frustrated. In a fine passage Cotton
Mather mentions non-Puritan settlements:

" The designs being aimed at no higher than the advancement of some
worldly interest, a constant series of disasters has confounded them, until
there was a plantation erected upon the nobler designs of Christianity;
and that plantation, though it has had more adversaries than perhaps
any one on earth, yet, having obtained hope from God, it continues to
this day." (*Magnalia,* Vol. II, p. 315 f.)

---

[1] Winslow's was " the sole authentic Pilgrim portrait " (1651). It is reproduced by Willison in *Saints and Strangers.*

[2] See Longfellow's " Rhyme of Sir Christopher " (*Tales of a Wayside Inn*).

One unfortunate by-product of these Church-and-King episodes was a deepening of Puritan gloom, a fixed idea that there was no room for the lighter side of life, on moral as well as economic grounds; Cavalier adventurers in America had certainly tended to be men of loose conduct. There is truth as well as exaggeration in Hawthorne's complaint: " When the Puritans met in conclave, it was never to keep up the old English mirth, but to hear sermons three hours long. . . Their festivals were fast-days, and their chief pastime the singing of psalms. Woe to the youth or maiden who did but dream of a dance! The selectman nodded to the constable; and there sat the light-heeled reprobate in the stocks; or if he danced, it was round the whipping-post—the Puritan 'maypole'." When it was maintained that Miriam danced (and David) authority replied: " These Instances are not at all to the purpose!" The Cavalier attempt to acclimatise the joy of life in the frosty atmosphere of New England failed. Did repression produce a wholesome social life ? Human instincts, denied a lawful outlet in innocent recreation, found abnormal expression in drunkenness and immorality. Too late, Governor Bradford (and others) realised that if " streams are stopped, or damed up, when they gett passage they flow with more violence".

Paradoxically, it was none other than " the Merry Monarch " who presented a bouquet to the second generation of Pilgrims. When a Royal Commission was sent to New England in 1664, they found Plymouth the most tractable of the " plantations ". Charles II sent them this message: " Your carriage seems to be set off with the more lustre by the contrary deportment of Massachusetts, as if, by their refractoriness, they had desired to heighten the merit of your compliance."

4. From the Fall of the Wilderness Zion to the Great Awakening

Massachusetts was a " totalitarian state " on Old Testament lines for about sixty years. Its authority, built on a basis of Puritan oligarchy, owed much to the " Mather dynasty ". The founder was Richard Mather, who preached Puritanism in the sequestered district of Toxteth Park, near Liverpool; this " Ancient Chapel of Toxteth " still exists (in Unitarian hands). When unwelcome " visitors " called by order of the Archbishop of

York, he explained that he had never worn a surplice for fifteen years. Whereupon they suspended him (one of them remarking that " it had been better for him that he had gotten fifteen bastards "). Persuaded by John Cotton and Thomas Hooker, Richard Mather sailed for the Bay Colony, where he became minister of Dorchester, one of the earliest settlements. His son, Increase (or Crescentius) Mather[1] was an ecclesiastical statesman comparable to Cardinal Carstares, who saved Scottish Presbyterianism at the Revolution of 1688. He well deserves the title bestowed by Dr. Murdock, his modern biographer, " The Foremost Puritan ".

Massachusetts assumed an independent attitude towards the mother-country from her foundation. She was practically a Puritan Republic, as jealous of the Long Parliament and Cromwell as of Charles I. In government, finance, trade and territorial expansion she claimed to exercise her own rights, safeguarding the smaller New England colonies against home interference. The English Government of course resented this independent attitude, which found a natural ally in the stormy Atlantic. The Restoration brought into power a régime utterly out of sympathy with the ideals of a Puritan Church-State. A clash was inevitable, sooner or later.[2] The storm so long feared by the ministers and magistrates of the Bible Commonwealth broke over their heads in 1684, when the Charter of Massachusetts was revoked. Two years later under James II there arrived Sir Edmund Andros, first royal Governor, with instructions to unify the provinces of New England and New York in the interests of autocracy.

Andros first shook hands with a velvet glove, but in a short time the community felt an iron grip. The legislature was abolished, the democratic " town " jurisdiction ignored, arbitrary imprisonment and fines imposed. Joseph Dudley, a judge of the Jeffreys stamp, told the citizens that their only remaining privilege was " not to be sold as slaves ". A new seal was adopted, showing his Sacred Majesty, James II, receiving from two kneeling figures, tribute and a petition. The Bostonians feasted their eyes on

---

[1] The names of Harvard graduates were Latinised, as at Edinburgh, e.g., Josephus Cookaeus, Marigena Cottonus (for Seaborn Cotton).

[2] Massachusetts was accused of usurping royal prerogative in coining money. Sir T. Temple, deputed to meet Charles II, produced a " pine-tree shilling ", with the politic explanation that it was the " Royal Oak ". The King was delighted and praised the New Englanders as " a parcel of honest dogs ".

novelties—gay equipages, brilliant uniforms and routs; less pleasing was the unwonted sight of an English clergyman in a surplice, reading the Prayer Book to a select audience in the " Old South " while the regular congregation had to wait in the street till he had finished. When would the whole apparatus of prelacy be imported?

The five ministers of Boston have been compared to " the steel point of the spear which Massachusetts held steadily before her breast ". Foremost was Increase Mather, who has been unjustly vilified by Brook Adams, the Puritan-baiter.[1] Selected by the General Court to present the case of the Bay Colony, he eluded arrest, boarded a ship in disguise and reached England safely. Soon after his arrival the Glorious Revolution of 1688 wrought a transformation-scene. " Who knoweth whether thou are come to the kingdom for such a time as this ? "

Increase Mather succeeded in obtaining as good terms as possible from Parliament for the Bay Colony, though the Charter of 1691 fell far short of his theocratic expectations. It permitted the Congregational Churches to remain the " Standing Order ", but insisted on freedom of worship for other orthodox Protestants. It gave the King the right to appoint a Governor for Massachusetts, but allowed appeals to higher English Courts. It confirmed the framework of the colonial legislature and local " town meetings ", but substituted a property qualification for Church membership as a test for voting. The Charter was reasonable, even generous, but it failed to satisfy the Massachusetts theocrats, just as the Revolution Settlement in Scotland failed to satisfy the more extreme Presbyterians.

Connecticut was more fortunate in one respect. She retained her privilege of electing a Governor; and this prevented the possibility of a royal nominee fostering a royalist, Anglican faction. When Governor Andros, during his brief dictatorship, demanded the surrender of the Charter at Hartford (1687) tradition says that the candles were extinguished and the precious parchment disappeared; it was safely preserved in a tree, " The Charter Oak ". When the Connecticut Constitution was confirmed at the Revolution, no provision was made for an official Episcopal chapel (which in Boston was regarded as not merely a blot on the Puritan scutcheon, but as a potential " Trojan horse").

Increase Mather married the daughter of the great John Cotton.

[1] *The Emancipation of Massachusetts* (1887).

Their son, Cotton Mather, became the best-known of the later Puritans, even more theocratic than his father, determined, if possible, to regain ground lost by the Charter of 1691, and to restore the fallen " Wilderness Zion ". This " Puritan Priest " found an able defender in Professor Barrett Wendell. He also interested Professor Parrington, but only as " an attractive subject for the psycho-analyst ".

Cotton Mather's industry was phenomenal. The most garrulous of men, he urged others, " Be brief ". His own motto was " Be fruitful ". He certainly lived up to it, for he produced 380 books and pamphlets. From the press rolled an endless procession of sprawling, rumbling sentences, heavily laden with the pedantry of his age. His style, like his speech, was " very emphatical ", according to a contemporary. His *magnum opus*, the *Magnalia Christi Americana*, in content and spirit, is a theocratic interpretation of New England history ranging from the landing of the Pilgrim Fathers in 1620 till 1698. It was published at London in 1702. Curiously enough, the first American edition did not appear till over a century later (2 vols., Hartford, 1820). The best epitome is furnished by the author—the Matherian equivalent of publisher's " blurb " :

" I write the *Wonders* of the CHRISTIAN RELIGION, flying from the Depravations of Europe to the American Strand. . . I do report the *Wonderful Displays* wherewith Providence . . . hath *irradiated* an Indian *Wilderness*.

I first introduce the *Actors* . . . and give *Remarkable Occurrences* in the lives of many *Magistrates* and of more *Ministers*.

I add thereunto the *Notables* of the only *Protestant University* that ever shone in . . . the *New World*.

I introduce then . . . a rich variety of *Synodical* and *Ecclesiastical* Determinations . . . Let my Readers expect all that I have promised them, in this Bill of *Fair*; and it may be that they will find themselves entertained . . . above and beyond their expectation, deserving likewise a room in *History*."

The modern reader of the *Magnalia* is likely to be " entertained" in another sense than the author intended; Southey read the unabridged edition[1] in a post-chaise between Nottingham and London (" one of the most amusing books I have ever seen "). Boston is the hub of Mather's universe. His forgotten worthies

[1] See *Selections from Cotton Mather*, edited by K. B. Murdock (New York, 1926).

are boldly compared to the leading lights of classical, Scriptural and ecclesiastical history. Mr. Adam Blackman is " our Melancthon " (largely on etymological grounds!), Mr. Peter Prudden is " Prudentius ", Mr. Samuel Stone is " Doctor Irrefragabilis ", Mr. Thomas Cobbet is " Eusebius ", Latin and Greek quotations embellish each encomium, adorned with verse and culminating in *Epitaphium*. The eulogist is an adept punster. Thus Mr. Ralph Partridge is compared to King David, " hunted like a partridge among the mountains ". This good pastor, " notwithstanding the *paucity* and *poverty* of his congregation, was so afraid of being anything that looked like a *bird wandering from his nest* that he remained with his poor *people* till he took wing to become a bird of paradise, along with the winged seraphim of heaven. *Avolavit* —he has flown away! " To continue the aviarist metaphor, most of Cotton Mather's swans are geese.

The following plum is one of many worth quoting. It refers to Thomas Hooker, founder of Hartford, Connecticut:

" When Toxaris met with his countryman Anacharsis in Athens, he gave him this invitation, ' Come along with me, and I will show thee at once all the wonders of Greece ': whereupon he showed him Solon . . . I shall now invite my readers to behold at once the ' wonders ' of New-England, and it is in one Thomas Hooker that he shall behold them: even in that Hooker, whom a worthy writer would needs call ' Saint Hooker ', for the same *reason* (he said) and with the same *freedom* that Latimer would speak of Saint Bilney [the martyr].

" 'Tis that Hooker, of whom I may venture to say, that the famous Romanist, who wrote *De Tribus Thomis*—meaning the Apostle, Thomas Becket, and Sir Thomas More—did not a thousandth part so well sort his Thomas's, as a New Englander might, if he should write a book, *De Duobus Thomis*; and with Thomas the Apostle joyn our celebrious Thomas Hooker: my *one* Thomas, even our apostolical Hooker, would in just balances weigh down . . . rebellious Archbishops or bigoted Lord Chancellors. 'Tis he whom I may call, as Theodoret called Irenaeus, ' The light of the western churches '."

When we turn the pages of the *Magnalia* we realise that a certain amount of its history is hysteria; nevertheless it is of enduring value as a window through which we may see Puritan ideals and ideas, extolled by a rhetorical Josephus, whose aim was to record the living past of his own people. Cotton Mather could write clearly when he chose. Consider his *Bonifacus: Essays to do good*. Published at Boston in 1710, it impressed even Franklin, who fled from Puritanism, and provoked him to write an impish

parody, *Mrs. Silence Doogood. Bonifacus* was reprinted at Glasgow
as late as 1825; this was appropriate, for had not the University
given its author a D.D.? He was very proud of his signet-ring,
bearing a tree (Psalm 1)—" Glascua rigavit ". A hostile pamphleteer commented:

> To Britain's northern clime he sends,
> And begs an Independent boon from Presbyterian friends;
> Rather than be without, he'd beg it of the fiends
> . . . To write C. Mather first and then D.D.

Cotton Mather's immense erudition was spoilt by his provincialism.[1] He was Boston born and bred, whereas his father,
Increase, had studied at Trinity College, Dublin, and served as
an army chaplain in Guernsey long before his London experience
as New England envoy. Cotton Mather, however, was a man of
scientific interests. He suffered from a stammer in youth and
therefore studied medicine; it was only when he overcame this
defect that he was able to proceed to the Ministry and succeed
his father in the Second Church, Boston. At the close of his life
he became a pioneer in recommending inoculation for smallpox,
for which he was execrated by those who might have known better.
A Fellow of the Royal Society (1713) he was largely responsible
for the Salem Witchcraft Trials (1692). This is one of the strange
paradoxes that make his life so interesting from a psychological
point of view.

Like the more extreme English Puritans and Scottish Covenanters, Cotton Mather was a man who fasted and wrestled in
prayer and saw visions. Diabolic agency was very real and must
be vanquished. He had a learned theory that America was the
special domain of the Devil who, served by his deluded subjects,
the Indians, was engaged in a ceaseless campaign against the
Puritan invaders of his appointed kingdom. Unfortunately, the
" Puritan Priest " was not content to confine these speculations
to his study; he was too " practical ". He believed that it was his
bounden duty to be continually informing, exhorting and warning
the public. In his *Wonders of the Invisible World* (1693) he

---

[1] To some extent inevitable. " While Boyle, Newton, and other founders
of the new scientific age in England, were tracing the reign of law, the intellectual leaders of New England were . . . gathering collections of ' remarkable
providences ', ranging from the sudden death of a Sabbath-breaker to the evi-
dent marking out for destruction, out of a whole library, of a Prayer Book, by a
mouse evidently brought up in the ' New England way '." (J. Truslow Adams,
ibid., p. 453).

solemnly accepted at face value old wives' tales of demonic agency. He was responsible for working up popular credulity to the pitch of fanaticism, culminating in the Witchcraft Trials—a New England tragedy, whose atmosphere is well conveyed in Longfellow's drama, *Giles Corey of the Salem Farms*.

History needs no dramatising. The Rev. Samuel Parris of Salem village wrote in his church records on 27th March 1692: "The Devil hath been raised up amongst us and his rage is vehement . . . and when he shall be silenced the Lord only knows." Inspired by the sincere but credulous Cotton Mather, Parris hatched a witchcraft conspiracy. His tools were his daughter, Elizabeth (aged 9), his niece, Abigail Williams (aged 11) and the parish clerk's daughter, Ann Putnam (aged 12). These children were apt mimics. Witchcraft was in the air and they took to it. Like sedulous apes, they practised the most blood-curdling gestures in private. One Sabbath they demonstrated publicly in the meeting house. Abigail called on the preacher: "Stand up now and name your text!" Ann shouted: "There's a yellow bird on your hat!" (which hung on the pin of the pulpit). As the sermon proceeded, interruptions went on: "Now, there's enough of that!" People (and physicians) were concerned about these "afflicted children". They refused to answer questions, but on being pressed, gave the names of persons guilty of sorcery. Acting under the control of Parris, they became witch-finders. Many years later they confessed their fraud.

A special Court was summoned by the Governor of Massachusetts to deal with "spectral evidence", which it accepted, following English precedent. After four months the judges gave their verdict. Twenty people were hanged, fifty who confessed were liberated, and one hundred and fifty were imprisoned. Anti-Puritan propagandists have made the most of these horrors, without bearing in mind contemporary conditions abroad. Lutheran orthodoxy, like the Papacy, considered that witchcraft was a crime; a woman was executed for diabolism in Germany as late as 1793, and a "witch" was burnt at Seville sixty years after Salem. In Scotland torture was used to secure convictions; two women were executed in Sutherland (1727); the death penalty was not abolished till 1736; Professor Forbes of Glasgow seriously discussed "spectral evidence" three years before the death penalty was abolished (*Institutes of Scots Law*, 1733); the Seceders con-

sidered that any relaxation of the anti-sorcery law as the sign of
" a carnal, back-sliding age ". In England John Wesley believed
in the reality of witchcraft. Nearly a century after the Salem
Trials the great Blackstone declared that to deny witchcraft was
to fly in the face of the Bible and experience.

It is to the credit of Robert Calef, a New England merchant,
that he succeeded in turning public opinion against the Salem
verdicts. He ridiculed Mather by publishing in London *More
Wonders of the Invisible World*. The highest legal authority of
Massachusetts rejected the findings of the Special Court, and the
Legislature appointed a Day of Fasting: " Help us, O Lord,
wherein we have done amiss, to do so no more." The persecutors,
men of the highest station, once convinced of their delusion, gave
relief to the victims' families. Judge Sewall even stood as a voluntary penitent in the crowded meeting house while his minister
read aloud his confession (*Diary*, 11th January 1697). However
much the Puritans erred, a number of them made amends.
Cotton Mather's influence declined and a wave of revulsion swept
the educated class against the theocracy; were they not blind
leaders of the blind ?

Thomas Brattle, associated with Calef and other enlightened
men, built a new church in Boston. The " Brattle Church " (1699)
witnessed for a humaner theology, more liberty in private life,
and enrichment of the bare Puritan worship. These liberals considered that young people should be admitted to full communion
without having to make public confession of their religious experience; and that baptism should be refused to no child provided
the parents promised to provide a Christian education. They
called to their pastorate the Rev. Robert Colman, ordained by the
Presbytery of London (" a wandering Levite who has no flock ",
according to Cotton Mather). Colman was not interested in such
curious speculations as Wigglesworth's " Who can tell the plagues
of hell and torments exquisite ? " He preferred " to err on the
charitable side " and his style was Addisonian. To the Mathers,
Brattle Church was a " cave of Adullam "; and what was most
vexing was the fact that the rich merchants tended to gravitate
there. As far back as 1663 a divergence between the theocracy
and plutocracy had been clearly indicated in an " Election Sermon ", preached in state before the legislature and duly printed:
" New-England is originally a plantation of religion, *not of trade*

. . . Let Merchants and such as are increasing Cent per Cent remember this." Another preacher remarked acidly: " New England hath many godly men—but few honest." By the early eighteenth century prosperous merchants were less docile in accepting such home-truths from the pulpit. The idea of worldly success as a road to ruin seemed nonsense.

How did the theocrats deal with this lamentable " hankering after new and loose ways " ? Increase Mather, during his visit to London after the Revolution of 1688, noticed that Presbyterians and Independents were negotiating a kind of Union. It occurred to him that the ministerial " Associations " of New England might be converted into Presbyteries with authority. Cotton Mather liked to think of the Congregational Churches as " Reformed Churches, nothing in Doctrine, little in Discipline, different from that of Geneva ". Massachusetts had little liking, at a time of nascent emancipation, for " ecclesiastical discipline, rightly ministered ". Proposals to give definite authority to " associations " were defeated largely through the efforts of an able publicist, the Rev. John Wise of Ipswich, who had been imprisoned under the Andros régime for refusal to pay arbitrary taxes. Wise's ideas, far in advance of his age, were destined to exercise a powerful influence at the time of the American Revolution.[1] Although a minister of the " Standing Order ", " he was a pioneer in recognising the injustice of the law that required all citizens to pay taxes towards the stipend of the parish minister ".[2]

A secular spirit was certainly in the ascendant. In Boston the magistrates discouraged week-day religious meetings as detrimental to business, though the " Great and Thursday Lecture " lingered as a venerable institution till the middle of the nineteenth century.[3] A sailor of Marblehead expressed widespread feeling when his minister " laid on " too hard: " Our ancestors came not here for religion: their main end was to catch fish." The theocracy seemed to be dying on the coast: might not the " hinterland " redress the balance ? Connecticut was still sound in the faith.

[1] See p. 146.
[2] The best known of his trenchant tracts are: *The Churches' Quarrel Espoused* (1710), and *A Vindication of the New England Churches* (1717).
[3] Latterly " none came but the saints, and these not with jubilant feet ". It was crowded for the last time in 1844 when Theodore Parker, Unitarian iconoclast, stood up to knock down all that the Puritan tradition had revered.

H

In 1708 the Governor of the Colony, the Rev. Gurdon Saltonstall[1] (a Congregational minister, of course), summoned a synod which enacted the " Saybrook Platform ".[2] The local Associations were more closely knit into " Consociations ", one or more in each county. These Councils were to function like presbyteries (but tell it not in Gath) " upon all occasions ecclesiastical ", including the ordination, installation and dismission of ministers. This applied, doubtless, to the Massachusetts Associations, but in Connecticut the Presbyterian tendency was definitely stressed. In order to strengthen the position of Calvinism, an inexpensive alternative to Harvard was founded. Yale College (1701) was named after Elihu Yale, son of a New Haven merchant who had amassed a fortune in India, eventually becoming Governor of Madras. This philanthropist had been contacted by the London agent for Connecticut, and flattered by a letter from Cotton Mather. The new institution, peripatetic for several years, was eventually established at New Haven. Its students were classified according to social status, as at Harvard, but its theological position was even more conservative. " Ask for the old paths and walk therein " (Jeremiah, 6.16).

This programme was being put into effect when an unexpected blow fell. Rector Cutler astounded the college trustees at Commencement 1722. He declared that he and several of his colleagues had decided to sail for London, to receive " Holy Orders ", which only a Bishop could confer, for the Congregational ministry lacked " Apostolic Succession " (such arguments were more usual just over a century later, when Anglicanism had been renewed by the Oxford Movement). A conference was summoned to deal with the Yale case, the dignified and Reverend Governor Saltonstall presiding. The Connecticut divines were well up in Calvinistic controversies, but rusty on Episcopal claims. The Revs. Timothy Cutler and Samuel Johnson were well primed with arguments derived from a collection of Anglican books[3] belonging to Elihu Yale; these had been unwittingly despatched to New Haven by Jeremiah Dummer, the colony's London agent. Dummer's consignment proved to be a veritable Pandora's box.

---

[1] Ancestor of Leverett Saltonstall, an outstanding public man of contemporary New England, a rich Unitarian.

[2] Named after a town settled by the Puritan Lord Saye and Sele.

[3] Johnson's pulpit prayers (much admired in his Congregationalist phase) were Anglican collects memorised and adapted.

The upshot was the organisation of a small but aggressive Episcopal Church in Connecticut, assisted by the English " Society for the Propagation of the Gospel ". Its agents took advantage of local feuds to plant Anglicanism; frequent disputes over meeting house sites provided many an opportunity of winning over discontented minorities. The prevailing brand of Episcopalianism was High Church, no mere appendage to a royal Governor's Court; it was the product of honest Connecticut convictions, no " sect of the Herodians ". The rector and his colleagues were " excused " further academic duties; after an uncomfortable voyage they were ordained in London (March 1723) and returned to New England as Anglican clergy. Yale survived the defection. Stringent doctrinal tests were imposed on the staff, and there soon were enough Calvinists for " the supply of all our synagogues ".[1]

It is now time to survey the New England scene with reference to Church and Ministry in the eighteenth century. The extreme " laic " views of the Pilgrims and Puritans were either abandoned or modified, e.g., the conviction that a " call " by a congregation was all that was necessary for the installation of a minister, and that he lost clerical status when he ceased to serve a particular parish. By the time that Cotton Mather wrote his *Magnalia* (1702) such individualism had become " plebeian ". Arch-Puritan as he was, he also believed in Church Order. His *Ratio Disciplinae* provides that " the laying on of hands must be done by those who are themselves of the same order ", and " by this consecration " the ordinand is " to be owned as admitted into the order of pastors through the whole Church of God ". In Massachusetts, as in Connecticut, " Ecclesiastical Councils " were advised of all calls to vacant churches and took part regularly in ordinations. Thus the Church at Northampton sends " Letters Missive " (25th January 1727) to neighbouring clergy, " requiring their presence and assistance to ordain Mr. Jonathan Edwards this day three weeks ".[2]

The " Standing Order " was organised on a territorial basis. Every New England " town " (urban or rural) was legally respon-

---

[1] It is pleasant to state that Johnson sent his son to Yale after all. Some Episcopalians reminded him that this involved compulsory chapel and extempore prayers. He replied that " incomplete prayers " were not injurious, and would only confirm the youth's preference for the Prayer Book.

[2] Such traditional forms of address are still carefully maintained in New England.

sible for supporting a parish minister. Citizens of all sects and corporations holding land were directly taxed to provide his stipend.[1] When the population increased so that one pastor was inadequate, a " town meeting " would petition the legislature; permission would be given to carve out a " second parish ", when the local authorities had guaranteed their ability to meet the extra cost. When there was only one meeting house,[2] the name " Congregational " was not usually applied. When there was more than one the title would be " First Parish in X——" or " the First Church of Christ in Y——". " First Churches " were historic;[3] " Second " and " Third " Churches carried diminishing ecclesiastical—and social—prestige. " Center Church " at the heart of the community would be supplemented by sanctuaries named after the points of the compass, the " Old South " being the most popular. Later churches were named after streets, as in English Dissent—" Maple Street ", " Dale Street ", " Tompkins Avenue", etc. The exact location of new meeting houses was a fertile source of disputes and schisms. Thus, disagreement over the settlement of a minister over the " New North " in Boston caused malcontents to hive off and erect a rival sanctuary (1720); they seriously intended to call it " The Revenge Church of Christ ", but eventually contented themselves with the humdrum label of " New Brick Meeting ". New Englanders avoided dedicating their places of worship to Saints (even those of the New Testament); they waited till they had saints of their own, such as Eliot, Shepard, Edwards, etc. Only occasionally does one find originality—the city of Providence being appropriately blessed with a " Beneficent Church ". The Founding Fathers are now remembered with many a " Plymouth Church " and many a " Church of the Pilgrims ".

Dr. S. D. McConnell, historian of American Episcopacy, referring to clerical " professionalism " in his own communion, generously admitted: " the debt which Anglicanism owes to Puritanism on both sides of the Atlantic is the restored reputation of the Ministry." During the eighteenth century the New England

---

[1] " The magistrates are nursing fathers and nursing mothers to the churches" (Cambridge Platform, 1648). This principle was axiomatic in the Church of England and in Lutheran Germany.

[2] " Church " was seldom used till well into the nineteenth century to denote the edifice, and country folk still speak of " goin' to meetin' ".

[3] In Britain we are familiar with the title " First Church of Christ Scientist ". It was probably adapted from New England usage, though we find " First Presbyterian " churches in Ulster.

minister was still revered for his integrity and his learning.[1] As the leading light of the community, he was known as " the parson", a formidable figure, complete with wig, cocked hat and gold-headed cane.[2] It was jocosely said that when teamsters drove past the parsonage they would put their best wheel on the nearest side ! At the close of the century the Chief Justice of Massachusetts declared that the right to glebe, parsonage and stipend from the town was " as permanent as the law could make it ". Pastor and people took continuity for granted. Taking Massachusetts, for example (1776) we find that 223 ministers retained their parishes till death, and only 48 severed the pastoral tie by resignation or transference to other churches. The Congregational tradition, however, was individualistic, and a new democratic tendency was stirring among the laity. During the War of Independence the Rev. Mr. Thacher of Malden declared that " no people under the government of Jews, Turks or pagans, were so badly off as the clergy of New England, on the supposition that power of dismission lies with the people ". The law could not prevent congregations from contracting with ministers that the pastoral tie be dissolved by, say, a two-thirds majority. People spoke of " hiring a minister ". Democracy destroyed the remnant of clerical authority.

As early as 1658 a certain Lieutenant Fuller was fined 40s. for asserting that when the Church and State laws of Massachusetts were framed, " the devil sat at the stern ". A century later this opinion was shared emphatically by dissenters from the " Standing Order ". The grievance affected their pockets directly, for the whole community (not merely landowners as in England and Scotland) were responsible for stipend, meeting house and parsonage. That did not mean that the official clergy were adequately remunerated,[3] but it did cause trouble. From 1719 onwards the

---

[1] During the eighteenth century " The Reverend " was substituted for " V.D.M. ", usually inscribed on portraits and pamphlets (*Verbi Dei Minister*); " Master " was also commonly used (implying M.A.).

[2] From 1685-6 two functions prohibited by the Puritans could henceforth be performed by ministers—officiating at marriages and funerals. Till then, civil marriage was compulsory in Massachusetts and funeral services were forbidden (like the Scots, they feared " prayers for the dead ").

[3] Economic depression after the Revolutionary War often involved payment of stipend in kind (crops, firewood, etc.). " Living low " and " scrabbling along " were accompaniments of Establishment. The financial position of the clergy improved after Disestablishment, as the people learned to give " as the Lord had prospered them ".

law was relaxed for Episcopalians, Baptists and other dissenters;
a reluctant town treasurer would transfer their Church tax to
their own sect, but only if it was organised locally. The law made
it easier to " sign off " from the Establishment than to obtain
permission from the legislature to sub-divide a parish by building
a new meeting house. The " Standing Order " thus lost supporters needlessly through local feuds. Episcopalian parsons who
had no compunction about taking taxes from dissenters in New
York, complained bitterly when the tables were turned in New
England. Thus we find the Rev. Mr. Muirson protesting to the
S.P.G. about the Congregational authorities: " How severely they
treat our people, by taking their Estate by distress when they do
not willingly pay to support their Ministers." Yet the position
of Episcopalian dissenters in New England[1] was much more
favourable than that of Congregational dissenters in England.
The Baptists were the most consistent in disclaiming state patronage and control under any circumstances. Quakers won an
important test case in 1724.[2]

The old Puritanism was declining in the eighteenth century.
It had lost the freshness of a crusade and was fast hardening into
a tradition. Among the farmers, patriarchal Old Testament ideas
survived in quaint forms. Drought was the penalty of neglecting
" ordinances ", and plenty was the reward of honouring them.
" Wa'al," remarked a typical husbandman, " our minister gives so
much attention to his farm and orchard that we get pretty poor
sermons, but he is mighty movin' in prayer in caterpillar and
cankerworm time." The poorer people thought it no sin to anti-
cipate marriage in the traditional practice known as " bundling ".
It was said that as much liquor was consumed at a New England
Ordination as at a Southern barbecue.[3] In 1765 Parson Smith
described an ordination at New Gloucester as " jolly . . . we
lost sight of decorum ". Despite denunciations of " promiscuous

---

[1] One rector of King's Chapel, Boston, wrote home to England, lamenting
his isolation but assuring Churchmen that he was " maintaining an offensive
attitude towards all " !

[2] Two Quakers were appointed " Assessors " at Dartmouth and Tiverton,
Mass. On refusing to collect the stipend-tax, they were imprisoned. Their
appeal to the Privy Council was sustained and their heavy fine remitted; for
all that, they spent a year in jail.

[3] " Raising the frame " of timber churches was a community effort, demand-
ing spirituous refreshment. As late as 1823, in the rural parish of Webster,
N.H., the expenses included $7\frac{3}{4}$ galls. W. Indian Rum, $8.62; $4\frac{3}{4}$ galls. New
Eng. Rum, $2.37; 3 lbs. sugar, 90 c.; 209 lemons, $8.71.

dancing " these were not uncommon, though ministers were not always present. The graver sort would allow " pyrrhical or polemical saltation " (whatever that might be) and dancing of men with men and women with women; these had Biblical precedent—but not " gynaecandrical " dancing. Censors complained that " women smoke in bed and whilst they're cooking ". As early as 1722 a public billiard room was opened in Boston. Cards became fashionable, in spite of the fulminations of divines like Cotton Mather. Lack of lawful recreations resulted in hard drinking among all classes, as well as the popularity of cock-fighting. The " playhouse " was the institution most unsparingly denounced. Not till 1793 was a theatre permitted in Boston, when *The School for Scandal* was performed, disguised as a " moral lecture ". Had a theatre been tolerated earlier in the century, it would doubtless have been patronised by the more enlightened clergy who would have been discriminating in their judgment of the stage.[1]

It will be remembered that in 1691 the Charter of Massachusetts was renewed only on condition that the vote be not confined to Church members—result, a definite fall in the number of communicants. To meet this growing laxity, parish ministers found it necessary to acquiesce in a " Half-Way Covenant ". This was a declaration made by baptized parents who were not communicants and could give no public evidence of regeneration. They were allowed to have their children baptised, if the grandparents had been communicants. Those who were willing to " own the Covenant " thus far, were to be met " half-way ". Although this innovation can be traced back as far as 1657 in New England, it was fiercely contested as a sign of degeneracy. Nevertheless, by the second quarter of the eighteenth century, it was being accepted in parishes where zeal was cooling and communicants were declining.

This " Half-Way Covenant " had been accepted even by patriarchs like the Rev. Solomon Stoddard. In 1726 Mr. Stoddard's grandson was elected as his assistant and successor in the parish of Northampton, Massachusetts. This young man was destined to resuscitate the dying Calvinism of New England, just as another young man, also born in 1703, was called to revive Evangelicalism in England. Jonathan Edwards was as Calvinistic as John Wesley

[1] In Scotland, John Home had to resign his parish because he had dared to write a play (1756). But so many ministers flocked to see Mrs. Siddons in *Douglas* that the meetings of the Assembly had to be altered to suit.

was Arminian; they were both ambassadors of Christ to a century that was too " enlightened " to accept revealed religion.

The Rev. Timothy Edwards of East Windsor, Connecticut, had eleven children. Jonathan's boyhood was lonely and austere by choice, not by necessity. A precocious lad, he wrote in his twelfth year an essay on flying spiders, remarkable for keen observation and vivid style. " I have seen a vast multitude of little shining webs, and glistering strings, brightly reflecting the sunbeams, and some of them of great length, and of such a height that one would think they were tacked on to the vault of heaven, and would burn like tow in the sun." The hard theology of Yale did not destroy his love of nature, so uncommon before the Romantic Movement. There was a pantheistic strain in the piety of young Edwards. Often he would withdraw to the woods and spend hours in meditation, soliloquy and prayer. He was oppressed by the hard dogmas of Election and Reprobation. One day he was perusing *First Timothy*, when he reached the ascription: " Now unto the King eternal, immortal, invisible, the only wise God, be honour and glory for ever, Amen." As he read these words, his soul was flooded by a divine current that fused tenderness and strength. The soul appeared to resemble " a little, white spring flower, low and humble on the ground, opening its bosom to receive the pleasant beams of the sun's glory; rejoicing as it were in a calm rapture, diffusing around a sweet fragrancy; standing peacefully and lovingly in the midst of other flowers round about ". Paul Elmer More has cited this passage as " worthy of Augustine at his best ".[1]

" They say there is a young lady in New Haven who is beloved of that great Being who made and rules the world, and that there are certain seasons in which this great Being, in some way or other invisible, comes to her and fills her mind with exceeding sweet delight." Edwards wrote these lines when he was twenty and Sarah Pierrepont was thirteen. He became urgent later and thus admonished his beloved: " Patience is commonly esteemed a virtue, but in this case I may almost regard it as a vice." They were married, and the conditions of harmony were provided by lineage, culture, temperament and mystical affinity. In this respect Edwards was a great contrast to John Wesley. The New England divine was not merely able to enjoy a marked detachment

[1] *A New England Group (Shelburne Essays,* Vol. XI, p. 39 ff., Constable).

from the outward turmoil of life; his wife profoundly influenced his subtle thought.

The strange thing about Edwards was this. How could a man who blended the philosophical, dogmatic and aesthetic temperaments so uniquely,[1] be capable of preaching such a sermon as "Sinners in the Hands of an Angry God"? Combustible materials and lurid metaphors were only too common in Puritan preaching, but seldom has calm deliberation achieved such an effect on worshippers—weeping, groaning and pleading. "The God that holds you over the pit, much as anyone holds a spider, or some loathsome insect over the fire, abhors you and is dreadfully provoked; his wrath towards you burns like fire." With calm Calvinistic deliberation he calls for silence as he elucidates his text: "Their foot shall slide in due time" (Deut. 32.35). His calm tenseness and motionless poise was punctuated only by the mechanical gesture of turning the pages of a closely written and carefully corrected manuscript. "It would be no wonder if some persons, that now sit here in some seats of this meeting house in health, quiet and secure, should be in hell to-morrow." When Isaac Watts read this discourse, he described it as "a terrible sermon". The modern visitor to Enfield will find it difficult to recapture the mood of this sermon; the beautiful village with its "elegant" Greek Revival temple seems utterly remote from hell-fire.[2]

The preaching power of Edwards defies analysis. His biographer, Dr. A. V. G. Allen, thought that "he was almost too great to let loose upon other men in their ordinary condition. He was like some organ of vast capacity whose strongest stops or combinations should never have been drawn." He was consumed by a passion for the sovereignty of God; an uncanny, volcanic power possessed the gentle scholar almost as completely as if he had been a coarse fanatic dealing damnation round the land. "If you had the History of my Life from the Beginning 'tis probable the very things which now appear mysterious to you would be explained." Dr. Alexander Whyte understood this secret when he entitled one of his lectures on Puritan saints, "The autobiographical element in Edwards".[3]

[1] C. H. Faust and T. H. Johnson, *Jonathan Edwards, Representative Selections* (Cincinnati, 1935).
[2] When Professor Lyon Phelps was lecturing on Edwards a few years ago on a public occasion, his reading of the famous hell-fire passages was realistic enough to terrify the negro waiters!
[3] See Sir Leslie Stephen's essay on Edwards (*Hours in a Library*, 2nd Series).

Northampton was on the frontier when Jonathan Edwards and Sarah Pierrepont made their home there. The townsmen within living memory lived in the fear of the Indians as much as in the fear of the Lord, but now the fortifications were grass-grown. About 200 unpainted wooden houses clustered around a formidable square meeting house. The population were not all uncouth frontiersmen, however; a number of them were people of substance, education and good birth. Northampton was the most flourishing town in the upper Connecticut Valley, and the parish was an important one. The neighbouring ministers spent much of their spare time farming; on the Sabbath they would castigate the age for its declension from the standards of the Puritan fathers. Twice a year they would meet at the " Hampshire Association " (Edwards being the librarian), and there they would discuss such diverse questions as:

" Whether it be Lawful to eat Blood ? "
" What is the sin against the Holy Ghost ? "
" In what sense are we to Understand That Expression in ye Apostles' Creed, He descended into Hell ? "
" Is the Institution of Deacons of Divine Origin ? "

Edwards did not treat religion as a mere insurance against a day of reckoning, or as a reward. He fervently believed that it was " man's chief end to glorify God and to enjoy Him forever ". His mystic fervour attracted all who had suffered from a " famine of the Word ". By the winter of 1733, 300 people had been converted and admitted to Church membership. Too Puritan, however, were the standards demanded by the preacher of his people. There was to be no more " frolicking "; the reading of novels like Richardson's *Pamela* was branded as sin. Abnormal excitement and morbid symptoms were often mistaken for conversion. Children were " young vipers " (he had a quiverful of them) " if not Christ's ". He singled out for approval a mite of four years old, " wreathing her body to and fro like one in anguish of spirit ". After " wrestling " for some time, she said with a smile: " Mother, the kingdom of heaven is come to me! " Thereafter she loved " to hear Mr. Edwards preach " and had " a great concern for the good of other souls ". Such incidents abound in Edwards' *Faithful Narrative of the Surprising Work of God . . . in Northampton* (1737).

This revival in a small town of western Massachusetts was destined to release a spiritual flood, soon to sweep through the American colonies, submerging landmarks and breaking through provincial and denominational barriers with an impetus unknown before. " True religion is a powerful thing . . ." said Edwards, " a ferment, a vigorous engagedness of the heart." This conviction, that " Christianity is an inner experience or it is nothing " stands out as basic to any adequate understanding of revivalism, which was to form the dominant pattern of American religion for well over a century.[1]

[1] Ola Elizabeth Winslow, *Jonathan Edwards*, 1703-1758, p. 212 ff. (New York, 1940).

BOOK II

UNIFICATION

CHAPTER I

THE GREAT AWAKENING

Lo! by the Merrimac WHITEFIELD stands . . .
A homeless pilgrim, with dubious name,
Blown about on the winds of fame;
Now as an angel of blessing classed,
And now as a mad enthusiast . . .
Up and down the world he went
A John the Baptist crying—Repent!

WHITTIER

WHITEFIELD, unlike Wesley, was the Apostle of two continents. Not content with his preaching triumphs in England, he sought new fields of conquest for the Gospel. The
amazing thing is that he, an Englishman, set his mark on America
more permanently than on his native land. His preaching put new
life into aging Calvinism in the new world. An Anglican clergyman,
he painfully crossed the Atlantic to awaken the descendants of the
Puritans and the Ulster Scots, who had recently fled to escape
Anglican oppression. And it was among these " dissenters ", not
the people of his own Church, that he preached with such tremendous effect. He seemed to feel perfectly at home in the new
environment. " As there is here the same sun, so there is here the
same God—in America as in England. I bless God all places
are equal to me." All sects were equal to him also. As soon as
he reached Philadelphia in the late autumn of 1739 he started
preaching from the balcony of the court-house; every note of his
sonorous organ-voice was carried four hundred yards to the ships
on the river at the foot of Market Street. " Father Abraham,
whom have you in heaven? Any Episcopalians? No. Any Presbyterians ? No. Any Independents or Methodists ? No, no, no.
Whom have you there ? We don't know those names here. All
who are here are Christians—men who have overcome by the
blood of the Lamb and the word of his testimony. Oh, is this

the case ? Then God help us, God help us all, to forget party names, and to become Christians in deed and truth."

Philadelphia was the largest town in British North America[1] and the most progressive. On Quaker foundations, the " city of brotherly love " rose to prosperity, amenity and culture.[2] Its leading citizen was Benjamin Franklin, printer, publisher and publicist. The first " typical American ", destined to be the greatest American of his age, he was more interested in business than in preaching; and he was a Deist. In spite of all this, Franklin could not help admiring the quixotic enthusiasm, the overflowing vitality, of this young crusader aged twenty-three. He procured him all the publicity he wanted and even undertook to get his sermons published. Did respectable citizens dislike being elbowed by a crowd of mechanics as he held forth in the streets ? Let them build an auditorium to accommodate any stranger with a message; " so that even if the Mufti of Constantinople were to send a missionary to us, he would find a pulpit at his service ". Franklin's *Pennsylvania Gazette* gave full accounts of Whitefield's tempestuous preaching and opened its columns to candid correspondence on this burning question.

Instead of expounding doctrines (like most preachers of his era) Whitefield used every conceivable device to touch the emotions of his hearers. His English biographer, Dr. A. D. Belden, entitles him " The Awakener ". He would raise his hands high above his head, stamp his feet, burst into tears when speaking of Peter weeping bitterly (drying them with a fold of his gown). Preaching extempore, he would illustrate vividly from such incidents as a thunderstorm, a passing cloud or a burst of sunshine; or he would quote admonitory passages from a contemporary murder-trial. His melodious voice would play on the feelings of his hearers and fuse them into unity; falling under his spell, they would hold their breath, laugh, sob or respond with violent bodily movements. Philadelphia was so enthralled by young Whitefield's dramatic power, that the theatre, the dancing school and the concert room were closed, " as inconsistent with the Gospel ". The educated classes felt that this was going too far. Members of the Anglican Church wondered how a clergyman of the English Establishment

---

[1] Its inhabitants numbered 32,000 compared to New York's 23,000 and Boston's 16,000. Pennsylvania, fifty years after its founding, had about 50,000 (1732). By the middle of the century New England had over 400,000 inhabitants.

[2] See Struthers Burt, *Philadelphia* (London, 1947).

could lower himself to such a degree of enthusiasm. The Friends were not friendly to a religion so different from theirs. As Whittier explained in his poem of " the Great Awakening" (*The Preacher*):

> The Quaker kept the way of his own—
> A non-conductor among the wires,
> With coat of asbestos proof to fires . . .
> But holding as in his Master's sight
> Act and thought in the inner light,
> The round of his simple duties walked,
> And stroved to live what the others talked.

Whitefield had a way of extracting money for his schemes as well as collecting vast congregations. Franklin tells of a Quaker who had taken the precaution to attend the preaching with empty pockets. Unable to resist the appeal, he whispered to his neighbour about a loan. The latter seems to have been one of the few present who maintained their professed firmness, for he replied: " At any other time, Friend Hopkinson, I would lend thee freely, but not now, for thee seems to be out of thy right senses." And has not Franklin told the story how he himself resolved to give nothing to the collection for Whitefield's orphanage, although he had in his pocket a good deal of loose change ? " As he proceeded I began to soften and concluded to give the copper. Another stroke of his oratory made me ashamed of that and determined me to give the silver, and he finished so admirably that I emptied my pocket into the collection, gold and all."[1]

Whitefield's philanthropy was secondary to his primary aim— preaching the Gospel throughout the colonies. " Field-preaching is my plan; in this I am carried on eagles' wings." This plan was much more difficult to execute than in relatively compact England, but he carried it out—from Georgia in the south to the northern towns of Massachusetts. " Do you ask what I am doing ? " he wrote to John Wesley: " I answer ' ranging and hunting in the American woods after poor sinners '." Sometimes he " read prayers " and preached in Anglican churches, but usually he was not wanted there. The Commissaries of the Bishop of London growled at his " intrusion ", his readiness to hold forth in con-

---

[1] Even Lord Chesterfield, heartless man of the world, found Whitefield irresistible. When the preacher pictured a blind man approaching a precipice, he interrupted: " For heaven's sake, Whitefield, save him! "

I

venticles, and his addiction to extempore prayer. For a clergyman
of the Church of England it was all very irregular. Yet the
common people heard him gladly and in their thousands assembled
under the open canopy of heaven. In Williamsburg, the capital
of Virginia, he dined with the Governor and admired the College
of William and Mary: " The present masters come from Oxford.
Two of them were my contemporaries there. I rejoiced at seeing
such a place in America." There were few towns in the South,
which abounded in scattered plantations. Negroes and white
" indentured servants " had few opportunities of hearing the
Gospel; " and if they pretend to serve God, their masters, Pharaoh-
like, cry out, ' Ye are idle, ye are idle '." During this tour Whitefield carried on a varied correspondence with friends in England
and Scotland. To the Rev. Ralph Erskine, the Dunfermline
Seceder, he wrote: " Although I profess myself a minister of the
Church of England, I am of catholic spirit, and if I see any man
who loves the Lord Jesus in sincerity, I am not very solicitous to
what outward communion he belongs." Whitefield did not
approve of Erskine's insistence on Presbyterianism and thought
it would lead to persecution. " Our dear friend, Mr. Gilbert
Tennent, thinks this will be the consequence, and said he would
write to you about it." This was Whittier's

> Celtic Tenant, his long coat bound
> Like a monk's with leathern girdle round,
> Wild with the toss of unshorn hair,
> And wringing of hands, and eyes aglare
> Groaning under the world's despair.

Tennent, a perfervid Ulster Scot, joined Whitefield on his way
to New York, and showed him with pride his " log-college " at
Neshaminy. The Presbyterian Synod, afraid of " enthusiasm ",
directed Presbyteries to ordain only graduates of New England
or European colleges. The visitor noted frankly: " the meanest
building ever erected for such a purpose—it reminded me of ' the
schools of the prophets ' in the Old Testament." Tennent did
the Great Awakening more harm than critics who pelted it with
" strictures ". A hot-gospeller without discrimination, he was no
suitable companion for the young English evangelist who had
drunk too deep of that heady wine, American applause. Franklin,
Deist as he was, proved a better friend.

In New Jersey, Whitefield found an ardent fellow-worker in

Domine Frelinghuysen,[1] whose zeal was ballasted by Dutch stolidity. Frelinghuysen was effectual in rousing the Reformed Church from its Rip van Winkle slumbers. Advancing into New York province, Whitefield became popular among the Presbyterians; they encouraged him to strike the true Calvinistic note. In Boston, a leading Congregational minister, Dr. Colman, took up his pen and wrote to Isaac Watts: " America is like to do Mr. Whitefield much honour. He proposes to see Boston before his return to Europe . . . our town and country stand ready to receive him as an angel of God. Ministers and people, all but his own church, speak of him with great esteem and love. He seems spirited from on high, in an extraordinary manner assisted and prospered " (16th January 1740).

In September he preached in Dr. Colman's meeting house, Boston, to 4,000 and to 15,000 on Boston Common. A minority disapproved.[2] " I am sorry to see you here," said Dr. Cutler, with asperity. " So is the devil! " was the characteristic reply. At Newburyport he preached in a thunderstorm. " Hark! " said he, raising an admonitory finger, " the voice of the Almighty as He passed by in his anger! " As the sound died away, he covered his face, absorbed in prayer. The sun burst out, throwing across the heavens the arch of peace. Rising and pointing to it, he exclaimed: " Look upon the rainbow and praise Him who made it. It compasseth the heavens about with glory and the hands of the Most High have bended it." When asked to publish the sermon, the preacher replied with a flash of humour: " I have no objection, if you will print the lightning, thunder and rainbow with it."

The climax of Whitefield's tour was his visit to Jonathan Edwards at Northampton, in western Massachusetts. Edwards, above all others, had prepared the way by a series of revivals, which might have remained local but for the mighty English evangelist. Edwards had effected "a great concern about religion". He had almost extirpated recreation. He had surpassed himself in such themes as " The Eternity of Hell's Torments ", " Men Naturally God's Enemies " and " Wicked Men Useful in Their Destruction Only ". Whitefield, with a sure touch of insight,

---

[1] For Theodore Frelinghuysen and other personalities of the Awakening, see W. W. Sweet, *Revivalism in America* (New York, 1944).

[2] Tutor Flynt observed with Harvard *hauteur*: " He has the old New England and Puritanic way of thinking and preaching about regeneration and conversion, original sin, etc." Whitefield described Harvard as " scarce as big as one of our least colleges at Oxford—and not superior in piety. "

recognised that the scorched soil of Northampton needed planting, not further fire. " I found my heart drawn out to talk of scarce anything besides the consolations and privileges of the saints and the plentiful effusion of the Spirit upon believers." When he left New England in January 1741 for old England, he had caused streams of revival to flow from Georgia to the borders of Canada. He had unified the Great Awakening, which may well be defined as the first great spiritual movement that overflowed the boundaries of the separate North American colonies. No longer were the provinces entirely self-contained units.

The tragedy of the Great Awakening was the fact that it set agoing the fierce sectarian spirit afterwards so characteristic of America. Whitefield was an Anglican of the broadest type ecclesiastically, but theologically he was a narrow Evangelical, and ethically a throw-back to seventeenth-century Puritanism. In England the leaders of orthodox dissent were well aware of his conceit and lack of discretion. Watts warned him against making too much of " impressions " assumed to be divine; Doddridge considered him " an honest man, but weak, and a little intoxicated with popularity ". Once the glamour of his personality was removed from the American scene, it became clear that the heavenly treasure he had disclosed was contained in definitely earthen vessels.

Whitefield's faults were exaggerated in the behaviour of his followers. Gilbert Tennent warned his hearers of " the Danger of an Unconverted Ministry ". Any minister who did not see the truth as he did was " unconverted ". The use of manuscript in the pulpit was denounced (for many years usual in New England). Uneducated exhorters were encouraged to take up preaching and prided themselves on their superior sanctity. Dr. Timothy Cutler, once rector of Yale College (before he became an Episcopalian) described Tennent in uncomplimentary terms: " A monster! impudent and noisy, and told them there were all damn'd, damn'd, damn'd; this charmed them ". Tennent's attitude was criticised in the Courts of his Church; it was obviously at variance with the orderly spirit of Presbyterianism. In spite of censoriousness and hell-fire, Whitefield revivalism was popular among the Presbyterian laity. The Church split in 1745 into the " Old Side " and the " New Side ". Both sides were about equal, but by 1758 the O.S. ministers had decreased from 25 to 22, while the N.S. had shot up from 22 to 72. Meanwhile, the minute divisions of Scotland had been introduced. The various Secession shoots appeared, not to speak of the Reformed Presbyterians who felt that their mission was essential in a land that had not committed itself to the National Covenant of 1638.

In New England revivalist excesses burst the bounds of good sense. Among those who might have known better was the Rev. James Davenport, great-grandson of the founder of New Haven colony. Under the suggestion of " impressions ", " impulses " and texts " borne in upon his mind ", he abandoned his own parish in Long Island and devoted himself to a peripatetic ministry throughout New England, denouncing the regular Congregational clergy as " unconverted ", and urging the people to leave their churches. At New London he emulated Savonarola in calling the people to bring all their luxuries to a bonfire. Strangely enough the works of Matthew Henry, Flavel and other Puritan divines were added to the pile; and the flames were compared to those which their authors were still enduring in hell!

Edwards, faced with the awkward problem of mass hysteria expressed in faintings, convulsions and morbid fear of hell, found it necessary to add to his pamphlets on the meaning of the Great Awakening. His *Thoughts on the Present Revival in New England* (1742) minimise these " bodily effects " as by-products of divine visitation; even this gentle scholar justifies terror as sometimes necessary in preaching. His *Religious Affections* (1746) gave emotionalism theological direction, literary balance and psychological insight. Edwards was in some respects a forerunner of William James. He is numbered among " the children of the Second Birth ", whose religious experience has meant so much in the dominant Evangelical tradition of modern America. Critics of the Awakening were not convinced, however, that its promoters really subordinated the morbid " bodily effects " as true tests of conversion. The Rev. Charles Chauncy, of the First Church in Boston, dwelt on the unwholesome effects of the Revival —hysteria, hypocrisy, neglect of business, the breaking of home and family ties. His *Seasonable Thoughts on the State of Religion in New England* (1743) procured him a D.D. from Edinburgh— Scotland too was having trouble with Whitefield and his " Cambuslang wark ". Chauncy's *Enthusiasm Describ'd and Caution'd against* is a homiletic masterpiece. In an era when pamphlets and printed sermons were widely read, it was effective in discrediting revivalist methods among the more intelligent. Dr. Chauncy appealed to the public of eastern Massachusetts, which had been steadily leavened by the more humane theology that reached them from English latitudinarian circles. Henceforth, it was only in the Connecticut Valley and western Massachusetts that demonstrative revivalism could stampede the whole community. The breach was widening that would ultimately issue in the Unitarian schism.

Whitefield paid no less than seven visits to America, but his methods yielded decreasing returns. Boston was now allergic to his influence. Even evangelical Yale found it necessary to warn students against his " enthusiasm " and even his " conduct ". He preached his last sermon in Newburyport, on the New Hampshire border, in 1770. " I am tired," he said, " and must go to bed." Standing with a lighted candle on the staircase of the Old South parsonage, he saw the crowd pouring in, and began to preach. It was " the ruling passion strong in death ". The Awakener went on exhorting till the candle went out, burnt down to the socket. That night he died. A cenotaph in the Old South Presbyterian Church marks his resting-place.

The candle burnt down to the socket—this picture symbolised the whole situation in New England. The spiritual glow had not been maintained by Christian nurture and orderly worship. " New Light " teaching was carried to absurd lengths. In the year of Whitefield's death, President Ezra Stiles cited in his *Diary* the case of one Dawson, a Baptist minister in Newport.

" He preaches that it is sinful for the unregenerate to pray at all; to use the Lord's prayer in particular, for if they said the truth, they would say . . . ' Our Father which art in Hell '. As to attending his preaching, he asked the unregenerate what they came there for, he had nothing to say to them, only to tell them they were heirs of damnation. . . None but saints were the subjects of his preaching; and [he] forbid at length the promiscuous congregation to sing or pray with them—and only a dozen or so now sing. . . So that he does the thing thoroughly—he makes no pauses or reservations. Now this, at this time, is a very wonderful looking-glass! "

Not many Edwardian Calvinists were prepared to behold their creed distorted in this " looking-glass "; nor were they inclined to turn to the " Old Calvinists ", who maintained that though salvation was wrought by divine grace, regeneration might be attained by those who exposed their souls to the means of grace—prayer,

Bible reading and public worship. Ministers of the " Standing Order " who had embraced the principles of the Awakening did not secure immunity from its excesses. Wandering evangelists dislocated the parochial system by forming " Separatist " conventicles—a return to the early Independent pattern of the " gathered church ". They were rebels against an educated ministry and the formal meeting house with its pews assigned according to social status and its pulpit high over their heads, at what Lowell called " the natural angle of somnolence ". The " Separates " burned out in their very fanaticism, but the Baptists added to their numbers and flourished under pressure of mild persecution. " Believers' Baptism " was a logical conclusion of the Edwardian attitude to children.[1]

If the " Standing Order " lost supporters on the " left ", it suffered defections on the " right ". All over New England there were quiet people sick of controversy and religious excitement; they sought peace in the orderly Episcopal fold (men of similar temperament in Scotland did likewise in Disruption days). They would agree with the worthy whose faith was summarised by his epitaph in Copps Hill cemetery, Boston: " He was an enemy to enthusiasm "—meaning religious presumption, emotionalism and fanaticism. These converts to Episcopacy claimed to be " sober dissenters " from Established Congregationalism. They did not take the High ground of their predecessors who left the "Standing Order ": " We are all good Churchmen: we maintain an offensive demeanour towards them that are without."

Optimists in Established Congregationalism took a different view. They claimed that the fires of Revival were " banked " rather than extinct. They pointed to the evidence of statistics. Church membership had increased by 25,000 to 50,000; 150 new churches were built between 1740 and 1760. The " system " of periodic revivals and " protracted meetings"(!) had been incorporated in the New England way of life. " New Light Calvinism ", forged by Edwards and his supporters, became a formidable instrument of indoctrination. It certainly evaded some of the errors of the older Calvinism—fatalism and a bargaining spirit, that owed more to the Old Testament than the New. We shall

[1] A characteristic pamphlet on the other side was Samuel Webster's *Young Children . . . declared by Christ Members of His Gospel Church . . . And, therefore, to be visibly marked as such, like other Members, by Baptism. And plunging not Necessary* (Salem, 1773).

find that the galvanised " New England Theology " was a powerful
conductor of spiritual current. Its defects must be related to the
intellectual atmospherics of the eighteenth century.

The Great Awakening, as a tidal wave of religious excitement,
inevitably died down. The man who suffered most from its ebb-
tide was Edwards himself. He had outlived his popularity at
Northampton. Not only was he blamed for the excesses of the
revival; he insisted on searching tests of conversion before
admitting candidates to Church membership; he would leave no
stone unturned till he had uncovered the scandal of " bad books "
said to circulate among his young people. Psychologist as he was
in some respects, he was altogether too Puritanical in his endeavour
to keep his parishioners at a high-pitched spiritual altitude, all
the time, denouncing as sin any descent to Life's pleasant and
beautiful valleys. He would have been the better of Keble's
wise placidity:

> We need not . . . strive to wind ourselves too high
> For sinful man beneath the sky.

Beneath the surface of Edwards' views there was another factor
that made his position at Northampton insecure. " He always
had the wrong friends." His chief supporter was the Squire,
Colonel Timothy Dwight, while his opponents were men who took
up a democratic attitude and thought it high time to curb clerical
control. They had their way on the 22nd June 1750, when a large
majority of Church members voted for his dismissal (an " Ecclesiastical Council " of the nine neighbouring parishes had decided to
abide by the decision of the Northampton congregation). In his
valedictory sermon Edwards replied. He appealed to " our future
and solemn meeting on that great day of the Lord, the day of . . .
irrevocable sentence ". From the draft of his farewell letter he
carefully erased the word *affectionate* pastor.

At the age of forty-seven he was thrust out of his parish, discredited, in broken health, and with a large family to support.
Dr. John Erskine suggested a living in the Church of Scotland;
other Scottish friends offered " Calvin redivivus " financial help.
He accepted the modest post of missionary to the Indians at
Stockbridge on the western frontier of Massachusetts. There was
a gritty, practical strain in Edwards and he seems to have protected
the Housatonics against white exploiters. He was free from the

cares of a large parish like Northampton, with time to meditate. A Calvinist romanticist, he would ride daily into the forest and return after many hours with strips of paper pinned to his coat, bearing the recorded fruit of meditation. Despite his belief that the greater part of mankind was eternally " lost ", he developed an optimistic opinion that Providence had chosen America as his instrument for " the glorious renovation of the world "—the reverse of Cotton Mather's view that Jehovah had predestined the new continent as a suitable location for hell!

It was at Stockbridge among the wooded Berkshire Hills that Edwards wrote his *magnum opus*. This classic *Treatise on the Will* has been more often praised than read. His biographer, Dr. A. V. G. Allan (1889), has called it the literary sensation of the eighteenth century. Fichte afterwards hailed its author as " the most original thinker in America ". Dugald Stewart, of Edinburgh, described it as " a work which never was and never will be answered ". It was translated into foreign languages, including Arabic. " The only relief I had was to forget it," said Boswell; and Dr. Johnson closed the discussion with the epigram: " All theory is against the freedom of the will, all experience is for it." It is not easy to summarise the subtle speculations of Edwards, but Dr. G. G. Atkins has stated its main issue thus:

" If the will were free, then God's predestinations were at the mercy of capricious men, and his elections could be counted out. At the same time, how can any moral responsibility be justified without freedom to choose or to reject ? If man is God's puppet, then hell arraigns God's justice, and heaven is a divine caprice. These were burning questions then; Milton's fallen angels discussed them in their lurid dark, and the New England farmer in his rocky fields, not to speak of philosophers and theologians. . . Careful students of Edwards reduce his arguments to, perhaps, a too simple paradox: man is free as far as he is inclined, but his inclinations are determined for him."[1]

The Edwardian theology has been compared to the Maginot Line—it was by-passed; but there is this important distinction. The Maginot Line was of consequence for less than a year, whereas the Edwardian theology prevailed in America for well-nigh a century. If Professor Gardiner claims too much for Edwards in ranking him with Calvin and Fénelon, Augustine and Aquinas,

[1] Atkins and Fagley, *History of American Congregationalism*, p. 112 (Boston, 1942).

Berkeley and Hume,[1] some modern American critics claim too little. He was surely more than an " amazingly shrewd and intellectually resourceful Puritan, little better than Cotton Mather " (Charles Angoff).[2]

Honour came to Edwards too late. A few months before his death in 1758 he took up his appointment as President of Princeton College. He died from crude inoculation for smallpox shortly after his arrival. Among his last recorded words were: " Now where is Jesus Christ, my true and never-failing friend ? " When his grandfather and colleague, Solomon Stoddard, expired in 1729, the Boston *News-Letter* eulogised that Patriarch of Northampton as " too eminent a Person to be suffer'd to slip into his Grave in silence ". When Edwards passed on, his death was dismissed by the press in a sentence. This would certainly not have been his fate had he been removed at the height of the Great Awakening or even during the dismissal controversy at Northampton. He had passed into oblivion during his seven years of exile at Stockbridge, though his books were remembered.[3] His retirement to the wilderness occurred when his powers were most mature, compared to Moses, Paul and other men of God whose days of seclusion have been passed in their youth.

Jonathan Edwards did more than reset the sagging arch of Calvinism with a firmer keystone. He blended dogmatism, speculation, mysticism and romanticism to an unusual degree,[4] considering that his opportunities of study and of meeting men of first-rate intellect were so few. Crabb Robinson, Unitarian and man of the world, could not refrain from offering tribute: " The most tremendous of all metaphysical divines ". Edwards transmitted his transcendent intellectual vitality to generations yet unborn.[5] His fame would have been even greater had he been vouchsafed the

---

[1] Art., Edwards, *Encycl. Britannica* (11th ed.).

[2] Compare the *Selections* from Edwards and Franklin (ed. C. Van Doren, New York, 1920).

[3] Northampton made tardy atonement in building a Memorial Church in his honour, but its pulpit no longer echoes his doctrines. In 1891, Paul Van Dyke, at odds with Presbyterian orthodoxy in New York, was willingly accepted by the Edwards Church as pastor.

[4] It is surprising to find Edwards confessing: " I should not take it at all amiss, to be called a Calvinist for distinction's sake; though . . . I cannot justly be charged with believing in everything just as Calvin taught " (*Collected Works*, Vol. I, p. 3).

[5] Genealogical study of Edwards' descendants reveals a roster of over 100 lawyers, 100 professors, 60 doctors, 30 judges, 25 army and navy officers, innumerable ministers and missionaries.

privilege of European contact. He is remembered in Mansfield College Chapel (" the most Catholic place in Oxford," said Friedrich Heiler). The stained glass procession representing the " American Church " includes John Eliot, Roger Williams, Cotton Mather, William Penn and Jonathan Edwards, " greatest of New England theologians ".

The appointment of Jonathan Edwards to the Presidency of Princeton reminds us that this " College of New Jersey " had been founded by the revivalist party in the Presbyterian Church to replace the " Log College " at Neshaminy, which came to an end with the death of Gilbert Tennent (1746). The " Old Side " Presbyterians had endeavoured to require from ministerial candidates a degree from a New England " or European " college. The " New Side " believed that the urgent necessity of evangelism justified letting down the academic standards. The reunion of these two severed branches of the Presbyterian Church in 1758 gave new institutions better prospects ; the radicals were learning to appreciate the value of education and the conservatives were realising the need of evangelism. After being moved from one location to another, the " College of New Jersey " was permanently established at Princeton in 1754, though the name was not adopted till 1896. Funds were collected in Great Britain (£1,000 being gifted by the Church of Scotland) and it was seriously proposed that Princeton should rise to the position held by Harvard and Yale. For many years Princeton was more noted for evangelistic zeal than culture (even Whitefield declined an M.A., doubtless on the grounds that his enemies would ridicule his backwoods degree). Two centuries, however, have led to the realisation of the founders' ideals—and a good deal more. Stately Gothic buildings have arisen on quite the most beautiful campus in America, including a chapel of cathedral-like dimensions and dignity. The Presbyterian tradition has made Princeton. It is significant that the first President to be a layman was Woodrow Wilson, a minister's son and an elder of the Kirk.

The University of Pennsylvania also dates from the Great Awakening. When Whitefield electrified Philadelphia by his preaching, Franklin took the lead in building a lecture-hall for speakers " of any religious persuasion, who might desire to say something to the people of philosophy " (1740). Whitefield was allowed to add to the " New Building " a Charity School for " the

instruction of poor children gratis, in the knowledge of the
Christian religion and in useful literature ". From these modest
beginnings there developed an academy, then a college, finally
the University of Pennsylvania. This great institution has followed
the scientific bent of Franklin rather than the theological bias of
Whitefield, but both founders are commemorated by statues on
the campus—the work of Dr. Tait MacKenzie. The life-size
statue of the Great Awakener was dedicated at his bi-centenary in
1914. One of the inscriptions is Franklin's tribute: " I knew him
intimately upwards of thirty years. His Integrity, Disinterestedness and Indefatigable Zeal in prosecuting every Good Work I
have never seen equalled, and shall never see equalled." From
Franklin this was high praise. The Awakener was more than a
showman and a rhetorician. The education which he had acquired
with such difficulty at Oxford he sought to make available even
for those whose background had been the rude frontier.

It is paradoxical that the Great Awakening, which gave unpre-
cedented scope to the preaching of uneducated laymen, should
have stimulated education. An instance of this is Queen's
College, New Brunswick N.J. (now known as Rutgers), chartered
in 1770, and situated in the district where the Revival had its
beginnings. The President was Dr. John Livingston, a Reformed
minister who had been educated at Utrecht, but realised that the
Dutch language was an anachronism in Anglo-Saxon America;
the promotion of the Gospel was more important than the artificial
perpetuation of an ancestral tongue. " The triumph of the
Evangelical party," says Dr. Sweet, "undoubtedly saved the Dutch
Church from extinction." In New England it almost looked as if
the Evangelical triumph was going to make learning extinct, at
least in certain denominations. Rustics often preferred the extempore unction of the lay preacher to the " sapless preaching " of
the regular ministry. Among the Baptists there had always been
a marked prejudice against an educated ministry, and this was
intensified by the Great Awakening's accent on immediate conversion. The more enlightened Baptist congregations of the coastal
cities, who tended to Arminianism, were not quite so sure that
" the Lord eddicates his own preachers ".

The progressive spirit of Roger Williams lingered in Rhode
Island, the smallest of the New England provinces. A rich merchant family, the Browns, were concerned about the fissure that

tended to divide religion and culture. They determined to use their influence to free the Baptist denomination from the reproach of being " the preserve of ignorant and illiterate men ". These princely benefactors were responsible for building the First Baptist Church, Providence—a landmark in New England architecture (cp. p. 168 f). They also founded Rhode Island College (1764), now called " Brown University ". Its Charter was extraordinarily liberal for the time. " The public teaching shall in general respect the sciences " and " into this liberal and catholic institution shall never be admitted any religious test ". The second provision was confirmed by a regulation that although a certain number of Trustees and Fellows were to be Baptists, a goodly proportion was to represent other denominations (Congregationalists, Friends and Episcopalians).

King's College, New York (now Columbia University) was founded in 1754, based on the conviction " in which true Christians of each denomination are generally agreed ". The services, however, were Anglican; Samuel Johnson, the first President, was as strong a Tory and Churchman as his famous namesake. He had been one of the Congregational ministers at Yale who " went Episcopal " in 1722. Accustomed to plough a lonely furrow, he acted as sole Faculty for the first few years. As a pioneer of higher education,[1] he was far in advance of his Puritan contemporaries who enforced rigid discipline in the boarding schools, euphemistically called " colleges ". He anticipated Bushnell's ideals of religious nurture in applying such maxims as " Magna reverentia pueris debetur ". As an eighteenth-century humanist, his mental outlook was altogether more flexible than that of Presbyterians and Congregationalists who were obsessed with the revivalist dogmas of the Great Awakening.

Tiffany, the Episcopal historian, considered that " the true spiritual founder of King's " was Bishop Berkeley. His visit to Newport, R.I. (1729-31) was memorable. " All sects rushed to hear him; even the Quakers, with their broad-rimmed hats, stood in the aisles." He had come to negotiate about a proposed American University on Bermuda; the scheme fell through, as the Bishop of London failed to get Walpole to implement his promise of £20,000. His ideals were realised to a fair extent

[1] H. W. and C. Schneider, *Samuel Johnson, his Career and Writings* (New York, 1929). Vol. I contains his autobiography.

by the modest college at New York. Although Yale was Congregationalist, he presented the library with 1,000 books ("the finest collection ever brought to America").[1] He is commemorated by the coveted Berkeley Divinity Prize at Yale, by the Berkeley Divinity School at Middletown, Conn., and the title of the city associated with the University of California.[2]

The Revival was discredited in the eastern cities, but spread like wildfire on the frontier, particularly the South-West. After 1720 the flood of Scots-Irish began to pour down the Shenandoah Valley; they were destined to re-shape the destiny of Virginia, as they moved into the interior. Some laymen in Hanover County found copies of Whitefield's sermons. Few printed sermons produce revivals, but in this instance it happened. Hanover Presbytery became a centre for evangelising the frontier. In 1748 the Rev. Samuel Davies, a native of Newcastle, Delaware, became the spearhead of a new advance, ranging through seven sparsely-populated counties. Presbyterianism, which had languished since the death of Makemie in 1708, made rapid progress in Virginia. Davies was " plain and pungent " as a preacher, and his sermons were " peculiarly adapted to pierce the conscience and affect the heart ". They were also carefully prepared, direct and inspiring.[3] He became so well-known in England through his printed sermons that when he visited the old country to raise funds for Princeton, George II asked him to preach in the Chapel Royal—a unique honour for a Colonial and a Presbyterian. In 1755, the year of Braddock's defeat by the French, he praised " that heroic youth, Colonel Washington, whom I cannot but hope Providence has hitherto preserved in so signal a manner for some important service to his country ".

Davies declared that he had come to preach " the catholic principles of Christianity ", but to the clergy of the Virginian Establishment that meant Presbyterianism,[4] for he was rapidly emptying their churches. They pressed for a severe application of

---

[1] He wrote *Alciphron* in a Rhode Island valley in a natural alcove among hanging rocks, and built a house, " the Dean's farm ", which he left to Yale College.

[2] B. Rand, *Berkeley's American Sojourn* (Cambridge, Mass., 1932).

[3] Sometimes they culminated in a hymn; he was the first American hymn-writer, though only a few of his compositions are still sung.

[4] In a characteristic sermon (Acts 11.26) he called for " sincere practical Christians. . . Unless I succeed in this, I labour to very little purpose, though I should presbyterianize the whole colony " (*Sermons*, Vol. I, London, 1815). Nine English editions, 1761-1800.

the colony's laws restricting the activities of Dissenters from the Church of England, but he outwitted them by securing from Governor Gooch a proper legal status for Presbyterians. In 1758 Colonel Corwin petitioned the House of Burgesses to restrict the right of Dissenters to expand. " Several of 'em [in Hanover Co.] Subscribed to Raise a Sum of Tobacco," he complained, " to build a Meeting-House, and have agreed with an Undertaker for one. This Proceeding affrights our apprehension that Dissension may be the forerunner of Rebellion; a fatal Consequence! " He was right. The struggle for religious rights merged with a political campaign against the " tide-water " aristocracy, so that when the American Revolution broke out, most Virginians declared for Independence, as a means of attaining civil equality.

The Baptists were not satisfied with bare toleration; they demanded religious equality. Starting as a small sect with the Sandy Creek Association as a rallying centre (1760) they soon overran most of Virginia and fanned out into Kentucky and Tennessee. They had none of Davies' caution against " New Light " fanaticism. Whole communities were converted; there was tremendous excitement during mass immersions in streams, and " bodily effects " were manifest on a scale surpassing those provoked farther north by men like Tennent. These scenes reached their climax in the Kentucky Revival of 1800. Baptist preachers were mostly uneducated as well as unpaid—a state of affairs congenial to their hearers. The emotional, ill-educated masses preferred a religion that is " caught " to one that is " taught ". Professor W. W. Sweet, the leading American authority on the spiritual influence of the frontier, estimates that after the Baptist and Methodist revivals had reached their crest, Presbyterianism in the South-West retained only about one-third of its membership.

The Presbyterians, however, tended to make converts among those of the upper classes who were disgusted at the inert apathy of the Established clergy, whose habits, as Thackeray observed, were "not very edifying". Readers of *The Virginians* will remember Madam Esmond's visit to Williamsburg, the colonial capital. She was enchanted with Whitefield's eloquence, but soon became disenchanted with her Whitefieldian tutor-chaplain; "young Mr. Ward with his great, glib voice and voluble commonplaces " was not much better than " harmless Mr. Broadbent ". About the best that can be said of the Virginia clergy is that some were harmless, though others behaved as badly as in the old days before the reforming activity of Commissioner Blair. In the words of the historian, Cooke: " The planter and his family came in their coach, and the parson read his homily; and then all went back to their week-day pursuits but slightly edified. It was very much of a Drowsyland, and a trumpet blast was necessary to arouse the sleepers." The self-indulgent laymen who dominated the Church preferred to sleep, and the few who thought at all were influenced by Deism, remaining merely nominal churchmen. The laity got the kind of clergy they deserved.

A Virginian named Devereux Jarratt blew a trumpet blast to awaken and renew the Church of his fathers.[1] The impulse came to him while he was " teaching school " in Albemarle County, then on the frontier. A chance traveller left a volume of Whitefield's sermons in Jarratt's lodgings, which fired his imagination and conscience. As a tutor in a Presbyterian home that was ardently " New Light ", he acquired " some knowledge of divinity " and " some gift in extempore prayer ". He conducted religious meetings and thus came to think of the ministry as a vocation. Should he become a Presbyterian minister ? It was in a Presbyterian home that religion had become real to him, but when he learned that Whitefield and Wesley were Church of England clergy, he decided to follow in their steps. To take Orders it was necessary to make the long and expensive voyage to England. A timely legacy from his brother enabled him to do this in 1762. After being ordained by the Bishop of Chester, he collected the usual bounty of £20 allowed to clergy for Virginia. His return was delayed by the great frost which froze the Thames, but that enabled him to hear Wesley and Whitefield. Then he took the smallpox, and discovered that he had been robbed, but at last got friends to pay his passage.

On returning to Virginia, he was appointed rector of Bath parish, Dinwiddie County, where he remained till his death in 1801. He immediately began to preach salvation by faith and the urgent need of conversion. For a long time he stood alone among the careless, incompetent clergy of his native province. They abused him with the rich vocabulary of ecclesiastical vituperation: " enthusiast, fanatic, visionary, dissenter, Presbyterian." Laymen, starved of the Word, heard him gladly. In 1773 one of the early

[1] *The Life of Devereux Jarratt . . . written by himself* (Baltimore, 1806).

Methodist preachers from England spent a week with Jarratt. This good man, Robert Williams, assured him that " the Methodists were true members of the Church of England ". Whereupon he welcomed them as fellow-workers in Christ. He took pains to warn evangelists privately of the dangers of fanaticism " that our good might not be evil spoken of ". Had there been more clergy like Jarratt, Virginia might have dispensed with the services of a " Methodist Episcopal Church ".

The Established clergy, however, were usually the bitterest enemies of " enthusiasm "; the " people called Methodists " had scant respect for careless, worldly parsons, and the demand for the ordination of their preachers could not be indefinitely ignored. Devereux Jarratt renewed the life of the Virginian Church as far as one man could, but Methodism submerged his achievements. In later life this fervent evangelical rector preached to fifty people instead of to thousands, though " his eye was not dim, nor his natural force abated ".

The Great Awakening in the South and Middle colonies maintained a steady advance for many years. When the movement weakened, it received an infusion of fresh blood through Methodist preachers, who began to come over from England in 1766. That year two Irishmen started preaching—Philip Embury in New York and Robert Strawbridge in Maryland. A game of cards prompted the first Methodist sermon in New York. A small company were gaming in a private house when Barbara Heck (who was known to them all) swept the cards into her apron and tossed them into the fire. After admonishing them earnestly, she went to her cousin's house: " Brother Embury, you must preach to us or we shall all go to hell, and God will require our blood at your hands." " But where shall I preach, or how can I preach ? " " Preach in your own house and to your own company first." So Philip Embury preached to five people in his house, and they all sang and prayed. They afterwards rented an empty room adjoining the barracks. A contemporary observed:

" Few thought it worth while to assemble with them in so contemptible a place. Some time after that, Captain Thomas Webb, barrack-master at Albany, found them out. . . The novelty of a man preaching in a scarlet coat brought great numbers to hear . . . they then hired a rigging loft to meet in . . . there Mr. Embury used to exhort and preach frequently."[1]

[1] Townsend and Workman (eds.), *A New History of Methodism*, Vol. I, p. 58 (London, 1909).

K

Captain Webb was certainly the most picturesque of the early Methodist preachers. He wore a green patch over one eye (lost at Louisburg) and his right arm was scarred (wounded at Quebec). " Soldier of the cross and spiritual son of John Wesley ", the power of God was with him. " One of the most eloquent men I have ever heard " (1774) said John Adams, second President of the United States; " he reaches the imagination and touches the passions." Webb not only preached effectually but headed the subscription list for the first Methodist church in New York, Old John Street—the " City Road Chapel of America " (1768).

Meanwhile Robert Strawbridge was building a log chapel in the backwoods at Sam's Creek, Maryland. Wherever he went, he raised up preachers; and wherever he preached, sinners were converted. Maryland, founded by a Roman Catholic, was becoming Methodism's first conquest.

As the work proceeded independently in New York and farther south, Wesley began to receive petitions from America to send out " an able and experienced preacher, a man of wisdom, of sound faith, and a good disciplinarian; one whose heart and soul are in the work ". To this Macedonian cry Wesley responded by getting the Wesleyan Conference of 1769 to send out Richard Boardman and Joseph Pilmoor. They arrived safely in Philadelphia and started preaching in St. George's—the oldest building in America where Methodist worship has been continuously conducted. In this city the first American Methodist preacher was duly recognised, Edward Evans. That was important, for relations between the mother-country and the colonies were becoming strained. Wesley's " Calm Address to the American Colonies " did nothing to calm public opinion across the Atlantic. Methodist preachers were English agents, " Tory spies ". Even native-born Methodists were sometimes tarred and feathered. Yet the Wesley of America was an Englishman who associated himself with his adopted country. Francis Asbury reached Philadelphia in 1771. He remained in the United States after war broke out, while most of the English preachers returned home. Despite these obvious hindrances Methodist membership rose from 1,160 in 1773 to about 12,000 at the end of the War of Independence. Their centre of gravity moved southwards. If Boston was the centre of the Congregationalists, New York of the Episcopalians, Philadelphia of the Quakers and Presbyterians, Baltimore—farther south still

—became the centre of Methodist activity. Thence they advanced beyond the Mason and Dixon line. Stevens in his *History of American Methodism* refers to the itinerants as " evangelical cavalry ". Almost every page of his book tells of advance— "Methodism enters Kentucky ", " McKendree goes to the West", " Asbury itinerating in the South ". Asbury was no great preacher. He could not be compared for a moment to Wesley or Whitefield. He was rather " Field marshal of a mobile army, waging a never-ending campaign for righteousness on every American frontier ".

In spite of the Calvinism of Whitefield and Edwards, Dr. Thompson, the Presbyterian historian, has claimed that " the Great Awakening terminated the Puritan age and inaugurated the Pietist or Methodist age of American Church history ".

THE CHURCHES AND THE AMERICAN REVOLUTION

"The World Turned Upside Down" (March played by the band when Cornwallis surrendered at Yorktown).

"*Ex pluribus unum*"—Motto of the United States (Augustine's Confessions, Book IV, viii, 13).

THE Great Awakening produced inter-colonial leaders whose names linked up provinces and denominations hitherto divided by regional interests. Whitefield, Tennent and Edwards concentrated on preaching the Gospel, but indirectly their peripatetic ministry increased the consciousness that the people were Americans rather than inhabitants of Virginia, Pennsylvania or Massachusetts. The Revival spread like a flood over the thirteen provinces (afterwards to become States) sweeping away old traditions and stimulating independence and enthusiasm.

By the end of the Colonial era, the population of British North America numbered about three million. There were 3,105 congregations of all denominations. The Congregationalists led with 658 churches, mostly in New England. The Presbyterians numbered 543 and were to be found mainly in New York, New Jersey and Pennsylvania (the Middle Colonies). The Baptists, like the Presbyterians, had grown rapidly since the Great Awakening, especially in the South (498 churches). The Church of England had some 480 congregations, ranging from a few flourishing charges, mainly in the cities, to mission stations staffed by agents of the Society for the Propagation of the Gospel. The Quakers were losing ground (295 meetings). The larger foreign churches were mainly in the Middle Colonies—Dutch and German Reformed (251), Lutheran (151). Immigration had yet to swell the Roman Catholic total of 50 congregations (in Maryland and the larger eastern cities). Methodism had just begun its meteoric mission in America. Denominations that stressed independence were in a better strategic position than those which boasted of the British connexion. Three New England provinces (Massachusetts, Connecticut and New Hampshire) maintained Congregationalism as the " standing order ", but were democratically organised and tended to relax restrictions against dissenters. The six other Establishments were Anglican and in the South. The Church of England claimed to be the official religion in New York City and the three adjoining counties.

Professor Cross in his *Anglican Episcopate and the American Colonies* (London, 1902) has pointed out that the possibility of sending Bishops across the Atlantic was always a bogy[1] to non-Anglicans. Indeed, as strife between the government of George III and the colonies grew more tense, there were open protests. Dr. Jonathan Mayhew declared in 1763 that the aim of the S.P.G. was to " root out Presbyterianism ". Another Boston minister, Charles Chauncy, critic of the Great Awakening, turned to the task of vindicating non-Episcopal ordination[2] (had he been available in 1722, the Yale men who expressed doubts as to the validity of the Congregational ministry, might never have had to sail to England for " Holy Orders "). From 1766 onwards annual conferences were held between Presbyterians and Congregationalists " to prevent the establishment of an Episcopate in America ". They remembered the words of Cotton Mather: " It was not to be endured that prelacy, unmolested, should rear its mitred head." In 1769 appeared a striking cartoon in the *Political Register* (London). A prelate tries to land, but is greeted by shouts of " No lords spiritual or temporal in New England! " He is bundled into the ship, his mitre and crozier being thrown after him. One bystander hurls Calvin's *Works* at his head; another brandishes *Locke and Sidney on Government*; a Quaker points to Barclay's *Apology*. The Bishop climbs into the rigging—" Lord, now lettest thou thy servant depart in peace."

Not all " Churchmen " in the colonies wanted an Episcopate.

[1] Laud's design for American Bishops was abandoned owing to acute difficulties with the Kirk. Berkeley was the only Bishop to visit the colonies and he came on academic business. Bishop Butler's plan (1750) disclaimed coercion of non-Anglicans and excluded New England from Episcopal jurisdiction. Archbishop Secker attributed governmental failure to appoint bishops to fear of rousing Dissent.

[2] See Williston Walker, *Ten New England Leaders*, p. 289-95.

Some of them realised that the very idea was enough to " infuse jealousies and fears into the minds of Protestant Dissenters ". The laymen of the South, who controlled the Church through legislatures and vestries,[1] did not welcome the interference of an English ecclesiastic probably ignorant of American conditions (like some of the Bishop of London's " commissaries "). Only twelve Virginian clergy attended a convention to discuss the project. Four of them opposed it and were thanked by the provincial legislature for withstanding this " pernicious project ".[2] Even if the plan had been realised, would a typical Hanoverian prelate have been any use in a country that needed a working clergy rather than ornamental bishops with classical attainments ? Doubtless the S.P.G. missionaries hoped that one of their number would be consecrated, as a guarantee of zeal and activity, thus excluding misfits. When the political crisis came, the " Venerable Society " almost wrecked the Church beyond recovery by their loyalty to the Crown. The rector of Trinity Church, New York, in the year of the Declaration of Independence declared that the Society's agents " have to the utmost of their power opposed the spirit of disaffection and rebellion ". New Englanders were now convinced that the Episcopal Church, introduced by those perverts, Samuel Johnson and Co., in 1722, had been a " Trojan horse " intended to destroy ultimately their institutions.

On the outbreak of the American Revolution upwards of 80,000 " Church and King " Loyalists migrated to Canada and the West Indies. These were mostly property-holders, their dependents, and officials; poor Churchmen were more inclined to be American patriots.[3] The exiles included Dr. Inglis, rector of historic Trinity, New York, Dr. Caner, of King's Chapel, Boston, Myles Cooper, an Oxford man who had succeeded Samuel Johnson as President of King's College, New York, and Samuel Peters, of Hebron, the clerical adventurer who had made *opera bouffe* of the " Blue Laws "

[1] It has been claimed that when the Virginia Convention declared for American Independence in 1776, all but three members were vestrymen. Vestries were self-perpetuating bodies, yet they served as a useful school for apprentices in self-government.

[2] " Political freedom is the offspring of religious freedom," observed Campbell, historian of Virginia; " it takes its rise in the Church."

[3] Thus, at Eastchester, near New York, Rector Seabury and prominent parishioners joined the British, while the rank and file joined the American Army. On 18th April 1775 Parson Byles, Jr., of Christ Church, Boston, handed in his resignation; that very evening the sexton hung lanterns in the tower to direct Paul Revere, patriot, on his historic ride for freedom.

of Connecticut.[1] Even in Virginia, where a number of the clergy were natives of the province, only 34 parishes out of 90 had incumbents when the War was over. Throughout the colonies a limited number of Anglican churches remained open. Some clergy who remained at their posts indiscreetly insisted on praying for the King. They were not merely unpopular; they were often roughly handled, and some were deprived of their property. Several were fired at in the pulpit; at Newtown the sounding-board was hit by a ball, whereupon Mr. Beach merely repeated his text, " Fear not them that kill the body ". Such fortitude deserves all respect. It was a contrast to the conduct of Jacob Duché, of Christ Church, Philadelphia. Asked to " read prayers " to the Continental Congress, " he struck into an extempore prayer " to the surprise and delight of his hearers. (" I never heard a better," was the comment of Samuel Adams.) Duché afterwards changed sides and fled to the British camp. His successor, the Rev. William White, acted as chaplain to the Continental Congress. It is significant that two-thirds of the patriots who signed the Declaration of Independence were Anglicans—Alexander Hamilton, Patrick Henry, Madison, Marshall and Washington.[2] These liberal-minded laymen, many of them Virginians, had nothing in common with the outlook of their own clergy.[3] When Washington was in camp at Morristown, N.J., in 1776-7, he noticed that the Lord's Supper was being celebrated in an orchard, the communicants seated at tables according to the Presbyterian tradition. He then asked the minister if he might partake. " Most certainly," replied Dr. Johnes, " ours is not the Presbyterian table, but the Lord's table . . . and the Lord's invitation is to all his followers, of whatever name.'

[1] Peters induced a handful of clergy to nominate him Bishop of Vermont (1795), but no prelate would consecrate him. Pitt removed his name from the Pension List (1804). He afterwards returned to America and died in obscurity.

[2] A picturesque character was " Parson Weems ", who gave up his parish for a roving career as purveyor of morals and culture. He was equally at home in mansion, inn and country fair. In 1800 he wrote: " Washington is gone! Millions are gaping to read about him. I am nearly primed and cocked for 'em." Weems was the *fons et origo* of too-good-to-be-true Washington anecdotes; he had been parson near Mount Vernon. Cp. Van Wyck Brooks, *The World of Washington Irving* (Dent, 1945).

[3] A characteristic incident. At Bennett's Creek Church, Virginia, John Agnew, the Tory parson, preached against rebellion in 1775 (" Render unto Caesar . . ."). William Cowper, magistrate and vestryman, ordered him from the pulpit. He replied, he was doing his Master's business. " Which Master ? Your Master in heaven, or your Master over the seas ? " Threatened with force, Agnew left the pulpit and became chaplain of a British regiment, while Cowper was chosen to represent his county in the Virginian Revolutionary Convention of 1776.

The Rev. Peter Muhlenberg, son of the founder of American Lutheranism, had joined the Church of England. Like other Germans who had taken this step (largely owing to the fact that they had adopted English as their language) he did not fall in with the clerical politics of his adopted Church. One Sunday in 1776, Muhlenberg announced that there was a time to preach and a time to fight. Stripping off his gown after the benediction, he revealed a colonel's uniform. Drums beat and three hundred of his parishioners were enrolled in the American army. Had such incidents been the rule rather than the exception, the Anglican Establishments would probably not have collapsed as completely as they did in the South, where their prestige was shattered.

The Church in Virginia had roots deeply intertwined with the historic tradition of " the old Dominion ". It was less easy to disentangle Church and State. A beginning was made in 1779, when an Act of legislature was passed whereby the collection of " parish levies " for the upkeep of the Established Church could no longer be enforced. The Presbyterians would have been satisfied with " concurrent endowment " or a guarantee of complete toleration. Madison wrote to Monroe: " They seem as ready to set up an establishment which is to take them in as they were to pull down that which shut them out." Marshall, Washington and other " Virginian Fathers of the Republic " favoured a " General Assessment Law " whereby taxes were collected for religious teaching and ear-marked according to a citizen's own denomination. The Baptists, who had been " honoured with the dongeon " since the Great Awakening, stood out for the absolute separation of Church and State. Patrick Henry, whose oration " Give me liberty or give me death! " has been memorised by countless American schoolboys, made a telling defence of certain Baptists accused of being incorrigible dissenters. " May it please the Court, what did I hear ? Did I hear it distinctly—or was it a mistake of my own ? Did I not hear that these men are charged with—with —what ... *preaching the word of God* ? " Pausing amidst profound silence, he waved his papers thrice above his head, and exclaimed: " Great God! What laws have they violated ? " Bench, bar and public were deeply moved. The case was decided by the magistrate's order: " Sheriff, discharge these men ! "

Freedom of faith was supported by Virginian statesmen who were nominally Anglican, but at heart Deists and doctrinaire democrats. Such was Thomas Jefferson, who was destined to reverse Washington's aristocratic policy. When Disestablishment became law after a protracted, embittered campaign (1786) its leading advocate requested that on his tomb be inscribed: " THOMAS JEFFERSON, Author of the Declaration of Independence, of the Statute of Virginia for Religious Freedom, and Father of the University of Virginia."

If American Anglicanism was a house divided against itself, Presbyterianism was ultra-American. This was partly due to the strong infusion of Ulster-Scots, whose memories of the old country were charged with economic repression and religious persecution. They hated Episcopacy and English "Ascendancy".[1]

> And when the day of trial came,
> Of which we know the story,
> No Erin son of Scottish blood
> Was ever found a Tory.

The magnetic personality who moulded American Presbyterianism at the time of the Revolution was not the product of thrawn dissent. Dr. John Witherspoon (1723-94) was brought up in the manse of Yester, East Lothian. He held important charges in the Church of Scotland and was well known as a controversialist by 1753, when he wrote *Ecclesiastical Characteristics*, which was the sensation of the hour. This was a satire on the Moderate Party's maxim, " let sleeping dogmas lie ", and took the form of a parody of the Athanasian Creed. An outspoken Evangelical and defender of the rights of congregations against lay patronage, Witherspoon was limited in outlook to the tight little kingdom of Scotland. When Richard Stockton called to offer the Presidency of Princeton College, he found him without " any Tolerable idea of America ". Mrs. Witherspoon was even more reluctant to leave Scotland. That eminent Philadelphian, Dr. Benjamin Rush, fellow-citizen of Franklin, had actually to visit Paisley, to use his powers of persuasion on Mrs. Witherspoon. He was eventually successful.

When the new President took up his duties at Princeton in 1768, he devoted himself to his task of improving the curriculum,

[1] " The first public voice in America for dissolving all connexion with Britain came, not from New England . . . but from the Scotch-Irish Presbyterians. They carried to the New World the Spirit of the Covenanters " (Bancroft).

introducing post-graduate study for the first time. He met James Madison and other young Southerners, who were soon to become public men. Witherspoon was silent at first on political matters, as became a canny Scot, but he identified himself thoroughly with the land of his adoption. Once he had made up his mind about the justice of the American cause, he struck hard as controversialist. The loyal Hanoverian, who had raised funds for his local militia in Scotland during the '45 Rebellion, now became rebel himself. Jonathan Odell, a rhyming pamphleteer, who had fled from the rectory of Burlington, N.J., to the British lines, exclaimed:

> I've known him seek the dongeon dark as night,
> Imprisoned Tories to convert or fright;
> Whilst to myself I've hummed, in dismal tune,
> I'd rather be a dog than Witherspoon.
> Be patient, reader—for the issue trust;
> His day will come—remember, Heaven is just.

Elected as delegate for New Jersey in the Continental Congress, Witherspoon was the only minister of religion to sign the Declaration of Independence. " He applied the Presbyterian theories of republicanism to the new civil government." [1] He was to a large extent the architect of the new Presbyterian constitution, and was appropriately honoured by being asked to preach at the first General Assembly (May 1789). He achieved success in spite of his deficiency in oratorical gifts and personal charm. A critic described him as " an intolerable, homely old Scotchman ", whose " burr " called for the closest attention on the part of his hearers. Witherspoon himself doubted whether he would have gone so far, but for his British origin and Scottish education, which commanded considerable respect.

The other Reformed Churches adhered warmly to the American cause. Although the redcoats were active in New York, they found few friends among the Dutch, who were weary of the arrogance of Anglican governors and their official coteries. The German Reformed minister at Lancaster, Pennsylvania, preached to his fellow-countrymen in captivity, the Hessian mercenaries: " Ye have sold yourselves for naught; and ye shall be redeemed

---

[1] Out of 3,000,000 Americans in 1776 nearly 900,000 were Scots-Irish Presbyterians. Horace Walpole said: " Cousin America has run off with a Presbyterian parson." The Congregationalists and Baptists were mostly Calvinists. With good reason did Ranke, followed by André Siegfried, claim that Calvinism moulded American civilisation.

without money." In this Quaker country, the Friends were generally conscientious objectors; and those who paid war-taxes or
helped the war-effort in any way were expelled from the Monthly
Meeting. When the fury of war spread over their fair countryside,
they suffered at the hands of the combatants for failure to co-operate
with those who were in possession, and for refusing to take oaths.
There was a split among the Friends. " Free Quakers " were
willing to perform military duties. It is interesting to note that
Washington and Franklin subscribed to a new meeting house for
these " disowned Friends " which was erected in Arch Street,
Philadelphia.[1] Other bodies who held " passive resistance " views
like the Quakers were German sects like the Mennonites and Moravians. They were more leniently treated by the authorities, as they
were few and foreign, but shared in the usual misfortunes of war,
and in such exactions as having their buildings commandeered.

Had the Irish immigration to America set in sooner, we could
count as a certainty which side they would have supported in the
American Revolution. The French Canadians were loyal to the
Crown, for the Catholics of Quebec were granted full freedom of
worship after Wolfe's conquest of the province.[2] On the other
hand, the small Catholic community of Maryland had little cause
for being grateful to the English; they, pioneers of toleration, had
been officially degraded by penal laws. Led by the influential
Carroll family, they were unanimous in their support of the
Declaration of Independence. When the first French Ambassador
arrived in Philadelphia, he invited the American Government and
the public to attend a *Te Deum* in the Catholic chapel in honour
of the foundation of the United States. Thus the ancient Church
of Europe was acknowledged as one of the constituents of the
new world.

Among the smaller Protestant denominations, the Baptists were
strongest for American Independence; they had suffered most
from Anglican intolerance, and also from the contempt of the
governing class. They could no longer be ignored. Even in
Boston one of their ministers was honoured by being asked to

---

[1] See Dr. Weir Mitchell's *Hugh Wynne, Free Quaker* (New York, 60th
thousand, 1898). A brilliant novel, giving the authentic atmosphere of the times.
[2] Indeed, one of the reasons for estrangement from the motherland was the
fact that these benighted " Papists " had been permitted to celebrate their
unhallowed rites. Many American Protestants disapproved of religious toleration when it came to the Mass.

preach the " Election Sermon ". The Methodists, on the other hand, suffered from the fact that they were newcomers on the American scene, and their wandering preachers had by no means renounced the Church of England. John Wesley was a staunch Tory and supporter of George III. He was so impressed by Dr. Johnson's *Taxation no Tyranny* that he went out of his way to issue an abridgement of this pamphlet under his own name. This *Calm Address to the American Colonies* did not succeed in allaying excitement. When the War broke out, Wesley warned his preachers to " say not one word against one or the other side ".[1] Most of them had to return to England and many Methodists underwent the unpleasant experience of being " tarred and feathered " by the mob (a rough diversion worthy of a Nazi concentration camp). We shall hear more of one English preacher, Francis Asbury, who remained and thoroughly identified himself with the country of his adoption. In spite of political prejudice and suspicion it is remarkable that during these years of war the Methodists increased their American membership from 4,000 in 1775 to 13,000 in 1780.

Among the Congregationalists of New England, one of the few Tory sympathisers was Dr. Mather Byles, Sr., minister of Hollis Street Church, Boston. A typical eighteenth-century colonial man of letters, he corresponded with Pope and Watts in his youth. He was a brave man as well as a wit. When placed under house-arrest because he insisted on praying for the King, he remarked that his home was an " Observe-a-Tory ". When the sentry was withdrawn, Dr. Byles described himself as being " guarded, regarded and dis-regarded ". His daughters could never forget that they had walked arm-in-arm with General Howe and Lord Percy on Boston Common.[2] Another Tory of the " Standing Order " was the Rev. Matthias Burnett. His politics doubtless saved his church on Long Island from being burnt by the British. His congregation, however, showed no signs of gratitude; indeed, they called for his resignation. He had the last word, however, for he gave out what he considered the most appropriate psalm at his farewell service:

---

[1] " The American War ", wrote Southey, " made the Dissenters feel once more a political party in the State. New England was more the country of their hearts than the England where they had been born and bred " (quoted by Anthony Lincoln, *Some Political and Social Ideas of English Dissent* 1763-1800, p. 256 (Cambridge, Eng., 1938).

[2] A. W. H. Eaton, *The famous Dr. Mather Byles* (Boston, 1914).

> O might I fly to change my place,
> How would I choose to dwell,
> In some wild lonesome wilderness,
> And leave these gates of Hell!
>
> *Psalm* 120

Byles and Burnett were exceptional. The Congregational clergy, orthodox and heterodox alike, were overwhelmingly American in sympathy.[1] In Virginia, the revolt was led by laymen like Jefferson and Henry, while the clergy either fled to England or remained utterly passive till the war was over. In New England there was an instant response to John Adams' appeal, " Let the pulpits thunder against oppression! " They certainly did. No form of crisis sermon was more popular than an application of *Hebrews* 11 to the duty of standing for freedom against British tyranny, as the forefathers of New England had done in the past.

" *By faith* Brewster and Robinson fled to Holland from Scrooby, rather than abandon the service of their conscience.

By faith their company made its way across the solitary sea and pitched on the winter shores at Plymouth.

By faith Winthrop and Dudley and the men who prayed with them forsook the honours of England, that they might here found a Commonwealth more pleasing unto God.

By faith the men of Massachusetts dared greatly, and flung from power the tyrant Andros who was undoing all that holy sacrifice had wrought."[2]

The call to stand boldly for American Independence is remarkable when we consider that until the time of the abhorred " Stamp Act " (1766) the ministers of the " Standing Order " had prayed ardently for " the illustrious House of Hanover "; British liberty and French slavery they compared in heated rhetoric, as they exhorted their young men to march to Canada and capture Louisburg from the hated Bourbon. To-day, it seems reasonable enough that the American colonists should have been willing to pay their share of the heavy cost of protection against French aggression from the Mississippi Valley and Canada. If Wolfe had not captured Quebec in 1759, a Catholic French Empire would surely

---

[1] Readers of Bernard Shaw will recall his fighting New England minister in *The Devil's Disciple* (1897).

[2] See W. S. Davis, *Gilman of Redford*, p. 392 f. (Macmillan, 1927), an historical novel that throws much light on the ecclesiastical aspect of the American Revolution, with special reference to Harvard. " Dr. Gilman " was a patriot preacher.

have expanded and cut off Anglo-Saxon expansion westwards.[1]
What *did* seem unreasonable to these New England preachers was
the levying of taxes by the Westminster Parliament in an arbitrary
unilateral manner. Using a vocabulary enriched with Old Testament phrases, they appealed to " natural law " and the " civil
contract " theories of Sidney and Locke. Ever since the seventeenth
century " Election Sermons " had been preached at regular intervals before the Governor and legislature. These discourses were
usually published and widely read. Old pamphlets were reprinted
to meet the new political situation. Especially significant were the
works of the Rev. John Wise (1652-1725) whose political views
were diametrically opposite to his Mather contemporaries. Particularly popular were his doctrinaire declarations: " Power is
originally in the people . . . all men are born free " (see p. 101).[2]
At the close of the War of Independence President Ezra Stiles of
Yale preached on " The United States Elevated to Honor ". He
predicted a population of 50,000,000 in a century and 300,000,000
in three centuries. Some of his predictions were striking: " Probably English will become the Tongue of more People on earth,
than any except the Chinese ".

The American Revolution naturally popularised the idea of Congregationalism as " pure democracy ". This interpretation would
have shocked John Cotton and the theocrats, but had its roots in
the tradition of the Pilgrim Fathers and blossomed in the words of
John Wise: " Democracy is Christ's government in church and
state."[3] There was a renewal of the old " Independent " suspicion
of overhead organisation. Nathaniel Emmons, exponent of
Edwardian Calvinism, went back to Wise when he contrasted
the semi-Presbyterian polity of Connecticut (" Consociational ")
with the looser grouping of Massachusetts (" Associational "):
" Association leads to Consociation; Consociation to Presbyterianism; Presbyterianism to Episcopalianism; Episcopalianism to

---

[1] The last royal Governor, Thomas Hutchinson, was a native of Massachusetts, and its historian, a Congregationalist and a counsellor of moderation,
though a " loyalist ".
[2] Wise was a pioneer to suffer for the principle, " No taxation without
representation ". Under the Andros dictatorship (1687) he persuaded the
citizens of Ipswich, Mass., to withhold taxes (for which he was suspended and
arrested).
[3] The link between theocracy and democracy was the Christian Platonism
of Pierre Ramus, introduced at Cambridge, the seed-plot of Puritanism, as
early as 1580. He was a Huguenot, who got into trouble at the Synod of
Nismes (1572) for advocating Congregationalism.

Roman Catholicism." This emphasis on decentralisation diverged from the tendency of other denominations to organise on a national scale. It was a strategic blunder, as we shall discover from our study of the post-war period. Yet the autonomous instinct was characteristically American, for, as Dean Sperry has remarked, one-third of American Protestantism is built upon the basis of local units entirely self-governing.

The Baptists were incorrigible individualists. Their ancestry in America went back to Roger Williams, seventeenth-century pioneer of " soul-freedom "; but they only became a major denomination after the Great Awakening had fired them with evangelistic ardour. Each of their congregations was self-governing and suspicious of anything resembling overhead control. It was with difficulty that Isaac Backus persuaded his co-religionists in New England to form the " Warren Association " of churches, to extend their witness and defend their rights, in collaboration with Baptist groups in other parts of the country. Baptists were Dissenters in the North as well as in the South. The Episcopal Establishments had sealed their fate by loyalty to England, but the Congregational Establishments of New England had strengthened their position through espousing the patriot cause. Baptists also had fought for American Independence and considered it unjust that they should be forced to pay taxes to support Congregational ministers; it was as unreasonable, they urged, as the alleged right of the British Government to impose a tax of 3d. on every pound of tea! This was a cogent argument.

The Baptists were fortunate in possessing a leader who was a sound chronicler as well as an effective controversialist. Isaac Backus (1724-1806) was a self-educated farmer[1] with his roots deep in New England. Historian of his region as well as his denomination, he was an adept in ecclesiastical law. In his fight for religious equality he noted that the Massachusetts law of 1728 relaxed stringency by granting Baptists and Quakers exemption from the poll tax for ministerial support; they could not be arrested nor could their goods be distrained[2] provided they signed a register and attended their own meeting within a distance of five miles.

---

[1] He wrote racy pamphlets such as *A Fish Caught in His Own Net* (1768), in reply to an attack on the Baptists by the Rev. J. Fish.
[2] " Passive resisters " in England suffered imprisonment and distraint of goods, under Lord Balfour's Education Act (1902), which involved assessment for Anglican schools.

Backus' comment is worth quoting, showing his quaintly scriptural cast of mind:

" Here we may see that arbitrary power is always the same nature, in every age and every country. ' Go ye, serve the Lord: only let your flocks be stayed,' said Pharaoh. Let their polls be exempted, but their estates taxed, said Massachusetts. Herein they imitated him; but in two points they went beyond him. ' Go not very far away,' said Pharaoh; go but five miles, said Massachusetts; though many of their own parishioners, from that day to this, must go much farther than that to meeting. Neither did Pharaoh require a list of the people upon oath as these did."[1]

The only concession allowed by the new Massachusetts constitution of 1779 was the omission of the name " Congregational " in the article requiring " towns, parishes and precincts . . . to make provision at their own expense for public worship". The Standing Order had a certain amount of elasticity. Thus, if Baptists happened to command a majority in any community, they might elect a Baptist as minister of the town. In New Hampshire, room was made for a Scots-Irish *diaspora* being included in the scheme; and there are isolated instances of Episcopalians being appointed pastors by local authorities. This is an interesting parallel to the right acquired by the German princes to settle the official faith of each principality (*cujus regio, ejus religio*).

Backus and his Baptists refused to be appeased with fragmentary concessions. They called on the Continental Congress and then on the Federal administration to implement their promises of democracy. They even appealed to Washington (1796) complaining that religious inequality was " a clear demonstration of the narrow selfishness of mankind ". John Adams remarked: " They might as well turn the heavenly bodies out of their diurnal courses as the people of Massachusetts from their meeting houses." The " Standing Order " of the Bay State stood fast till 1834.

The American Revolution brought to an end the dependence of American denominations on ecclesiastical authorities in Europe. Gone was the link that bound the Episcopalians to the Bishop of London and the Roman Catholics to the Vicar Apostolic of London. John Wesley could no longer count on the unquestioning obedience of that nominally Anglican society—" the people called Methodists ". The Dutch and German Reformed had to reorganise as American Churches. The Lutherans were henceforth bound

[1] Backus, *History of the Baptists*, Vol. I, p. 577 f.

only by sentiment and fellowship to Halle Pietism (which had greatly declined since the early eighteenth century). The Presbyterians, who had never been too specifically thirled to the Church of Scotland, now rose to the status of a nation-wide American Church, with four synods and a General Assembly, not confined in its constituency to people of Scots descent. The Westminster Confession required to be adjusted regarding the authority of the " civil magistrate ",[1] but little modification was required in other respects. Indeed, the Presbyterian structure of graded, representative councils is said to have influenced the architects of the Federal Constitution.

" We are not republicans," said John Wesley, " and do not intend to be." This grand old man (then approaching the end of his life) had never revisited America since his unhappy sojourn in Georgia (1736); since then, he had learned much by experience, but had not given up his belief in the principle of personal leadership. Just before the American Revolution he had sent forth George Shadford with the following commission: " I let you loose, George, on the great continent of America. Publish your message in the open face of the sun, and do all you can." Despite the vast estranging expanse of the Atlantic, control was exercised over Methodist lay preachers who had to promise to be loyal to " Mr. Wesley ", strictly to avoid administering the sacraments (which were to be received in Anglican churches), and on no account to reprint any of Mr. Wesley's books without his authority (" when it can be gotten "). Francis Asbury, Wesley's faithful deputy, remained in America during the war at his own peril, often in concealment, directing evangelistic strategy as best he could under trying conditions.

When peace was declared in 1783, Wesley acted with decision, even anticipating sects in America that were in a better position to reorganise. He consulted Dr. Thomas Coke in his study at City Road, London, and unfolded a plan that was capable of meeting the emergency. The Episcopal Establishment was abolished and America separated for ever. Something must be done. Acting on the precedent of the ancient Church of Alexandria, he was going to ordain Coke as bishop or superintendent over the Methodist societies in America, with Whatcoat and Vasey as attendant pres-

---

[1] The Synod of New York and Philadelphia considered it necessary to allay rumours that the Presbyterians coveted the position of a National Church, by formally renouncing such claims of superiority.

L

byters (" elders " was the name actually used overseas). The following remarkable document was written with Wesley's own hand, 2nd September 1784:

" To all to whom these presents shall come, John Wesley, late Fellow of Lincoln College in Oxford, Presbyter of the Church of England, sendeth greeting.

Whereas many of the people of the Southern provinces of North America, who desire to continue under my care, and still adhere to the doctrine and discipline of the Church of England, are greatly distressed for want of ministers to administer the sacraments according to the usages of the same church: and whereas there does not seem to be any other way of supplying them with ministers.

Know all men, that I, John Wesley, think myself to be providentially called at this time to set apart some persons for the work of the ministry in America. And therefore, under the protection of Almighty God, and with a single eye to His glory, I have this day set apart as a Superintendent, by the imposition of hands and by prayer (being assisted by other ordained ministers) Thomas Coke, Doctor of Civil Law, a presbyter of the Church of England, and a man whom I judge to be well qualified for that great work."[1]

Thus accredited and armed with an explanatory letter, Dr. Coke and his clerical companions set sail and landed in New York on 3rd November. Eleven days later they were directed to Barrett's chapel, which had recently been erected in the midst of a Delaware forest. Scarcely had Dr. Coke finished his sermon that Sunday, than he perceived a " plainly dressed, robust, but venerable-looking man moving through the congregation. . . On ascending the pulpit, he clasped the Doctor in his arms; and, without making himself known by words, accosted him with the holy salutation of primitive Christianity. That venerable man was Mr. Asbury ".

The founders of American Methodism were men of very different background and experience. Thomas Coke was a D.C.L. of Oxford, the only son of a well-to-do gentleman; Francis Asbury was the son of a Staffordshire gardener. Coke crossed the Atlantic eighteen times and founded mission stations all over the world: Asbury settled in one continent, set upon it the impress of his own vigorous, austere personality and spent the rest of

[1] Charles Wesley questioned the propriety of his brother's action:
How easy now are bishops made
At man or woman's whim;
Wesley his hands on Coke hath laid,
But who laid hands on him ?

his life in the colossal task of transforming a despised English sect into the largest Protestant Church in the United States.

Asbury lost no time in putting Coke on the field. With characteristic realism he arranged his itinerary—merely a thousand miles to be covered in six weeks! He despatched Freeborn Garrettson, " like an arrow ", to summon the Methodist preachers to Baltimore for Christmas 1784. The plans for a Methodist constitution had already been made. They were ratified without protracted discussion, so urgent was the need for organisation. Wesley was the architect, though the details of his design had afterwards to be modified to suit American needs. The Church of England was the model; with all its accumulated lethargy and sterile conservatism, it was still to him " the best constituted national church in the world ". The XXXIX Articles were reduced to XXIV—by the significant excision of Calvinist teaching. Calvinism had hitherto been the granite which had contributed most to the building of American religion: it was destined to be supplemented to a considerable degree by a softer, synthetic product—Arminianism blended with experimental emotionalism and frontier democracy, and reinforced with evangelical Paulinism.

Wesley's abridgement of the Prayer Book was approved by the first Methodist Conference at Baltimore. It seems to have been generally used by the " travelling preachers " for the sacraments, but Wesley's advice " to administer the Lord's Supper every Lord's Day" was disregarded. "Morning" and "Evening Prayer" proved, as might be imagined, quite unsuitable for the newly evangelised people of the backwoods, but the Apostles' Creed and the Lord's Prayer were given a regular place in the Sunday service. A General Conference was established on the English Wesleyan model. Its membership was confined to the " clergy ",[1] although Methodist ministers, for many years to come, were little better educated than full-time lay preachers. This clerical monopoly was the cause of secessions, though on a less considerable scale than in England; not till 1872 did laymen appear in the elected conferences of American Methodism. One reason for this was the fact that a system of graded councils was dovetailed into hierarchy of officials. The " superintendents " indicated by Wesley were openly called bishops. Thus the " prelates ", so much dreaded by the

---

[1] Generally used by all denominations in the U.S. to-day.

colonists, were modestly introduced by a humble group of English clergy, loyal subjects of King George III.

John Dickinson (Eton and Oxford), founder of Cokesbury College, moved a resolution, suggesting the title, " Methodist Episcopal Church ", which was approved. A *Book of Discipline*, based on the Wesleyan *Large Minutes*, adapted English procedure to American conditions. Francis Asbury tactfully declined the office of Bishop or Superintendent, conferred on him by Wesley, until the first American Conference elected him of its own accord. He was duly elected and ordained Superintendent, after Christmas, 1784; Dr. Coke officiated in his surplice, and the other clergy in gown and bands. When Coke returned to England and corresponded, " The Rt. Rev. Bishop Asbury, N. America " was a sufficient address.

To the typical Anglican such a consecration was null and void. Wesley had once been a doctrinaire High Churchman, but had changed his views after reading Lord Chancellor King's *Primitive Church* on the road between London and Bristol in 1746. Later he declared: " I firmly believe that I am a scriptural *episcopos*, as much as any man in England: for the uninterrupted succession I know to be a fable which no man ever did or can prove." Wesley's views are of interest:

" It has indeed been proposed to desire the English bishops to ordain our preachers for America. But to this I object: (1) I desired the Bishop of London to ordain one, but could not prevail. (2) If they consented, we know the slowness of their proceedings; but the matter admits of no delay. (3) If they would ordain now, they would expect to govern them; and how grievously would this entangle us. (4) As our American brethren are now totally disentangled, both from the State and the English hierarchy, we dare not entangle them again. . . They are now at full liberty, simply to follow the Scriptures and the primitive church. And we judge it best that they should stand fast in that liberty wherewith God has so strangely made them free " (*Methodist Magazine*, 1785, p. 602).

It is heartening to observe that the Methodist Episcopal leaders kept the door open for reunion with the mother-church in America. Coke was personally ready to " connect the succession ". Asbury outlined a plan for the inclusion of Methodism as a society within the Episcopal Church, whereby Superintendents might surrender the title " bishop " to meet Anglican scruples. This olive-branch was rejected.[1] " Ethos " rather than " polity " was the dividing factor. The Episcopalian saw in the Methodist an unstable fanatic: the Methodist saw in the Episcopalian a worldly Laodicean. Had the negotiations proved successful, the dominant pattern of American religion would have been considerably modified.

The most sweeping triumphs of early Methodism took place in Maryland, founded by Roman Catholics on a basis of toleration. Charles Carroll, of Carrollton, the wealthiest citizen of the province was the only Catholic to sign the Declaration of Independence. " To obtain religious liberty . . . I entered zealously into the Revolution and, observing the Christian religion freely divided into sects, I hoped that no one would so predominate as to become the religion of the State."[2] His cousin, the Rev. John Carroll, S.J., reorganised the American Catholics (only 24,000), when political events severed contact with that remote dignitary. Fr. Carroll, after completing his education at the Jesuit Seminary, St. Omer, returned to America as " Superior " when English jurisdiction ceased in 1784. He was appointed by the Pope first Bishop of the Catholic Church in the United States (1789). Rome allowed two concessions. The American priests were given permission to elect their own prelate, and he was allowed to name his own see. On 15th August 1790 John Carroll was consecrated Bishop of Baltimore by the Vicar-Apostolic of London in the chapel of Lulworth Castle. To-day his archiepiscopal successor has the honour of primacy in the American hierarchy.

The comparative ease with which Methodists and Romanists adopted new constitutions was not experienced by American Anglicans. Their Church was in an exhausted condition. She had set herself against the Great Awakening which had brought new life to the other Evangelical Churches. She had set herself against American Independence, except in the South. To many citizens she was " a piece of heavy baggage which the English left behind them when they evacuated New York and Boston ". She was a fallen Church, deserted by many of her clergy before suffering

---

[1] Bishop Seabury did not even reply; he afterwards ordained Joseph Pilmoor and Bishop White ordained Thomas Vasey. These Methodist pioneers remained friendly to their former co-religionists.

[2] Roman Catholic historians claim that the Scholastic Philosophy was the arsenal whence Protestants found weapons to fight tyrants. In the seventeenth century Filmer remarked: " Cardinal Bellarmine and Calvin both look asquint this way."

disestablishment. She was the Church of the elderly and conventional, who were afraid of the " new order " of the Republic.

What about the Bishop of London, the traditional custodian of ecclesiastical affairs in America ? He might have stepped forward in this crisis to do his best for the scattered band of Anglicans, now cut off from the dim and distant comfort of a "father in God ". Franklin, a nominal " Churchman ", expressed public opinion in the United States when he wondered why devout and learned men should consider themselves dependent " on the permission of a cross old gentleman at Canterbury ". That old gentleman was in no accommodating mood and his mentality was complacently insular. Dr. White, rector of historic Christ Church, Philadelphia, was convinced that the emergency warranted " a temporary departure from episcopacy " (*The Case of the Episcopal Church considered*, 1782). In Maryland a Convention was summoned to decide how the Church's work was to be carried on. It was decided to approach the legislature so that the vestries might be charged with interim authority. In this petition the name " Protestant Episcopal Church " (afterwards the official title of American Anglicanism and a stumbling-block to High Churchmen) seems to have been first used. The moving spirit, the Rev. William Smith, was nominated bishop-elect. It was one thing to nominate, another to obtain valid consecration. Dr. Smith was a Scotsman of good family, a graduate of Aberdeen who had come to America as a tutor in 1751. He was ordained shortly afterwards, became Provost of the College of Philadelphia, and received a D.D. from his *alma mater*, also from Dublin and Oxford. Johnsonese rhetoric made him an impressive speaker and his sermon before the Continental Congress, denouncing " non-resistance " made him famous. He was praised by Priestley, blamed by Wesley. Patriot and man of affairs, he determined to salvage as much Church property as possible from the wreck. Critics complained that he was bibulous as well as secular-minded. The General Convention did not confirm his nomination by Maryland, but he was an able man, needed in difficult days of reconstruction.

The most outstanding clergyman was certainly Dr. William White of Philadelphia.[1] Washington, Franklin and Morris " sat

---

[1] Dr. S. A. Temple has published extracts illustrating *The Common Sense Theology of Bishop White* (New York, 1947). This gives a good idea of the beliefs of an eighteenth-century Episcopalian, but White was a statesman, not a constructive theologian.

under him " in Christ Church; Hamilton and Madison were his friends. The son of a Londoner, White had enjoyed the opportunity of spending eighteen months in London, on crossing the Atlantic for ordination (1770); there he became acquainted with Johnson and Goldsmith. In 1777 he was appointed joint-chaplain of Congress, in fellowship with Dr. George Duffield, a Presbyterian. Dr. White was a wise, resolute and courteous statesman, anxious to do his best for the Church of his fathers. He deserved Wordsworth's eulogy:

> Patriots informed with Apostolic light
> Were they, who, when their Country had been freed,
> Bowing with reverence to the ancient creed,
> Fixed on the frame of England's Church their sight,
> And strove in filial love to reunite
> What force had severed. Thence they fetched the seed
> Of Christian unity, and won a meed
> Of praise from Heaven. To thee, O saintly WHITE,
> Patriarch of a wide-spreading family,
> Remotest lands and unborn times shall turn.
>
> *Ecclesiastical Sonnets*, xv.

One churchman was not prepared to salute "saintly WHITE" as " Patriarch of a wide-spreading family ", nor was he disposed to follow his plan of welding divergent elements into unity, before procuring the blessings of Apostolic Succession. This was Samuel Seabury, a Loyalist who had been imprisoned by the Americans during the War owing to the vigour of his controversial *Farmer's Letters*; he had fled to the British lines and became an army chaplain.[1] A small company of Connecticut clergy (the most " churchly " to be found in the United States) assembled in December 1785 and selected Seabury as their future bishop. From the American point of view, this was a blunder, for the average citizen would regard such a candidate as a traitor. On the other hand, might not such a choice prove tactful with a view to conciliating England ? This approach failed. The Archbishop of Canterbury, complete Erastian, could not see his way to consecrate any American as bishop who failed to take the oath of allegiance to the Crown.

Another approach was made. Dr. George Berkeley, son of the

---

[1] Paradoxically, his church (St. Paul's, Eastchester, N.Y.), has been restored as a " national shrine ", on the grounds that it had been used as polling-place in 1733 at an election leading to the " Zenger Case ", in which the freedom of the press was vindicated against Cosby, the autocratic royal governor.

philosopher-bishop who had visited America in 1729, suggested
that the United States might welcome bishops consecrated in
Scotland by "apostolic bishops" who were not lordly prelates of
a State Church. Bishop Skinner of Aberdeen, as representative of
the Scottish Nonjurors who cherished Jacobite and High Church
sentiment, sympathised with a struggling minority-Church whose
position resembled that of the Scottish Episcopalians. The consecration took place in Aberdeen (14th November 1784), Seabury
having no "nolo episcopari" modesty. Bishop Skinner preached
in his humble chapel (consisting of two rooms thrown into one).
The printed sermon caused much comment south of the Tweed;
for the Scottish bishops "paid more attention to the Acts of the
Apostles than to Acts of Parliament".

Seabury returned to the United States, after ordering a mitre
in London (none could be found, for the English bishops preferred
other headgear to suit their "cauliflower wigs"). On arrival he
exhibited the mentality of Laud.[1] "I, Samuel, by Divine permission Bishop of Connecticut . . . hereby request every one of you,
the Presbyters and Deacons . . . to make the following alterations
in the Liturgy." His ordination of a priest in Boston amazed the
congregation, who had no idea that a bishop communicated the
Holy Ghost by breathing on the candidate. He also addressed an
appeal to "the Presbyterian and Independent persuasions". They
should return to the fold—by relinquishing those errors which
they, through prejudice, had imbibed". Dr. McConnell, the
Episcopal historian, remarks drily: "This sort of treacle catches
no flies."[2] New Englanders, of course, were accustomed to putting
down upstarts. Seabury wrote to President Stiles of Yale, announcing that he would be present at "Commencement"; he hoped
that "he would be received with proper distinction, and that his
precedency would be allowed". Dr. Stiles replied courteously:
"They should be very glad to see Bishop Seabury, but that he
could not promise him any such mark of distinction as he expected.
One thing, however, he could engage for—that he would meet
with a hundred and ninety-one as good bishops as himself!"

[1] High Tory fanaticism even to-day occupies a tiny niche in the P.E. Church.
A New Jersey rector was selected to preach in London at the 300th com-
memoration of "Saint Charles the Martyr" (1649).

[2] American Episcopalians have generously renovated the Episcopalian Cathedral, Aberdeen. The ceiling of one aisle is decorated with the coats-of-arms of
Jacobite families; the other, inappropriately, with insignia of the various American states (who regarded Seabury as a traitor).

The unilateral attitude of Seabury almost caused a split in American Episcopalianism. Outside Connecticut, his narrow Churchmanship could count on slight support, but what line of action should be taken ? On 27th September 1786 a Convention of clergy and laity at Philadelphia decided to send Dr. White and Dr. Provoost to England, with a view to their consecration as Bishops of Pennsylvania and New York. The American Ambassador, John Adams, went out of his way (as a Congregationalist) to secure them a more cordial reception at Lambeth than they expected; he had already used his good offices to facilitate the ordination of clergy by Danish bishops, when candidates could not travel to London during the War. White and Provoost found the Archbishop more orthodox than they had expected; they had to make doctrinal concessions (see p. 167) as the price of their consecration, which eventually took place in Lambeth Palace on 4th February 1786. They reached New York as the bells of Trinity were proclaiming Easter. They could claim to have brought " peace with honour ". Unity with the Church of England was conserved and the mysterious blessings of " Apostolic Succession " transmitted.

In 1789 an ecclesiastical constitution was adopted which asserted the Church's independence of all foreign authority, denied the power of the civil magistrate in all purely spiritual matters, and introduced a democratic element which emphasised the influence of the layman. Instead of Archbishops, there was to be an elected " Presiding Bishop " (corresponding to the Primus of the Episcopal Church in Scotland). The House of Bishops was to be offset by a House of Deputies, giving clergy and laity equal representation. In each diocese there were to be elected synods on somewhat similar lines. Anglicanism, like Lutheranism, thus achieved conciliar self-government which the mother Churches of England and Germany were slow in attaining. The analogy of the American constitution, with its federal Senate and House of Representatives at the apex and its subordinate State legislatures, is obvious. Like the Presbyterians, the Episcopalians borrowed democratic elements from the secular sphere, but hallowed them by the infusion of the Christian spirit.

Over against the influence of the Churches on the American Constitution must be set definitely secular influences. Theodore Roosevelt dismissed Tom Paine as a " filthy little atheist ", yet

the *Common Sense* of this obscure English pamphleteer " turned
thousands to independence who, before, could not endure the
thought " (Sir G. O. Trevelyan). Defender of *The Rights of Man*
against Burke, Paine fled to France, where he wrote *The Age of
Reason* while awaiting the guillotine, under the Jacobin tyranny.
Liberated after the death of Robespierre, he sought refuge in the
United States, where he found himself far from popular, partly
owing to his Deism, partly owing to his advocacy of reforms that
went far beyond the horizon of Washington and the founders of
the conservative republic—abolition of slavery, emancipation of
women, free education, etc. Mr. W. E. Woodward, Paine's latest
biographer,[1] has emphasised the contrast between Paine's remarkable influence in moulding American thought during the War,
and his unpopularity after the new institutions had taken shape.
He was hooted in the cities, denied the right to vote, consigned to
hell by preachers, and turned into a bogy by mothers to intimidate
refractory children. His private life was mercilessly attacked (and
unjustly): if he drank too much, it was not surprising, considering
the circumstances. President Jefferson, who had given him a
cordial welcome to America, cooled off when he realised the
hostility that Paine's tactlessness had aroused among the populace,
the clergy and men of property. In the camp-meetings they sang:

> The world, the Devil and Tom Paine,
> Have tried their force, but all in vain,
> They can't prevail, the reason is,
> The Lord defends the Methodist!

Thomas Jefferson, author of the Declaration of Independence,
like Paine, accepted " Nature's God " and not the God of the
Anglican or Puritan, but he believed most in human Reason.
Religion was treated negatively in the Federal Constitution.
Article VI prohibited the imposition of religious and theological
tests for office-holders and Amendement I enacted: " Congress
shall make no law respecting the establishment of religion." That,
of course, did not prevent the States from retaining their own
Established Churches (also the case in the German *Reich* of 1871).
The Federal Constitution is secular in tone, taking Franklin's
view of religion as " a private affair, which right-thinking men do

---

[1] *Tom Paine: America's Godfather* (London, 1947). One of Paine's few
appreciative biographies. Earlier outstanding *Lives* were by Moncure D.
Conway (1892) and Hesketh Pearson (1937).

not care to discuss ".[1] Yet each House of Congress had its Chaplain who holds prayers daily. The President issues a Thanksgiving Day Proclamation, calling on the people to attend their respective places of worship; he appoints National Days of Prayer. Christmas is now a public holiday, celebrated even more intensely than in England. Some of the State Constitutions, while prohibiting ecclesiastical Establishments, disqualify from office anyone denying the existence of a Supreme Being (several add " future rewards and punishments "). Others retain laws against swearing and Sabbath desecration (seldom enforced except in " test cases "). All places of business are closed on Good Friday in many States. Despite controversy the Bible is read in many State schools, and churches are exempt from taxation.

A body of Christian opinion continues to regret that the Federal Constitution, drawn up in a deistical age, omits the name of Jesus Christ. Efforts have been made from time to time to insert the Name that is above every name. Indeed, the Reformed Presbyterian Synod, a small body that maintains the Scottish Covenanting heritage, refuses to allow its members to vote or to hold office till such a declaration is unequivocally written into the Constitution.

Nevertheless, Christianity is to a large extent a part of the American common law. Lord Bryce, who understood American institutions better than any British subject, devoted important chapters in his *magnum opus* to the various religious bodies in their social environments. He considered that the effects of the separation of Church and State were wholly beneficial.[2] Fortunately the nation was not split into two strata, one of them preserving at all costs " our happy Establishment ", and the other entering politics to cast it down. Theological and ecclesiastical differences were not deepened by social snobbery, nor did the clergy of Churches

---

[1] While many English travellers criticised the absence of a State Church, several eminent Scotsmen, seeking emancipation from Erastianism, enlarged on the advantages of the separation of Church and State, claiming that voluntary Churches provided adequately for evangelism, pastoral care, clerical efficiency, education and philanthropy. Cp. Dr. Dunmore Lang (founder of Australian Presbyterianism), *Religion . . . in America*, (London, 1840); Rev. R. Baird, *Religion in U.S.A.* (Glasgow, 1844).

[2] Schleiermacher, thwarted by petrifying Prussian Erastianism (" that Medusa's head ") often longed for the freedom of American Churches; he never visited the United States. Bismarck, with a view to liberalising the Prussian Church, ordered a survey of American ecclesiastical law to be published in German and English. The result was Dr. J. P. Thompson's *Church and State in the U.S.* (Boston, 1873).

that were Established in Europe seek privileges at the expense of
other denominations in the United States. Bryce did not quite
realise the weak points of voluntaryism—the substitution of
shifting " denominations " for the ideal of the Holy Catholic
Church.[1] Yet we can accept, with qualifications, his conclusion:
" Christianity is in fact understood to be, though not the legal
established religion, yet the national religion " (*The American
Commonwealth*, Vol. II, p. 576 f., 1889 ed.).

[1] Dean Sperry of Harvard Divinity School is fully alive to this defect. The
average American thinks of " the Church " almost as a matter of course, as his
own particular place of worship (*Religion in America*, Chs. 3, 4).

CHAPTER III

POST-REVOLUTION EBB-TIDE

These are the times that try men's souls.—PAINE

Religion at a very low temperature.—WHITEHEAD

DURING the American Rebellion a significant incident occurred during a skirmish at Springfield, N.J. A Presbyterian chaplain, James Caldwell, ran to a nearby church in search of much-needed wadding for the muskets of his men. He returned with an armful of Watts' psalm books, shouting: " Put Watts into 'em, boys, give 'em Watts! " Not long afterwards this champion of the Church militant was killed by the British and his church burned. Caldwell probably used the old edition (1774), which was " accommodated " to the British connexion and fit for destruction in the eyes of patriots. Watts had once been considered advanced in making " David " voice sentiments of civil and religious liberty, extolling the House of Brunswick and the British Empire. He had even prefixed to Psalm 107 the caption, " A Psalm for New England ". Times, however, had changed and even the ideals of a stout English Dissenter had to be brought up to date. Thus the new edition of 1781 " applied " Psalm 75 to the American Revolution instead of the English Revolution of 1688. " David " was *now* not only a converted Christian; he was a naturalised American![1] " Watts " survived the Declaration of Independence. He was more of a household name than ever, an institution. "Put Watts into 'em" was the imperative of preachers, choir leaders and schoolmasters almost up to the middle of the nineteenth century.

The metrical version of Watts came as a godsend to Congregational and Presbyterian congregations in the eighteenth century. They were devoted to psalm-singing, but wanted something

[1] No " psalm " was more popular in camp than Billings' version of Ps. 137, "By the rivers of Watertown we sat down and wept, when we remembered thee, O Boston " (Boston being then held by the British).

smoother than the rugged rythms of *The Bay-Psalm Book* and its seventeenth-century competitors. Watts offered something " elegant " and in keeping with the spirit of the age. In 1719 appeared his *Psalms of David Imitated*. Was there any reason why the highest themes of the New Testament should be debarred from the sanctuary ? Sticklers for the old ways sneered at "Watts' whims ", Scots and Irish Presbyterians for some time held tenaciously to their 1650 version, but Watts' stock rose. Whitefield's triumphant evangelistic campaign spread enthusiasm throughout the colonies for " the new song in the house of the Lord ". It was as if sunlight had broken through leaden skies. The prejudice against " human composures " gradually broke down. Sometimes the reaction went too far. Jonathan Edwards, returning to Northampton from a journey in 1742, found that his people had turned to Watts " and sang nothing else, and neglected the Psalms wholly ". In most congregations the Psalms and Hymns of Watts were used together, though the editions were legion. There was much rivalry between " Watts entire " and " Watts select ". As late as 1831 the Presbyterian collection of 531 hymns allowed Watts 215. Even the editors of new books modestly claimed to provide " supplements " to Watts.

In Anglican congregations the " prose " psalms of the Prayer Book were read (chanting was unknown in America till 1786); the " singing Psalms " were also used, as in England. The rugged version of Sternhold and Hopkins (1562) sounded uncouth to the more cultivated Colonial congregations who replaced it by Tate and Brady (1696). This " New Version " was fashionable among those bred on " polite literature " of the Addisonian school which lingered in America long after it had become obsolete in England.

When John Wesley landed in Georgia and published seventy hymns he was charged with making unwarrantable innovations. Churchmen became more suspicious of hymn-singing when it became associated with the emotional excesses of the Great Awakening. It is strange that Wesley's hymns were so little known in America in days of revival. They only appeared as late as 1790 in the *Methodist Pocket Hymn Book*, issued in response to the decision reached by the first American Conference at Baltimore (1784): " How shall we reform our singing ? Let all preachers improve by learning to sing themselves, and keeping closer to Mr. Wesley's tunes and hymns." This pointed advice reveals a gulf between the high standard of hymnody desired by Wesley and his leading American associates, on the one hand, and the tendency of their followers to "fall for" cheap revival songs. American Methodist collections for many years were practically reprints of English Wesleyan hymnbooks and had slight influence on other denominations. Not till 1799 did the good popular hymns of Cowper and Newton reach America, the *Hartford Collection* containing many of the *Olney Hymns*. There were, to be sure, "folk hymns" that circulated among the illiterate, but these were not admitted into the sanctuary.

The all-sufficiency of Watts was hardly impaired by the derivative collections of Psalms and Hymns issued in 1801 by Joel Barlow and Timothy Dwight. "Watts" was still a household word among Congregationalists, Presbyterians and Baptists.[1] His hymns, along with those of Doddridge and other eighteenth-century writers, were bound up with Tate and Brady's Psalms, in the Episcopal *Prayer Book Collection* (1833-72). By the middle of the nineteenth century, however, "Watts" had ceased to be synonymous with hymnology. The flow of hymns could no longer be regulated by traditional locks. The sluice-gates were opened and all that remained of metrical psalmody was isolated psalm versions by Watts, Dwight, Tate and Brady, etc. These were swept into the hymnaries, along with "Old Hundredth". Among these fragments was President Dwight's translation of Psalm 137 ("I love Thy Kingdom, Lord") which is probably the oldest American hymn still popular on both sides of the Atlantic.

Watts, as an innovator, pointed the way to another advance in congregational praise—the use of musical instruments, which had been deemed un-scriptural by the Puritans. In spite of long-drawn local controversies, bass-viols, flutes, clarionets, etc., appeared in meeting houses as well as Episcopal churches. One congregation, eager for novelty, actually proposed to alter Watts' lines about "David's harp of solemn sound":

> O may my heart be tuned within
> Like David's sacred violin!

The first choir-master to introduce the bass-viol was William Billings ("the American Cyclops") a popular but eccentric personage whose *Fuguing Psalm Singer* revolutionised the time-honoured drawl. "Now the solitary bass demands the attention,

---

[1] Henry Wilder Foote, *Three Centuries of American Hymnody* (Harvard, 1940).

next the manly tenor, now the volatile treble. Now here! Now
there! Now here again! O ecstasy, push on ye sons of harmony! "
By some inexplicable magic, the various part-singers, racing after
one another, would eventually reach their desired haven together.
" With reverence let the saints appear, and bow before the Lord "
(" and bow-wow-wow, and bow-wow-wow " till each part had
bow-wow-wowed in turn). Many worshippers considered that this
was no improvement on unison singing led by a nasal deacon.
Were not old and new alike covered by the text, " The songs of
the temple shall be turned into howlings "? (Amos 8.3). There can
be no doubt, however, that mixed choirs enjoyed these " fuguing
tunes " and miscellaneous instruments as much as the English
village singers in George Eliot's day. In the early nineteenth
century Mrs. Beecher Stowe had pleasant memories of the choir-
loft at Lichfield, Conn.; but she makes it clear that the infectious
love of music did not emancipate New England from Puritan
prejudice against the observance of the Christian Year. She gives
a graphic description in *Poganuc People* of the sensation caused by
a young Episcopal rector who tries to attract the villagers from the
ancestral meeting house by his Christmas services. Dr. Cushing
cited an impressive chain of texts culminating in Clement of
Alexandria, to show that the date of Christ's birth was quite
unsettled, Christmas taking the place of a pagan solar festival in
the fourth century (25th December). The preacher enjoyed " the
success that a man always has, when he confirms the previous
opinions of his hearers ". Hiel Jones declares: " Mother, them
'piscopals got pitched into lively, now; the Doctor pursued 'em
even unto Shur, as the Scriptur' says."

Organs began to appear in the non-liturgical churches before
the Christian festivals got a foothold, but prejudice died hard, as
in Scotland. " I was at Mr. Brattle's; heard ye organs and saw
strange things in a microscope " (Joseph Green's *Diary*, 29th May
1711). This Puritan divine, like his brethren, had no objection to
" ye organs " in the homes of the people. Two years later, Thomas
Brattle, treasurer of Harvard College, bequeathed the instrument
to the congregation that he had founded; but not even the enlightened Brattle Street Church dared to accept the gift.[1] The
Dutch Reformed made history in 1724 by installing an organ in

---

[1] Given to the Anglican chapel in Boston, it still survives in usable condition
in St. Paul's, Portsmouth, N.H.

their New York church, the donor being Governor Burnet. Bishop Berkeley on his visit to America, presented one to Trinity Church, Newport, R.I., and the Episcopalians in the larger cities followed suit. An English gentleman offered £500 to the first " dissenting " congregation in America that should venture on the innovation. Ezra Stiles records in his *Diary* (10th July 1770): " Last month an Organ of 200 Pipes was set up in the Congregational Meeting in Providence. . . This is the first organ in a dissenting Ch. in America except Jersey College." Dr. Chauncy, of the " Old Brick Church " in Boston, a man of advanced views (theologically), felt he was too old to change with the times in this respect. " The people eager to get an organ waited on the Dr. who told them that it would not be long before he was in his grave . . . and they might do as they pleased." By 1800 there were not more than twenty organs in all New England, but the number rapidly increased after the War of 1812. In the Middle States the Moravians had cultivated music of all kinds since their arrival in the eighteenth century; in 1746 they erected a fine organ in their church at Bethlehem, Pennsylvania; this tended to break down the Quaker and Presbyterian tradition of opposition to instrumental music. The organ in Christ Church, Philadelphia, where Washington had a pew, was completed in 1766. Francis Hopkinson, secretary of the Continental Congress and himself a composer, delighted to listen to it, and waxed quite lyrical:

> . . . . Noble to the sight,
> The gilded organ rears its towering height.

In a number of New England churches the congregation turned their backs on the pulpit during singing and faced the rear gallery, containing choir and organ. In the nineteenth century they were saved the trouble, for organ-case and choir-loft were usually placed behind the pulpit, with the instruments of praise continually in view.

Apart from praise, the non-liturgical Churches maintained the Puritan tradition with slight modifications. While the Presbyterians were setting their house in order after the Revolutionary War, they appointed a committee to revise their seventeenth-century Westminster standards in the light of contemporary conditions. A draft Directory of Public Worship was submitted to the Synods of New York and Philadelphia in 1786. Opposition

M

was disarmed by the statement that there was no intention to confine ministers to printed forms; they were supplied with " specimens, not prescriptions " for public prayer. The Preface expressed high regard for the Reformed, Congregational, Lutheran and Episcopal Churches; there was a genuine, ecumenical spirit abroad at this time. In spite of friendly feeling, the Revised Directory was not adopted. " Forms " of all kinds (except written constitutions) were discounted by rising democracy. There was a republican idea, alien to the colonial tradition, that official costumes of any kind, including pulpit robes, were vestiges of " effete Europe ", and symbols of social distinction. As the conservative Federalism of Washington gave way to the doctrinaire democracy of Jefferson and the cruder equalitarianism of Andrew Jackson, this tendency grew more dangerous. It was also affected by a religious tendency—the pervading influence of Methodism, favouring an over-familiar style in prayer and preaching. It is one of the wonders of Wesley that his wishes were respected even across the Atlantic; for the Methodist Episcopal *Ritual* actually preserved the Anglican services for Sacraments and Ordinances, and handed them down to a generation that can appreciate them better.

The Church of England in America at the close of the eighteenth century used the Prayer Book, but in a lax manner—particularly in Virginia; there were no cathedrals and collegiate establishments to exemplify a higher standard. Dr. S. D. McConnell, in his *History of the American Episcopal Church* observed:

" The surplice was rarely used. There were probably not above a score in America. The ' gown and bands ' was the usual vestment. The congregation sat while singing; when standing was introduced in 1814, it was considered a portentous ritual innovation, requiring action by the House of Bishops. At the Prayers it was not the custom for any but communicants to kneel, the others sitting in a respectful attitude. The Holy Communion was celebrated quarterly, or, in a very few places, monthly; and the proportion of communicants to the congregation was very small. Confirmation, of course, could not be had, and the nature and purpose of the rite had well-nigh been forgotten. Bishop White was never confirmed, and it is doubtful if Bishop Seabury was " (p. 199 f.).

In 1785 a committee was appointed to revise the Prayer Book, consisting of one clergyman and one layman from each state. Within three days they presented draft proposals. Some changes were obvious—the substitution of prayers for President and Congress instead of for King and Parliament. There were changes of taste, e.g. the Marriage Service. There were anti-sacerdotal changes, such as omitting the sign of the cross in baptism, and substituting a declaration of forgiveness for priestly absolution. There were changes in the interests of liberty: the selection of Psalms and Lessons was to be left to the Minister's discretion. Most significant of all was the latitudinarian motive that dropped the Athanasian, Nicene and Apostles' Creeds. The " Proposed Book " was not finally adopted—partly owing to the High Church objections of Bishop Seabury, partly because the English Bishops would only ordain Drs. White and Provoost on condition that the Nicene and Apostles' Creeds were restored. The Prayer Book, as eventually accepted, conformed fairly closely to the English model; only a few additional prayers were provided, e.g. for " Thanksgiving Day ", the new American festival. No attempt was made to insist on an office for the Fourth of July, as proposed in the rejected draft; the sentiment of lingering loyalty to King George was too strong among " Churchmen " for that.

The setting for Anglican worship in the Colonies was usually simple, and only Americans who had visited England could visualise the majestic Gothic background of medieval cathedrals, college chapels and parish churches. American Episcopal churches of the normal type were usually timber structures, with or without a steeple,[1] the interior filled with box pews and galleries, facing a central pulpit. They differed only slightly from the meeting houses of the Congregationalists and Presbyterians. In Virginia there were a number of brick cruciform churches of historic interest; but these were neglected and often abandoned after the Revolution, destined to become ruins or to be occupied by Methodists and Baptists. Disestablishment in the " Old Dominion " was followed in 1802 by Disendowment. Glebes and churches were sold for a song. The proceeds, instead of being used for " any public purpose not religious ", were often embezzled by officials. " Churchmen " stood by or shared in the spoil. Planters drank from chalices and passed cheese in patens; they used sanctuary cushions for their " parlors " and marble fonts as horse-

---

[1] Not many have been spared by the Gothic Revivalists. These iconoclasts in 1858 destroyed the mother church at Stratford, where Samuel Johnson, founder of Connecticut Churchmanship, had laboured. Teams of oxen, attached by ropes to the quaint steeple, with the utmost difficulty pulled it down.

troughs.[1] In other parts of the South conditions were not quite
so bad. In sequestered glades you can still find charming old-
world interiors, like St. James's, Goose Creek, S. Carolina (1713).[2]
Queen Anne presented Communion plate, bells and other furnishings to struggling colonial churches, and throughout the
eighteenth century the S.P.G. agents continued to crave royal
patronage in such matters.

In the larger towns on the Atlantic coast the London City
Church of the eighteenth-century type was imitated in a simplified
form from Boston to Charleston. King's Chapel, Boston (1753),
is reminiscent of St. Bride's, Fleet Street, a full-blown Georgian
interior admirably preserved. Christ Church, Philadelphia (1727),
designed by Dr. Kearsley, physician and cultured citizen, demon-
strates how warmth and personal quality can be imparted by a
local material, such as rich-coloured Pennsylvania brick. Other
interesting Colonial churches in the same city are St. Paul's and
St. Peter's (the latter mystified Bishop Gore by the unusual
position of the pulpit at the west end, facing the altar at the east
end). The larger Colonial churches were planned by leisured
amateurs, who were acquainted with English manuals such as
Salmond's *Palladio Londiniensis* and Gibb's *Book of Architecture*.
If Wren was the grandfather of the Colonial Georgian church,
Gibbs was the father. When he designed St. Martin's-in-the-
Fields (1722) he little knew that he was erecting a model that was
to be widely followed across the Atlantic, with few competitors!

The non-liturgical churches slowly followed the Episcopal
example in building rectangular churches with a steeple at one
end[3] (the historic " Old South " in Boston was one of the first of
these, 1729). The " meeting house plan " was adhered to, however,
as in Scotland and in English dissent, viz., the placing of the
pulpit on the " long " side. The First Baptist Church, Providence,
R.I. (1775) marked a transition to the " church plan ", viz., the
pulpit at the " east end ", with the vague hint of a chancel. This
historic house of worship was much admired and copied throughout the colonies. The designer adopted one of Gibbs' alternative

---

[1] G. C. Mason's *Colonial Churches of Tidewater Virginia* (Richmond, Va.,
1947) tells the story of how the churches were built and administered, and the
pathetic sequel.
[2] Illustrated by Percy Dearmer in his *Story of the Prayer Book* (1933).
[3] Cp. " The Evolution of the New England Meeting House ", by A.L.D.
(Rl. Instit. of Br. Architects' *Journal*, June 1946).

steeple-designs for St. Martin's. Nearly forty years later Ithiel
Towne copied Gibbs' portico as well as his steeple in his design
for Center Church, New Haven—the Congregational church
associated with Yale College. Thereafter, the steeple astride a
portico became an established type throughout the United States
but particularly in New England.

There are at least two hundred meeting houses in New England
of surprising architectural charm, built mostly during the later
eighteenth and early nineteenth centuries, though popularly called
" Colonial ". The vast majority were built of wood by enterprising
carpenters (" workaday Wrens in aprons ") who had absorbed
the classical spirit through the careful study of builders' manuals.
Asher Benjamin's *Country Builder's Assistant* (eds. 1796-1833)
made Palladio speak not merely plain English but Yankee vernacular.[1] Good taste was universalised through good proportions
and a realisation that timber had its limitations as well as its
possibilities. At slight expense a regional type of church was
evolved that still expresses the New England attitude to religion—
in city square, among the elms of a village green, or crowning
eminences (hence the " templed hills " in " My country, 'tis of
thee "). During the early nineteenth century it became customary
to paint the exteriors white, with green shutters. The interiors
were often a grey-green, pews white, pulpits mahogany, windows
of clear glass suggesting " the glory of the lighted mind ". The
box pews were divided by a broad central aisle, which the minister,
in gown and bands, would traverse on his way to the pulpit (in
some parishes the congregation would rise and stand in reverence
until he had reached his place). At revivals, converts, marshalled
in the spacious vestibule, would advance in procession up this
aisle, to be welcomed at the Communion table by the minister
and deacons. About the middle of the nineteenth century dignity
and decorum lapsed. In many churches the central passage and
wine-glass pulpit disappeared. The meeting house became a
featureless auditorium. Towards the end of the century a starved
sense of beauty reasserted itself in perverted forms—crude stained
glass, stencilled walls, and veneered woodwork; " enrichment "
revealed itself in Gothic or Romanesque ornament of devastating
ugliness.

[1] Carpenters built houses, churches and boats. " The work of their craftsmanship was their prayer." See Mary E. Chase's fine novel of the Maine
coast, *Silas Crockett* (Macmillan, 1935).

After a century of neglect, these Georgian meeting houses have been restored with scholarliness as well as zeal. Thus in 1935 the historic First Church of Bennington was dedicated as " Vermont's Colonial Shrine ". Organisations and individuals of all kinds connected with the " Green Mountain State " contributed appropriate gifts. Had the architect of 1805, Lavius Fillmore, returned to view his masterpiece, he would have found nearly every feature of the original edifice reproduced, including the box pews and pewter candle-holders. Could meticulous " restoration " be carried further ? Like Victorian " Ecclesiologists " these New Englanders have taken seriously the motto, " Donec templa refeceris ". Some restorers, however, conscious of the bareness of even the best type of New England meeting house, have sought direct inspiration in Wren's City Churches, with arcades and chancel adding to internal interest.[1] The instinct to preserve has fostered the impulse to create a type of church building expressive of American Protestantism at its best. Palladian windows, fan-lights, decorative ironwork and plasterwork are reminiscent of the Adam Brothers; but a sense of breadth and simplicity evokes an awareness of American tradition.[2] As one of their own poets has said:

> The sight of a white church above thin trees in a city square
> Amazes my eyes as though it were the Parthenon.
> Clear, reticent, superbly final,
> With the pillars of its portico refined to a cautious elegance.
>
> AMY LOWELL

The final phase of the " post-Colonial Spring " was the Greek Revival (1820-50). It was simply a continuation of the native classical tradition, with cupolas instead of steeples, austerer detail, more sharply defined porticoes. Yet the Greek Revival was not purely academic, as in England. It flourished not merely among cool Unitarians and conventional Episcopalians; Calvinist Congregationalists welcomed it, and Presbyterians, and ardent Methodists.

[1] It is gratifying to find an English High Churchman, Dr. Leighton Pullan, paying a generous tribute to the American " meeting house " type in his Bampton Lectures, *Religion since the Reformation*.

[2] Charles Bulfinch, a cultured Bostonian who had made the Grand Tour set the imprint of his genius on the Colonial tradition in the early nineteenth century; the State House, Boston, and the Capitol, Washington, are his monuments. He influenced church design to a considerable extent. It is appropriate that the Rev. C. A. Place, who ministered in the First Church, Lancaster, Mass. (his ecclesiastical masterpiece, 1816) should have written one of the best American biographies—*Charles Bulfinch, Architect and Citizen* (Boston, 1925).

It was a popular movement that affected all parts of the United States; it was sacred and secular, public and private, adopted for modest homes as well as mansions.[1] These were days when higher education meant classical education, and men who had no Greek would read Plutarch in translation. Enthusiasm for ancient Greece, which blossomed during the French Revolution, flowered when Byron's exploits made Greece heroic. The " ideal Greece " of democracy and the search for a physical El Dorado in the West blended in the popular mind. Greek porticoes sprang up as frontiersmen moved from New England and New York into the Middle West, giving some justification for the new place-names—Athens, Syracuse, Ithaca, etc., which looked as if the contents of a classical dictionary had been indiscriminately released.

The most eminent advocate of classical ideals was Thomas Jefferson, who became President of the United States in 1800. He was a prophet of democracy, a doctrinaire believer in the French Revolution, the leader of all who thought that the American Revolution ought to have gone further. The " Federalists " under Alexander Hamilton represented the propertied classes who wanted to maintain something like a Court at Washington, as well as the cultured life of the old colonial capitals and estates. These political and social differences were intensified by religion. Jefferson was not merely a Deist, like so many of the educated classes who remained within the nominal border of the Church. He made no secret of his convictions as to " The Sufficiency of Reason " and " The Rights of Man ". He expatiated on free enquiry as opposed to revealed religion—" and I trust that there is not a *young man* now living in the United States who will not die a Unitarian."[2] Orthodoxy lined up with political conservatism, especially in New England, where Jefferson was pilloried in countless sermons as " Jeroboam the son of Nebat, who made Israel to sin ".[3] Not all Christian people felt like this, however. A popular " Election Hymn " numbered him among the noble company of patriots:

> May Jefferson, our Chief, in Cabinet and Field,
> Check vice and party feud, be Order's friend and shield;
> In virtue great, as in command,
> Deal justice with Impartial hand.

[1] Talbot Hamlin, *Greek Revival Architecture in America* (Oxford, 1944).
[2] *Jefferson Himself*, edited by Bernard Mayo, p. 323 (Boston, 1942).
[3] A minister named Samuel Eaton did not hesitate to allude to Madison, Jefferson's successor: " Thou hast commanded us to pray for our enemies. We would, therefore, pray for the President of the United States."

The presence in America of rationalist propagandists who had fled from England augmented the influence of French sceptic refugees:[1] Paine, Cooper and Priestley, were no mere "strangers within our gates" in the same sense as Talleyrand, Lafayette, and Louis Philippe (afterwards " Citizen King "). Paine's pungent pamphlets were sold at a few pence and widely circulated among the classes designated by New England ministers as " the rag, tag and bobtail ". Crudity, superficiality and lack of taste were no bar to their finding a public. Paine observed that Judas and Pilate ought to stand first in the calendar of saints, " for they were the persons who accomplished the act of salvation ". The Russian city of Perm has erected a statue to Judas, but Philadelphia refused to erect a statue to Paine in 1942. Thomas Cooper, a scientist and agitator who accompanied Priestley, did not follow his master to the banks of the Susquehanna but embarked on the academic life. While President of the College of S. Carolina, he read from the Bible whose authority he openly denied, and preached a God in whom he did not believe, with less of reverence than he would discuss a scientific hypothesis. Home-grown unbelief was trumpeted by Ethan Allen, a blustering frontier hero from Vermont, who had led his " Green Mountain boys " against the British; Reason, he was convinced, was "the only oracle of Man".

Philip Freneau, the poet of idealism, was as sure of his humanist creed as Addington Symonds a century later.

> And men will rise from what they are;
> Sublimer, and superior, far,
> Than Solon guessed, or Plato saw;
> All will be just, all will be good—
> That Harmony, "not understood ",
> Will reign the general law.

In spite of prophets, poets and doctrinaires, Deism left a smudgy imprint on the minds of the half-educated. Revivalism might flourish on the frontier, but the East still suffered from the reaction that followed the Great Awakening. States where the Episcopal Church had been officially recognised before the War " passed easily over to complete secularism ". Even among the clergy religious emotion was distrusted, and the spiritual

[1] Unbelief was sown thinly by British officers fighting the French in Canada (Seven Years' War). It was broadcast by French officers who fought for American Independence. It was harvested in the French Revolution era.

thermometer was not supposed to rise above " cool ". This was still true forty years later. Easy latitudinarianism failed to meet the needs of the age. Bishop Provoost resigned the See of Philadelphia in despair. Chief Justice Marshall feared that " the Church was too far gone to be ever revived ". Between 1805 and 1812 the depleted clergy of Virginia received but one accession, and he was no credit to the cloth. William Meade, afterwards Bishop of the " Old Dominion ", tells how he was on his way to his own ordi-nation at the dilapidated parish church of Williamsburg when he passed a number of students with dogs and guns. They looked at him with scorn. They could not understand how a sensible gentle-man could think of becoming a parson; they had just been debating " whether Christianity had been beneficial or injurious to mankind ".

Young men in other denominations were as indifferent. At Princeton only two students professed the Christian faith in 1782. Lyman Beecher, in his racy *Autobiography*, described Yale under the latitudinarian régime of President Ezra Stiles: " The college church was almost extinct. Most of the students were sceptical . . . That was the day of the Tom Paine school.[1] Boys that dressed flax in the barn, as I used to, read Paine . . . most of the class before me were infidels and called each other Voltaire, Rousseau, D'Alembert."[2] When Dr. Timothy Dwight was appointed Presi-dent in 1795, they handed him a list of subjects for disputation in class, assuming that he would evade free discussion. To their surprise he selected the question: " Is the Bible the Word of God ? " He heard all that they had to say with good humour. Then he embarked on a series of sermons, afterwards published and widely read in England (*Theology Explained and Defended*, 5 vols.). As " chapel " was compulsory the undergraduates had

[1] Stephen Girard, a French merchant, who became a citizen of Pennsylvania (1778), named his ships *Rousseau, Voltaire*, etc. He left most of his fortune to found an orphanage in Philadelphia: " No ecclesiastic, missionary or minister of any sect whatsoever . . . shall ever be admitted for any purpose. . . I desire to keep tender minds . . . free from clashing doctrines and sectarian contro-versy." Girard's heirs contested the will in 1836, encouraged by public opinion, and Daniel Webster made a famous plea for Christianity in the Supreme Court. He did not win his case, however; and in 1848 the splendid Greek Revival fabric of Girard College was erected.

[2] A. de Tocqueville, who wrote *Democracy in America* (1832), was sent by the French Chamber of Peers to study American institutions. He visited markets, courts and legislatures, but not till he entered their churches did he learn the secret of democracy; it was no doctrine of " the Rights of Man ", but " the soul-elevating and equalising gospel of Christ ". For want of this, democracy in France had failed.

every opportunity of absorbing his " system " every Sabbath for four years. Grandson of Jonathan Edwards, Dwight was endowed with " pith and power of doctrine ". His style was pointed and perspicuous, logical and polished, with enough rhetoric to stimulate and not enough to bore. Dependence upon God was reconciled with personal responsibility. Students who had been in the habit of forming rationalist societies now came to prayer-meetings. " Infidelity skulked and hung its head." "New School" Calvinism was rejuvenated. Yale graduates streamed forth to lead the Second Great Awakening of 1800.[1] Their influence on public life is illustrated by John C. Calhoun's recollection of the time when natives of Connecticut, led by Yale men, came within five of making a majority in Congress.

President Dwight, once eulogised and then neglected, has recently served as a target for the " de-bunker ". Angoff, the literary historian, will only admit that he was a " useful man " in rejuvenating Yale, organising a Medical School and appointing scientists like Silliman to Chairs. On the literary side Dwight was certainly vulnerable. His *Essay on the Stage* (London, 1824) might have been written a century earlier; actors were " the very offal of society ". He denounced fiction on the grounds that " the consciousness of virtue, the serene remembrance of a useful life, and the hope of an interest in the Redeemer . . . are never to be found in novels ". Like his British contemporaries, he wrote tedious Biblical epics in unending cantos, which he compared to the *Iliad*; American heroes were portrayed as Hebrew heroes in a naively provincial style, following Cotton Mather. His *Conquest of Canaan* pointed to the future of freed America, but his roots were deep in the ruts of eighteenth-century English versification. Like a stiff Tory of the British " Anti-Jacobin School ", he and his " Hartford Wits " hammered away in denunciation of the French Revolution. Infidelity and democracy went hand in hand. It was " presumption little short of blasphemy to assert that sinners are competent to manage the temporal affairs of society " (sinners included Jeffersonian democrats and deists). Connecticut had not suffered like Massachusetts in the War of Independence; might not the vanished theocracy of the Mathers be resuscitated, with the saints in control ? The Federalist party in

---

[1] For a spirited account of Dwight's "Conquest of Infidelity" see C. E. Cuningham's biography (New York, 1942).

politics corresponded to the " standing order " in religion, with men of substance in key positions. " Compulsory Religion " would be effectively propagated since " the schools, high and low " were " essentially Church schools ". As a man of affairs, Dwight was admirably qualified to pursue this programme. He was a keen observer of nature, social customs, agriculture and industry. " Belles-Lettres " did not reduce him to a purveyor of " elegance ". The sacred and the secular were always linked. His *Travels in New England and New York* (London, 1823) is still worth reading, and reminds us of the celebrated *Statistical Account of Scotland* to which parish ministers contributed.

As Puritan Pope, President Dwight naturally made enemies. Grandson of Jonathan Edwards, he drove home the practical points of neo-Calvinism, instead of dwelling on its mystical and speculative aspects. Dwight's mind was set in too rigid a mould, and he lacked imagination. He did not take account of the changing spirit of the age and the need of fresh expression; nor did he realise that a prolonged war, rather than wilful popular degeneration, has an exhausting reaction on religion and morals. Nevertheless, he is an interesting character for all who understand his country and his times. He undoubtedly succeeded in rehabilitating the Christian faith by his zeal and unquestioned sincerity. His influence spread far beyond New England. Although an American military chaplain in the War of Independence, he called the War of 1812 " unnatural ". He valued Anglo-American friendship and asserted that France had injured the United States " ten times where Britain injured us once ".

A portent rather than a poet, Dwight wrote satirical verses that give a delightful flavour of social life. His lines on " The Smooth Divine "[1] might easily have been written by an eighteenth-century Evangelical in England or Scotland, as an acid sketch of a " Moderate " or " Latitudinarian " clergyman.

> There smiled the Smooth Divine . . .
> No terrors on his gentle tongue attend;
> No grating truths the nicest ear offend.
> That strange new birth, that methodistic grace,
> Nor in his heart nor sermons found a place.
> Plato's fine tales he clumsily retold,
> Trite, fireside, moral see-saws, dull as old.

[1] See *The World's Great Religious Poetry*, ed. C. M. Hill, p. 369 (Macmillan, 1926).

. . . 'Twas best, he said, mankind should cease to sin:
Good fame required it; so did peace within.
Their honours, well he knew, would ne'er be driven;
But hoped they still would go up to heaven.
Each week he paid his visitation dues;
Coaxed, jested, laughed; rehearsed the private news;
Smoked with each goody, thought her cheese excelled;
Her pipe he lighted and her baby held.
Or, placed in some great town, with lacquered shoes,
Trim wig, and trimmer gown, and glistening hose,
He bowed, talked politics, learned manners mild,
Most meekly questioned, and most smoothly smiled;
At rich men's jests laughed loud, their stories praised,
Their wives' new patterns gazed, and gazed, and gazed;
Most daintily on pampered turkeys dined,
Nor shrunk with fasting, nor with study pined;
Yet from their churches saw his brethren driven,
Who thundered truth and spoke the voice of heaven.
. . . " Let fools," he cried, " slave on, while prudent I
Snug in my nest shall live and smug shall die."

There was a sense, however, in which Dwight himself wanted
New Englanders to live and die at home. " As a bird that wandereth from her nest, so is a man that wandereth from his place "
(Proverbs, 27.8). The President of Yale was altogether opposed
to the restlessness that urged the people of Connecticut (" land
of steady habits ") to venture into the new and open lands of
Ohio. These migrants are " not fit to live in regular society.
They are too idle; too talkative; too passionate; too prodigal and
too shiftless to acquire either property or character. They are
impatient at the restraints of law, religion, or morality; grumble
about the taxes by which Rulers, Ministers and Schoolmasters are
supported. . . They are usually possessed, in their own view, of
uncommon wisdom; understand medical science, politics and
religion better than those who have studied them through life.
After censuring the wickedness of their superiors in many a
kitchen and blacksmith's shop, they become discouraged . . . and
betake themselves to the wilderness ". A New England minister
who had actually lived on the frontier, Timothy Flint, replied with
spirit to the imputations of the "learned and virtuous Dr. Dwight ".

BOOK III

SECTIONALISM

CHAPTER I

• NEW ENGLAND SPRING

" Calvinism has passed its meridian and is sinking to rise no more. It has to contend with foes more powerful than theologians. . . Society is going forward in intelligence and charity, and of course is leaving the theology of the sixteenth century behind it."

WILLIAM ELLERY CHANNING

JOHN CALVIN has had no followers more devoted than the New Englanders. For two hundred and fifty years they devoted themselves to the exposition, "improvement" and enforcement of his theology. Not only did " the System " provide " iron rations " for the soul of a frugal people: it furnished material for the minds of thinkers who found pleasure in metaphysical subtleties as well as in dogmatism. Calvinism was exported to New England by John Cotton (b. 1565); it was expounded by Richard Mather, Increase Mather and Cotton Mather (d. 1728). This patriarchal procession passed out, only to give place to a new line of doctrinal specialists. The " Old Calvinism " was dying when Jonathan Edwards providentially appeared as a " repairer of the breach ". " New Light Calvinism " became an arsenal for the wayfaring and warfaring Puritan spirit. It smote latitudinarianism, Arminianism and Deism. It prevailed against Unitarianism, save in once-holy Boston. Channing, like John Hales of Eton in the seventeenth century, "said goodnight to John Calvin"—but long after Channing's death, many a young man greeted the great Reformer with a loyal " Good morning!" Consider "the Edwardian dynasty ". Ola Elizabeth Winslow, in her recent biography of Jonathan Edwards, claims that it would be easier to derive him from his posterity than from his ancestors. From Edwards (b.1703) to Professor Edwards Amasa Park (d. 1900) stretched a procession of witness. Dr. Park married the great-grand-daughter of Edwards, and gathered together the remnants of " Old " and " New School Calvinism ". He was the last of the Edwardians. When the

National Congregational Council assembled at Plymouth Rock in
1865 to honour the Pilgrim Fathers, they drew up a Declaration
of Faith which contained articles that would have astounded the
Mathers, e.g. The Gospel Ministry " implies no power of government ". References to Calvinism were filial and respectful; they
were worthy of a funeral and the site was appropriately named
Burial Hill. When the International Calvinistic Congress met at
Edinburgh in 1938 there was not a single New Englander present
—" Ichabod, for the glory is departed from Israel! " This is
somewhat surprising when one considers that the spiritual descendants of Edwards' Presbyterian friends from Princeton were vocal,
much to the fore and all out for Calvinism.

One thinks of the heyday of German Protestantism in the nineteenth century when the theologians engaged in continual question
and answer from generation to generation. We find the same
phenomenon in New England, with the significant qualification
that Calvinism was taken for granted. Within this limited sphere
active theologians vied in purposeful activity, in " delineating and
improving the System ". As readers can well imagine, their
speculative resourcefulness was sharpened by the fact that " the
System " meant Calvinism, and any other -ism was heresy.
Tracts, treatises and pamphlets were not only published but read
and closely discussed by the laity. Of this vast, long-withered
literature, few pages can be perused to-day without effort. The
modern reader would find some interest, however, in the occasional
protest of humanity against rigid theology carried too far. An
instance of this is a genial dialogue by Samuel Webster of Salis-
bury, Mass.

*Winter-Evening's Conversation upon . . . Original Sin . . . wherein the
notion of our having sinned in Adam, and being on that account ONLY
liable to eternal damnation, is proved to be unscriptural, irrational, and
of dangerous tendency.*

He asks, how can a good, holy and just God send infants to
hell from their mother's womb ? " What! make them first to
open their eyes in torments; and all this for a sin which certainly
they had no hand in . . . and all this from the *holiest, justest and
kindest* being in heaven and earth! Mayn't we venture to say
'tis impossible! "

Many of the New England divines, like Webster, were country
ministers. There was Bellamy at Bethlehem, Conn., and Emmons

at Franklin, Mass. These were eminent men who found sufficient scope in parish, pulpit and study.[1] They not only wrote but taught. Their parsonages became " schools of the prophets " like the Scottish manses of " John Brown of Haddington " and " Lawson of Selkirk ". Students for the ministry would take Arts at the University, but study theology mainly under one of the recognised pundits, whose " sayings are like nails driven home; they put the mind of one man into many a life".[2] Edwardian Calvinism could be effectively preached, despite its doctrinal defects. Emmons' influence was considerable, though he spent most of his 54 years' ministry protected from intruders by a formidable hook on the study door; and as he meditated and fulminated, paced up and down, making a well-defined track on the floor. The exponents of " the System " were men who knew how to pass on their experience. " Do you mean to preach another sermon ? " Emmons asked a student. " Yes, sir," said the astonished youth. " Then what can you say ? You have already preached the whole system of theology." Memorable was Emmons' caustic comment on a pulpiteer famed for fluency: " It is a great blessing to be able to preach a half hour about nothing. The great body of *extempore* preachers are *pre tempore* preachers." The fatal fluency of Methodism might easily have prevailed in the American pulpit generally, but for the sound homiletics of these " New School " Congregationalists. They deserved the tribute that " Rabbi " Duncan of Edinburgh paid to Edwards: " His doctrine was all application, and his application all doctrine."

It should be noted that the names of Joseph Bellamy (1719-90), Nathaniel Emmons (1745-1840) and Samuel Hopkins (1721-1803) were known in Europe. Bellamy received his D.D. from the University of Aberdeen. Continental Calvinists endeavoured to distinguish " Emmonsism " and " Hopkinsianism ". The New England arsenal furnished quite a few weapons to British Evangelicals, who wanted Calvinism brought up-to-date and made efficient (one thinks of Chalmers in Scotland, Andrew Fuller and Robert Hall, among the English Baptists). Newman complained that Evangelical rectories were inundated with what he called " American dissenting divinity ". Some men were attracted, others were repelled. Those fortunate enough to know them-

---

[1] When Bellamy received a call to New York church, an " ecclesiastical council " decided that the needs of Bethlehem had priority!
[2] Ecclesiastes 12.11 (Moffatt's tr.)

N

selves among the elect, " through intellectual conviction or the mystical certainty of re-birth ", saw light: those who were not in that favourable position dwelt in the shadow of doubt or despair.

Modern readers who lack the inclination to go to the original sources or even to consult Dr. F. H. Foster's lucid study of " the System " in its successive phases,[1] will get a good idea of the mental and spiritual climate that conditioned later Calvinism if they will turn to *The Minister's Wooing*, by Harriet Beecher Stowe (1858). The daughter of Lyman Beecher could not help preaching in her novels, but she is never dull. In her girlhood she absorbed the authentic New England atmosphere. A devotee of Sir Walter Scott, she romanticised Puritanism rather than the Middle Ages, spicing her sentiment with racy humour.[2] She was far better at theology than Scott, but was sensible enough not to dispense it too lavishly. *The Minister's Wooing* was enjoyed by readers as diverse as Gladstone, Ruskin, George Eliot and Lady Byron. Mrs. Stowe actually succeeds in making a hero of Dr. Samuel Hopkins of Newport, who carried Edwardianism to its logical extreme. We watch the good Doctor toiling at his rock-ribbed " System ". Some of his friends enquired whether it might not be abridged with advantage. His reply was final: " If the public will not be at the expense of printing it *as it is*, let them do without it till the Millenium; then it will be read with avidity." It was published in 1793. Whether the readers were edified or appalled would depend on the state of their souls. The author was uncompromising in his conclusions. The best intentions and actions of the " unconverted " (even their prayers) are hateful to God. The felicity of the redeemed will be completed by the sight of ever-lasting smoke rising from the damned; " and all this display of the divine character will be most entertaining and give the highest pleasure to all who love God." Dr. Hopkins, the very embodiment of " plain living and high thinking ", was far from encouraging the saints to live at ease in Zion. " Men must be willing to be damned for the glory of God."[3] This " disinterested benevolence " was designed to make Christianity something more than a system

---

[1] *A Genetic History of the New England Theology* (Chicago, 1907).

[2] Mary Lyon, pioneer educationalist and head of Mt. Holyoke Female Seminary, declared: " Fun is a word no young lady should use."

[3] This became a test question at ordinations. One candidate, exasperated by clerical hecklers, declared that though not personally willing to be damned for the glory of God, he was perfectly willing that the Ordaining Council should be!

of rewards and penalties. Christians should "live dangerously". Hopkins sought the high paradoxical path of speculation, while holding fast to orthodox railings. He gloried in hyper-orthodoxy, while he gazed right and left into an abyss of heresies.[1] He entitled his first treatise: *Sin through Divine Interposition an Advantage to the Universe; and Yet, This No Excuse for Sin or Encouragement to It*. Such diction makes literary historians like Charles Angoff declare that the style of the New England divines was as crabbed as their theology, and that both were medieval, in spite of Puritanism. Dr. Hopkins and his colleagues were "painful Christians", but they were better than their creed.[2] Under a hard exterior there often glowed a loving heart and a tender conscience. This was not always true of the men who broke loose from "the System".

The New England Theology, like the medieval cathedral, was built on balanced thrusts, the work of many generations. As the craftsmen were putting the finishing touches to the topmost arches and pinnacles, the mighty fabric was shaken by an earthquake.

．　　　．　　　．

When Oliver Wendell Holmes, practitioner of the art of living, received an ovation in England, a Cambridge undergraduate asked him if he had come over in the "one-hoss shay". This referred, of course, to the genial doctor's satire on the ancestral Calvinism of New England. The allegory tells how "The Deacon's masterpiece" was a chaise or gig designed to last for ever. The good Deacon had noticed that many a vehicle "breaks down, but doesn't wear out". The weakest place has to stand the strain, and "the way to fix it" is "only just t' make that place uz strong uz the rest". With diaconal craftsmanship a "hahnsum kerridge" was

---

[1] He might have welcomed the "limerick":

> There was a young lady of Lynn,
> Who was deep in original sin.
>> When they said, "Do be good!"
>> She said, "Would if I could",
> And straightway went at it again.

[2] The Doctor's great-nephew, Mark Hopkins, President of Williams College (d. 1887), exercised phenomenal influence by personality. He became a legend.

> Mark Hopkins sat on one end of a log
> And a farm-boy sat on the other . . .
>> All through lecture time and quiz,
>> "The kind of a man I mean to be
> Is the kind of a man Mark Hopkins is."

constructed. A century passed and it was still serviceable. On the hundredth birthday of this " wonderful one-hoss shay " a minister was driving in it, thinking out his Sunday's text. When he reached *fifthly* he felt a shiver, then a shock, and found himself upon a rock, " at half past nine by the meet'n house clock "! It was exactly a century since the Lisbon earthquake. The parson pulled himself together and found the shay, reduced to minute fragments, as if ground to pieces. It had been kept going by logical clever resourcefulness, but this was no guarantee of perpetuity in a changing world.

> In fact, there's nothing that keeps its youth
> So far as I know, but a tree and truth.

Thus Dr. Holmes saluted the collapse of Calvinism, as fabricated by Jonathan Edwards, master-craftsman. The strength of " the System " consisted in its perfect balance of interlocking supports and strains. The linch-pin was not removed; the breakdown was not so complete as the " shay's "; but some of the key-supports were so loosened that the fabric was beginning to give way at other points.

Unfortunately for Calvinism, its weak point was Boston, " the hub of New England ". Back in 1726 Cotton Mather had reassured those who feared innovations: " I cannot learn that among all the Pastors of Two Hundred Churches, there is one Arminian; much less an Arian." An Arian did appear even in Boston in 1747. This was Jonathan Mayhew, whose father, Experience Mayhew, had modestly submitted that " the best actions of the unregenerate are not properly called sins " (*Grace Defended*, 1744). When Jonathan was installed some city ministers refused to dine with the ordaining council, and one cautious cleric advised his barber not to risk hearing such a heretic. Mayhew, more outspoken than his colleague, Charles Chauncy, did not trouble to unravel the " five points " of Calvinism; he cut them. His name soon became known across the Atlantic, for he received a D.D. from Aberdeen when he was only thirty. Unlike the Scottish Moderates, however, he did not " let sleeping dogmas lie "; he prodded them till they woke up and fought. By 1780 there was only one Congregational minister in Boston who was an unqualified Calvinist. The others were influenced by latitudinarian English thought. The sermons of Bishop Tillotson were widely read, also the works of " Taylor of Norwich ", a Presbyterian divine who claimed to be " a mere Christian " rather than an adherent of any sect or school. A trickle of Arminianism became a stream of Arianism, culminating in a flood of Socinianism.

The new Unitarianism of Theophilus Lindsey (ex-Anglican rector) and of Joseph Priestley (dissenter and discoverer of oxygen) reached Boston in treatises and pamphlets.[1] Priestley, provoked by the mob outrages to which he had been subjected owing to his sympathy with the French Revolution, decided to emigrate to America in 1794. It was a disappointment to his Boston friends that he elected to settle in a remote region of Pennsylvania, the Susquehannah Valley (favoured by Southey and Wordsworth for their experiment in " Pantisocracy "). As far back as 1783 the Rev. William Hazlitt, father of the essayist, had visited America, reporting the existence of Unitarians in Philadelphia and Charleston as well as Boston. Some of these groups were inspired by " democratic vistas " rather than by real religion, and this became more marked as the influence of the French Revolution penetrated the United States. Even after fighting for Independence, New Englanders were slow to realise the incompatibility of autocratic Calvinism and progressive politics.[2] The backwash of English rationalism contributed a good deal to the silent advance of Liberal religion in America, but when the tide brought in Deistic propaganda, there was a marked reaction. Tom Paine's *Age of Reason* (1793) was good ammunition for the orthodox, proof positive that radical politics and irreligion were close bed-fellows.

In England Unitarianism was the religion of the " extreme left ", who held advanced views on all questions. In New England it was destined to become the religion of the class that were conservative in everything except theology. Even then, the appeal was to Scripture rather than to rationalistic ideology. One of the most conservative congregations in America led the way. King's Chapel, Boston, the stronghold of Tory Anglicanism,[3] was a strange nest for hatching the first New England Unitarians. Circumstances, however, were abnormal. The British Governor and the rector having departed, the members elected Churchwarden

---

[1] See T. Belsham, *Memoirs* of Lindsey (Centenary ed., London, 1873).
[2] Mrs. Beecher Stowe deals with this issue in all its aspects (*Old Town Folks*, Ch. 29).
[3] H. W. Foote, *Annals of King's Chapel* (Boston, 1882).

Freeman as " Reader ", and asked him to revise the Prayer Book[1]
in a Unitarian sense (1783). He still wanted to remain in the
Episcopal Church. Bishops Seabury and Provoost could hardly be
expected to ordain a man who had " expurgated " their incomparable Liturgy. Whereupon the congregation installed Mr. Freeman themselves.[2] Had they accepted the usual New England
custom, they would have summoned an " ordaining Council " of
neighbouring ministers, but no Episcopal congregation followed
their example. Change of creed did not make King's Chapel any
less fashionable. Indeed, a century later no person in humble
life would have thought of entering King's Chapel any more than
they would have dared to enter a Beacon Street residence.

The Congregational ministers of Boston, left to their own
devices in public worship, had no need of a revised liturgy to
draw attention to their views; they simply ignored doctrines which
they could not accept. The appointment of a pronounced Unitarian, the Rev. Henry Ware, to the Hollis Professorship of
Divinity at Harvard, brought matters to a head (1805). The first
blast of the orthodox trumpet was blown by the Rev. Jedidiah
Morse (whose son invented the Morse code). The alarm was
raised: " To your tents, O Israel! " The challenge was rapped
out: " Are you of the Boston religion or the Christian religion ? "
This was a crucial question to which a Boston layman replied in
characteristic Yankee style by the counter-question: " Are you a
Christian or a Calvinist ? " The wordy warfare resounded in the
reports of the *Panoplist*, the *General Repository*, etc.; published
sermons were scorched by strictures and " Replies " were met by
" Rejoinders ". An orthodox bastion, Park Street Church, Boston,
was thrown up in 1808. The same year Edwardian Calvinists
joined forces with " Old School " Calvinists in founding Andover
Theological Seminary (1808) to serve as an arsenal of orthodoxy.
The lines were closely drawn. A fissure separated friends and

---

[1] Revision was in the air. A few years later a copy of Watts' *Divine Songs*
was discovered in a Boston shop, with the Trinity and Divinity of Christ carefully excised. The discoverer exposed this edition in a newspaper article,
" Beware of Counterfeits!"

[2] Liberals rejoiced. Here is a gem of party rhetoric by Dr. Belknap, Federal
Street church: " Then was cut the aspiring comb of prelatic pride—then was
undermined the pompous fabrick of hierarchical usurpation—then was
pricked the puffed bladder of uninterrupted succession; while the eye of
liberty sparkled with joy, and the modest face of simple, unadulterated Christianity brightened with the conscious smile of a decent, manly, substantial
triumph."

families. Ministers ceased to exchange pulpits. " Human fila-
ments, more vital than ecclesiastical bonds, were torn asunder."[1]
After the second war with Britain (1814), religious controversy
became more bitter in press, pulpit and platform.

When the smoke cleared in 1825 the outlines of a new sect
could be discerned—the American Unitarian Association. One
hundred churches in Massachusetts went over to " Unitarianism ",
but only about twenty in other New England States. There was
some point in speaking of " the Boston religion ", for its influence
was limited to a radius of thirty-five miles from the city. Within
these limits the Unitarians swept the board. As Lyman Beecher
put it: " All the literary men were Unitarians; all the trustees of
Harvard College were Unitarians; all the élite of wealth and fashion
crowded Unitarian churches; the judges on the bench were
Unitarians " (*Autobiography*, Vol. I).[2]

The last item is significant. Disruptions usually involve litigation over property; one thinks of the minute Free Church minority
in Scotland appealing to the House of Lords and being allocated
what obviously belonged to the newly-formed United Free Church
(1900). In eastern Massachusetts a miscarriage of justice also
occurred on a smaller scale. Unitarians took advantage of the law
that vested church property, not in the hands of communicants
but of " the town ", or an " ecclesiastical society " constituted
locally for the maintenance of public worship. A test case occurred
at Dedham in 1820. The usual arrangement by which the parish
minister was elected by the church members and sanctioned by
the " town ", had broken down. The town of Dedham insisted
on appointing an avowed Unitarian, against the wish of two-thirds
of the communicants. When the latter appealed to the Supreme
Court of Massachusetts, Chief Justice Parker declared that a town
had the sole right to elect a minister; tax-payers paid for the
upkeep of the church, therefore they had the right to control it.
Further, he drew this astounding inference: however large the
majority of communicants withdrawing from ecclesiastical authority, the seceders lost all title to the property and even the name
of the church.

The wheel had certainly revolved since the heyday of the
theocracy. In those saintly days only church members could vote

[1] G. G. Atkins and F. L. Fagley, ibid., Ch. 9.
[2] Cp. G. W. Cooke, *The Unitarians in America* (Boston, 1902).

at a political election. Now, the churches were at the mercy of the electors, whose decisions were confirmed by the civil courts.

For ten years a press and pamphlet controversy raged. Every vacancy occasioned litigation and disruption. At Brookfield all but two members seceded, yet the law secured the name and property of the church to the town. Throughout eastern Massachusetts the historic " First Churches ", dating back two centuries to the founding fathers of the commonwealth, passed into Unitarian hands. Those who were faithful to the principles of their forebears saw meeting houses, communion plate and parsonages handed over to men who rejected historic Christianity. By 1836 Trinitarians in 81 congregations had to start afresh, leaving $600,000 to 1,283 Unitarians. Unitarians spoke blandly of "the parish theory " and community religion! It is a euphemism of some American historians to label this grievous schism " The Unitarian Departure ".

The Scottish Free Church received messages of sympathy from all over the world in 1843. The Evangelicals of Massachusetts received scant encouragement even from their own countrymen. Episcopalians objected to their defective constitution; Presbyterians attributed their troubles to lack of Church Courts; Baptists attacked their Church and State principles. These orthodox Congregationalists bowed before the gale that followed the rustling of thirty printed pages. They had nothing now to gain by the Establishment of religion. They acquiesced therefore in the separation of Church and State, which was voted in 1834 by 32,234 to 3,273. The " Standing Order " had been vindicated a few years before by a plebiscite, but the abuse of secular power by the Unitarians had discredited the historic relationship of Church and Commonwealth. Disestablishment had already taken place in Connecticut and New Hampshire by 1819, apart from a Unitarian schism. The influx of other Protestant denominations, not to speak of the Irish Catholic invasion, would have made Disestablishment inevitable later in the century.

Sectarian divisions were needlessly duplicated by the fact that a parallel movement to Unitarianism had been fermenting since about 1770. John Murray, one of Whitefield's lay preachers, went through highway and byway proclaiming a simple Gospel of liberation. Universal redemption, he declared, was the essential message of the New Testament; God was the Father of all and

Christ died for all. At the close of the century Murray's message
was carried further by Hosea Ballou, also a self-educated man.
The British reader will wonder why two parallel columns arrayed
against Calvinism did not join forces. Broadly speaking, the Universalists were Unitarians and the Unitarians were Universalists;
compared to their modern successors they were fairly conservative,
most of them believing in miracles and the deity of Christ. They
both rejected the old Calvinistic creed of God's wrath, man's
depravity and " inability ", impending doom and eternal torment.
Why then did they not march in step ?

The distinction between them has been stated thus: " The
Universalists believed that God was too good to damn men, while
the Unitarians held that men were too good to be damned." The
differences depended on class-stratification as well as theology.
The Universalists were obscure folk, many of them living in
villages and small towns; their leaders were earnest men of medi-
ocre education who disposed of Calvinism by asserting, " Every
man is elected who votes for himself." The Unitarians were
mostly " Boston Brahmins "—polished, reticent, well-bred; and
their leaders were Harvard men. The two classes did not meet.
Moreover, the enthusiasm of the Universalists would not have
been considered " good form " by the Unitarians. The Cabots
and Lowells set the tone, which prevailed for generations. Not
long ago a lady admonished a young minister, " One does not
speak of sin in Boston " (Browning once spoke of " the hub " as
"a hole"—that would have been the unpardonable sin to a "proper
Bostonian ").

The first book to be published in Boston was a sermon by
Increase Mather, entitled " The Wicked Man's Portion " (1675).
In the early nineteenth century Boston abounded in books, but
most of them would have been burnt by the Mathers and their
Edwardian successors, for they breathed confidence in human
nature and its possibilities. A fresh spirit pervaded Massachusetts
Bay. Her ships sailed the seven seas, bringing home cosmopolitan
culture as well as wealth to the former Puritan Mecca. Charles
Bulfinch, son of an eminent citizen (physician and warden of
King's Chapel) returned from the Grand Tour in Europe and
proceeded to re-plan the backward old town. New terraces,
crescents and churches appeared—even a theatre, all designed in
a style elegant yet unpretentious, reminiscent of Robert Adam's

manner. Grace and propriety in architecture intimated that the
Boston mind had crystallised and found appropriate form. Mr.
Van Wyck Brooks, in his *Flowering of New England*, 1815-1865
(Dent, 1936), has re-created a fascinating panorama of the Boston
scene in the years that followed Waterloo. He has compared
Boston to " Modern Athens ", the Edinburgh of Scott, Jeffrey,
Cockburn and Dugald Stewart.[1]

Boston gained a world-reputation for culture, which lasted well
over half a century. The significant fact is, that most of her
literary men were Unitarians—Bancroft and Bryant, Longfellow
and Lowell, Holmes and Hawthorne. Parkman, historian of the
Jesuits, was the son of a Unitarian minister. Dr. Holmes was the
son of an orthodox minister, ousted by Unitarians; that did not
prevent the " Autocrat at the Breakfast Table " from preferring
the " Boston Religion " to the piety of " the whey-faced brethren ".
Indeed, the genial doctor was a militant Unitarian, as readers of
Elsie Venner and his other " medicated " novels will discover.[2]
A man of the world, he was as conservative in his politics as he
was radical in his theology. Social status meant as much to him
as to an Englishman of the upper middle class. " In certain
localities," he explained, " it is expected of persons of a certain
breeding that they shall be either Episcopalians or Unitarians."

If Oliver Wendell Holmes represented the hard-headed Unitarian layman, William Ellery Channing was the supreme example
of the Unitarian minister of warm heart and tender conscience.
His monument in the Public Garden of Boston bears the significant inscription: " HE BREATHED INTO THEOLOGY A HUMANE
SPIRIT ". New England had long waited for a theologian of this
calibre.

Channing's work was mostly done in Boston, but he was born
in Rhode Island (1780), the colony that Roger Williams had
founded to advance the sacred cause of " soul freedom ". Channing had the advantage of good birth and a comfortable home,
his father being attorney-general of his State. There was something in the free atmosphere of Rhode Island that was friendly to
enlightened religion. As a boy William was taken to hear a famous
preacher; so sulphuric was the sermon that a " curse seemed to

[1] Cp. M. A. De Wolfe Howe, *Boston—The Place and the People* (London,
1903).
[2] See A.L.D., " New England Puritanism in Fiction " (*London Quarterly
Review*, Jan. 1946).

veil the face of nature ". As they left the church, his father greeted
an acquaintance, " Sound doctrine, sir! " They drove away in
silence, but his father whistled and settled down at home to enjoy
a blazing fire. The boy was disturbed. Could such a doctrine be
true ? If not, should it be preached ? The Channings belonged
to the Second Congregational Church of Newport, whose minister,
Dr. Ezra Stiles (afterwards President of Yale), was a fine specimen
of eighteenth-century clergyman—literary, enlightened, dignified;
if classifiable as Calvinist, he was certainly of the " mitigated "
type. Not so his neighbour, Dr. Samuel Hopkins, of the First
Church, who carried the consistent Calvinism of Edwards to
logical extremes. Hopkins, however, was much better than his
creed, and won the respect of all good men by his brave stand
against slavery and his theory of " disinterested benevolence ",
which he certainly practised. William Channing would pore over
his father's books in his little garden-house. " His evening lamp
frequently vied with Dr. Hopkins a few rods away as herald of
the dawn." The patriarch and the youth were both sincere Christians, though their study of theology led them in diametrically
opposite directions.

It was fortunate for William Channing that his father allowed
him to go to liberal Harvard, instead of sending him to conservative Princeton, his own *alma mater*. The student's mind found
room to expand in a free atmosphere. A period of tutorship in
enervating, slave-holding Virginia, broke both his health and his
spirits. In 1803 he was called to Federal Street Church, Boston,
where he remained for the rest of his life.

Marriage and improved health contributed to Channing's gradual rejection of even " mitigated " Calvinism. He shrank from
controversy, and modestly disclaimed the title of " Liberal Christian " for fear of monopolising a virtue that belonged to men of
different schools of thought (1815). Four years later, finding
himself thrust into leadership by those who looked up to him, he
preached a decisive sermon at the ordination of Jared Sparks in
Baltimore. This was a manifesto of " Unitarian Christianity ".
By Unitarian, he meant " all who believe that there is no distinction of persons in God ". It is a pity that he used the label
Unitarian at all, for he realised that Unity was as abstract a term
as Trinity, though the modern interpretation of diversity in unity
had not yet appeared above the horizon. To Channing's genera-

tion, " Trinity meant baldly three *persons* in one in the prosaic
Boston sense . . . hence they supposed it necessary to deny the
Trinity in order to affirm the Unity of God." They were only
too ready to make reason the standard by which religion is to be
judged, " imposing common sense on every Biblical writer—a rule
of thumb for agonies and exultations of the spirit". This was a
natural enough reaction from the unbridled and often unethical
revivalism that had been so prevalent; but failure to plumb the
depth of Evangelicalism inevitably brought Liberal religion into
the shallows of rationalism.

Channing's positive contribution to theological progress was his
appreciation of the dignity of human nature and the Fatherly
relation of God to man. His study of Adam Ferguson's social
theories led him to re-read the New Testament in the light of
God's Kingdom on earth. Hence his campaign against war,
slavery, corporal punishment and all social evils that degraded
Man made in the image of God.[1] His definition of intemperance
was characteristic: " It is the *voluntary* extinction of *reason*." He
was an ardent advocate of world peace, penal reform, education,
and the amelioration of poverty through " levelling-up ". As a
forerunner of " the Social Gospel " he avoided the rabid partisan
attitude of the " Abolitionists " in the slavery issue; even so he
alienated a number of his well-bred parishioners by " interfering
with the rights of the individual " in business and social life.
He taught his generation that " divine service " is not confined to
the Sabbath, but implies the hallowing of all life.

The preaching of Channing was ponderous with the rhetoric
of his era, but his printed word was amazingly effectual in reaching
Hungary, Italy and Russia, as well as the British Empire. His
works were translated into many languages. Among his admirers
were Coleridge, Wordsworth, Sydney Smith, Dean Stanley and
Robertson of Brighton.[2] The Emperor of Brazil reverently visited

---

[1] One of the most effective Unitarian publicists was J. R. Lowell. His
biting wit served Abolition better than Whittier's almost hysterical verse—
" Libbaty's a kind o' thing thet don't agree with niggers." In the *Biglow Papers*
he punctured inflated imperialism and " manifest destiny " with shrewd realism
blended with Christian idealism. Who can forget his snapshot of a smart
Yankee, reckoning that Christianity did not explain everything in the universe ?
But John P.
Robinson he
sez they didn't know everything down in Judee!
[2] For a fine centenary estimate, see Dr. Sparrow Simpson's article in the
Church Quarterly Review (Oct.-Dec. 1942).

his grave. Baron Bunsen, leading layman of Germany, hailed him as the prophet of Christian consciousness. Renan, arch-sceptic of France, deprecating undue eulogy, paid tribute to his social idealism and nobility of character.[1] His sphere was provincial and limited (" the Boston religion "), but his influence was international. Could an American preacher ask for more ? If he " breathed into theology a human spirit ", it may also be claimed that he breathed into literature and life a religious spirit. He broke down the barrier between the sacred and the secular. Longfellow, crossing the Atlantic in 1842 and not knowing of Channing's death, greeted him as an international hero.

> Well done! thy words are great and bold;
>   At times they seem to me
> Like Luther's in the days of old,
>   Half-battles for the free.

Channing's sermon, " Unitarian Christianity most favourable to Piety " (1821) is a *locus classicus*. It reveals a " devout Biblicism ", a " rational supernaturalism ", that would have been considered as fairly conservative in many respects by " Modernists " a century later. His views on miracles and the Inspiration of the Bible were more akin to those of historic Christianity than those of his English co-religionists, Belsham and Priestley. One regrets that he severed relations with historic Christianity, by repudiating the Trinity instead of re-stating it. The followers of Channing might well have continued to act as " left wing " Congregationalists. On the other hand, principle prevailed through the parting of friends. A sect was provided to meet the needs of those who rejected historic Christianity. Henceforth, there was no excuse for men remaining in Congregationalism who had " everything in common with Unitarians except their honesty ".

Unitarianism has been described as an " unsectarian sect ". After its rapid expansion in eastern Massachusetts it made no further advance, like other denominations. It acted as a leaven of liberalism in churches that were still creed-bound, but did not seek to make proselytes on an extended front. It flowered with New England culture, and enjoyed its Indian summer. It produced essayists, publicists, novelists, philosophers, prophets, poets, even hymn-writers. In this respect American Unitarianism has a

[1] Renan exalts him to the company of Spinoza, Calvin, A-Kempis, St. Francis and Marcus Aurelius in his *Leaders of Christian and Anti-Christian Thought* (London, n.d.).

noble heritage. Over-influenced, however, by the "spirit of the age" it became too contemporary, losing grip of Christian essentials. Channing vainly hoped to stabilise Unitarianism on the "left centre". Once the fulcrum of Christ's Divinity was taken away, nothing could prevent Unitarian thought from moving to the extreme left. "Unitarian orthodoxy" had to deal with two heresiarchs—Ralph Waldo Emerson and Theodore Parker.

Emerson was born in Boston in 1803, and his clerical descent stretched back to a sturdy Puritan, Peter Bulkeley, who left the rectory of Odell, Bedfordshire, in 1634, to found Concord in New England. Morley described the Sage of Concord as " the ripened product of a genealogical tree that at every stage of its growth had been vivified by Puritan sap ". His father, minister of the First Church, Boston, died when he was eight years of age, and the large family had to undergo much hardship. " The angels that dwelt with them were Toil and Want and Truth and Mutual Faith." There was another angel in their home, " Aunt Mary ". Mary Moody Emerson was no Unitarian like the parents. She was " a dumb Dante of New England Calvinism, who transcendentalised the fiery faith into a poetic worship of the Infinite ". To the Emerson boys she was a searching counsellor, a stimulating influence that bade them "scorn trifles, lift your aims, do what you are afraid to do ". It was largely owing to her that Ralph Waldo threw off the distasteful routine of " teaching school " and refused to be " the nursling of surrounding circumstances ". He entered Harvard and in 1829 was elected minister of the Second Church of Boston. After three and a half years he resigned on the unusual grounds that he did not see his way to dispense Communion, even in a merely memorial sense.[1] He did not think that the Founder intended the feast to be permanent. As far as he was concerned, it was an outworn form. The congregation urged him to remain, he administering the Lord's Supper in his sense, the people receiving it in theirs. Emerson did not see his way to accept this compromise and resigned. Some time after he remarked: " I would not discourage their scrupulous observances. I dare not speak lightly of usages which I omit." Of the Puritans he said: "I belong by natural affinity to other thoughts and schools than yours, but my affection hovers respectfully about your retiring

[1] English travellers in the early nineteenth century were impressed with the splendid Communion plate of the Boston churches. These were the days before the "individual cup", an American invention inspired by Hygeia.

footsteps, your strict platforms and sad offices, the iron-grey deacon and the wearisome prayer rich with the diction of ages."

At Christmas 1832 Emerson sailed for Europe, seeking enlightenment from a continent branded by most of his countrymen as " feudal " and " effete ". He came to see, not universities, but men of light and leading—Landor, Wordsworth, Coleridge and Carlyle. As he walked on the moors near Craigenputtock, Carlyle said: "Christ died on the tree: that built Dunscore kirk yonder; that brought you and me together. Time has only a relative existence." Forty years later they met again in London. Emerson still ignored the fact of sin and suffering. The sage of Chelsea is said to have shown him round the worst slums of the metropolis —" And do ye believe on the deil noo ? " The sage of Concord shook his head in gentle denial.

Emerson settled in 1834 at ancestral Concord, a spot as peaceful as its name. There he stayed for the rest of his life, preaching occasionally when requested and lecturing frequently on such themes as Biography, the Philosophy of History, Human Life and Destiny. Indeed, he founded a new profession—that of peripatetic lecturer; he set a fashion for public lectures on miscellaneous subjects; all who were eager to pick up crumbs of learning would resort to " lyceums ", ready like the Athenians of old " to hear some new thing ".

Emerson's oration to the Phi Beta Kappa fraternity at Harvard (1837) was an intellectual " Declaration of Independence ", calling on the American scholar to strike out on his own, eschewing subservience to the European tradition. The following year he showed his independence again, this time without his usual tact and courtesy. Addressing the graduating class of Harvard Divinity School as guest preacher, he did not limit himself to affirming that there was a spark of the true light in everyman. He denounced historic Christianity and incisively criticised absolute reliance on the personal authority of Christ. " The old is for slaves. Go alone. Refuse the good models, even those sacred in the imagination of men. Cast conformity behind you, and acquaint men at first hand with deity."

The Sage did not reply to the protests that followed this " Divinity Address ". Henceforth his dealings with " Unitarian orthodoxy " were few. He had no liking for " this ice-house " and preferred to walk by himself. For the rest of his life he preached

from press and platform, and the world was his parish. In his
Essays he distilled the quintessence of his faith—" Self-Reliance ",
" Compensation ", " The Over-Soul ", etc. In his *Journals* we
overhear him talking to himself.[1] " If our dormant intuition
answers to his," remarks Paul Elmer More, " we are profoundly
kindled and confirmed; otherwise his sentences may rattle ineffec-
tually about our ears."[2] Running through his words and writings
gleams the New England conscience, deprived of its concrete
deity and buoying itself on insight and suggestions of divine
beauty and holiness derived from the East as well as Christendom.
One of the most remarkable tributes to Emerson came from an
unlikely quarter. " Father Taylor ", the picturesque Methodist
preacher who held forth in his " Seamen's Bethel "[3] observed in
characteristic vein: " Mr. Emerson is one of the sweetest creatures
God ever made; there is a screw loose somewhere in the machinery,
yet I cannot tell where it is, for I never heard it jar. He must go
to heaven when he dies, for if he went to hell, the devil wouldn't
know what to do with him." He was prophet, sage, poet and
lover of beauty. He related time to eternity and reared

> A temple, neither Pagod, Mosque, nor Church,
> But loftier, simpler, always open-door'd
> To every breath from heaven, and Truth and Peace
> And Love and Justice came and dwelt therein.

Emerson's serene sweetness was qualified by an astringent strain
of Yankee shrewdness, which his followers did not usually possess.
" We are a little wild here," he wrote to Carlyle in 1840; " not
a reading man but has a draft of a new community in his waistcoat
pocket." Carlyle afterwards made the acquaintance of Margaret
Fuller,[4] intellectualist and enthusiast, who manifested " such a
determination to *eat* this huge universe ". Hawthorne idealised
this " priestess of Transcendentalism " as " Zenobia " in his
Blithedale Romance (1852). What was " Transcendentalism " ?
In his modern version of the Pilgrim's Progress, Hawthorne explained that those " vile old troglodytes, Giants Pope and Pagan "
had been replaced by another terrible Giant, who seizes travellers
and fattens them for his table with meals of smoke, mist, moon-

---

[1] See *The Heart of Emerson's Journals*, ed. Bliss Perry (London, 1927).
[2] *A New England Group*, p. 73 f. " Shelburne Essays " (Vol. XI).
[3] See Herman Melville's *Moby-Dick, or The Whale* (Chs. 7-9).
[4] A kind of American Madame de Stael, she married an Italian, Baron
Ossoli. They lost their lives at sea, on returning to America (1850).

shine, raw potatoes and sawdust. " Giant Transcendentalist is a German[1] by birth; but as to his form, his features and his nature generally . . . neither he for himself, nor anybody for him, has ever been able to describe them." Judging by papers contributed to *The Dial* Hawthorne's satire is justified. What can one make of such jargon as " harmonic unity ", " Energising about the hecatic sphere ", etc. ? One of the arch-transcendentalists was Bronson Alcott, whose daughter is still remembered as the author of *Little Women*. Alcott was a venerable Don Quixote whom no one could help liking for his oddities; he once asked Emerson: " You write of Plato, of Pythagoras and of Jesus: why do you not write of me ? " The Sage of Concord attracted by his beacon a number of bats and owls, sometimes mistaken for feathery angels. Long after his death Emersonianism was diluted and mixed with other notions to produce fancy religions like " Christian Science " and " New Thought ". Sin and evil were evaded. Order was the absolute law of the Universe; one had only to align one's thoughts aright and life would be irradiated by healing currents. The key-words of right thinking were Inspiration—Health—Power (capitals had a mystic meaning). To estimate the influence of Emerson, we must consider not merely his immediate following, but his root-ideas which in simplest form acted like leaven in American popular thinking, producing a facile optimism in social and religious life.

Readers who seek the atmosphere of Emerson's time will find interest and entertainment in the exuberant pages of Sylvester Judd's *Margaret* (1845). Chaotic as a novel, it is yeasty of " the fabulous 'forties ". Social reforms of every kind are boldly broached, Christian unity enthusiastically advocated. Seldom has Unitarianism been invested with such glowing colours. " Boston Brahmins " must have been surprised to see their religion presented as a guide to a Utopian community whose shape is dimly seen through a fog of Transcendentalism. That reminds us of the " Brook Farm Experiment ", which lives in fiction as Hawthorne's *Blithedale Romance*. The art of living and working together in a self-supporting community was just the last thing of which the Transcendentalist group were capable. In early colonial days the Scottish observer, Robert Baillie, noted that the

[1] Octavius Frothingham's *Transcendentalism in New England* (N.Y., 1876) traced the movement to Fichte, Goethe and Schleiermacher; Coleridge, Carlyle and Wordsworth. Frothingham in old age confessed that this " new religion " had deeply disappointed his hopes.

o

New Englanders were inclined to " differ from all the world, and from one another and shortly from themselves ". That remark fitted Emerson's circle precisely. They were born individualists. Thus Thoreau retired from the world of men to the forest and refused even to pay his taxes. " Know ye, all men by these presents, that I Henry Thoreau do not wish to be regarded as a member of any incorporated society which I have not joined."

Brook Farm was in the parish of West Roxbury, where the minister was a practical reformer as well as a mystic. Theodore Parker (1810-1860) has been called " the Paul of Transcendentalism ". Emerson, his master, took down idols of all kinds so tenderly from their pedestals that his iconoclasm almost seemed like an act of worship.[1] Parker meted out judgment in summary fashion. A burly and bearded Boanerges, he was the son of a skilled mechanic and did not belong to the same class as urbane Unitarians and Transcendentalists. He worked his way through Harvard. Entering college as an orthodox Unitarian or " rational supernaturalist ", he left it a complete radical. Far from being edified, he dismissed Harvard as " an embalming institution ". He followed Emerson's advice and determined to be independent. A born linguist, he read the latest sceptical theology in German. The infallibility of the Bible, miracles and the exclusive claims of Christianity seemed less likely than ever, after the study of Strauss' *Leben Jesu*. He was cautious for a few years after his settlement in the little Unitarian parish of West Roxbury (1837). Four years later he dismissed discretion to the winds in his Boston address, " The Transient and Permanent in Christianity ". Little of permanent value was left after Parker the iconoclast had wielded his sledge-hammer.

There was a sensation. No publisher would print this sermon. Unitarian pulpits were closed to him—as effective as excommunication " by bell, book and candle ". Even the unconvenional declared that his paradoxes were in execrable taste, e.g., " If Christianity be true at all, it would be just as true if Herod or Catiline had taught it." But Parker refused to be silenced. His 7,000 supporters (the classical number who would not bow the knee to Baal) hired a Boston music hall, where he held forth every Sunday to a miscellaneous company of seekers after truth, dis-

[1] After Emerson's lecture on Immortality, the newspaper *Alta California* sententiously observed: " All left the church, feeling that an elegant tribute had been paid to the Creator."

ciples, enemies and cranks. He boldly abolished the distinction between sacred and secular, for he was " a Universal Reformer ", a crusader against social evils of every kind.

He was an " intellectual gourmand " as well as an agitator. He translated, he wrote, and his books were read in Europe. He found time, in spite of his manifold activities, to do more than most American and British professors of his era—to study contemporary German theology at first hand, to visit German theologians like Ewald and De Wette. Professor Commager, in a first-rate biography (Boston, 1936), emphasises the fact that he was one of the first Americans to assimilate current Continental theology. He had a sound knowledge of Syriac, Arabic, Coptic, etc. His scholarship, however, was linked with such negative views that he perpetuated the orthodox association of Biblical Criticism with unsound views of Christianity. As a social reformer, likewise, he alienated moderates by reckless political passion. His anti-slavery polemics, in particular, inflamed prejudice against the very cause he sought to promote.

Another notable " Abolitionist " was Charles Follen (1796-1840), whose views lost him the German Chair at Harvard. Follen was a contrast to most Lutheran immigrants from the Fatherland. A victim of political reaction in Germany, he reached America in 1824, Ticknor having procured him a post at Harvard. The Unitarians befriended him, but were soon alarmed by his radical views. This able thinker served for some years as Unitarian minister at East Lexington, Mass. (where the " Follen Church ", a curious octagonal edifice, is still pointed out). Like Margaret Fuller, Follen perished at sea, returning from a lecturing tour. He is still remembered as a kind of Teutonic Theodore Parker.

By the time Parker had done with the Christian faith, there was little left of it save three " instinctive intuitions "—God, the moral law and immortality. So extreme were Parker's views that he was disowned by most of the Boston Unitarians. When the National Unitarian Conference met in 1865, the majority expressed belief in " Our Lord Jesus Christ, gifted with supernatural power, approved of God by miracles ". The minority refused to limit membership to professed disciples of Jesus. They organised a " Free Religious Association " on rationalistic lines (German idealism flavoured with mysticism). Emerson was the first to sign the roll of the new Association, which stressed the scientific study of theology, "fellowship in the spirit" and co-operation with ethnic faiths. This radical group, after some desultory years of separation, merged with the main body before the end of the century.

American Unitarianism faces two directions. Its right wing is socially conservative, as becomes its " Brahmin " descent. Theologically, it is Christo-centric; anxious to maintain fellowship with Trinitarians, it exchanges pulpits with them to a greater extent than in England. The layman who is familiar with Congregational or Presbyterian services would find little difference in tone. Moderation and culture have not enabled the Unitarians to hold their own ground, even in their homeland, eastern Massachusetts; indeed, some of the historic Boston congregations seem to be slowly dying out and losing members to Broad Church Episcopalianism. The impulse to evangelise seems lacking.[1] In the middle of the nineteenth century Unitarianism was still dominant in greater Boston,[2] which was rapidly expanding, but no attempt was made to welcome young men from the country. D. L. Moody came to Boston from a Unitarian home and a Unitarian church at Northfield. Had he remained a Unitarian in the city during the impressionable years of youth, American evangelism might have developed along very different lines.

The gradual liberalisation of big Protestant denominations that used to emphasise hell has removed much of the *raison d'être* of Universalism and Unitarianism, the aboriginal tiger of orthodoxy having evolved into a harmless domestic cat. Universalists and Unitarians, so diverse in social origins, have practically joined forces. If the former can recapture their old zeal for men's souls, and the latter can translate their humane theology into vital religion, there may yet be room for Liberal Christianity.

Left-wing Unitarianism has become vocal in the cities of the Middle West. Its congregations have been largely recruited from discontented elements in orthodox churches; they are radical both theologically and socially, determined on a complete break with the past. Some of these groups are little more than ethical societies, "forums" for the discussion of current industrial and inter-

---

[1] Unitarianism might have done better had it possessed more men of a virile, practical, organising type like Edward Everett Hale (1822-1909). As a writer and humanitarian, his name for many years was a household word.

[2] It was said that Unitarians believed in " the Fatherhood of God, the Brotherhood of Man—and the Neighbourhood of Boston."

national questions, with emphasis on " sharing with other faiths "[1]
and the compatibility of religion and the latest scientific theories.
If the conservative wing of Unitarianism represents the " Boston
Religion " of Channing in twentieth-century dress, the radical
wing may be described as the " Chicago Religion ", for much of
their strength lies in this region among the *intelligentsia*. Their
line of descent is by way of Theodore Parker and Emerson, but
the shadow of bleak, impersonal science lies athwart their paths
in contrast to the sunny, individualistic optimism of their Victorian predecessors. Many of them prefer the name of " Liberal "
to that of Christian. Not all are consistent, however. Shivering
in the outer darkness of unbelief, they take refuge in neo-Gothic
sanctuaries bright with warmth and colour, rather than in appropriate " machines for worshipping in "—the stark mechanistic
architecture of Frank Lloyd Wright.

Whatever may be said of American Unitarianism theologically,
it has been fruitful from a literary, philosophical and philanthropic
point of view. From the day that Theodore Parker wrote " O
Thou great Friend to all the sons of men " up till the present,
its hymnological contribution to Christendom has been outstanding. Its spirit is surely embodied in the noble lines of
Samuel Johnson:

> Life of ages, richly poured,
>   Love of God, unspent and free,
> Flowing in the prophet's word,
>   And the people's liberty!

.   .   .   .

Returning to the " Unitarian departure " (*c.* 1820-25) we en-
quire—what happened to the remnant that clung to historic
Christianity ? Orthodox congregations, stripped by the law of
fabric, plate and endowment, proceeded to rebuild. Opposite the
" First Parish Church " in most towns of eastern Massachusetts
(complete with steeple, portico and mahogany furniture) there
would rise a more modest " Second Church " (Trinitarian). In
Boston, only one of the historic congregations, the Old South,
remained orthodox. Evangelical Christianity, however, procured
a champion in the person of Lyman Beecher, who was called from
Litchfield, Conn., to Hanover Street Church in 1826.

[1] They were prominent in the " World's Parliament of Religions " (Chicago,
1893), when Christians, Buddhists, Moslems, etc., joined daily in the Lord's
Prayer and took as their text of unity: " Have not we all one Father ? " (Mal. 2.10).

Lyman Beecher was no ordinary man. The son of a Connecticut blacksmith, he was deeply influenced by the zeal of President Dwight at Yale. A son of thunder, he was intensely narrow in his earlier phase. He submitted his fiancée, Roxana Foote (granddaughter of a Revolution general) to the supreme test of Calvinism by asking her point-blank whether she was prepared to rejoice, should God damn her for His own glory. An Episcopalian, she replied that the idea was monstrous, unworthy of God's nature. " Oh, Roxana, what a fool I've been! " His orthodoxy had received its first blow. He continued to advocate revivals, but when converts protested that they were willing to be damned for the glory of God, he shocked them by shouting, " Be damned then if you want to be! " His *Autobiography* (London, 1865) gives an intimate picture of his personality against a varying social background. His first parish was East Hampton, Long Island, where cackling geese wandered up and down the grass-grown street. The houses had all sanded floors, but the Beechers had a carpet in their parlour. Old Deacon Tallmadge called and stood on the threshold, afraid to enter. " Walk in, Deacon, walk in," said the minister. " Why I can't thout steppin' on't ". After surveying the carpet with admiration, he paused and asked: " D'ye think ye can have all that an' Heaven too ? "[1] Beecher's feelings may be imagined when it is explained that he had to support a large family on $400 (£80) a year.

His next charge was the delectable town of Litchfield, Connecticut, famous for its girls' finishing school and Judge Reeves' Law School (an old French Count, one of the students, used to say half a century later, " The society of Litchfield was the most charming in the world "). In this sophisticated environment, Beecher learned that there were other things of value in the world besides revivals and " protracted meetings ". He learned better manners; he learned how to relax, engage in sport and even read novels. He became known as a human divine as well as a powerful preacher, although he was still incorrigibly ultra-Calvinist. He repeated an earlier mistake by reading to his second wife, Harriet Porter, Edwards' classic sermon, " Sinners in the Hands of an

[1] The remark can be traced back to Matthew Henry. It supplied Rachel Fields with the title of her famous novel, *All This and Heaven Too*, in which the brilliance of Paris is contrasted with demure parsonage life in " Early Victorian " New England. This is factual fiction. H. M. Fields (d. 1907), Hartford graduate, rescued and married the heroine, Henriette Des Portes. Their wedded life lasted twenty-four years.

Angry God ". The beautiful bride rose and swept out of the room: " Dr. Beecher, I shall not listen to another word of that slander on my heavenly father! " This incident, followed by a breakdown in health, led him to develop a " clinical theology "; he amazed earnest enquirers at revivals by asking what exercise they took and how their digestion worked. There was a relation between dyspepsia and depression, he learned by personal experience.

" Lyman Beecher was a reformer, not because of his theology but in spite of it ".[1] He believed in the speedy Second Coming of Christ; his creed was strictly Pauline, and he was not inspired, like Channing, by such texts as " Jesus went about doing good ". Indeed, he would have assented to the hymn-writer's assertion, " doing is a deadly thing, doing ends in death ". There could be no reform without regeneration. Beecher's practice broke through the limitations of his theology. He attacked national sins and social evils. When Aaron Burr, wayward grandson of Jonathan Edwards, killed Alexander Hamilton, the eminent statesman, Beecher's sermon against duelling (which was on the increase) made a widespread impression. Shocked at the prevalence of drinking habits among the clergy, especially at ordinations, he founded the " American Society for the Promotion of Temperance " (1826), which advanced from the moderate position of Dr. Rush (1745-1813)[2] to the advocacy of teetotalism. Beecher did not see eye to eye with his friend, Dr. Leonard Bacon, who declared himself " the relentless foe of the liquor traffic, and equally of the false philosophy that hopes to eradicate it by statute " (the failure of Prohibition a century later confirmed the wisdom of his contention). Both reformers agreed that the solution of the slavery problem was gradual emancipation, not immediate abolition; unfortunately die-hards in the South and reckless agitators in the North made a constructive settlement impossible.

About the only " Lost Cause " espoused by Beecher was the attempt to stave off Disestablishment in Connecticut (1818). There was no Unitarian element to complicate the situation, but the ministers and deacons of the " Standing Order ", drilled by " Pope Dwight ", had committed themselves too whole-heartedly to the Federalist party. Their opponents, a motley crowd of

---

[1] Lyman Beecher Stowe, *Saints, Sinners and Beechers*, p. 390 (London, 1935).
[2] Professor of Medicine, Philadelphia—a pioneer in noting the effects of alcohol (*Inquiry*, 1785). In his " Moral Thermometer ", he approved of ale and wine but not spirits.

Methodists, Baptists, Episcopalians and unbelievers, assisted by
the " rag, tag and bobtail " of the cities, assembled under the
Jeffersonian banner. Reputable Democrats were embarrassed by
the taunt that they were in charge of an ark full of creatures clean
and unclean. The " Toleration Party " won, though Disestablishment was carried by a much smaller majority than in Massachusetts (13,918 to 12,364). Beecher was mortified by this breach
with the past, but wasted no time in lamentations. He " let the
clerical cocked hat and gold cane float down stream "; henceforth
the Church should be a " Standing Order " of the Gospel alone.
He afterwards admitted that separation from the State was " the
best thing that ever happened to old Connecticut ".

Lyman Beecher's Boston ministry was a striking success. He
did not allow the harness of Puritanism to interfere too much with
the circulation of warm blood through his system. In many ways
he was a pioneer, particularly in awakening the interest of young
men and women, by starting societies where they were allowed to
discuss current issues. His buoyancy appealed to them, and older
men were reassured to notice that it was ballasted by sound
experience. Daniel Webster described him as " the most keen-
sighted man in the United States ". He was one of the few parsons
who realised that orthodox preaching was needlessly dull (" like
Passover bread ", said Dr. Holmes, " holy but heavy "). Nor
were Unitarian sermons much better, if Emerson's experience of
them is to be treated as serious evidence. Even in Boston their
cold rhetoric and marmoreal periods had no chance against Lyman
Beecher's " arrowy sentences " and memorable epigrams. His
sayings were frequently quoted, like Franklin's. On pulpit and
platform he energised his hearers by " logic on fire ". The very
titles of his sermons made an irresistible appeal to his generation—
" The Government of God ", " The Faith once delivered to the
Saints ", " The Building of Waste Places ". His name is kept alive
by the periodic appointment of outstanding American and British
preachers to deliver the " Lyman Beecher Lectures " at Yale.

In 1830 the Hanover Street church went on fire. The firemen
stood idly by, refusing to work the engines, singing:

> While Beecher's church holds out to burn,
> The vilest sinner may return.

One of the basement rooms had been let to a merchant, who

(unknown to the minister) had stored it with liquor. The firemen watched the conflagration and demonstrated their delight by cheering " Beecher's broken jug! "

This event led to the Doctor's decision to accept the Presidency of Lane Theological Seminary, Cincinnati (1832)—a frontier Divinity School. He had never been converted to the correct opinion that " Boston was the hub of the solar system ". Attracted by " the Call of the West ", he felt drawn to a wider field; he was too ardent and energetic a personality to appeal indefinitely to the conventional East. Nevertheless, he had done his work in bearing testimony for the Gospel in Boston; he made orthodoxy vital again. Strangely enough, he was regarded as a heretic by the " Old School " Presbyterians of the West. His influence touched American life at many points and gave it lustre, although his academic career was a record of disappointment and frustration.

Theologically, the neo-orthodox reply to Unitarianism was hardly convincing. Lyman Beecher, Leonard Bacon and Nathaniel Taylor made Calvinism more " practical " by dispensing with fatalism and putting the accent on immediate conversion. This gave a certain impulse to theological progress, but could never satisfy the demand for it. Hell-fire Evangelicalism scorched the humane approach to God, for which the Unitarians had rightly contended. The layman was tormented by dilemmas, which were burlesqued as follows:

> You will and you won't, you can and you can't,
> You'll be damned if you do, you'll be damned if you don't.

Lyman Beecher's brilliant son, Henry Ward, was afterwards to simplify the issue by declaring that " the elect are—whosoever will: the non-elect are—whosoever won't."[1] For the first half of the nineteenth century, however, this solution would have been considered as childish, if not wildly heretical, by the vast majority of New Englanders, who preferred " the high *a priori* path ". When Dr. Leonard Woods succeeded in blending the " Old School " Calvinism and the " New " (Edwardian), the foundation

---

[1] This satirical attitude affected even those Calvinist stalwarts, the English Baptists. Robert Hall (d. 1831), challenged to preach more frequently on pre-destination, replied: " Sir, I perceive that nature predestinated you to be an ass, and what is more, I see that you are determined to make your calling and election sure." Later in the century Spurgeon used to pray: " Lord, hasten to bring in all Thine elect, and then elect some more!"

of the Andover Theological Seminary (1808) was laid to make the resulting fabric permanent. This united front was consolidated in Massachusetts, but it cracked in Connecticut. " Dyed-in-the-wool " Calvinists were not at all sure whether Professor Nathaniel W. Taylor was " sound ". From 1822 onwards he was lecturing to large and enthusiastic classes at the Yale Divinity School. His Chair was appropriately entitled " Didactic Theology ". Were not some of his " improvements " the thin end of the Arminian wedge, doomed ultimately to destroy the sacrosanct System ? Those who trembled for the Ark founded a new institute at East Windsor (1834) supported by annual subscriptions from sympathetic congregations, with Dr. Bennet Tyler as President (now the Hartford Theological Seminary). To-day, Taylor and Tyler seem like Tweedledum and Tweedledee. Only a theologian trained in the metaphysical subtleties of American Calvinism could detect the difference; but if Connecticut had been Presbyterian, and not Congregational, the Church would certainly have split.

Both Andover and Hartford were designed as fortresses of God, defended by formidable heretic-proof creeds. These defences were only effective against old-fashioned frontal attack. When weapons changed, obsolete fortifications proved an embarrassment to future defenders of the faith. The cast-iron creeds of Andover and Hartford were increasingly difficult to manipulate as the century advanced; " dead-hand requirements and living scholarship " made an uneasy combination; there was endless trouble (and in the case of Andover, much litigation) before freedom could be achieved.[1] The strategy of die-hard Calvinists was revealed, a " Maginot Line " mentality, an obtuseness utterly unimaginative, blind to the possibilities of by-passing and outflanking.

At the funeral of Dr. Leonard Woods of Andover (1854) his published lectures were eulogised as " a monument more enduring than Parian or Pentelic marble ".[2] This marmoreal claim has not been sustained by history even as regards the greater Edwardian divines—Hopkins, Bellamy, Emmons. Their works gather dust on the top shelves of libraries, to be occasionally examined by research students who seek material for Ph.D. theses on the New

[1] The result of which paved the way for the affiliation of Andover and the Harvard Divinity School (once mutually antipathetic). For transition from ultra-Calvinism to Liberal Evangelicalism, see *The Hartford Theological Seminary* (1834-1934) by Curtis M. Geer.

[2] See Williston Walker, *Ten New England Leaders*, Ch. 9 (New York, 1901).

England Mind and its theological preoccupation.[1] One regrets the immense amount of hard thinking and earnest convictions that produced such tomes. They are dreary because they substituted controversy for investigation; they argued within the closed circle of Calvinism; they had no sense of proportion, perspective or style. The assured finality of these men ruled out understanding of that pivotal text: " The letter killeth, but the Spirit giveth life." The divines who produced these works were utterly sincere, but usually narrow and unimaginative. Donald G. Mitchell, who knew the life of the New England parsonage from within, has left us a representative picture of " an orthodox minister of Connecticut ":

" He was utterly inaccessible to the graces of life; no bird ever sung in his ear; no flower ever bloomed for his eye . . . staggering through life with a great burden of theologies on his back, which it was his constant struggle to pack into smaller and smaller compass. Let us hope that the burden, like that of Christian, slipped away before he entered the celestial Presence."[2]

Horace Bushnell was the liberator of the New England conscience. He did not take the short cut of Unitarianism; he was well aware of the dangers of rationalising on the " left " as well as on the " right ". Instead of " logicking " in the interests of a " system " he acquainted himself with religion at first hand. He sought life rather than consistency. He preached what he felt, then he interpreted what he had experienced. He started writing a century ago, yet his books are still read; they belong to the abiding " Literature of Power ".

Bushnell was a New Englander through and through, despite his adventures beyond the limited boundaries of the New England theology. He was born in 1802, the son of Ensign and Dotha Bushnell, in a village with the singular name of Bantam, among the lovely Litchfield Hills associated with Lyman Beecher. Although his parents belonged to the Congregational Church, they were not High Calvinists; his mother had been brought up an Episcopalian, and his paternal grandmother was a Methodist. Horace was " raised " in a cheerful, happy home. His boyhood was not altogether a round of unending " chores " on the farm. He climbed hills, boated by moonlight, swam, skated and sang

[1] e.g. Joseph Haroutunian, *Piety versus Moralism: the passing of the New England Theology* (New York, 1932).
[2] *Doctor Johns* (New York, 1864, 1883). A novel of historical value, as readable as Harriet Beecher Stowe's New England books.

glees with other young people. He built stone walls, constructed dams, surveyed the countryside. He seemed a born engineer. Head, heart and hand co-operated in that " Age of Homespun " to co-ordinate " Work and Play " (to name his later unforgettable essays). The foundations of attractive Christian character were not merely laid in boyhood; they were crowned with a love of nature that afterwards enabled him to see the supernatural afresh, and declare from his heart: " The Gospel, a gift to the Imagination."

Horace entered Yale in 1823 with " sound health, a clear conscience, strong home affections and pure tastes ". After a sceptical phase he entered the Yale Divinity School. Professor Nathaniel Taylor seemed to him to be thrashing old straw—was not Calvinism in *any* form a vain attempt to define the undefinable ? He profited far more from Coleridge's *Aids to Reflexion*, and thus became an intuitive searcher after divine truth, though he never lost the evangelical spirit and the New Englander's love of the Bible. In 1833 he was called to the North Church, Hartford. The capital of Connecticut, so attractive in pre-industrial days, was his home till his death in 1876.

Like Johann Neander, Bushnell realised that " the heart makes the theologian ". When revivals were the characteristic American institution he denounced them as a " machinery system ", " artificial fireworks "; it was a poor kind of Christianity that could only be lifted out of dull routine by flashes of lightning from the bottomless pit. Calvinism did not know what to do with young people except to save them from " night-walking ", " frolics ", novel-reading and other forms of carnal pleasure; they were either " lost " or " candidates for revivalistic regeneration ". Calvinism had little or no place in the Church for the child. Bushnell had to teach his generation the elementary truth of Christ, " Suffer little children to come unto me ". After a year in Europe, due to his breakdown in health, Bushnell returned to write his epoch-making book, *Christian Nurture* (1847). He did not deny the fact of Conversion. He did deny what was universally held in New England—that it was the *normal* experience for a young Christian. His key-thought was: " The child is to be brought up a Christian, and never know himself as being otherwise." This was a reversion to the pre-Edwardian conception of the family covenant, stated in a modern way. It was a seed-plot of ideas for the education of the future, creating free and happy personalities, blending " sacred " and " secular " (cp. p. 336).

One morning early in 1848 Bushnell had a mystical experience. His wife looked at him and saw a new light in his face—" What have you seen ? " He replied simply, " The Gospel." Out of this fresh vision issued *God in Christ*, the *Vicarious Sacrifice* and other creative books. One of his most thought-provoking works was *Nature and the Supernatural* (1860) in which he broke down hard-and-fast distinctions between the normal and the miraculous. Perhaps his most valuable insight was his recognition of the real distinction between theology and religion. Had this been done some generations earlier, much controversial ink might have been spared, especially in polemical New England. Bushnell explained that theological terms are not like chemical formulae, exact and precise; they are merely words capable of expressing religious experience and thought in approximate, poetical, " symbolical " language. Here was a prophet and a psychologist in the camp of the system-grinders. " What does Dr. Bushnell mean ? " asked the Connecticut clergy, perplexed as well as shocked. They would have liked to silence him, but fortunately Congregationalism did not facilitate heresy trials. His own congregation forestalled any such move by withdrawing from the local " Consociation ".

The seer of Hartford was too original, too thoughtful, to attract crowds, but as " the preacher's preacher " he is still read in many a manse and rectory on both sides of the Atlantic; " he being dead yet speaketh."[1] The very titles of his sermons are suggestive:

" Every Man's Life a Plan of God " (Isaiah 45.5);
"The Dignity of Human Nature Shown from Its Ruins " (Romans 3.13-18);
" Loving God is but Letting God Love Us " (1 John 4.16);
" The Dissolving of Doubts " (Daniel 5.16);
" Spiritual Dislodgements " (" Moab . . . hath not been emptied from vessel to vessel, therefore . . . Jeremiah 48.11).

Bushnell's study windows commanded wide views of earth as well as heaven. When it was proposed in 1847 to bring water-power to Hartford from the Connecticut River, he enlarged on the text: " This same Hezekiah also stopped the upper water courses of Gihon and brought it straight down to the west side of the

---

[1] His outstanding discourses are collected in *The New Life* (1862) and other volumes still to be found in the second-hand book shops of Britain.

city." During the panic of 1857 he preached a week-day sermon
to the business men of Hartford from Acts 27.15: " And when the
ship was caught and could not bear up unto the wind, we let her
drive." Here was a minister who glorified in being a " citizen of
no mean city ". He did his utmost to make Hartford a worthy
capital for his native state, giving " beauty for ashes " by transforming an expanding slum into a public park in the heart of the
city. He watched over the interests of Hartford as closely as Dr.
Chalmers in Glasgow. A forerunner of social Christianity, a per-
sonalised municipal conscience, he is appropriately commemorated
by the Bushnell Memorial Hall, erected a few years ago at a cost
of $1,500,000. No church in Hartford is yet named in his memory.

Bushnell's treatment of the great Christian doctrines lacks
exactness; his elucidation of the Trinity, Incarnation and Atonement may even be criticised as amateurish. Yet he gave American
theology impetus. " He was a theologian as Copernicus was an
astronomer," said his biographer, Dr. Munger; "he changed the
point of view, and thus not only changed everything, but pointed
the way towards substantial unity on theological thought." He
led his generation from the Christ of the creeds to the Christ of
experience. Dr. John W. Buckham, in his *Progressive Religious
Thought in America* (1919) has not merely claimed for him " a
greatly enhanced estimate of his part in theological advance "; he
has testified to a " fresh sense of the inexhausted treasures of his
productive personality ". It is largely owing to Bushnell that we
can speak of the " enlarging Pilgrim faith ".

FROM THE ERA OF GOOD FEELING TO SECTARIANISM

" In things essential, unity; in things non-essential, liberty; in all things, charity.—*German saying* (seventeenth century)

" Every sect is a moral check on its neighbour. Competition is as wholesome in religion as in commerce."—LANDOR

THE attainment of Independence by the United States involved, as we have seen, the reconstitution of the various churches in relation to the new order. American civilisation, nevertheless, was still dependent on Europe for imported goods; and not even the most ardent patriotism could improvise a new art and literature; it is difficult to create, even in a new world. In religion the tendency was to build up new organisations on conservative lines, and for some years " Americanisation " was a slow process. The denominations had all suffered from the effects of protracted war in various ways—property, prestige, moral and spiritual leadership. The Evangelical Churches were exhausted. They needed a regime of national unity so that they might consolidate their position. In national politics the " era of good feeling " started with the inauguration of Washington as President (1789) and ended with the triumph of Jackson, the hero of the masses (1829). In religion, quite as much as in politics, this was an " era of good feeling ". The churches had shared common suffering. They were conscious of each having a part to play in the building of Christian America, the enterprise involving co-operation. The keynote of the period was toleration and accommodation. The average man was inclined to believe with Franklin: " Churches are like clocks. No two of them agree; but they all approximate to the true time." Churches of German origin, such as the Lutheran, were ready to adopt the American way of life. Congregationalists and Presbyterians joined forces to evangelise the West. Episcopalians exchanged pulpits with non-liturgical preachers. Strangest of all, Roman Catholics (numerically feeble as yet) showed a genuinely fraternal attitude to Protestants, sometimes sharing the same buildings. Jesuits in some instances actually served as trustees of Protestant colleges. It appeared as if Catholicism itself was to be Americanised, through the use of English in worship and the control of church property by elected boards of laymen. Even to-day the term " pastor " (ultra-Protestant in England) is used by American Romanists, as synonym for " priest ".

A wave of missionary enthusiasm swept over denominational barriers. Most of the early missionary societies resembled the " American Board " (1812) in being organised on an inter-Church basis. This was true of the American Bible Society (1816), the American Tract Society (1825) and the American Sunday School Union (1824).

As in England, elementary education owed its origin to Christian effort, but America was spared the acrid controversies of " Churchmen " and " Dissenters ". As early as 1790 the " First Day or Sunday School Society " was founded in Philadelphia. The leader was a well-known philanthropist, Dr. Benjamin Rush (a Universalist); the directors included Bishop White (Episcopal), Matthew Carey (R.C.) and Joseph Sharples (Quaker). The plan was to give poor children a general education on Sundays for want of opportunity during the week. Out of this practical experiment there emerged a movement for public elementary schools, which were established in Pennsylvania (1834) and gradually adopted by other states. Professor Calvin E. Stowe (husband of Harriet Beecher) and other educationalists visited Europe to study various school systems and report. Some of the best features were adopted and wrought into the fabric of American Protestant tradition. By the middle of the nineteenth century, sectarian catechisms had disappeared from the schools of New England and the Middle States, but the Bible, the Lord's Prayer and the singing of hymns remained.

The Congregationalists were foremost in higher education,[1] but

[1] Their colleges, starting in New England (e.g. Dartmouth, Williams, Bowdoin, Amherst and Middlebury) were planted like stepping-stones through Ohio towards the Pacific. Protected by Charters from sectarian or State interference, they were witnesses to sound scholarship. See D. G. Tewkesbury, *American Colleges . . . before the Civil War* (New York, 1932); particular reference to religious influence.

the Methodists were the pioneers of Sunday Schools in the modern sense, which became common after 1816. They also realised the need of providing courses for semi-literate teachers as well as reading for children and adults. They blazed the trail of Christian publishing when they founded the " Methodist Book Concern " (New York, 1789). Every travelling preacher was a book-agent in an expanding network of circuits. The " circuit-rider " tradition was strongly prejudiced against higher education (" The Lord eddicates his own preachers") but in 1831 " Wesleyan University " came into being at Middletown, Conn. A Divinity School was actually founded as far west as Chicago (1855), but only on the understanding that it should be camouflaged as the Garrett " Biblical Institute ".

Even in the East, theological " seminaries "[1] only date from the early nineteenth century. They were intended to provide a more specialised curriculum for the Ministry than could be obtained by taking an Arts course (heavily laden with theology), followed by study under a single Professor of Divinity or in the parsonage of a Hopkins, a Bellamy or an Emmons. The first Protestant Seminary was established at Andover, Mass., in 1808, as an indignant gesture against the appointment of an avowed Unitarian to the Hollis Chair of Divinity at Harvard (founded by a London merchant of that name in 1722). One of the first Andover professors was Dr. Moses Stuart, whose *Hebrew Grammar*, dictated to his students (1813) won fame even in Oxford, edited by Pusey (1831). Stuart's study of German theology aroused the suspicion and distrust of his colleagues; here was a man who dared to be independent even in a creed-bound seminary; he was one of the few theologians who attempted to keep in touch with Continental research, and his books were honoured in manse and rectory on both sides of the Atlantic.

Controversy rather than specialisation accounted for a number of denominational seminaries, which sharpened the frontiers of sectarian division.[2] Harvard, however, initiated a fresh line of advance—the establishment of a liberal University Divinity School, open to all (1819). Yale retorted by founding a similar School on

---

[1] Among Protestants the term is peculiar to U.S. The Sulpician Fathers organised the first " seminary " at Baltimore (1791).

[2] New Brunswick, N.J., Dutch Reformed (1810); Princeton, Presbyterian (1812); " General Seminary ", New York, Episcopal (1817); Gettysburg, Lutheran (1826).

P

definitely Calvinistic principles; but time mellowed its angular outlines. More influential than either of these Faculties was Union Theological Seminary, New York, a Presbyterian foundation (1836), which broadened out into the most progressive School of Religion in the United States.

The argument that theological education unfitted men for the work of a strenuous ministry was squashed when graduates from the seminaries of the East pledged themselves to a period of missionary service in the West; witness the " Illinois Band " from Yale (1828) and the " Iowa Band " from Andover (1828). When Lyman Beecher gave up a Boston church to become President of a frontier seminary at Cincinnati (1830) he gave a tremendous impetus to " the Call of the West ". Many a poorly-equipped log college developed into a modern University within half a century, thanks to Christian initiative.

.   .   .   .

About 1830 the " era of good feeling " in American public life gave way to an era of controversy, in which national unity was endangered by excessive " sectionalism ". The doctrine of " State Rights " carried much weight with Southerners, whose economy tended to rest exclusively on slave-produced cotton. The North was becoming a land of business men, though the wheels of the Industrial Revolution moved as yet but slowly. The centre of gravity was moving West. This economic trend was politically demonstrated when the frontier farmers swarmed into the White House in 1829, giving a vociferous welcome to their idol, Andrew Jackson, who was pledged to extirpate the obsolete ideal of the gentleman (his slogan, " to the Victors belong the Spoils!"[1] was of course no novelty; the politicians of Georgian England who appointed Colonial officials knew all about it).

In religion, sectarianism corresponded to sectionalism in political, economic and social life. Gone was the readiness to subordinate denominational advantage to the common well-being of Christianity. Gone was the courtesy that " agrees to differ ". Coarse invective infected religious journalism. Controversy was

[1] Before Jackson's inauguration, Robert Little (a leading Unitarian) preached from the text, " When Christ drew near to the city he wept over it ". The ladies of the capital had good reason to weep over the crude manners of the Jacksonians. It was a far cry to the semi-regal pomp of George Washington. The use and abuse of Scripture texts by American preachers would furnish material for an instructive Ph.D. thesis.

apt to take a very " personal " line, in the pulpit as in politics.
Partisans " sold religion " like commercial travellers with the aid
of " clap-trap ". In Home and Foreign Missions, even in philanthropic enterprise, sectarian organisations tended to replace co-
operation. The Roman Catholics founded parochial schools to
indoctrinate their children and keep them isolated (compulsory
since 1884); the Lutherans did likewise, and the " Old School "
Presbyterians tried to do so.[1] Churches that differed from the
prevailing pattern of American religion no longer tried to " accommodate themselves " to their neighbours, but asserted themselves
aggressively. This was particularly true of the Presbyterians,
Lutherans, Episcopalians and Roman Catholics.

American Lutheranism presents the unusual case of an immigrant Church merging its inheritance and traditions in new
surroundings until spurred by the pressure of new waves of
immigration to recover what it had lost.

It will be remembered that German Pietism was transplanted
by Muhlenberg. At the end of the eighteenth century, however,
Halle University had gone rationalist, and had lost its missionary
interest in America. Lutherans supported the War for Independence. Denominational consciousness declined. In 1792
the oldest provincial Synod (the Pennsylvania *Ministerium*)
omitted all reference to the Augsburg Confession. The New York
Ministerium gave the English language official recognition in 1807.
English hymns came into general use. The Lutheran liturgical
tradition was giving way to the American demand for spontaneity
in worship, especially in rural districts. The New York *Ministerium* resolved to unite with the Episcopalians in view of " the
identity of their doctrine and the near approach of their discipline "; where the services of the sister Church were available,
no new Lutheran congregation was to be recognised. Both
Churches tended at this time to tone down dogma and were at
one in their attitude of tired laxity. The negotiations were not,
however, completed. In Pennsylvania Lutherans co-operated with
the German Reformed in managing Franklin College at Lancaster;
their congregations often used the same building for worship, and

---

[1] With Princeton support, 264 schools were organised (1846-53). They were
more successful in indoctrination than in general education. The Civil War
wiped out the scheme, a few years before the Church of Scotland entrusted
her schools to the State; the financial drain was excessive. Cp. L. J. Sherrill,
Presbyterian Parochial Schools, 1846-70 (Yale, 1932).

issued a *Common Hymnbook* (1817) as a preliminary to organic union.

" Unionism " received a check when the *Evangelisches Magazin* was started in 1812, with the two-fold aim of " conserving the German language and fighting rationalistic unbelief ". Actually, rationalism had found its way from the Fatherland *via* a limited number of pastors who were in a position to understand its theological bearing; but it was good propaganda to depict English as the language that clothed itself with unbelief and German as the bulwark of happy homes and sound faith. Slowly but surely the tide of Lutheran consciousness reached the shallow and stagnant pools of indifferentism. In 1820 a " Plan of Union " was adopted that linked into a federation the *Ministeria* of New York, Pennsylvania and the South. This " General Synod " was not merely an act of consolidation. " The Lutheran Church had no intention of dying or moving; she liked the Western World and meant to live here " (C. P. Krauth).[1] The General Synod, however, was only saved from disintegration through the exertions of Samuel S. Schmucker, the most scholarly among the younger ministers, son of the first President of the Gettysburg Theological Seminary.

About 1830 most of the American Churches passed from the " era of good feeling " to an " era of hard feeling "—controversies, schisms and heresy trials were the ecclesiastical equivalent of " sectional " jealousy and party bitterness in politics. This phase lasted till about 1870. In American Lutheranism the pendulum swung decisively from latitudinarianism to dogma, from " accommodation " to self-assertion. By 1850 the return to historic " confessionalism " was well under way.[2]

The " advance guard " of belligerent Lutheranism came direct from Germany in 1839—Lutherans of a very different type from the gentle Pietists of Halle, led by Muhlenberg. In Saxony, Pastor Martin Stephan of Dresden decided to bring his sympathisers over to America. Attracted by glowing accounts of Missouri, he organised an exodus of 750 earnest Lutherans. They would be free from the restrictions of State Church bureaucracy and of a rationalist liturgy; no one would interfere with their project of ecclesiastical autonomy, linked with self-imposed bonds

[1] Dr. Krauth was the first American Lutheran theologian of note. His *Conservative Reformation and its Theology* (1872) clearly expresses his viewpoint.
[2] Cp. Vergilius Ferm, *The Crisis in American Lutheran Theology. A Study of the Issue between American Lutheranism and Old Lutheranism* (1927).

—the various creedal codes that tightened up the Augsburg Confession in the sixteenth and seventeenth centuries. Shortly after
arriving at St. Louis these good Saxon folk discovered that their
spiritual guide had embezzled their funds. They were stranded
at the edge of the American frontier. Fortunately, a young pastor
who had accompanied them stepped into Stephan's place.
C. F. W. Walther restored confidence. He founded a mother-
church at St. Louis, with daughter-churches wherever his followers settled. What centre could have been more strategic than
St. Louis? Streams of German immigrants passed through the
city in the '40s and '50s.   Ambition to make a fresh start and
political persecution had impelled them to leave the Fatherland.
Their motive was seldom selfless, but Walther shepherded many
of them into his " Missouri Synod " when they arrived at that
great clearing-house for the frontier, St. Louis on the Mississippi.
Walther was a man of tremendous energy. He built churches
and parochial schools, defended orthodoxy of the strictest type,
and advanced his views by means of a popular paper, *Der
Lutheraner* (1844). By the time of his death in 1887 the Missouri
Synod had grown to about 1,500 congregations and nearly 1,000
ministers.

Another group, kindred in spirit to the Missouri Lutherans,
left Germany for Buffalo the same year (1839). They were " die-
hards " who had refused to fall in with the formation of the
Prussian United Church by Frederick William III in 1817, the
tercentenary of the Reformation. These " Old Lutherans "
would have nothing to do with the Reformed element and underwent considerable persecution at the hands of the Prussian
Government. Pastor Grabau of Erfurt brought a thousand settlers
to western New York a few months after the Saxon detachment
had reached St. Louis. An attempt was made to link the two
kindred groups, but both these ultra-orthodox sects suspected
each other's motives. The Missouri Synod accused the Buffalo
Synod of " hierarchical tendencies ", and the Buffalo Synod
accused the Missouri Synod of " disintegrating congregationalism ".
A well-known German divine, Dr. W. Löhe of Bavaria, became
interested in guiding American Lutherans along the right lines.
Walther went to Germany to interview him. Löhe's High Church
opinions irritated the Missouri men. Some of them, however,
sympathised and separated to form an " Iowa Synod " (1854).

Thus reference to a German authority on Lutheran polity merely precipitated another schism.

The main point about these ultra-Lutheran Synods in the West is to remember their tremendous influence in gathering in the immigrants from Germany, who numbered nearly 1,000,000 between 1850 and 1860 (4,731,000, 1820-92). Valuable welfare work was carried on by American Lutherans among the newcomers, inspired by the achievements of the " Inner Mission " in the Fatherland. Hospitals, orphanages and deaconess institutes were founded, which set an example to individualistic Anglo-Saxons. It is estimated that one-third of the German immigrants were Catholics, one-third Protestant, and one-third " freethinkers " (most of them political refugees victimised by the repressive governments after the failure of the Revolution of 1848). A large proportion of these Germans settled in the Middle West. Others joined Lutheran churches in the East and swelled the orthodox element in the " General Synod " that embraced New York and Pennsylvania.

The German influx was instrumental in altering the balance of Lutheranism in the United States.[1] Dr. Samuel Schmucker, advocate of an Americanised Lutheranism co-operating with Anglo-Saxon Evangelicals, lost the leadership. He had started by claiming that Lutherans ought to be " positive " in holding to their particular principles, but had no idea that they would be pushed so far. To his chagrin rigid orthodoxy gained ascendancy. He witnessed reactionaries disinter the crass scholasticism that had discredited German Lutheranism in the seventeenth century. Confessions, catechisms and outmoded liturgies were almost elevated to the level of the Bible. " Orthodoxism " (as Pusey christened this exaggerated orthodoxy) made for a new Pharisaism among pastors. The slightest deviation from simon-pure Lutheranism met with immediate condemnation. Parochial schools were established to isolate children from young Americans, see that they spoke German, and drill them mechanically in catechism and Luther-lore. Irenical persons were warned off by the notice, " LUTHERAN PULPITS AND LUTHERAN ALTARS FOR LUTHERANS ONLY! " (the " Galesburg rule ", 1875).

Between 1870 and 1910 Lutheranism increased its membership

[1] The Lutheran immigrants acquired " activist " traits in the land of their adoption, notably the church-going habit, to which they had not usually been addicted in the Fatherland.

from less than 500,000 to nearly 2,250,000. It moved from fourth to third place in the numerical scale of Protestantism, being only exceeded by the Methodists and Baptists. During these years over 1,750,000 Scandinavians migrated to the United States. Not all these northern Lutherans kept the faith; many of the Danes were secularists; only a third of the Swedes and Norwegians maintained their church membership. Even so, Lutheranism was much strengthened by these accessions, particularly the ultra-orthodox section. It is curious that these incomers with their State Church traditions made little attempt to introduce Episcopacy, which could have been procured from home;[1] but in every other sense they were thoroughly conservative. The original Scandinavian " Augustana Synod ", which separated from the " General Synod " in 1860, split into Swedish, Norwegian and Danish segments.

Lutheranism in the United States thus developed a stiff spirit of isolation, except in the Old South, which did not attract many continental immigrants after the Pietist exodus in the eighteenth century. The prevailing pattern of confessional orthodoxy is due to nineteenth century settlers.

The Protestant Episcopal Church resembles the Lutheran in experiencing a decisive change from the attitude of " accommodation " to self-conscious assertion.[2] The quarter of a century that followed American Independence found this Church at its lowest ebb. The English connexion, so long a source of prestige, now proved an embarrassment; the fixed liturgy and hierarchical order seemed ill adapted to the needs of a new country. Bishop Provoost, who was as ardent a patriot as he was lax in Churchmanship (brought up among the Dutch Reformed) declared that all the Episcopal Church could ask for was toleration; he thought it would die out with the old Church-and-State families. On the other hand, there was a certain influx of Lutherans who wanted to use the English language. When Zion Church, New York, expressed unwillingness to continue services in German, the New York *Ministerium* informed them that " they might join the Episcopalians "—which they proceeded to do in 1797. These new-

---

[1] The Episcopal Church tried to win over Swedish Lutherans who had been brought up under Episcopacy. In 1874 Bishop Whitehouse proposed the union of the Augustana Synod with the Protestant Episcopal Church.

[2] W. W. Manross, *The Episcopal Church in the United States*, 1800-1840 (P. S. King, 1938).

comers received a warm welcome from General Peter Muhlenberg, son of the founder of American Lutheranism, who had been ordained by the Bishop of London, and yet raised a German regiment for Washington. Henceforth the Episcopal communion was enriched with many German names. A number of old Dutch families also conformed to a denomination which they considered "respectable"; one of the best-known New York churches, St. Mark's-in-the-Bowery (now extremely "High") was built by Mr. Stuyvesant, great-grandson of the last Dutch Governor.

The fortunes of the Episcopalians brightened at the very time when one would least have expected—during the War of 1812-14 between Britain and the United States. So far as New England was concerned, semi-political causes operated in favour of a Church traditionally associated with English Toryism. Episcopalians, campaigning against the privileged position of the Congregational Establishment, were compelled by circumstances to line up with the Democratic party of Jefferson, which was anti-English (their Federalist opponents being against the War of 1812). Bishop White, who had guided his church through the difficult years that followed American Independence, maintained cordial relations with other Evangelical Churches, though he was loyal to the Liturgy and had little sympathy with explosive revivalism. White had no use for the words "priest, altar and sacrifice". Very different was the attitude of J. H. Hobart, whom he consecrated as Assistant Bishop of New York in 1811.

Bishop Hobart had no doubt whatever as to the divine origin of Episcopacy, although he was descended from Parson Peter Hobart, who quitted England in 1635 to avoid the "blackening cloud of prelatical impositions". J. H. Hobart was as uncompromising in his principles as his Puritan ancestor. Tired of having to defend himself against the charges of "visionary and enthusiastic devotion", he rejected the current conception of the Episcopal Church as the preserve of gentlemanly decorum. "Give me a little zealous imprudence!" He received much support from stiff Connecticut Churchmen who walked in the steps of Johnson and Seabury. He gave his views publicity by publishing *Companion Manuals* for "the Altar", "the Prayer Book" and the "Feasts and Fasts of the Church". These High Church opinions antagonised many people within and without his own communion.

Oil was poured on the waters by the consecration of two Evan-

gelical Bishops—Griswold for New England (1811) and Moore
for Virginia (1814). The result was the creation of a new and
earnest Bible-loving party in sections of the country that had
hitherto known only Episcopacy as " high-and-dry " or as slack
and worldly. No bishop could have been more unprelatical than
A. V. Griswold; brought up on a Yankee farm, he wore no mitre,
lived plainly, and even held prayer-meetings. Prejudice was so
completely disarmed that after his death New England provided
material for five dioceses.

The church revived in the South. On Bishop Moore's decease
(1841) Virginia claimed 100 clergy and 170 churches. The days
of Jarratt Devereux, it seemed, had returned. Had he belonged
to the next generation, he would have seen the cause of the Gospel
triumphing in the Virginian Church, where Bishop Meade continued the Evangelical succession.

Bishop Hobart had no intention of continuing the " era of good
feeling "; he wanted to see an end of all fraternising with " dissenters " in missions, religious education and philanthropy. He
noted with satisfaction " a decided and increasing attachment to
the peculiarities of our communion ". His sermon at the consecration of Bishop H. U. Onderdonk at Philadelphia was the
American equivalent to Keble's historic discourse on " National
Apostasy " (1833). Hobart's *High Churchman Vindicated* (1827)
was a clarion-call—" Apostolic Succession! "—" Only the Episcopal Ministry valid! "—" The Prayer Book the only divinely
approved form of worship ! " This manifesto was actually published before the Oxford Movement. The Rev. John Hall, of
Ashtabula, Ohio, accused of being a Puseyite, made inquiries,
obtained the Oxford *Tracts*, and asserted: " Dr. Pusey is a Hallite.
I have held these principles throughout my ministry."

Bishop Hobart visited England in 1823 and corresponded with
the future Tractarians before his death in 1830. Stephens, in his
Life of Dean Hook says that " he perplexed not a few . . . by his
mixture of Republican and High Church principles." Frank,
impetuous and fearless, he was forthright in expressing his views.
He praised what was " churchly " in Anglicanism, but did not
hesitate to criticise the government appointment of bishops, the
holding of " livings " as private property, and the scanty opportunities for advanced study in such a richly endowed church.
This attitude appealed to young men like W. F. Hook, afterwards

well-known as Vicar of Leeds;[1] Scottish and American Episcopacy was purer without official patronage and prestige. Pusey, however, did not care for Hobart's tone. Newman wanted to export eminent divines to propagate the Catholic tradition in New York with an authentic Oxford accent. It was decided to dispatch a complete set of Patristic works to the General Theological Seminary. This was the suggestion of Hook, who afterwards invited Bishop George Washington Doane to preach at the opening of his new church in Leeds. In 1834 Doane edited the first American reprint of Keble's *Christian Year*, which helped to melt frigid Churchmanship by gentle Romanticism. "Puseyism" and "Newmania" flourished in his see of New Jersey; the *Tracts for the Times* were given full publicity,[2] and Tractarian novels familiarised the Episcopal layman with the setting of the Oxford Movement.[3]

On the English side, Samuel Wilberforce wrote a *History of the American Church*, before his consecration as Bishop of Oxford (1844). He had never visited the United States, but his conclusions register the impressions of English Churchmen. He complained that in America "the pew-holders are the parish, which has no territorial existence". The poor were excluded by high seat-rents, except in New York churches blessed with endowments; and the clergyman was "the hired servant of the pew-owners". Wilberforce was disquieted by notices in American papers testifying to cordial relations between Episcopalians and other denominations; these ranged from the use of "unconsecrated" places of worship during building operations to the admission of non-Anglicans to occasional Communion, which was "gladly witnessed and affectionately encouraged". To Bishop Wilberforce such fraternising with "Dissenters" was deplorable. There was more point in his criticism that American churches were too lavishly upholstered ("like splendid drawing rooms"). The altar (often a mere board projecting from the reading-desk) was browbeaten by the massive pulpit. Bishop Hobart had introduced

[1] In the American Episcopal Church, "vicars" are the incumbents of "chapels" founded by big congregations. Trinity, Mother-Church of New York, had many offshoots.

[2] Dr. J. W. Nevin, of the German Reformed Church, from a casual reading of the Tracts, "caught his first glimpse of what the church spirit really meant." The Liturgy must be "in the fullest sense an altar service—churchly, sacramental and in proper measure priestly."

[3] Cp. my art. "Fiction and the Oxford Movement", *Church Quarterly Review*, April 1945.

the improvement of transferring the Communion table to the front of the pulpit, instead of leaving it almost hidden behind. In the 'forties, however, this " Hobart chancel " yielded to the real thing.

" Ecclesiology " was imported into the United States, along with other furnishings of the English High Church Movement. A " show " church was erected at great expense in the heart of New York. Historic " Trinity " was replaced by a Perpendicular edifice—the first genuine Gothic church to be erected in America, complete with vaulting and solid masonry throughout (1846). The architect was a young Englishman named Upjohn who had settled in America, bringing with him the living tradition of English Gothic. Another masterpiece was Grace Church, New York (1845), more eclectic in style with a slender German spire; it was designed by James Renwick, who built St. Patrick's Cathedral after the Civil War for the Roman Catholics. For some years to come, however, Protestant Episcopalians had to be satisfied with " pro-cathedrals ", like their co-religionists in Scotland. The expense of maintaining a large staff of clergy was as yet beyond their means, and in many sees the Bishop had to be a working rector. Churches like Trinity and Grace were as good as any Gothic Revival achievements in England, but few congregations could afford such splendour. Architects like Upjohn and Renwick made the mistake of erecting flimsy churches elsewhere in grotesque " carpenter's Gothic " which were preferred by clergy and building committees to the dignified classical tradition of native American craftsmanship. Gothic was required as the setting for the fashionable type of service imported from England—surpliced choirs, in chancels, chanting, frequent Communion.[1]

These aesthetic attractions lured the laity and appealed to proselytes from other denominations, but Evangelical churchmen were sensitive about the theological implications of " ecclesiology " and ritual. Bishop Manton Eastburn of Massachusetts refused to conduct Confirmation in churches that indulged in such " superstitious puerilities " as altar crosses, candles and the " eastward position ".[2] Bishop McIlvaine of Ohio refused to consecrate a

---

[1] This era lives in E. M. Upjohn's *Richard Upjohn, Architect and Churchman* (New York, 1939).

[2] The vestry of the Church of the Advent, Boston, in 1844 submitted that their Communion table was of pine, with four unmistakable legs, the candles being burnt only at night in preference to " gas fixtures ". But the Bishop was not appeased.

church furnished with an altar instead of a table standing on legs (1846). A war of pamphlets and newspaper correspondence ensued. The teaching of the General Theological Seminary, New York, was arraigned as " Puseyite ". In the same city there was a " scene " at an ordination. Two of the examiners (prominent clergy) publicly protested against the candidate's High Church views, and left the sanctuary. Bishop Onderdonk over-ruled the objection and proceeded. The placid surface of Protestant Episcopacy was disturbed by other storms.[1]

The spirited opposition of the Evangelicals did not arrest for long the advance of the High Church Party.[2] By a kind of " gentleman's agreement " guileless Low Churchmen made an incredibly foolish compromise in 1835; they arranged to concentrate on Foreign Missions, leaving Home Missions to their ritualist rivals. This short-sighted bargain, as suicidal as the one between Congregationalists and Presbyterians (p. 254 f) determined the type of Episcopalianism that was to be planted in the West. Evangelicals doubtless felt that it was a forlorn hope to extend westwards when they needed to consolidate in the East.[3] In any case, it seemed unlikely that the Prayer Book, even if backed by powerful preaching, would be suited to the frontier.

It was through chance reading of the Prayer Book at Dartmouth College that a young New Englander with the singular name of Philander Chase, was led to dedicate his life as a home missionary to the West. In the years that followed Waterloo he laboured in Ohio. His career has been dramatically depicted in stained glass by the late Mr. C. J. Connick (the Douglas Strachan of America). We see him leaving Hartford by coach, snow on the ground; then on horseback, armed with a lantern (" He braved the perils of

[1] Bishop Smith was tried for " inveracity ", with 198 specifications; verdict, " Guilty but without the least criminality "(!) Two bishops were suspended for moral delinquency. Bishop Doane was acquitted of the charge of mismanaging the funds of church schools.

[2] Horatio Southgate, a convert from Congregationalism, and afterwards a Bishop, was sent out east to establish contacts with the Greek Church, etc. (1844-9). He became so High as to cause consternation in the Protestant Episcopal Church. Cp. P. E. Shaw, *American Contacts with the Eastern Churches* (Chicago, 1937).

[3] Yet in New England, Bishop Hopkins of Vermont was an uncompromising Tractarian. He entered the church with slight theological training, passing from a law office to the rectorship of Trinity, New York. A self-made man, he differed from his fellow-clergy in being a facile platform speaker and extempore preacher, able to " put across " his ideas and gain a hearing from the common people.

the Wilderness "); he drives across the cracking ice of the Great Lakes; he visits the Mohawks; and he preaches to the settlers, using all that was possible of the Prayer Book (" the few present ' admired ' the prayers—it would have been better if they had joined in them "). These windows beautify Kenyon College, Gambier, Ohio. It was founded as a Log College in 1824. Chase went to England to collect funds. His rugged simplicity and earnestness touched the hearts and unloosened the purse-strings of his hearers. The chief benefactors were Lord Kenyon and Admiral Gambier (one of the commissioners who negotiated peace between Britain and the United States in 1814).

Philander Chase became the pioneer Bishop of Illinois in 1835. He was followed by successors of a more pronounced High Church type; these men gave the prevailing tone to congregations in the Middle West, who had never come across any other kind of churchmanship. Missionary priests would sometimes celebrate the Eucharist on " rude altars of rough stones distinguished by a rustic cross ". Generally, however, they missed the apostolic glory of not building on other men's foundations. They laboured, not with the advance guard of Methodists, Baptists and Presbyterians, but after the cruder sects had already broken ground and built settlements. Then they profited by the mistakes of their forerunners by offering a religion that made *some* appeal to man's latent sense of beauty; they exalted the sacraments; they avoided the sensational tricks of evangelism. They had to endure a certain amount of ridicule when they first appeared. Curiosity would draw frontier folk " to hear the night-gown preacher pray and his wife jaw back at him ". In course of time, however, the Episcopalians won proselytes as well as respect; they were joined by many American settlers of the second generation who had made a comfortable home for themselves and hoped to rise in the world; for many years they were about the only Protestant body that valued dignity and reverence in worship. Unfortunately, this encouraged their clergy to magnify the sacerdotal differences that separated them from their neighbours.

In the East, a number of recruits came into the Episcopal Church from Germans who had settled for several generations. Foremost among these was the great-grandson of the Pietist Apostle who ministered to incoming Lutherans in the eighteenth century. William Augustus Muhlenberg came to New York in

1846 as rector of the Church of the Holy Communion.[1] This
was an early " free " church—there were no pew rents. The poor
were made welcome and Muhlenberg (a rich man) embarked on
an energetic campaign to reach the people through deaconesses,
sisterhoods, hospitals and schools. It is a curious irony that the
descendant of a good German should have introduced into the
United States an imitation of the English " public school " for
the well-to-do.[2] These " Church schools " multiplied, the best-
known to-day being Groton, Massachusetts and, St. Paul's, New
Hampshire. Muhlenberg called himself an " Evangelical Catholic ". He claimed to have passed beyond the mere Tractarian
stage; he was a pioneer Broad Churchman who stressed in modern
manner the sacramental view of life. In 1853 he persuaded the
Episcopal General Convention to accept a memorial embodying
his ideals of a truly comprehensive Church.

By this time the Low Church party had declined so much
that the future of Evangelicalism seemed to be mere toleration
in a communion increasingly dominated by the agressive High
Church party. No opportunity was lost of arraigning clergymen
who co-operated with other denominations. During the meeting
of the World Evangelical Alliance in New York (1873) the Dean
of Canterbury, Dr. Payne Smith, and the Bishop of Kentucky,
George D. Cummins, took part in a united Communion service
in Fifth Avenue Presbyterian Church. Dean Smith paid no attention to High Church criticism, but Bishop Cummins wrote to the
presiding bishop of the Protestant Episcopal Church, intimating his
" purpose of transferring his work and office to another sphere ".
Nearly seven months before his trial and deposition, he organised
the " Reformed Episcopal Church ", in communion with other
Evangelical churches, but retaining the episcopate " as an ancient
and desirable form of church government rather than of divine
right ". Cummins consecrated Dr. C. E. Cheney of Chicago as
fellow bishop, thus securing episcopal continuity. The Prayer
Book was used, as before. In spite of sound claims to represent

---

[1] American Episcopalians adopted a new line of nomenclature, e.g. " Cathedral of the Incarnation ", " Church of the Transfiguration ", " Chapel of the
Beloved Disciple ". Evangelical parishes preferred " Calvary " and " Grace ".
Conventional English Churchmen visiting America often recorded disapproval
of such names.

[2] The Congregationalists were also to the fore in founding boys' boarding
schools, less consciously modelled on English precedent, e.g. the Phillips
Academies at Andover and at Exeter, N.H.

historic Anglican Protestantism, the Reformed Episcopal Church has only 9,000 communicants; the " Free Church of England " (1844) has an even smaller membership. Anglicanism may lose adherents, but does not have the urge to reproduce its doctrine and discipline in seceding bodies, after the manner of non-episcopal churches.

Some years earlier a split was feared when the Rev. Dudley Tyng, a fervent Evangelical, was reprimanded by his bishop for preaching in a Methodist church.[1] An anonymous Low Church-man of New York diocese expressed his view of the situation in vigorous verse:

> I saw a bishop lying flat,
>   Choking in gasps of agony,
> Trying to swallow down a gnat
>   That in his gullet chanced to fly.
> The insect had, while on the wing,
> Seemed buzzing out Tyng Tyng Tyng Tyng.
>
> Again I looked. With mouth agap
> The bishop takes a stertorous nap,
> When lo! a camel staggers by
> Loaded with priestly panoply;
> Bales of vestments on his hump,
>   While here a crucifix appears,
> A box of candles galled his rump,
>   And smoking incense scorched his ears.
>
> Before, behind, a savory crowd
>   Of greasy monks, with alb and cope,
> Intoned and chanted, crossed and bowed
>   Like Father Agapius or the Pope.
> The bishop slept; he took no note;
>   The caravan marched down his throat!
>
> .   .   .   .
>
> Was't Rome I saw, or was it not her ?
> Or did I dream, dear Bishop Potter ?

A very different bishop was Phillips Brooks, who was enthroned in the affections of all denominations before he was consecrated to the See of Massachusetts in 1891. Brooks outgrew the narrow Evangelicalism of his youth, like Robertson of Brighton, but with-

---

[1] His last message, after a fatal accident caused by farm machinery, was—" Tell them to stand up for Jesus; now let us sing a hymn." This inspired his friend, George Duffield, a Presbyterian minister, to write, " Stand up, stand up for Jesus ", which was sung at the memorial service.

stood the growing priestly tendencies of his own communion. He
was a loyal Episcopalian, but had definitely reformed convictions.
With warmth he opposed suggestions that the name " Protestant
Episcopal " be altered to grandiose titles such as " American
Catholic " or " American Church ". He preached in Presbyterian,
Baptist and Methodist Churches. He invited all Christians to
Holy Communion. He did not refuse spiritual fellowship to Unitarians. He followed the usual American custom of not wearing
clerical attire except at services. He did not deny the High
Church party the privilege of practising their own rites, but he
would not let them dominate a communion that was both " Protestant " and " Episcopal ". The broad, inclusive Churchmanship of Phillips Brooks not merely broke down cold aloofness, but
strengthened American Anglicanism far more effectively than
the nervous isolationism of ecclesiastics who trembled for the Ark.
" It is the spirit that quickeneth; the flesh profiteth nothing ".

   Although the Oxford Movement has leavened the Protestant
Episcopal Church for the past century, it has not furnished a
large annual quota of recruits to Rome like the Church of England.
Bishop Levi Silliman Ives of N. Carolina crossed the Rubicon in
1852 after much vacillation, along with a few young clergymen.
In the United States there was no exodus of laymen, such as
followed the secession of Newman and Manning (1845, 1850).
Ecumenically-minded Englishmen realised that what had become
a cloistered sect in their own land was " The Church " on the
Continent; and even in England a section of the nobility and
gentry had remained loyal to their ancestral faith. In America,
Catholicism had no such status; it was the religion of ignorant
immigrants. Even to-day, Dean Sperry writes: " Making one's
submission to Rome in this country . . . carries with it acceptance
of a predominantly Irish hierarchy and priesthood. Theological
issues quite apart, the readjustment of racial and cultural affilia-
tions . . . is more radical here than in England " (*Religion in
America*, p. 111). Again, Anglo-Catholicism, so popular in certain
quarters in the old country, has no exact " Americo-Catholic "
equivalent; save for the very elect, it has no propaganda-value;
" Catholicism without the Pope " is meaningless to most Americans, to whom a Catholic means a Romanist. However " High "
Churchmanship may become, it functions within a communion
definitely entitled " Protestant Episcopal ".

It was not till the Irish invasion of the 'forties that Roman Catholicism became a significant factor in the United States. Hitherto, the small English and French nuclei in Maryland and Louisiana had pursued a policy of accommodation rather than aggression. By 1880 some four and a half million Irish landed in America, burning with hatred against Anglo-Saxon hegemony.[1] Numerical increase bred self-confidence; a priesthood predominantly Irish had no reason to cultivate friendly relations with Protestants, and was well equipped to make successive swarms of foreign Catholics at home in the land of their adoption.[2] The hierarchy did not, however, find the Irish element altogether submissive. The laity showed a turbulent democratic spirit in one respect. They appointed trustees to hold church property; and these trustees claimed the right to appoint and dismiss priests. What was this but the recalcitrant spirit of Protestantism ? Bishop Hughes of New York set his face against such " Americanisation " (1837). Five out of the eight Catholic churches of the city went bankrupt and were sold by the sheriff. Hughes boldly bid in his own name, and afterwards got the faithful to make themselves responsible for the debt. In Philadelphia the Catholic bishop had to launch an interdict to secure control of his own cathedral.

When these ecclesiastics had set their house in order, they made use of the Irish vote to demand state support for their own voluntary, " parochial " schools. Protestants were alarmed. A native American party was started, with the object of restricting immigration in order to limit the number of religionists " subject to a foreign power ", the Papacy.[3] The " Know Nothing " movement was a secret organisation that made considerable headway between 1850 and 1860. If a member was interrogated, he said he " knew nothing about it ". The more reputable element of this party was concerned with the defence of American institutions against priest-ridden foreign immigrants, determined to score by " pressure politics". The less reputable element was concerned with the " Protestant underworld " that circulated propaganda of

[1] Foreign Catholics followed. In Chicago to-day there are 124 " English " R.C. churches, 35 German, 12 Italian, 8 Czech, 38 Polish, 9 Lithuanian, 10 Slovak, 4 Croatian, 5 French and several Mexican.
[2] Dr. Sweet considers that if " Protestantism saved the restless and reckless frontier from sinking into barbarism, Catholicism was the largest factor in keeping the American cities from becoming veritable Sodoms " (*The American Churches*, p. 48, London, 1947).
[3] R. A. Billington, *The Protestant Crusade*, 1800-1860 (New York, 1938).

Q

a sensational type. Maria Monk claimed to disclose convent horrors; she was exposed as a fraud, but never lacked supporters (the same kind of anti-Popery agitation flourished in England during the early Victorian period).[1] Riots occurred in the big eastern cities between " Native American " mobs and Irish hordes. A convent was burnt down near Boston and a Jesuit was tarred and feathered in Maine. The " Know Nothing " party was eclipsed by the Civil War in 1861, but many of its ideas were afterwards adopted by the Ku Klux Klan. It was one of the influences that contributed, through fear of Catholicism, to the largely prevalent American tradition that public education must be strictly secular. There were faults on both sides. An echo of this political-pressure-in-religion controversy was the rejection of " Al " Smith (R.C.) as Democratic candidate for the Presidency in 1928. No Roman Catholic as yet has been elected President.

During the Civil War, Bishop Hughes, himself the son of an immigrant, proved to be an eloquent advocate of the Union in European cities, the Catholic equivalent of Henry Ward Beecher. His achievements in the task of justifying the North against the Slave Power vindicated the patriotism of his co-religionists. Before the War, he had to fill his churches in New York with armed men, to protect them against a hostile mob. When peace came, he won tolerance for Catholic worship and crowned his work by the completion of St. Patrick's, a huge French Gothic cathedral in the heart of the metropolis (1879). Eventually Archbishop, he won public respect as a " good American ", while he was successful in checking the demand among some of his people for an autonomous " American Catholic Church ".

It is significant that the most notable American converts did not pass over the " bridge Church ", but reached it by swimming from one raft to another. Orestes Brownson[2] was never an Episcopalian. He was an enthusiastic Transcendentalist, a typical " universal reformer " of Emerson's generation. After being a Congregationalist, Universalist and Unitarian minister, he went over to Rome; as restless as ever, he proved an embarrassment rather than a trophy to the hierarchy. Another unusual convert was Isaac Hecker (1819-88). Hecker,[3] " a seven-footer with a

[1] Edward Hutton, *Catholicism and English Literature* (London, 1942).
[2] Professor A. M. Schlesinger, *Orestes A. Brownson, A Pilgrim's Progress* (Boston, 1939).
[3] Fr. Walter Elliott, *Life of Father Hecker* (New York, 1891).

divided beard ", was a social reformer of mystical tendencies; he took part in the Brook Farm experiment. The son of a German immigrant, he passed from Lutheranism to Methodism before being " received " in 1844. He was even more American in his outlook, than his New England friend, Brownson.[1] A thorough " activist ", Hecker's fond desire was to transform the Church of his adoption by substituting self-reliance and reason for passive obedience and authoritarianism. After being ordained in London by Cardinal Wiseman, Hecker founded the " Paulist Fathers " to carry out his democratic ideals. In Europe many liberal Catholics were influenced by the sincerity of his appeal, " let us go to the people! " In the United States his wide-awake, constructive mind and broad sympathies produced, for a time, a return to the happier relationships of Protestants and Roman Catholics which existed after the American Revolution. Archbishop Keane of Washington read papers at Protestant gatherings; Cardinal Gibbons opened the " World's Parliament of Religions " with prayer. The new orientation was not destined to last. Leo XIII expressly condemned " Americanism " (22nd January 1899). This put an end to " broad " interpretation of dogma, the attempt to bring together religion and science, and to fraternise with Protestants. The passive virtues were pointedly extolled: " Christianity is docility."

Thus Hecker's democratic movement was numbered with the " lost causes " a decade after his death. It was his avowed aim to " catholicise America " as well as to " Americanise Catholicism ". In 1868 he predicted that the United States would be a Catholic country by 1900. Had his " Americanism " prevailed, his Church might have registered further gains. It has held its own, but not outdistanced Protestantism,[2] for even in the heyday of immigration not all Catholics from central and southern Europe kept the faith. It is estimated that accessions to Roman Catholicism from outside the fold amount to about 40,000 annually, but this is

[1] Immigration has made Romanism the religion of two-fifths of New England, only about one-fifth being now Protestant. Cp. D. C. Brewer, *The Conquest of New England by the Immigrant* (New York, 1926).

[2] Dorchester proved by statistics and graphs that the Protestant increase in membership exceeded R.C. growth, their losses in New England being more than balanced in the S.W., etc. (*Christianity in U.S.*, 1895). H. C. Weber has confirmed this trend (1800-1900), adding that immigration restrictions have caused a sharp decline in R.C. annual increase (*Evangelism : A Graphic Survey* (New York, 1929).

balanced by leakages to unbelief and to Protestantism. Some 60,000 ex-Catholics are grouped in small denominations (Methodist, Episcopal, Baptist, etc.) according to nationality (Polish, Italian, Magyar, Mexican, etc.).[1] The Roman Church, weakened by the reduction of immigration to a mere trickle, has become less palpably foreign owing to the operation of the melting-pot. Superficially it is assimilated to the American way of life; but culturally it lags behind.[2] This solid minority, one-third of the population, is an emphatic and persistent protest against the dominantly Protestant pattern of American religion.

[1] T. Abel, *Protestant Home Missions to Catholic Immigrants* (Instit. of Social and Rel. Research, New York, 1933).

[2] In 1932 R.C.'s numbered only 3% of the names in *Who's Who in America*.

BOOK IV

THE FRONTIER AND THE FAITH

THE SOUTH WEST

" The psychology of the frontier corresponds in many respects with the faith of the disinherited."—H. RICHARD NIEBUHR

CHARLES and Mary Beard in their massive but eminently readable *Rise of American Civilisation* (1930) have given a full account of the moving frontier that transformed the original thirteen states into a nation whose centre of gravity tended to shift steadily westward. Manifold motives impelled millions to pack up and venture all—economic depression in the East, frustration among poor whites in the South, land hunger, desire for a freer life. The years that followed the promulgation of the United States Constitution saw a series of westward trails opening up. There was the Mohawk Valley, leading from New England, and the Valley of Virginia; passes led through the Appalachian Mountains into Kentucky and Tennessee (which had become states as early as 1792 and 1796). By way of western New York the settlers poured into the " North Western Territory " (soon to become Ohio), and down the Ohio River they sailed in great flat boats. The sale of Louisiana by Napoleon opened to unimpeded American traffic the " father of waters ", which was quickly transformed into the easiest of highways.

On the frontier flaming sins and cultural crudity flourished. Even weddings and funerals degenerated into drunken orgies. Horace Bushnell diagnosed the situation in a searching pamphlet, *Barbarism the First Danger* (1847). Transplantation denuded settlers of social sense. "All the old roots of local and historic feeling—the joints and bands which minister nourishment—are left behind."

Evangelism called for " the expulsive power of a new affection ". Boanerges succeeded where Apollos would have failed.

The Presbyterians had been to the fore in the Great Awakening, but could not adapt themselves to frontier conditions as strategically as the Baptists. The Congregationalists were not hampered, like the Presbyterians, by the restrictions imposed by Church Courts, but insisted on maintaining their ideals of an educated ministry and the ordered methods of settled parishes. The Baptists flourished on the frontier despite the rigid independency of their congregations. They were almost as Calvinistic as the Presbyterians and Congregationalists. " Election " was capable of being given a democratic interpretation; in New England the doctrine tended to enhance the power of the clergy and the well-to-do. On the frontier, rough preachers made it clear that God's choice of " the elect " had nothing to do with worldly position. " The illiterate son of the border might just as well be a divinely chosen vessel as the cultured gentleman." The Methodists, latecomers compared to other sects, were hindered by no scruples about the " limitation of the atonement " and the " natural inability " of the sinner to repent. They preached full and free salvation to all. Their nominal theology, Arminianism, they derived from their Episcopalian parents. Poor child of an aristocratic Church, Methodism was ardent, while her mother was cool and conventional. Formal theology meant little on the frontier; it was the emphasis, the tone and the understanding of backwoods psychology that mattered most. Earnestness, fluency and adaptability carried most weight; the theological subtilty that appealed to seasoned New England farmers cut no ice on the frontier.

Broadly speaking, we may say that on the *Northern frontier* " New School Calvinism " prevailed, provided that Evangelical ardour irradiated doctrinal scholasticism, whether the missionaries were Congregational or Presbyterian. The *Southern frontier* was the chosen sphere of Arminians, who had the requisite emotional drive, appealing to the heart rather than the mind, whether the missionaries were Methodist or Baptist.[1]

In this chapter we shall deal with the frontier in the South and South West. Here there was close rivalry between the Baptists and Methodists. The latter had the joint advantages of centralised direction and mobility. Methodist circuit-riders were under orders, working to plan in co-operation with their fellow-preachers,

---

[1] Professor Sweet compares these two approaches to the settler in *Revivalism in America* (New York, 1944).

and not subject to the authority of their flocks, like Baptist pastors. The marvel of Methodism is its unique, rapid success in a new country to which it was an entire stranger.

Methodism made comparatively few converts in New England except among the poorer classes; and even then, political cross-currents had some influence in drawing the unprivileged from the " Standing Order " with its Federalist bias to a dissenting body that found Jeffersonian democracy more congenial. In the South Methodism advanced rapidly, making a host of converts among the nominal adherents of the Church of England. In some Southern cities, notably Baltimore, Wesley's way attracted even the educated classes. Methodism in its early phase was essentially of the South; in 1779 all but 319 of the growing membership lived across the " Mason and Dixon line ". From the Southern base, the hosts of Methodism set out for the winning of the West.

In the chapter on the Great Awakening we dealt with the arrival of Methodist missionaries from England, and marked their progress, despite the rupture between the United Kingdom and the United States. We then proceeded to describe the landing of Bishop Asbury and the organisation of the Methodist Episcopal Church. We are now in a position to consider his achievements as arch-evangelist.

Francis Asbury, Englishman though he was, knew well how to evangelise frontier folk. A graduate of the " university of life ", he had no time to waste on theological controversy. Since his arrival in America in 1771, he excelled even Wesley in " journeyings oft ", since the obstacles of nature surpassed anything to be encountered in England. For forty-four years this apostle with white locks flowing over his shoulders traversed mountains, rivers, swamps and forests. When he and his fellow-Methodists were under suspicion as Tories and Englishmen during the American Revolution, they retreated to the " back settlements ". Necessity proved to be a door of opportunity, for when peace came in 1783 " the flame of religion spread far and wide ".

Asbury's appointment as " Superintendent " of the new " Methodist Episcopal Church " involved no retirement to city headquarters. He continued to itinerate, adding supervision to his missionary task. No " ornamental bishop ", he travelled over 250,000 miles, claimed 300,000 converts and ordained 4,000 preachers. Like Wesley, he read assiduously on his arduous journeys and carefully recorded his experiences in a Journal.[1] He had every qualification for his task, it appears, save a sense of humour. His austerity found no place for the ordinary comforts and graces of life. As early as 1780 he became a teetotaller and pressed his itinerants to follow his example, about fifty years before total abstinence ceased to be regarded as an oddity. Like Wesley, he believed in personal authority rather than in committees, but never asked his preachers to submit to hardships which he was not prepared to undergo himself. His task was not to *find* Methodists among the settlers, but to *make* them out of raw material. Nor was his influence limited to Anglo-Saxons, for a collaborator, Wilhelm Otterbein, did much to spread Methodism among his German fellow-immigrants, founding the " United Brethren in Christ " (1800).

The following scheme, based on Wesleyan precedent, was devised by Asbury. Each " preacher " (carefully selected and supervised) was to itinerate round twenty to thirty places in his " circuit "; and every preaching-post would be a nucleus of Evangelism, the people being enrolled according to age in small groups under " class-leaders ". The circuits were arranged in districts, each in charge of a " Presiding Elder " (always an ordained man); he visited every circuit quarterly, conferred with the class-leaders, preached, and administered the sacraments; the visit of the Presiding Elder was always a happy event breaking the monotony of the daily round.

A " circuit-rider " had to be tough as well as fervent, accustomed to deal with bullies and drunkards, and capable of soundly converting men more familiar with the bowie-knife than the prayer-meeting. He started off on horseback, with his library at hand (Bible, Hymnal and " Discipline "). " He plunged through swamps, swam swollen streams, lay out all night with his saddle-bags for a pillow and his old big coat for a blanket. Often he slept in dirty cabins, on earthen floors, before the fire; ate roasting ears for bread, took bear-meat or wild turkey for breakfast, dinner and supper—if he could get it." This is a transcript from the daily life of Peter Cartwright, who preached for about seventy years in Illinois. His shrewdness and wit, faith and courage, remind us of another Illinois man, Abraham Lincoln. We turn the pages of Cartwright's utterly sincere *Autobiography* (New York,

[1] *The Heart of Asbury's Journal*, ed. Tipple (New York, 1904).

1856)[1] and the man is embodied before our eyes. He probably provoked the proverb commonly repeated in wintry weather, " There is nothing out to-day but crows and Methodist preachers." Peter Cartwright was a short, thickset man with a fine head but black beady eyes and dishevelled hair. He was not prepossessing, but he won the hearts of the frontiersmen. With engaging frankness, he confessed: " We murdered the King's English at almost every lick. But there was a divine unction . . . and the Methodist Episcopal Church was planted firmly in the western wilderness." It was not surprising that Methodism forged ahead and outstripped denominations that were less mobile in their methods.

Cartwright was a veritable " Friar Tuck ". When personal appeal and humour failed, he had other resources—a sharp tongue and a kind of holy " knock 'em down power " that was often irresistible. On one occasion he was attacked by a mob, whose ring-leaders carried loaded whips. His supporters faltered, the magistrates fell back, and the situation was only under control after he had taken the lead.[2] He quelled the riot, ordered the trumpet to be blown and the encampment lighted up. He then stepped forward and preached from the text, " The gates of hell shall not prevail! " " In about thirty minutes," he explained, " the power of God fell on the congregation . . . not less than three hundred fell, like dead men in a battle, strewed all over the camp-ground. Our meeting lasted all Sunday night, and Monday, and Monday night, and when we closed on Tuesday there were 200 who had professed religion, and about that number joined the Church."

Cartwright had grown up in Logan County, Kentucky, which was known as " Rogues Harbor " because an actual majority of its " citizens " were horse-thieves, highway-robbers, counterfeiters and murderers. It was to Logan County that the Rev. James McGready came in 1796 to storm this stronghold of Satan. His amazing ministry culminated in the first great " Camp-Meeting ", held on Cane Ridge in August 1801. An army officer estimated that there were 20,000 present.

" The remembrance of that fateful gathering lingers in Kentucky after the lapse of a century. Nothing was lacking to stir to their profoundest depths the imagination and emotion of this great throng of

---

[1] The *Autobiography* does not mention the fact that Cartwright was twice a member of the Illinois legislature; he " ran " against Lincoln unsuccessfully.
[2] Methodist preachers were prominent in politics, e.g. Tiffin, first Governor of Ohio, after whom a city is named.

men, women and children. It was at night that the most terrible scenes were witnessed, when the camp-fires blazed in a mighty circle around the vast audience of pioneers bowed in devotion. Beyond, was the blackness of the primeval forest; above, the night wind and the foliage and the stars. As the darkness deepened, the exhortations of the preachers became more fervent and impassioned; their picturesque prophecies of doom more lurid and alarming; the volume of song burst all bonds of guidance and control, and broke again and again from the throats of the people; while over all, at intervals, there rang out the shout of ecstasy, the sob and the groan."[1]

Not only so. Weird " motor automatisms " appeared and inhibitions disappeared under the influence of mass hysteria. Votaries would crawl on all fours; in groups they would surround a tree and proceeded to yelp, bark and snap; this exercise was called " treeing the devil ". A more nervous paroxism was known as " the jerks ": the head was shaken violently, the body bent double, and the feet so affected that the victim would jump about like a frog! Cartwright saw 500 people " jerking at once " and noticed that the morbid contagion possessed even those who came to scoff.[2] Bishop Asbury was much more sympathetic to these emotional extravagances than his master, John Wesley.[3] Yet Lorenzo Dow, craziest of evangelists,[4] actually crossed the Atlantic and shocked cautious Wesleyans by utterances, attire and behaviour reminiscent of the more primitive Hebrew Prophets. Obviously the " Camp-Meeting " as a revival technique required considerable adaptation for English conditions.[5]

In America many religious leaders were afraid to discourage "manifestations" owing to their popularity, hoping devoutly (like St. Paul) that " by *all* means some might be saved ". The " Second Great Awakening " (1801) spread rapidly throughout the United States. It assumed its most characteristic, intense form in the South West. Territories like Missouri were settled mainly by poor whites from the South, and these frontiersmen were illiterate, superstitious and desperately poor. Methodism

---

[1] F. M. Davenport, *Primitive Traits in Religious Revivals*, p. 75 (New York, 1905). A standard book, sociological and psychological.
[2] For an illuminating analysis, see Dr. G. Steven's *Psychology of the Christian Soul*, 2nd ed., (Edinburgh, 1911).
[3] According to Asbury's latest biographer, Herbert Asbury—*A Methodist Saint* (New York, 1927).
[4] Dow could be incisive at lucid intervals. He nicknamed the Calvinists " A-L-L Part men " (where *all* occurs in the Bible, they read *part*).
[5] The Camp-Meeting at Mow Cop, Staffordshire (1807) caused the Primitive Methodist secession from Wesleyanism.

brought them the Gospel hot and strong. Like the Christians of Corinth in St. Paul's time, they " got religion ", and felt it coursing through their veins—" a conquering, new-born joy ", They wanted " celebration rather than cerebration ", and thus ousted the Presbyterians who had been first on the field. They were too staid, these Presbyterians—what douce elder would revel in " jerking, barking, and the holy laugh " ? And what Presbyterian pastor would like to hear an educated ministry described by Cartwright as " a lettuce growing under a peach tree " ?

Some Presbyterians, however, felt the burden of conventional restrictions and hived off to work on lines more suited to the frontier. Thus in 1810 a number of them left the mother church to form the " Cumberland Presbyterian Church " in the backward mountain district associated nowadays with the " hill-billies ".[1] Revivalists who emphasised the universal appeal of the Gospel naturally found difficulty with the Calvinist doctrines of Election and Predestination. In Kentucky the " New Lights " felt like this. Barton W. Stone therefore seceded and with five ministers formed the " Springfield Presbytery ". After a few years, however, they dissolved their presbytery[2] and replaced it by a loose grouping of congregations, which they modestly called " The Christian Church ".[3] Elder Stone, re-examining the New Testament, found that it taught Immersion. This brought him into line with the Baptists. These sturdy individualists had arrived early on the frontier scene.[4] They eschewed the authoritarian organisation of the Methodists, though they had their " Associations " which licensed and ordained candidates for the ministry. Their preachers, however, were uneducated men who accepted no salary and farmed five or six days in the week. Baptist congregations usually built their little log chapels on the banks of rivers which were useful for immersion—hence the names of the churches—" Gilbert's Creek ", " Big Crossing ", etc.

[1] The majority of this sect recently rejoined the Presbyterian Church.
[2] Leaving a document which is an ecclesiastical curiosity, " The Last Will and Testament of the Springfield Presbytery " (1804). His *Autobiography* was published at Cincinnati (1847).
[3] It is surprising that their organ, the *Herald of Gospel Liberty*, is the oldest religious paper in America. It was published continuously from 1808 to 1931, when it was incorporated with the *Congregationalist* (the surviving " Christians " having joined forces with those of the Pilgrim faith).
[4] They have had a tendency to split on proof-texts. Thus we find " Seventh Day Baptists ", " Free Will Baptists ", " Hard Shell Baptists " and " Soft " ditto., even " Glory Hallelujah Baptists "

Another Presbyterian group was finding that the Revival type of religious experience and a preference for simple New Testament teaching in place of creeds and confessions drew them towards fellowship with the Baptists. They would not have agreed with the Free Church minister in Ross-shire, who, finding himself in difficulties with the knotty points of the day, addressed his expectant congregation: " Ah, my friends, these things are difficult. They are dangerous. They are not for you. They are for theologians, like myself! " On the frontier every man was his own theologian, and the most ignorant was often the most dogmatic. Earnest desire to return to the essentials of the Apostolic Church merely produced another sect. There is a striking instance of this tendency in the " Disciples of Christ ", which has grown to the stature of almost a major American denomination.

One autumn morning in 1808 the *Hibernia* was wrecked off the Hebrides on her way from Ireland to America. Among the immigrants was a Mrs. Thomas Campbell and her seven children. As her oldest son, Alexander, watched the women and their babies being taken ashore, he meditated on the theme: " How transitory are all worldly security and ambition! " On the spot he dedicated himself to the spiritual realities that could never be wrecked. Several hours before the ship sank, the youth had been reading that searching seventeenth-century classic, *The Marrow of Modern Divinity*, which had so marked an influence on the Scots Seceders of the eighteenth century. It was providential for Alexander Campbell that the family had to postpone their voyage till the winter was over. He was twenty years of age and of an enquiring mind. What could be more appropriate than a session at Glasgow, the University frequented by Ulstermen and his father's *Alma Mater*? To Glasgow he went, and there he toiled at study, rising daily at four a.m. What really mattered, however, was his contact with sects that modified his strict Presbyterian tradition. The followers of the Haldanes[1] taught him the value of lay-leadership in Evangelism. The Glasites taught him to go back to the Apostolic Church and restore such primitive rites as weekly Communion.[2]

[1] The Haldane Brothers, prevented from evangelising India, spent their fortune by training lay preachers for Home Missions. Leaving the Kirk, they became Independent, latterly Baptist.

[2] Had Campbell reached Glasgow twenty years later he would have found Irvingites, who claimed restoration of the " gifts " and " order " of primitive Christianity. It would be interesting to speculate how far Campbell's contact with the " Catholic Apostolic Church " would have modified his views.

Alexander's father, Thomas Campbell, had been an "Old Light Anti-Burgher" minister and teacher at Richhill, County Armagh. Weary of his impossibly narrow congregation and financially embarrassed, he decided to start afresh in the United States, leaving Alec to take charge of the school, till he could afford to bring the family over. Thomas brought his credentials to the Anti-Burghers of Philadelphia, whom he found even more rigid than in Ulster. Guilty of "violating their seal and testimony", he organised a "Christian Association" at the frontier settlement of Washington, in the "Redstone Country" of Pennsylvania. Weary of creeds and confessions, he sought relief from Protestant scholasticism by the simple expedient of accepting "the Bible and the Bible only" (to use Chillingworth's classic phrase). Like the disciples at the Transfiguration, he "saw Jesus only"; he was pained by the rival watchwords of "Paul, Cephas and Apollos". This "Back to Christ Movement" he inaugurated by publishing a *Declaration and Address*: "Where the Scriptures speak, we speak; where the Scriptures are silent, we are silent." This manifesto was in the printer's hands when news came that his family had arrived safely in America (1809).

"Father, I accept that plea for Christian union," said Alexander; "I believe it implicitly and now I devote all that I am or hope to be to this cause." The youth went ahead. He preached his first sermon in July 1810 and married Margaret Brown, daughter of a prosperous farmer at Bethany (now in the state of West Virginia). This made him financially independent. The Campbells organised the "Brush Run Church" at Bethany (1811). Shortly afterwards they introduced Immersion, which brought them into communion with the Baptists. Thomas liked to speak about "our brethren of all denominations". It was not long, however, before Alexander incurred the displeasure of the Redstone Baptist Association. He opposed their ultra-Calvinism; but apart from that, he was not inclined to pull together with any but docile followers; he was controversial, iconoclastic, and cranky. Yet his preaching was lit up with flashes of real insight, e.g. his *Sermon on the Law* (1816), which declared that Christians were entirely emancipated from the law of Moses. On the other hand, he attacked such "human innovations" as Sunday Schools and Missionary Societies. As editor of the *Millenial Harbinger* he opposed the anti-slavery movement for some years, taking the pessimistic view that evil must take its course till routed by the imminent Second Coming of Christ.

The Campbellite movement might never have come to anything but for certain notable accessions and alliances. A Dumfriesshire man named Walter Scott, an Edinburgh graduate, landed in New York and fell in with a proselytising companion on the road to Philadelphia. Scott was converted to the views of Alexander Campbell, joined him, and proved an ardent and successful evangelist. The " Feeble Disciples " were not long in adding to their number. They contacted the revivalist group that had already detached itself from the Presbyterian Church under Elder Barton W. Stone (see above p. 241). These good people had aligned themselves with the Baptists (like the Disciples) but derived no satisfaction from their fellowship. They called themselves by the modest title of " Christians " (pronounced *Christ-ians*). What more natural than a union of these two groups of " primitive Christian " believers ? They came together at Lexington, Kentucky, in 1832. Campbell insisted on the title " Disciples of Christ ", but agreed to the use of Stone's alternative name, " Christians ". The brethren set before them Apostolic precedent: " They continued stedfastly in the apostles' doctrine and fellowship, breaking bread . . . with gladness and singleness of heart."

The united fellowship had a stormy course, although its origin was irradiated with something like the cheering light of the Early Church. Everyone was " brother This and sister That ", but individualism made for selfishness. Extreme undependency was pushed so far that disintegration seemed inevitable. Those who protested against " legalism " would do nothing unless expressly sanctioned in the New Testament. Those who accused the regular Churches of " sectarianism " proceeded to found a new sect and then split again![1]

Alexander Campbell defined the church as " essentially, intentionally and constitutionally one ". Paradoxically, this Apostle of Christian Unity spent his life in controversy. His grandfather

---

[1] In 1906 the U.S. Census listed the statistics of the body in two sects— " Disciples of Christ " and " Churches of Christ ". The latter title is used in the British branch. " We do not claim to be ' the only Churches of Christ ' but ' Churches of Christ only ' " (Principal Robinson, *What Churches of Christ stand for*, Berean Press, 1929). It is interesting to note that Lloyd George only became a Baptist because he could find no " Church of Christ " in London, like that in Wales. (" I learned all my democracy from Alexander Campbell and Abraham Lincoln.")

revolted from the Church of Rome, his father revolted from
Anglicanism, and he himself revolted from Presbyterianism. We
think of him as editor of the *Millenial Harbinger*, arguing inces-
santly that the Second Coming would occur in 1866 (the year of
his own death). We watch him debating publicly, in approved
Victorian style, with bishops,[1] Presbyterian divines, and unbelievers like Robert Owen.

Campbell was a queer mixture, almost defying analysis. His
attacks on the clergy as " stall-fed " and " agents for milking
schemes " did not come well from the richest man in West Virginia, a farmer too. Frontier ministers were usually a cadaverous,
ill-clad and ill-fed class! B. L. Smith, Campbell's eulogistic biographer (1930), thinks that his attitude was " largely responsible
for the lack of respect shown to-day to Protestant ministers ".
His criticism of culture as the foe of plain godliness did not prevent him sitting for twenty-five years in the President's chair of
Bethany College, West Virginia. His suspicion of synods carried
him to absurd tirades against organisations for making Missions
effectual (reminding one of Edward Irving's attacks on modern
methods in the foreign field). Campbell re-galvanised the old
Presbyterian prejudice against organs, which in America was sub-
siding. He wrote a *Christian System* (1835), yet declaimed against
the metaphysical subtilties of creeds and confessions. Dogmas
were but " inferences and deductions from the Scriptures, not
formally binding on the conscience " further than the devout
Christian could " perceive the connexion ".

This foe of " innovations ", this advocate of " the Restoration
of the Ancient Order of Things ", incurred the hostility of nearly
all Protestants by departing from generally accepted views of
Scripture. He insisted that the Bible was an historical book,
varying in value according to periods, and not a uniform collection
of " proof-texts ". He stressed the New Testament to such an
extent that the Baptists accused him of " throwing away the Old
Testament ". He did not appease them by translating *baptizo* as
" immerse " in his revision of the New Testament (*Living Oracles*,
1826). Most people at that time were shocked at the very idea of
correcting the King James Bible by a modern translation. N.T.

---

[1] His disputation with Bishop Purcell (R.C.) attracted so much attention
that 15,000 copies of the proceedings were sold within a year. Both contro-
versialists hit hard, but became personal friends till death. This kind of thing
could happen in America, hardly in Europe.

R

emphasis led him to deny the binding force of O.T. institutions (e.g. the letter of the " Sabbath", in contrast to the spirit of the " Lord's Day "). Those who observed the Lord's Supper only a few times each year were surprised at his plea for a weekly Communion—when this is not done, he announced, " New Testament worship ceases ". Evangelicals were disconcerted by his emphasis on the ethical teaching of Jesus (" to obey the Gospel " was a favourite phrase). Orthodox Protestants had almost lost sight of the practical teaching of Jesus in their devotion to Pauline terminology. Campbell drew attention to the concrete, vivid imagery of the Gospels, which had been so much neglected. Without being in any sense drawn to Unitarianism, he simplified belief, making it personal rather than doctrinal. Christians should accept " the Christ, the Son of the living God ", rather than a body of abstract doctrines about Him—which reminds us of John Oxenham's lines—" Not what, but Whom I do believe."

It will be realised that Alexander Campbell anticipated many of the trends worked out in detail by the Higher Critics; his insight laid bare approaches to the right understanding of Christ and the Bible which are now accepted by most Reformed Churches. What Tennyson said of King Arthur may be applied to Campbell's influence on the Disciples. " He laid his mind upon their minds, and they believed in his beliefs." While rejecting infant baptism as " baptism by proxy ", Disciples accept immersion, not in an exclusive sectarian sense, but as " the primitive confession of Christ "; they assent to the conviction of the Nicene Creed: " We believe in one baptism for the remission of sins." They now avoid the extremes of emotional Revivalism and Modernism. Professor D. E. Walker says of his co-religionists: " The Disciples are a pragmatic people; they refuse to take theology very seriously. Every opinion is subjected to two tests: Is it in harmony with the Scriptures ? and, Does it square with common sense ? And the verdict is returned, not in a court of law, but in open discussion before all the brethren."[1]

The Disciples have outgrown to some extent the crudities of their frontier origin. They have no longer an undiluted horror of culture and symbolism.[2] The line of demarcation between minis-

---

[1] *Adventuring for Christian Unity*, p. 39 (Berean Press, Birmingham, 1935).
[2] There is a great difference between their rural and city churches. Their University Church and " Disciples' Divinity House ", Chicago (associated with Professor E. Scribner Ames, the psychologist) represent the progressive wing.

ters and laymen is indeed thin; for many years they objected to the titles " Reverend " and even " Pastor ", allowing only the ambiguous name, " Elder "; they have a lingering prejudice against D.D.'s (salutary in a country where honorary degrees are too easily granted). Disciples claim to recapitulate in their own experience what the first generation of disciples underwent. This apostolic spirit implies fellowship and considerable informality, Congregationalism being carried to its extreme limit. Their fidelity to the early Christian precedent of a weekly Eucharist has corrected egocentric egotism in the pulpit; unfortunately their preaching service follows the Communion, thus reversing the historic analogy of an ascent from instruction (" Synagogue ") to the intimacy of the Upper Room. The Lord's Supper is celebrated as a feast expressing Christ's real presence, not simply observed as a memorial.

After little more than a century the Disciples have spread to thirty-five countries. In the United States, they now number over two million (fifth largest membership in the Union); this is significant in view of the fact that in most of their churches only immersed believers are counted as " members ". Their leaders have claimed that there has been no case of such rapid increase since the Apostolic Age of a body so loosely organised. The Disciples are democratic to the core. Here is a product of the frontier that has had within its fellowship the capacity to meet spiritual needs that remain when the frontier of the " wild west " has ceased to exist.

CHAPTER II

" THE PLAN OF UNION " (1801)

" All America seems to be breaking up and moving westward."
EMERSON (1817)

FROM the American Revolution to the close of the Napoleonic wars we notice a striking contrast between the ebbing of religion in the East and its floodtide in the West. Economic forces urged men westwards, offering fresh opportunities and producing a different attitude to life. The East was orderly, conservative, conventional: the West was rough, experimental, democratic. The East was still influenced by the cultural standards of Europe: the West had no time for anything save the satisfaction of the rudimentary needs of body and soul.

New England Congregationalism was in a strong position when the United States became a nation. It had been the spearhead of American Independence among the churches. It survived as a " Standing Order ", while the Anglican Establishments of the South collapsed. Yet this virile, compact body had somehow lost the adventurous spirit of the Pilgrim faith; it lacked confidence in the conviction that its future lay in the West. Potentially national in its combination of Evangelical doctrine and democratic autonomy, it shrunk for a time to the level of a regional church. Its leaders had no sense of " manifest destiny ". They doubted whether Congregationalism was adapted to the rough-and-tumble of the frontier. They looked towards New York and Pennsylvania, where the Scots-Irish were forging ahead; Presbyterianism seemed to be an instrument better adapted for the winning of the West. Had New Englanders looked further South than the " Middle States " they would have realised that the Baptists, the most successful frontier denomination, were incorrigibly Congregationalist in their insistence on local autonomy. That was no insuperable barrier to advance, even in competition with the " drive " of centralised Methodism.

Were New Englanders entirely preoccupied with doctrinal controversies, political feuds and post-war rehabilitation ? Their own sons and daughters were crossing the Hudson in increasing numbers towards the close of the eighteenth century, and pushing into the fertile land of Ohio. The Ordinances of this " Western Reserve " (1787) prohibited slavery and set aside 640 acres for the support of religion and a similar amount for education. It was obvious that the descendants of the Pilgrims and Puritans had inherited ancestral vigour and resourcefulness. If Thomas Hooker led his congregation from Boston to Hartford across the wilderness in the seventeenth century, Manasseh Cutler, of Hamilton, Mass., led his flock in 1786 a great deal further without modern transport. He was instrumental in opening up the " North-west Territory ". Cutler was citizen, scientist and preacher. He had scarcely founded Marietta, Ohio (named in honour of Marie Antoinette, 1788), than he planned a University. By 1821 Ohio was the fifth largest state in the Union; and of twelve new states, ten lay west of the Alleghany Mountains. The settlers included a much larger number of educated men than the frontier further South—intelligent farmers, business men, teachers and mechanics. As the " Middle West " filled up, New England institutions were planted on the prairie—the elm-shaded village green with steeples and cupolas, its meeting house, school (often an " academy "), and court-house. In a remarkably short time the crudity of frontier life gave way to order, decency and neatness.[1] Even beauty flowered in Greek Revival architecture, spacious squares and tree-lined streets. Dr. Truslow Adams, the historian, surveying America from the Hudson to the Pacific, observes: " Wherever we find Congregationalism, town government and the village school, we may trace the triple influence straight to New England." Was there any weighty reason why the " Pilgrim Faith " should not march west ? New England had a population of over a million at the close of the Revolutionary War, one-third of the federated states. A considerable majority of the citizens were Congregationalists: they belonged to a fertile stock well able to hold its own with any other. Why, then, this lack of confidence ?

---

[1] Naturally, there was another side to the picture. When H. W. Beecher was installed in Brooklyn (1847), a strict New England minister asked if he believed in " The Perseverance of the Saints ". " I used to . . . but when I went out West and saw how the New England Saints behaved when they got there, I gave it up." The Ecclesiastical Council questioned him no further.

In 1801 the General Association of Connecticut concluded a remarkable " Plan of Union " with the Presbyterian General Assembly (they had already co-operated during the " Bishop " scare in a " plan of union for preserving " their religious liberty, 1766-75). It was not fusion or federation, but a " gentleman's agreement " as to the future relationship of Congregationalists and Presbyterians. Presbyterians pledged themselves to seek no future extension in New England. That was a pledge easy to keep. In a region where there were only small pockets of Scots-Irish (e.g. around Londonderry, New Hampshire) there was no point in starting feeble Presbyterian causes in competition with the regular parochial system of the Congregationalists. Congregationalists, on the other hand, were to co-operate with Presbyterians in working out a " mixed " polity (only to apply to the new areas of the West).[1] We shall examine this " Presbygational " system set up by the Act of Union and discover just why this scheme made Congregationalists tributory to Presbyterians.

It was not merely the challenge of Home Missions that drew Congregationalists and Presbyterians together. There was doctrinal unity, Calvinism; and there was more affinity in church government than might be supposed. Some of the early Puritans, John Eliot, for instance, were drawn towards Presbyterian polity. Later leaders of the theocracy, like Cotton Mather, felt likewise. In 1708 Connecticut accepted the " Saybrook Programme ", whereby " Consociations " were to set up (one or more in each county); they had practically the authority of Presbyteries, and indeed the name Presbyterian was freely used throughout the province. right into the nineteenth century.[2] Massachusetts, on the other hand, was not enamoured of Presbyterianism; she advanced from Independency to " Association ", but would not go so far as " Consociation ". This line of division coincided to a large extent with divergent doctrines. Eastern Massachusetts, which was influential in population, wealth and culture, " went liberal " in the eighteenth century. It was susceptible to winds of doctrine that blew across the Atlantic—Arminianism, Socinianism, and finally Unitarianism. It had no sympathy with the hide-

---

[1] Even the Congregational Home Missionary Society (founded 1826) advised young preachers going West to get Presbyterian ordination.

[2] Hartford North Consociation claimed for Connecticut " the essentials of the Church of Scotland or Presbyterian Church in America, particularly as it gives a decisive power to Ecclesiastical Councils ".

bound Calvinism, the Edwardian revivalism of the backward *hinterland*. Western Massachusetts and Connecticut had no sympathy with heretical movements in the " East ". Men like Timothy Dwight and Jonathan Edwards the younger were naturally drawn towards the Presbyterians who gloried in the same rigid doctrine. The Great Awakening (and its sequel of 1797-1802) fused " New Light " Congregationalists and " New Light " Presbyterians; they felt that they could go forward with confidence to the joint enterprise of winning the West by avoiding fratricidal competition. " Old Light " Presbyterians did not look with much favour on fraternising of this kind. It upset the balance of the church of their fathers, it introduced alien practices. If, however, the alliance were to be confined to the frontier it might not prove so dangerous. After all, the united front presented by the " Congregational, Consociated and Presbyterian Churches " before the Revolution had been one of the means of preventing the establishment of an Anglican Episcopate in America (1766-75).

The " Plan of Union " ushered in the nineteenth century of Home Mission activity and must be judged as a missionary expedient rather than as a careful attempt to fuse two classic polities. It was laid before the General Association of Connecticut by three Presbyterian delegates and " promptly ratified without alteration " (1801). Massachusetts and the other New England States were not consulted. " The Connecticut Association committed with the best of intentions the westward movement of Congregationalism to the control and consequence of the Plan, and for the simplest of reasons: it held the keys by geography and precedence in missionary enterprise to the gateways of the West for New England."[1]

The " Plan of Union " provided that Presbyterian ministers could be called to Congregational pulpits and *vice versa*. " Mixed churches " were to be administered by a " standing committee ", which was to appoint one of its members to sit and act in the Presbytery as a ruling elder. This was un-Presbyterian practice, but the major advantages worked out in favour of the more highly organised body. The voluntary " Associations " did not materialise, but faded into the background, while Presbyteries became solid realities. On Congregational principles, a church might vote

[1] G. G. Atkins and F. L. Fagley, *History of American Congregationalism*, p. 144 (Boston, 1942).

itself into a *willing* Presbytery: on Presbyterian principles, it could not extricate itself by a majority vote of communicants. These are the bare outlines of the Plan of Union. The consequences were striking. Up to two thousand churches, in origin and usages Congregational, were transformed into Presbyterian charges (the actual statistics are still debated, but not the effects). The Middle West was lost to the men of the " Pilgrim Faith ".[1]

Dr. H. M. Dexter, the Church historian, has spoken of " Presbyterianised Congregationalism and Congregationalised Presbyterianism ". The former was the product of the Plan of Union. Yet not all Presbyterians were satisfied with their triumph. They complained that Presbyterianism was being Congregationalised. " Committee-men " were being allowed to sit in the Courts of the Church, in spite of the fact that they were simply delegates, not ordained elders. The " Old School ", like the " Old Side " in the eighteenth century, were concerned about the preservation of Presbyterian Order, which they felt was being infringed by this infusion of Congregational democracy; frankly, it reinforced their opponents, the " New School ". This conservative party made its weight felt as never before. It was concerned at the efforts of Congregational theologians to revise Calvinism, and of Congregational evangelists to substitute Arminianism, which was better adapted to revival preaching.

A series of measures restricting the right of Congregational " committee-men " to sit in Church Courts (1832) culminated in the crisis of 1837. In that year the " Old School " gained a majority in the General Assembly. After a long and sharp debate the Plan of Union was abrogated without qualification. The four synods containing the churches founded under the pact were solemnly " excinded " (Western Reserve, Utica, Geneva and Genesee). In other words, they were declared to be " out of ecclesiastical connexion . . . not in form or in part an integral portion of the Presbyterian Church ". The following year the " New School " attempted to face the situation as resourcefully as possible. To their amazement, they found themselves excluded also. They had no option but to withdraw and form another denomination, taking with them the " mixed " churches formed

---

[1] Even in the Colonial period there was a tendency among some of the theocrats to think of a New England as an Israel with definite boundaries; the Hudson was their Jordan. Cotton Mather spoke of settlers who crossed the line as men " on the wrong side of the hedge ".

under the Plan of Union. The " excinded " congregations numbered 533, with a membership of 100,000 communicants.[1] They duly constituted themselves the " New School Presbyterian Church ".

The " Old School ", in their jealousy for the ark of the covenant, had cast off, not a small coterie but four-ninths of the total membership. This *coup d'église* (1837-8) was a quick and easy way of ensuring pure doctrine and good churchmanship. It is a striking contrast to the Disruption of the Church of Scotland in 1843. In the Mother-Church the battle for spiritual independence had been going on for a century. The Ten Years Conflict culminated in the formation of the Free Church mainly because the English-controlled government refused to treat Scottish problems seriously; there seemed no prospect whatever of protecting the Kirk from State interference. In America, on the other hand, neither the State nor a tradition of continuity was available to act as a moderating influence. There was nothing to prevent the church from being rent asunder by an opportunist majority. The American Disruption of 1837 could have been avoided far more easily than the Scottish Disruption of 1843. It was healed in a much shorter time (1870 compared to 1929), but it split the Presbyterian Church, just when unity was most needed. A visitor from Scotland, the Rev. Robert Baird, noted the folly of the schism in his impressions of *Religion in the U.S.A.* (Glasgow, 1843). Presbyterianism was equal to the task of winning the West, but threw away the opportunity through reckless sectarianism, masquerading under the name of churchmanship and orthodoxy. We have already noticed that self-assertion superseded " accommodation " in the case of the Lutherans and Episcopalians from about 1830 till the Civil War. Narrow denominational loyalty tended to replace willingness to co-operate on a united Protestant front.

The " Old School " Presbyterians attained their aims after the schism of 1837-8. They cleared the Church Courts of all save ministers and *bona fide* elders. They placed Home and Foreign Missions under Church Boards, instead of leaving them to inter-denominational societies. They enforced rigidly the dogmas of classic Calvinism. That did not mean that they went far enough to

---

[1] By 1837 the Church had grown in 120 years from one presbytery to 135 presbyteries; there were 2,865 churches, 2,140 ministers and 220,557 communicants.

conciliate the small Presbyterian sects, the " Reformed Presbyterians " and Seceder offshoots, who imported their hair-splitting " testimonies " from Scottish dissent. The " solid South " had been largely responsible for the " Old School " breakaway in 1837, and thus were able to enforce the order, " hands off slavery!"

" New School " Presbyterians tended to be anti-slavery in sentiment, but did not go far enough to please their thorough-going Congregationalist friends. Theologically, there was a fair degree of toleration in the " New School ". Orthodoxy was less crass. Albert Barnes, minister of the First Presbyterian Church, Philadelphia, who had been indicted for heresy in 1836, was allowed after the breach to continue his ministry. He was the first American Presbyterian theologian to become widely known abroad. When scripture exposition was at its lowest ebb in Scotland and England, ministers found refreshment in his lucid, practical commentaries. A million copies of his *Notes on the New Testament* were issued before his death in 1870.

The " New School " Presbyterians did not find it easy to maintain " two sets of agencies and two conceptions of ecclesiastical order " in their new congregations planted in the West. The Congregationalists, hitherto so passive, began to grow restive in the 'thirties. At last, they wondered why *they* had done all the " accommodating ". " We have been well called ' the Lord's silly people '," said one of their leaders. There was a renewal of denominational consciousness. Even in Connecticut, opinion was changing. In 1750 Jonathan Edwards had written to Dr. John Erskine of Edinburgh: " I have long been out of conceit with our unsettled, independent, confused way of Church government in this land; and the Presbyterian way has ever appeared to me most agreeable to the Word of God and the reason and nature of things." Things were moving in the opposite direction by 1850 in Connecticut. Dr. Leonard Bacon was preaching the virtues of Congregationalism from a New Testament and a democratic point of view. The hybrid " Presbygational " system of Connecticut was gradually breaking down, in favour of a looser fellowship. These convictions of the value of decentralised polity became so prevalent that a General Council of American Congregationalists was summoned to meet at Albany, N.Y., in 1852. It is significant that this was their first united gathering since the Cambridge Synod of 1646-8. The Albany Convention by unanimous vote abandoned the Plan of Union. One of the members remarked that their former team-mates had " milked our Congregational cow but made nothing but Presbyterian butter and cheese! " A new programme of expansion was planned for the West. The growing national consciousness of Congregationalism thereafter took shape in periodic " General Councils ", State Conferences, etc., that knit the scattered churches of the " Pilgrim Faith " into a fellowship that linked the Atlantic and the Pacific. At last the New England tradition broke loose from regional confines.

The final chapter of the fateful Plan of Union was written in 1870, when the " New School " Presbyterians severed their relations with the " American Board for Foreign Missions " and other organisations that had become practically part of the Congregational fellowship. Presbyterian churches in the areas where the Plan formerly operated were required to complete their organisation by adding Sessions where these did not exist. Most of them complied and the fateful " Plan of Union " passed out of history.

These events facilitated the reunion of " Old School " and " New School " Presbyterians. Both these bodies had learned much in isolation and both had suffered from secessions owing to the Civil War. The Southern Church remained apart in chilly isolation. So did the " United Presbyterian Church ", formed in 1858 by a merger of small sects that claimed to conserve Covenanting principles, and maintained the ban on organs and hymns. Incomplete as it was, the Union of 1870 made Presbyterianism once more a power in the land. The northern Presbyterian Church is now easily the largest Presbyterian Church in the world.

Are we to treat the Plan of Union as a fruitful experiment in Christian unity, or as a disaster that crippled one partner and mutilated the other? Between 1801 and 1830 the Plan undoubtedly furthered Home Missions and prevented a wasteful duplication of agencies. It imparted to the Presbyterianism of the Middle West a progressive and open-minded outlook not to be found in Pennsylvania, the home of Scots-Irish Presbyterianism. It illustrated certain phases of idealism in the " Pilgrim faith ". In a day of bitter sectarianism the Congregationalists set a noble example of disinterestedness; they were ready to put the Gospel before denominational interests; and it was only after their partners had pulled out that they decided against running in double harness. The Plan of Union, in the perspective of history, seems a makeshift arrangement. Two alternatives would have been better—either to allot separate zones to each denomination, or to have built a new church out of New England Congregationalism and Scots-Irish Presbyterianism. Had such a church been successfully reared, it would have to-day a corporate power and distinction which neither body now possesses and would come near to constituting a national American Church. The temperamental factor, however. tended to make a gap. The New Englander is more speculative, more ready to try untrodden paths than the traditional hide-bound Scots-Irish Presbyterian.[1] On both sides there was an antipathetic element which would certainly have sabotaged corporate union. In the nineteenth century, at any rate, such sections would not have served as durable materials for any architect of a United Church; indeed, they would have mixed no better than the proverbial oil and water.[2]

[1] The Congregationalists have just decided (1949) to unite with a German body of predominantly Presbyterian, but partly Lutheran composition—the Evangelical and Reformed Church.

[2] One result, however, has been permanent. New Englanders crossing the Hudson into New York State join the Presbyterian Church as a matter of course, and the converse is equally true.

CHAPTER III

MIDDLE WEST AND FAR WEST

" Go West, young man, and grow up with the Country."

HORACE GREELEY (1850)

W E have watched successive waves of immigration pour westward through Ohio in the early nineteenth century, reproducing the neat homesteads and orderly townships of New England. The migrants brought their educated ministers and teachers. They were indeed a contrast to the poor whites who were driven by hunger from the Southern States through the gaps of the Appalachian Mountains, and settled in remote places under conditions that long continued to be crude. On the Southern frontier we expect emotionalism and find it. We are surprised to discover all the phenomena of revival hysteria on the Northern frontier also.

By 1820 New York had become the most populous State in the Union. The English traveller landed at " the Empire City ", but as he passed westwards he gradually lost the amenities of " the East ". The frontier began in central and western New York, which became known as " the burnt-over district ", so called because it was continually being swept by waves of religious excitement resembling forest or prairie fires. There was always enough inflammable material left for new evangelists ready to satisfy an abnormal craving for religious thrills. Some of the original settlers of the " burnt-over district " were " men of rather unsavoury fame ". They were followed by earnest and industrious artisans from the East. The mingling of these diverse elements produced an amalgam of constructive idealism and eccentric religiosity. " They have revived all the irregularities of the Corinthian Church," reported Messrs. Reed and Matheson, deputies of the English Congregational Union, " as though they had been placed on record to be copied, and not avoided " (1836).

The revivalist who set his mark on Evangelism in this area was

Charles G. Finney. A frontier lawyer, he knew the men of " up-state " New York. His only book was Shakespeare and he did not even own a Bible till he was thirty. He underwent a thorough-going conversion in 1818 and adopted the usual Puritanical hostility towards personal adornment, the theatre, secret societies and other " worldly " practices. He began to preach in the surrounding villages (Rome, Utica, etc.), but refused to listen to the plea of neighbouring ministers who urged him to go to a theological seminary. His Presbytery, however, agreed to license him in 1824. He had been brought up in the keen-edged tradition of Edwardian Calvinism, which stressed revivalism, but he had no use for academic divinity of any kind. He preached " full and free salvation " in homely, everyday speech, illustrated by incidents that would appeal to his hearers. He used his lawyer's training to good purpose; he made God, sin, atonement and repentance as real as houses and lands. He had something of the quick logic, humanity and wit of Abraham Lincoln. He treated of sins in the concrete with a clinical knowledge of motives possessed by few evangelists. In his famous sermon on the " Seared Conscience ", he analysed the problem exhaustively, naming no less than 95 specific instances. Nor did he hesitate to give straightforward ethical addresses on the sin of borrowing tools and failing to return them.

Finney's fame soon spread to New York, where an " elegant circular edifice in the Greek style ", Broadway Tabernacle, was built to his own design to accommodate the crowds that wanted to hear him (1834).[1] A year later, however, he was called to organise a frontier college at Oberlin, Ohio. A nucleus was formed of his own converts and forty theological students who had been expelled by the trustees of Lane Seminary, Cincinnati, for expressing their anti-slavery opinions. Oberlin became a " station " on the " underground " that transported fugitive slaves to Canada; it welcomed coloured students as well as white, women as well as men; emancipation was its motto. Oberlin College (1850) was appropriately named in honour of the Alsatian pastor whose fame in blending evangelism and social reform had spanned the Atlantic. Here was an institution adapted to the frontier, yet capable of developing into the most progressive college of the Middle West.

Finney's educational interests did not interfere with the spec-

---

[1] Forerunner of the huge " auditoriums " afterwards so common in big American cities, it avoided their obvious architectural blunders.

tacular evangelistic tours fully described in his *Memoirs* (New York, 1876). These campaigns were promoted intensively during the 'forties and 'fifties. He attracted big audiences in England and Scotland. His *Lectures on Revivals* had a wide circulation (80,000 copies of the British edition were sold before 1850); it was through reading Finney that George Williams, a young London shop assistant, was inspired to start the Y.M.C.A., which was soon copied in America. The way was prepared for Moody and Sankey a generation later.

Finney had a lawyer's ability of presenting his case to men of various occupations, including his own; he seems to have been one of the few evangelists to make any impact on distillers and brewers. His converts became his fellow-workers. Rich men like the Tappans used their wealth as Christian philanthropists through his influence. The weak point in Finney's evangelism was the fact that he preached his own experiences without discrimination. In 1843 he underwent " a fresh baptism of the Spirit " (" so far as I could see, I was in a state in which I did not sin "). This " Higher Holiness ", akin to the " perfectionism " of primitive Methodists, was far from wholesome for the populace of Up-State New York; the psychology of this " burnt-over district " was suggestive, credulous, nervous and unstable. Lyman Beecher, apostle of the West, preached hell-fire and believed in continuous revivals; but even he did not approve of Finney's " new measures " —the " Anxious Bench " and similar technique. Both men were New Englanders by birth.

It is a strange phenomenon that New England, pre-eminent in the United States for a high average level of intelligence and practical evangelical religion, should have proved in the nineteenth century such a fertile seed-plot for various freakish cults. William Miller, herald of the Second Advent, was a native of Massachusetts; Joseph Smith, the prophet of Mormonism, was a Vermonter; J. H. Noyes, the priest of Perfectionism, was a convert of Finney, and also came from Vermont; Mary Baker Eddy, founder (and proprietor) of Christian Science, came from New Hampshire. Only the last of these " uplifters " can be said to have reached the sensible, Bible-reading and church-going people of New England. They " sprouted in the revival-singed soil of western New York, among an uncouth people pitifully eager for signs and wonders ".

William Miller was a recruiting sergeant in the War of 1812. On retiring from the army in 1815 as captain, he joined the Baptist Church at Low Hampton, Washington County, N.Y. Farmer and earnest Bible student, he began to lecture on " unfulfilled prophecy " in 1831, about the same time as Edward Irving was creating a sensation in London. Miller's theme, however, was Christ's return to judge the world and its date, rather than the preliminary signs—the gift of tongues, etc. Working on a formula taken from Daniel and Revelation, the prognosticator calculated that the end of the world would arrive on 21st March 1843. Encouraged by the curious phenomenon of meteoric showers (" celestial fireworks " scientists called them), Miller was asked to preach and lecture in the larger cities. Second Advent papers built up a large body of supporters in town and country—*The Midnight Cry* (New York), *The Signs of the Times* (Boston) and the *Philadelphia Alarm*. As 1843 approached enthusiasm mounted. " This year—the long-looked for year of years! The best! It has come! " When the fateful 21st March dawned, the Millerites greeted the Day on house-tops and hills, clad in white muslin. Nothing happened. " Father Miller " explained that his error was due to an error in calculating the date (he had followed Hebrew instead of Roman chronology). His followers accordingly girded their loins for 21st March 1844; believers sold their shops and closed their homes. The appearance of a comet confirmed their hopes. Nevertheless, nothing happened. Miller revised his figures and postponed his date till 22nd October; this time, positively, he would be right! The old enthusiasm flared up. Men sowed no crops. Newspapers issued " last editions ". The faithful took their stance in strategic positions—graveyards were popular, through association with a physical resurrection of the body. Despite the scoffing of the unregenerate, believers awaited the midnight cry, ready to ascend skywards. Alas, failure for the third time! Poor Miller was prostrate, and died a few years later.[1] Strangely enough, the sect that he founded was not ignominiously dispersed. It merely split into half a dozen smaller sects, of which the Seventh Day Adventists are at present the most flourishing. It is computed that Miller had at least 50,000 followers in his life-time (some claimed 1,000,000). A century later there were about 150,000 Adventists in the United States alone. We may

[1] Clara E. Sears, *Days of Delusion* (Boston, 1924).

smile at Miller and his disciples as ignorant fanatics, but many educated people in England, long after his day, listened to the Rev. Dr. Cumming who declared that 1867 would see the end of chronology, and when this failed, merely postponed his date.

Another product of the revival-singed soil of western New York was Mormonism, which sprouted about the same time as Miller-ism. When Joseph Smith was a lad of fourteen, his parents moved from Vermont to a small farm near Palmyra, N.Y. His father used a divining-rod to find hidden treasure and the proper place to dig wells. Joseph's grandparents were superstitious, neurotic cranks; they were seers of visions, hearers of celestial voices, believers in miraculous cures. When Joseph was eighteen (2nd September 1823) he claimed that the angel " Moroni " had appeared to him three times at night; this was the revelation—the Bible of the Western Continent was buried in " the hill Cumora " (now known as Mormon Hill). It was not till 1827 that he claimed to have dug up a stone box containing the new revelation, inscribed on gleaming golden plates, accompanied by " supernatural spec-tacles " to decipher the mystic writing in the " reformed Egyptian tongue ". Not being very literate, Smith employed his wife and three witnesses, to whom he dictated (behind a curtain) " The Book of Mormon ". This inspired record was attested genuine and published at Palmyra in 1830.

The new revelation claimed to tell the story of religion in America from its original settlement by " Jaredites ", dispersed at the Tower of Babel. We read of the " Lamanites " (=the Red Indians) and their struggle with the " Nephites " (= God's chosen people). The latter, however, apostasised and were nearly all annihilated in a battle said to have been fought in Ontario County, N.Y. (384 B.C.). Only Mormon, his son Moroni, and a few others escaped.

The *Book of Mormon* consists of sixteen books, forming a com-pact volume of some 500 pages, the modern editions being printed like the Bible, with similar chapter and verse divisions. Not only is the style scriptural; some passages are " lifted " from both Testaments in the King James Version, errors and all. Here you will find chunks of the Westminster Confession; there, exhorta-tions from a nineteenth-century camp-meeting[1] put into the

---

[1] Joseph was astute in keeping frontier psychology in mind. He omits reference to cities and to music, although there were Biblical precedents, just because these things would be unfamiliar to his converts.

mouths of primitive Indian chiefs. The " Gentile " reader soon
wearies of ploughing through the pseudo-Biblical narratives of
Mosiah, Alma, Helamen, Fourth Nephi;[1] and when he comes to
The Book of Ether he will feel like calling for chloroform ! Yet
this farrago of nonsense was accepted by a number of honest
dupes and a " church " was formed at Fayette, Seneca County,
N.Y., in April 1830.

Smith was joined by Sidney Rigdon, who had been a Baptist
preacher and latterly a follower of Alexander Campbell's " Disciples ". These adventurers got into trouble with the law and
removed to Kirtland, Ohio. They built a large stone temple in
1836 and gathered a compact body of supporters. There they
were joined by Brigham Young from Vermont, a glazier by trade,
who soon became one of the " Twelve Apostles " (perhaps they
got this idea from the Irvingites). The Mormons did not limit
their activities to apostolic persuasion, however. Smith preached
a gospel of " extermination ", and organised storm troopers
(" Danites ") who came into conflict with the state militia. From
Ohio the " Saints " were driven to Missouri, and thence to
Nauvoo, Illinois. There they settled in 1840 permanently, it
appeared; for the Illinois politicians, angling for the Mormon vote,
issued a charter for Nauvoo, which gave Smith almost unlimited
power, with a " Legion " to enforce his will. This " New Jerusalem " extended rapidly, a temple was erected, even a " university ". Then the Leader received a revelation authorising " plural
marriage " (July 1843), although polygamy had been forbidden by
the Book of Mormon. The opposition crystallised. An insurrection broke out, the Nauvoo Legion surrendered, Joseph and his
brother Hyrum were captured, imprisoned at Carthage and shot
by the mob, who broke into the jail on 27th June 1844. Further
disorders between " Saints " and Gentiles led to a Mormon
exodus from Illinois.

Brigham Young, who had survived " fightings without and
fears within ", proved a most capable leader. He organised the
migration across prairie and mountain with a resourcefulness that
wins respect—the epic of " Deseret " in the Rocky Mountains
deserves to be remembered like the voyage of the *Mayflower*. By
the application of large-scale irrigation, the Mormons made the
wilderness blossom like the rose. They anticipated the " town-

---

[1] In *II Nephi* 1.14 is an echo of Shakespeare's " undiscovered country ".

planning movement " when they laid out the spacious tree-lined and slum-less Salt Lake City. They defied one of the Puritan taboos in erecting a theatre as one of their first public buildings. They justified the experiment of a theocracy in modern times that should be efficient and yet basically religious. They made provision for the growth of a thrifty, frugal people—so abstemious that they " abjured the use of tea, coffee and tobacco " (as the Tabernacle guides tell you). Not till 1890, however, did the Mormon authorities acquiesce in the surrender of " plural marriage ". Ever since the Union Pacific Railroad reached Utah in 1869, the power of the United States government encroached on the " peculiar " institutions of the Latter Day Saints; and " Gentiles " filtered into the Holy City in increasing numbers. The Mormon hierarchy could no longer act as an autocratic machine. The last Church-State in America lost power, like the Puritan Theocracy two centuries earlier. Brigham Young died in 1877, leaving an estate of $2,000,000 and at least twenty-five wives and forty children. " For daring, he was a Cromwell; for intrigue, a Macchiavelli; for executive force, a Moses; and for utter absence of conscience, a Bonaparte."

It is tempting to enlarge on this remarkable experiment, which has produced a flourishing and stable community of over half a million members, based on such a dubious spiritual and ethical foundation. Despite the prominence given to Jesus Christ in the title of the cult, the claim to be a Christian Church cannot be admitted. Mormonism is a reversion to pre-Christian ideas of primitive anthropomorphism. As Dr. Weigle says, " The frontier community, like the embryo, tends to recapitulate the history of the race."[1]

The Mormon migration is an epic. The settlement of Utah was an enterprise economically successful, yet based on faith. Missionaries were sent to England as early as 1837, to the Jews of Constantinople and Jerusalem in 1840; the same year they actually reached Australia and the East Indies. By 1851 some 17,000 English converts, fired with glowing reports of Zion, braved the

---

[1] Through the universe there drift disembodied spirits, offspring of deity, whose sole hope is to be born on earth and grow into the *physical* likeness of God. This provided a theological justification for the revival of polygamy. Famous men in history can be given the benefit of Mormon baptism by proxy. " Baptism for the dead " (I Cor. 15.29) takes place in the great Temple, Salt Lake City; also, marriage, which can be " for eternity " as well as " time ". Gentiles are excluded from these esoteric rites, but may attend preaching services in the vast Tabernacle, noted for its dish-cover roof and perfect acoustics.

perils of the wilderness, many of them pushing their possessions in hand-carts.[1] Those who succeeded in reaching their Mecca usually prospered, though a number were disillusioned by experience of autocracy in action and "plural marriage" in practice. Lord Bryce described the Mormons as "chiefly recruited from Europe; one finds few native Americans in Salt Lake City, and those few from among the poor whites of the South". Not till 1887 did the Federal authorities put an end to this unique "Perpetual Emigration Scheme". Seldom has a fraudulent faith, palmed off on a credulous people by designing, ill-educated leaders, and promoted without the backing of wealth, achieved such vitality, winning ultimate respect and producing such solid results. It is a striking illustration of the economic success of heterodoxy, combined with a shrewd business instinct and a strong sense of community.

During the 'thirties and 'forties the United States continued to ferment with all kinds of idealistic, utopian schemes for the benefit of mankind. This marked a reaction from individualistic other-worldliness; but the method was a separation of the elect rather than an attempt to raise the standards of the country as a whole by leavening it. Fourier, Robert Owen and other Europeans had suggested self-supporting colonies where social ideals could be realised in seclusion. What more natural than free experiment in America, which had still the reputation for being an El Dorado, where mankind was not bound by tradition, and advance along fresh lines was therefore invited. A definitely Evangelical tinge characterised some of these "Bible Communists", such as Noyes' "Oneida Community".

John Humphrey Noyes (1811-86), like many founders of new sects, was a New Englander, but a man of good birth and education. After graduating at Dartmouth College, he studied Divinity at Andover with a view to the Congregational ministry. A convert of Finney, Noyes was influenced by a protracted revival in 1831; he was drawn into the "perfectionism" so prevalent at that time, and had his licence revoked by the New Haven Association. At Putney, Vermont, he gathered associates around him who were prepared to share a community life on perfectionist lines. A New England village, however, was not the most sympathetic milieu for such a radical experiment. The society withdrew to the more congenial atmosphere of "up-state" New York. At Oneida they

See Susan Ertz, *The Proselyte* (London, 1933), a brilliant novel.

formed " The Oneida Community ", based on corporate devotional life and business enterprise. Unlike the Brook Farm community of the New England Transcendentalists (satirised by Hawthorne in his novel, *The Blithedale Romance*, 1852) Oneida was thoroughly practical. Its promoters were pioneers in canning vegetables and fruit; they manufactured steel traps for killing animals, and went in for various manufactures. Unlike the Mormons, they had no trouble in getting on with their neighbours: " their word was as good as their bond." Among themselves, they insisted on holding property in common, following the example of the Apostolic Church. The Perfectionist ideas of Noyes were carried as far as having wives in common—which went further than the " plural marriage " of the Mormons. It was only about thirty years after the founding of the community that public agitation became clamant, the churches of Syracuse, N.Y., taking the lead. Noyes fully expected this protest. In 1879 he proposed that they should " give up the practice of Complex Marriage ", not from conviction " but in deference to public sentiment ". The members agreed.[1] It is somewhat surprising that two years later they decided to transform the altruistic Oneida Community, based on Bible Communism, into a joint-stock company!

A parallel and contrast to Oneida is the " Harmony " experiment of George Rapp. a south German pietist who emigrated to western Pennsylvania with his followers in 1803. In 1815 he moved to New Harmony, Indiana. This farm community soon presented a picture very different from the usual frontier settlement—" a garden of neatness " with gabled buildings, pretty church, orchards and vine-clad hills. Patriarchal simplicity, neighbourliness and Evangelical religion of a warm-hearted Moravian kind, held sway. The community, however, seemed to suffer from the *wanderlust*. In 1824 they sold out to Robert Owen, the famous English experimenter in communal ventures. This time the Rappites retraced their steps eastwards and founded Economy, some seventeen miles from Pittsburgh. Prosperity was repeated. Unfortunately, the colony decreased from 522 members in 1827 to 385 in 1844. Eventually only three persons were left, and the concern was eventually purchased for several million dollars by a Pittsburgh syndicate. Here, surely, we find evidence of the

[1] More recent separate communities have proved much more eccentric, e.g. Purcell's " House of David " and Dowie's " Zion City ", both on the shores of Lake Michigan.

petering out of the ideal of Christian brotherhood, which was much to the fore in the fermenting 'forties. Religious motives gave the impetus, but gradually faded out before commercial realism. Oneida and New Harmony were alike in this respect. The difference lies in the fact that whereas the former stressed " complex marriage ", a free association of the sexes, the latter was on a celibate basis and depended on adequate intake of persons intent on remaining single.

One of the quaintest communistic sects, the Shakers, were definitely celibate. They followed " Mother Ann " Lee across the Atlantic in 1774; " Ann the Word " was a blacksmith's daughter from Manchester, a " shaking Quaker ". Her " United Society of Believers in Christ's Second Appearing " spread through New England as well as the South West. Settlements were founded at Mount Lebanon, New York, and Union Village, Ohio, where they conducted home industries, clad in a weird uniform, the men wearing their hair long. Sex was taboo; the brothers and sisters were equals. Lafayette and other foreigners made a point of watching them at their religious exercises—Sabbath dances in which men and women approached one another with odd twitching and whirling movements. The upturned palms represented a gesture of receiving divine blessings through the hands: the shaking of the hands turned down symbolised the shaking of sin and evil magnetism through the finger tips.

The Shaker movement, before its decline, enjoyed a last flash of publicity in 1847, near Palmyra, N.Y., the birthplace of Mormonism. The brethren and sisters recognised as familiar mysterious " rappings " in the house of Margaret and Kate Fox. Horace Greeley, the eminent journalist, " thought there was something in it ". Literary celebrities like Cooper, Bryant, Poe and Mrs. Stowe became interested. Table-turning, automatic writing, phrenology and mesmerism were all the vogue during the 'fifties and 'sixties. Books and magazines publicised the movement. Séances became fashionable, and clairvoyants like A. J. Davis (the " Seer of Poughkeepsie ") exploited the cravings of the credulous, like their Mormon predecessors. Spiritualism became a recognised cult.[1] As many as 2,000,000 adherents were claimed

---

[1] Laurence Oliphant, scion of an ancient Scottish family, traveller and M.P., fell under the ascendancy of Prophet Harris; he worked in his Spiritualist brotherhood at Lake Erie as a farm labourer, and believed for ten years that Harris was deity incarnate (*Ency. Brit.*, 11th ed.).

in 1873, but in 1926 only 126,000 persons were registered as professed Spiritualists.

Such freakish cults were thrown up by frontier revivalism—the products of designing leadership working on credulity, the flame often fanned by persecution. A specialist in " wild religions "[1] classifies them into five (over-lapping) groups: (a) *Pessimist*: the world so wicked that an imminent Second Advent is the only remedy; (b) *Perfectionist*: absolute holiness possible even in this world to the Elect; (c) *Charismatic*: miraculous " gifts " of the Apostolic Church still essential, e.g. " unknown tongues "; (d) *Communistic*: cultivation of the " higher life ", involving a separate community (and sometimes Antinomian practices violating accepted Christian ethics); (e) *Legalistic*: the zealous preservation of certain practices on Biblical grounds, e.g. mutual foot-washing in public.

. . . .

Religion, in following the frontier, was " Americanised ". Protestant Churches had to accommodate their message and methods to frontier mentality. Those who refused to do so failed—or attained only a measure of success after relatively settled conditions of life had been achieved. A Scottish visitor[2] noticed the gulf that yawned between Congregationalist, Episcopalian and many Presbyterian preachers, who " read their sermons more or less closely " and the excited extemporising of Methodists and Baptists. Refinement, which was highly esteemed in the East, created ridicule in the West. (British travellers like Mrs. Frances Trollope did not seem to have appreciated this distinction.) The loneliness of western life naturally drew folk together. Gregariousness made a bifurcated appeal. The rough element made the saloon their club, while the tamed element concentrated on the conventicle as their place of fellowship; the " church supper " became an institution, which still holds its own in more sophisticated days. Those who " got religion " wanted it " hot and strong " from preachers who were not separated from them by cultural barriers.[3] They responded readily to emotional stimulus, too readily—for founders of new sects who understood popular psychology exploited it shamefully to gain proselytes.

[1] Elmer T. Clark, *The Small Sect in America* (Nashville, Tenn., 1937).
[2] R. Baird, *Religion in the U.S.A.* (Glasgow, 1844).
[3] The Romanists sent to the frontier priests of superior education, many of them French *emigrés*; they were successful and their culture was respected.

The frontier saw ethical questions clear-cut in black-and-white. Such tracts as *The Swearer's Prayer* were widely circulated and supplemented crude local newspapers as food for starved minds. The vices of the pioneer—gambling, drunkenness and sexual laxity—provoked an ultra-Puritan reaction that went even further than New England. Not only was dancing banned, with other "worldly amusements": even smoking was taboo in Methodist and Baptist circles, doubtless in revulsion from the spitting habit which Dickens and other Englishmen found so offensive in the States. This readiness to lay down hard-and-fast regulations for the control of personal behaviour can still be clearly discerned by consulting the Methodist *Book of Discipline* or by noting the activities of their "Board of Temperance, Prohibition and Public Morals". The Middle West has still circles that retain traces of the mentality castigated by Mrs. Trollope in her *Domestic Manners of the Americans* (1832). She had the opportunity of meeting New Englanders of a good type who were busy transplanting their institutions and culture on the frontier. One of her few friends in Cincinnati, the Rev. Timothy Flint, was a leader in this enterprise. Mrs. Trollope, however, like Dickens, did not carry away happy memories of her sojourn; her dominant impressions were of raw, complacent provincialism. She could never forget being addressed by a scholarly gentleman of Cincinnati: "Shakespeare, madam, is obscene, and thank God we are sufficiently advanced to have found it out!" Revivalist religion fostered prayer-meetings, Bible classes, lectures on "improving subjects" and later, innocuous "sociables" on week-nights in Church premises. The cant phrases of Methodism long outlived spontaneity, e.g. "I indulged hope", "I gave myself away to the Saviour"; "And how is your soul, my sister?" There was a mawkish strain in Methodism, yet a virile character like President Theodore Roosevelt could claim that it was "peculiarly congenial to a hardy folk, democratic to the core, prizing individual independence above all earthly possessions, and engaging in the rough and stern work of conquering a continent." This might be said of the Baptists also, who have thriven on their frontier in spite of the extreme autonomy claimed by local congregations. Taking the United States as a whole, the Baptists are five times as numerous as the Lutherans; there are seven Baptists to every Presbyterian, and ten to every Episcopalian.

Churches that were run on democratic lines had the ball at their feet when frontier ideas of social equality prevailed. When the " Middle West " became gradually urbanised, however, after the Civil War, ideas altered. The intensity of the pioneer had to be harnessed to farming on more scientific lines, or switched to business. Specialisation replaced the tendency for men to drift from one occupation to another. Distinctions emerged between employers and employees, educated and uneducated. The coming of the railroad across the prairie broke down isolation, improved amenities and pointed to imitation of the East and its settled ways. Wealth was available to end the reproach of illiteracy. High Schools, Denominational Colleges and State Universities were rapidly planted.

How did the churches adapt themselves to new conditions ? By the second quarter of the twentieth century religion had been sadly commercialised by business interests. In a scientific study of " Middletown ", a typical mid-Western city of 38,000,[1] we find that business men support the church to a large extent because it gives security to investments and allays social discontent. The " go-getter " attitude secularises religion. An educator, coming to reside in the city, was warned, " No matter what you think, you'll have to become a regular churchman to get along in Middletown." Prosperity has modified social standards. We find " Methodists of the Gothic type "[2] gravitating towards stylish Presbyterians and Episcopalians. Poor Methodists (and Baptists), repudiating as " worldly " social practices beyond their means, and reluctant to slough off the frontier suspicion of all " book larnin' " " have tended to join sects where they would feel more at ease, with full liberty to indulge in " corybantic Christianity ". These statements need qualification, but the Middle West certainly offers some illuminating examples of religious sociology. " One joins a sect, but is born into the church." Yet the sect, in the second generation, often loses its intensity, adopts " churchly " practices and loses its more ardent members, who again hive off.

Anglo-Saxon Protestantism naturally accommodated itself to the frontier more readily than Continental Protestantism transplanted. The churches of the immigrants were naturally poor, in the first generation. German, Dutch and Scandinavian parents

[1] *Middletown*, by Robert S. and Helen M. Lynd (New York, 1930).
[2] Sinclair Lewis' phrase. See *Main Street*, *Babbitt*, and his other Mid-West novels

valued their church as one of the few links with home, along with
the mother-tongue. Their children, however, got accustomed to
American ways and wanted to accommodate themselves to the
new customs and attitudes. There was therefore a tendency in
the second generation to adopt English in church services and to
modify the ritual, whether Lutheran or Reformed, in accordance
with the freer American usage. Few immigrants had the historic
sense imparted by a relative degree of education. They belonged
to the dispossessed classes. They had nothing to lose economically
by emigrating, and everything to gain in a land of promise, once
they got over the initial obstacle of not knowing the language and
customs of America. To the average German immigrant, Goethe
and Nietzsche were mere names, but Luther and his Bible
were realities. The more orthodox Lutheran denominations
that made full use of the German language could count on the
support of many who clung in inarticulate loyalty to the ancestral
tradition.

The linguistic tradition also caused the Scandinavians to organise Swedish, Norwegian and Danish Lutheran Churches distinct
from the German Lutherans. All these national groups were
influenced by the American tendency to split into rival sects.
This was facilitated by the fact that there was no Establishment
(as in the home-land) to hold rival parties together under the
shelter of a National Church. Further, the fact that there were
no State endowments forced these foreign denominations to maintain themselves on a scale undreamt of in Europe; they had to
depend on publicity to gain more members. Voluntaryism stimulated zeal; the members were responsible for their church, not
external authorities. Their pastors they elected; they were not
the functionaries of an official Establishment. Swedes like Pastor
Hasselquist rejoiced in the freedom of the new environment.
Immigrants who had been nourished on the somewhat passive
doctrine of " salvation by faith alone " were stimulated by changed
circumstances (aided by the American climate of the Middle
West). Their zeal was released and flowed into active channels
of missionary, philanthropic and social activity. They might still
subscribe to the Augsburg Confession, but they recited the catechism and sung the hymns in a different accent; particularly in
the sermons did there sound a new note of urgency, which evoked
a response of " immediacy " in the pews.

In the Dutch Reformed Church, Domine John H. Livingstone, one of the first pastors to preach in English, wrote in 1754 that this was the only way of avoiding extinction. In spite of indignant protests that he wanted to hand over the Dutch Church to the Presbyterians, the policy of " accommodation " was followed with success and the English language prevailed. Nineteenth-century immigrants from Holland, dissatisfied with the toning down of distinctive traits and traditions, organised " The True Dutch Church ", which stressed confessional orthodoxy, the metrical psalms as opposed to hymns, etc. But even the " True " Dutch Church eventually dropped that title in favour of " The Christian Reformed Church ". Americanisation was almost inevitable to avoid extinction, but there are always diehards.

.   .   .   .   .

On the two-hundredth anniversary of the landing of the Pilgrim Fathers, Daniel Webster delivered one of his great orations. He pictured New England farms, villages, and churches flourishing two thousand miles westward from the rock where the founding fathers landed. " Ere long the sons of the Pilgrims will be on the shores of the Pacific." Fifteen years after Webster's oration, a New Englander arose to blaze the trail to the extreme North West, and to open a door of opportunity for the missionary as well as for the trader and the settler.

In 1831 five Indians from distant Oregon reached St. Louis, on an unusual venture. They came, not to sell furs but to ask for " the white man's Book of Heaven ". Volunteers were called for. A young physician, Marcus Whitman, was accepted by the American Board of Commissioners for Foreign Missions. He was ordained and rode to Oregon early in 1835. After making preliminary investigations he came home, married Narcissa Prentiss, and returned to Oregon with his wife, the Rev. H. H. and Mrs. Spalding, and Mr. W. H. Gray. The " Oregon Trail " was a terrible ordeal for white women, but they survived it. Their waggon train was said to be the first to cross the Rockies. After passing the " Continental Divide " they stopped at the furthest west point reached by Whitman a year earlier. There they knelt in prayer and claimed the land " in the name of Christianity and the mothers of America ". It was no empty gesture when they planted the Stars and Stripes, for after settling near Walla Walla they discovered that a chain of trading posts was being established by the Hudson Bay Company, with a view to the annexation of Oregon by Canada. This inspired Whitman's epic winter ride to Washington, D.C. Owing to snows and hostile Indians, he had to travel by a southern detour, the Santa Fe trail. A dishevelled, emaciated figure, he appeared in Daniel Webster's office at Washington, wrapped in a buffalo coat. He needed all his powers of persuasion to convince the authorities that the country which he had opened up was worth saving for Uncle Sam. This is the story according to popular American tradition. Some historians have minimised Whitman's part in the Webster-Ashburton Treaty of 1842, which resulted in Canadian claims to Oregon being set aside and the territory being annexed by the United States. There is no doubt, however, that his part in opening up a vast tract was considerable. He was " Gaius, mine host " to countless pioneers, who preceded the covered waggon through the Rockies.

Whitman was not merely a pioneer of " manifest destiny ". He was a pioneer of medical missions. His settlement at Waiilatpu (" place of wild rye ") was a house of mercy for exhausted white men on the move and Indians seeking the advice of the medicine-man. The Cayuse tribe was particularly indebted to the Whitmans, but instead of greeting them as benefactors they execrated them as traitors responsible for the flood of white men who were going to rob them of their land. When epidemics broke out among the Cayuse (doubtless brought by the whites) it was interpreted as an evil spell cast by the doctor. On 29th November 1847 these bad Indians surrounded the mission station and murdered the people who had come to help them. Among the martyrs were Marcus and Narcissa Whitman.

Professor W. W. Sweet, the leading American authority on the frontier in its impact on American religion, has given a high place as " Christian Pathfinder " to Sheldon Jackson. His name is unfamiliar to most British readers, but deserves to be remembered along with Marcus Whitman's, as an Apostle of the Far West.[1]

Sheldon Jackson was born in the Mohawk Valley of central New York (1834), the son of a Presbyterian elder. He was educated at Princeton. The news about the martyrdom of missionaries during the Indian Mutiny inspired him to dedicate his life

[1] *Makers of Christianity from John Cotton to Lyman Abbott*, Ch. VI (New York, 1937).

to Evangelism. Rejected by his Church's Board for the foreign field, on grounds of physique, he accepted an appointment from the American Home Missionary Society to the churchless village of La Crescent, Minnesota. One of his characteristics was a " broad interpretation of his assignments ". Far from confining his ministry to La Crescent, he extended his parish over eighteen counties, which he traversed often on foot. He was not long in planting preaching stations and Sunday Schools, and in distributing Christian literature. His opportunity came when the flood of immigrants poured west after the end of the Civil War in 1865. Nine days after the last spike was driven on the Union Pacific Railroad, Jackson started work as Superintendent of Missions. The commission named Nebraska, Idaho, Montana, Wyoming and Utah—" or as far as our jurisdiction extends ". With his headquarters at Denver City, he appointed a team of missionaries and ranged over the Rockies through the 'seventies. He was often in danger from Indians; once he was mistaken for a highwayman; and on another occasion he jumped from a stage coach, as it rolled down a mountain side to destruction. Journeys of 1000-2000 miles were not uncommon; he was able to do this by getting passes from the railways and coaches. Where he could not go himself, he sent others—or his newspaper, *The Rocky Mountain Presbyterian* (posted free to every member of the General Assembly for ten years). Timber for churches was hard to get in the prairie parts of his " diocese ", so he had " prefabricated " chapels sent out from Chicago.

Sheldon Jackson believed in " lengthening his cords " as well as " strengthening his stakes ". The Presbyterian Board of Home Missions limited its work to English-speaking people. He believed that it should be extended so as to include the Indians and Spanish-speaking South West. Seven years of persuasion failed to change the official attitude of the Board; he therefore called a convention on his own at Pittsburgh to devise means of covering this vast field of operations. He had to create a new organisation, but in time it developed into a most effective evangelistic agency, The Presbyterian Woman's Board of Home Missions.

Sheldon Jackson's crowning glory was his work in Alaska (1882-1907). Here again, he received little encouragement from the missionary authorities in his own Church, but went ahead till his leadership compelled support. He was appointed by the

United States Government to organise schools in Alaska. On each
of his twenty-six journeys to that ice-bound land he travelled
17,000 to 20,000 miles, and by his books and reports he tried to
interest his fellow-countrymen in the needs of the natives. The
whale, the walrus and the seal, on which they largely depended
for food, were quickly disappearing. In 1890 he advocated the
introduction of reindeer. By this means " a barbarian people on
the verge of starvation " could be elevated to " comfortable support and civilisation ". Frustrated by the delay of the politicians
in Washington, he acted (as usual on his own). He imported
a herd of 171 reindeer from Siberia. That set things going and
induced the United States to import reindeer in large numbers.
The statesmanship and philanthropy of this Christian Pathfinder
in Alaska deserved lasting fame; yet his name is not even to be
found in the index of the *Encyclopaedia Britannica* (the great
eleventh edition, and an American publication).

Sheldon Jackson did not lose touch with Home Missions in his
own country during his Alaska journeys. By 1906 he had founded
six synods, thirty-one presbyteries, and 886 churches with 77,105
communicants. In half a century he had travelled a million miles.
He co-operated freely with Roman Catholics and the Greek Orthodox Church. In 1897 the Presbyterian Church in the United
States called him to the Moderator's chair. A journalist once
described Sheldon Jackson as " short, bewhiskered, and bespec-
tacled. By inside measurements a giant."

Sheldon Jackson lived to see the end of the frontier. His
apostolic achievement recalls the lines of Bishop Berkeley, one of
the few great philosophers genuinely interested in America.[1]

> Westward the course of empire takes its way,
> The first four acts already passed;
> A fifth shall close the drama with the day,
> Time's noblest offspring is his last.

[1] Kant, to eke out his small salary, used to teach geography. He would
speak of the various Indian tribes—Iroquois, Narragansetts, etc., adding:
" There are also a few Englishmen scattered in settlements along the shore of
the Atlantic."

CHAPTER IV

HOME AND FOREIGN MISSIONS

"Enthusiasm is the genius of sincerity, and truth accomplishes no victories without it."—LYTTON

To record the epic of Christian expansion in North America would call for the pen of a Latourette. One could write volumes on the romance of Catholic missionaries and explorers. One thinks of the French pioneers who traversed the forests and swamps between Canada and Louisiana during the seventeenth and eighteenth centuries. They established a chain of frontier posts between the St. Lawrence, the Great Lakes and the Gulf of Mexico (one of which was Detroit, 1701). They traded with the Indians, preached to them, and sometimes intermarried with them. It looked as though a French, Catholic Empire was going to take shape in the Mississippi Valley, developing out of this network of forts, trading posts and missions. Wolfe's capture of Quebec, the advance of British frontiersmen across the Alleghany Mountains, and the sale of Louisiana by Napoleon to the United States, changed the course of history. The romance and heroism of the French has been told for all time by Francis Parkman, himself an intrepid explorer and the son of a New England minister. Thanks to him the names of La Salle and Father Marquette will not be readily forgotten. Many of the great French missionaries were Jesuits. It was the suppression of the Jesuit Order in 1767 and its subsequent expulsion from the Spanish dominions in America that led the Franciscans across the South West from Mexico to California. Twenty-two days after the signing of the Declaration of Independence, the first white men broke ground at San Francisco (27th July 1776). It was the aim of Fra Junípero Serra "to plant one of God's milestones at the end of every day's journey." Fra Serra, Apostle to the Indians, set himself the task of building them into orderly community life.

275

" Spanish Missions "—we can picture a sun-drenched land, padres at their breviaries within the shady cloister, natives busy in their workshops, children drilled in creed and catechism—the rhythm of routine tuned by the sweet chimes from high cupolas that summoned the whole community into a Baroque church, ornate with flowing curves yet homelike in adobe and local tiles. The years that intervened between the Independence of Mexico in 1821 and the annexation of California by the United States (1848) saw the disintegration of this idyllic paternalism. The " gold rush " completed the chaos begun by the emancipation of the Indians and the consequent secularisation of Church property.

It is with regret that we turn aside from the fascinating panorama of Catholic Missions in North America. Space compels us to proceed to Protestant Missions among the Indians. Here, we can record no architectural triumphs, for the Puritan mind did not approach Evangelism from that angle. Yet the mere task of preaching the Gospel to the natives involved the task of civilising them in some measure. The process of semi-civilisation unfortunately did little to arrest the decline of the Red race. During the nineteenth century the institution of " Reservations " by the Federal government has enabled them to maintain their own customs and survive, in patches, mostly in the West and South West.

The evangelisation of the natives was sometimes used in England as a decoy to get subscriptions from the pious for commercial ventures. Most of the colonial Charters give prominence to missionary aims as one of the objectives. The seal of the Massachusetts Bay Company was an Indian, a label issuing from his mouth with the S.O.S., " Come over and help us ". In Virginia, the earlier colonists endeavoured to carry out evangelisation. One of the earliest buildings at Harvard was for the use of Indians. The only colony where conciliation with the natives was not at once followed up by Evangelism was Pennsylvania under William Penn; could this be due to Quaker faith in the sufficiency of " the Light that lighteneth every man that cometh into the world " ?

John Eliot, " the Apostle of the Indians ",[1] was a Cambridge graduate who arrived in New England in 1631. By a curious coincidence he sailed in the *Lyon*, the same ship in which his predecessor in Indian Missions, Roger Williams, had crossed the

---

[1] Excellent chapters on Eliot in Williston Walker's *Ten New England Leaders* (1901) and S. E. Morison's *Builders of the Bay Colony* (1930).

Atlantic the year before. Eliot was inducted to the parish of Rox-bury where he remained pastor for fifty-seven years. Although no great preacher, he had a gift of " improving the occasion " which appealed to his Puritan hearers. Calling on a business man one day he noted that his religious books were in a case against the wall, but his account books were on a table before him. " Sir, here is earth on the table, and heaven on the shelf; let not earth by any means thrust heaven out from your mind." Eliot's pastoral labours did not deflect him from the difficulty of learning Indian dialects, which involved sitting in filthy wigwams and eating loathsome food. He followed Paul's advice in adopting " all means . . . that some might be saved ". His zeal was quickened by the firm belief that the Red Indians were the Ten " Lost " Tribes of Israel. In 1646 he started to preach to the red men, and suc-ceeded in arousing their interest. He was thanked by the General Court of Massachusetts, who awarded him £10 " in respect of his greate paines and charge in instructing ye Indians in ye know-ledge of God ". Villages were built near Boston for these native converts, the wigwams being grouped in an orderly way round the meeting-house, which also served as a school. The inmates aban-doned polygamy and Sabbath-breaking; duly instructed in Puritan theology, they imitated their white preceptors by subscribing their names to a " covenant ". Natick was the principal village of the " praying Indians ". The native community has long since dis-appeared, but the town owns a copy of Eliot's Indian Bible. This is significant as the first Bible of any kind to be printed in America before 1782; Britain rigorously required that every English Bible must be imported. Eliot's Catechism (1653) was the first book to be printed in an Indian tongue. His complete Indian Bible appeared in 1663—a triumph of scholarship achieved in the face of almost insurmountable difficulties. Apart from religion it is a labour of love, a cultural landmark. Yet those secular-minded historians, the Beards, do not so much as mention Eliot's name in the index of their portly *Rise of American Civilisation*.

Long before this, news reached England of Eliot's remarkable success as a missionary, Thomas Shepard's pamphlet proclaimed *The Day-Breaking if not the Sun Rising of the Gospell with the Indians* (London, 1647). In 1649 the Long Parliament established " The President and Society for the Propagation of the Gospel in New England ". Under the direction of Cromwell a fund of

T

£11,000 was raised at home and invested in real estate. This was the first Foreign Missionary Association in England—would that the impulse had not flagged after the Restoration of 1660! By 1658 the Society was spending £520 a year in New England (including Eliot's salary of £50). Books, tools and clothing were despatched overseas. By 1674 you might see no fewer than 33 villages of " praying Indians ", clustering around Boston and dotted over the island of Martha's Vineyard. Unfortunately, the Narragansetts and other tribes of southern New England were strongly suspicious of the missionaries' intentions. They rose against the white man in " King Philip's War " (1675-6). Murder, fire and robbery cost the New Englanders 600 lives and ravaged 40 towns. Some of the " praying Indians " stood fast for their Christian faith, others joined their savage kinsmen as " preying Indians ". Fierce exaltation possessed the whites, akin to the frenzy that inspired Israel against Midian. Let them be put to the sword, and the remnant be reduced to " hewers of wood and drawers of water " to the Chosen People. Even saintly Shepard greeted the extermination of the Pequots as " a Divine slaughter ".

Disaster dogged Evangelism again and again. When all seemed to be prospering, the Indians would rise against the white man, and even earnest Christians would believe that there was something in the frontiersman's conviction that " the only good Indian is a dead Indian ". As time passed and the Red menace no longer threatened the East, the race faded away. At Natick, Mass., e.g., the natives decreased to 1666 persons in 1749; to 20 in 1797; and only one was left by 1855. Fortunately Eliot did not live to see the dying of the race he had befriended.

As the frontier moved westwards and northwards during the eighteenth century, a second wave of enthusiasm for the conversion of the Indians swept through New England. Fervid fire was kindled by the " Great Awakening ". A distinguished Yale student named David Brainerd, converted in 1739, dedicated his life to Indian Missions, and was supported by " The Society in Scotland for the Propagation of Christian Knowledge ". He had been expelled from Yale for attending a revival meeting of the " Separates ", but received ordination from the " New Side " Presbytery of Newark, N.J. He soon wore himself out by long missionary journeys in New Jersey and as far south as the Susquehanna Valley. His candle burned down to the socket and he died of consumption in his twenty-ninth year. His last days were spent in the parsonage of Northampton, in northern Massachusetts. He had been engaged to Jerusha, daughter of Jonathan Edwards. Edwards published Brainerd's *Life*, compiled from his " Journal ", which speedily became a missionary classic on both sides of the Atlantic. From a devotional point of view, it is a morbid, introspective book, exaggerating the defects of the Great Awakening through the religious experience of a consumptive. As a missionary tract, however, it had an immense circulation. John Wesley published it in abbreviated form for the Methodists. It stimulated the Moravians.[1] It inspired the impulse to the foreign field in Carey, Coke, Martyn and Marsden, who went out to India, the West Indies, Persia and New Zealand. Professor Sweet rightly claims that " David Brainerd dead became a greater influence for the spread of the missionary spirit than David Brainerd alive ".

Edwards' name was now well known in Britain. In 1746 he welcomed the suggestion of a group of Scottish ministers that Christians should unite in a " concert of prayer for the coming of our Lord's kingdom throughout the earth ". This was fifty years before enthusiasm for Missions burst into action among English-speaking Protestants. Edwards himself became a missionary at Stockbridge on the western frontier of Massachusetts (1751). He was in his forty-eighth year, and had just been dismissed after a bitter campaign by his congregation at Northampton. He preached to the Housatonics through an interpreter, as an agent of the London Society for the Propagation of the Gospel in New England (the Prince of Wales being leading subscriber). With all respect to Edwards his metaphysical cast of mind was hardly suited to the task. Like many of his predecessors, he was much too theological for the redskins. Yet he had the gift of inspiring missionaries who *were* successful. The Rev. Eleazer Wheelock was essentially a man of the Great Awakening. He started a modest school for Indians at Lebanon, Connecticut, about the same time as Edwards settled at Stockbridge. One of the Lebanon pupils, Samson Occom, a Mohegan, showed such promise that

---

[1] Their work among the redskins is a tragic story. David Zeisberger's settlement at Gnadenhütten (" Tents of Grace ") was founded on the Lehigh River, Pennsylvania (1746). Nine years later most of his missionaries were massacred. The Moravian Indians refused to take sides at the Revolution and suffered at the hands of both Americans and British. On one occasion, colonial militia massacred Christian Indians who practised non-resistance taught by the Moravians; 29 men, 27 women and 34 children perished.

he was sent to England to plead for his school cause. Occom preached three hundred sermons, caught the popular fancy and was instrumental in raising £10,000. This meant that Wheelock was able to enlarge the scope of the institution. It was incorporated as a college and came into being at Hanover, in the wilds of New Hampshire (1769). Named after Lord Dartmouth, chairman of the English board responsible for raising funds (a friend of Lady Huntingdon and a fervent Evangelical) the new foundation was intended for the training of missionaries to the Indians; it bore the appropriate motto, *Vox clamantis in deserto*. The decay of the Indian race meant that the original purpose of the Charter could not be maintained, but instead of closing down, Dartmouth College widened its scope still further, and is now one of the finest of New England Colleges, in a magnificent setting of mountain and forest.

One of the most successful, large-scale examples of Evangelism was in Georgia, where the Cherokee nation adopted Christian civilisation towards the close of the eighteenth century. They divided their territory into districts, with justice administered on American lines. They bred sheep and cattle. They cultivated farms, orchards and gardens. By about 1800 they were manufacturing cotton and woollen cloths, and carrying on an extensive trade with their white neighbours. Schools were flourishing in their village and the printing press was at work. The Christian religion was publicly acknowledged and consistently followed. Presbyterians, Methodists, Baptists and Moravians were well represented, by ardent disciples.

One might have supposed that the State of Georgia would have given all encouragement to this model community. Unfortunately, the Georgians preferred to break the tenth commandment. They coveted Cherokee land. The State actually parcelled it out in lottery tickets, distributed among white voters. Missionaries were arrested for preaching to Cherokees, and Cherokees were imprisoned and hung for holding on to their rights.[1] Actually, the State of Georgia had no right to interfere at all, for the Cherokees had placed themselves under the Federal government as far back as 1785. They had the status of a sovereign nation: they were not simply tenants at will. In 1823 their chiefs (mostly half-breeds) resolved " never to cede one foot more of land ". Presidents

[1] R. S. Walker, *Torchlights to the Cherokees* (New York, 1931).

Monroe and J. Q. Adams had treated the Cherokees with all courtesy, paying due respect to their Treaty rights. Andrew Jackson was a believer in democracy, to be sure, but democracy among white men; he sided with land-hungry frontiersmen and told the Cherokees that they must submit or emigrate. The exploited people carried their case to the Supreme Court of the United States, which in 1832 declared that the Cherokees formed a distinct community " in which the laws of Georgia have no force ", and that all claims to jurisdiction were null and void. The Governor of Georgia, acting on the theory of " State rights " (so dear to the Southern heart) declared that this inconvenient decision of the Supreme Court was " usurpation ". He acted with violence against the natives and defied the Federal authorities. President Jackson did not see his way to enforce the decision of the Supreme Court.

From all over the United States came petitions, remonstrances and indignant protests against this flagrant miscarriage of justice. Press, pulpit and platform roused the Christian conscience. When Congress considered the question, it appeared as if justice would triumph. In spite of earnest advocacy, the cause of the Cherokees was lost by one vote. Deprived of their rights, they were eventually removed by federal authority from the soil of Georgia (1838). Andrew Jackson, so-called champion of the common man, had failed them; he evidently did not want to lose popularity by taking up the cause of a coloured race. The great wrong of negro slavery, aided and abetted by no less a man than Whitefield, evangelist of two continents, had blunted the conscience and blighted the humanity of Georgia (see above, p. 23 f.). Crime against the black race led to crime against the red race.[1] The gates of hell triumphed. But thirty years later " the chivalry of Georgia " were vanquished in the Civil War at the battle of Missionary Ridge—a name that recalled the martyrdom of the Cherokee nation and their missionaries who helped them to build a Christian civilisation.[2]

Missionary work among the Red Indians stimulated endeavours

[1] The Indian had few friends, even among " nigger-worshipping " Abolitionists. General Sheridan, friend of the negro, used to say: " The only good Indian is a dead Indian."

[2] The Indian U.S. population is mainly grouped in Reservations and numbers about 500,000. Most of them are nominally Christian (Protestant in N.W., R.C. in S.W.). The new policy of encouraging Indian indigenous culture has somewhat embarrassed Missions by setting old superstitions in a more favourable light.

which sought a wider field. The formation of the (undenominational) London Missionary Society led to similar associations in
New York (1796) and in Connecticut (1798).[1] The latter started
operations by sending David Bacon, " afoot and alone, with no
more luggage than he could carry on his person " to instruct the
wild tribes in the Lake Erie region. The *Connecticut Evangelical
Magazine* (1800) sought to interest church members in Missions
" by exhibiting displays of the grace and mercy of God . . . rather
than to amuse the specialist and entertain the curious ". In 1802
the Presbyterian General Assembly took over the direction of
Missions from presbyteries, congregations, etc., anticipating the
Church of Scotland in entrusting leadership and control to a
standing committee. General stimulus was provided by the passage of British missionaries to the East, travelling *via* America,
e.g. Robert Morrison, the Apostle of China. It seemed probable
that the American societies might be able to link up with the
London Missionary Society. Then occurred a historic incident
that stirred American initiative to act on their own.

Williams College, among the Berkshire Hills in western Massachusetts, like the other New England colleges, Amherst and Dartmouth, had been moved by the Evangelical revival at the beginning
of the nineteenth century. It was under the lee of a haystack on
the campus of Williams that Samuel J. Mills and a group of
friends dedicated themselves to Christian service as America's
pioneer missionaries (1810). An August thunderstorm drove them
to the shelter of a haystack; and while the skies played an overture
to an epochal enterprise, Mills proposed that they should send the
Gospel to Asia. " We can do it if we will." This prayer group,
which has been compared to Wesley's Holy Club at Oxford, was
reconstituted at the newly-opened Andover Theological Seminary; it kept an invaluable record of its meetings in cipher (translated in 1819). At Andover, they were joined by several of a like
mind, including Adoniram Judson, who had just graduated at
Brown University, Providence. He was much impressed by *Star
in the East*, written by the famous East India Company chaplain,
Claudius Buchanan, whose father was schoolmaster at Cambuslang during Whitefield's revival. It was Judson who approached

---

[1] The English S.P.G. Missionaries ceased operations in America after the
War of Independence. They worked mainly to promote the interests of the
Anglican Church among the colonists, and to some extent for the conversion
of negroes.

the London Missionary Society; would they accept two or three unmarried men, liberally educated and " susceptible of a passion for missions " ? The reply was —providentially—unfavourable. The petitioners then looked to the General Association of Massachusetts. " Feeling their youth and inexperience ", Judson, Mills, Nott and Newell solicited " the attention of their Reverend Fathers " (June, 1810).

Next day a committee decided to institute " The American Board of Commissioners for Foreign Missions ". They in turn appointed a " Prudential Committee ", which seems to have lived up to its name for at first only one member approved of the venture as practical. Eventually, however, five young men were ordained in the Tabernacle Church at Salem (8th February 1812). The imagination of the congregation was kindled by the dramatic solemnity of the service; " the entire assembly seemed moved . . . as trees by a mighty wind ". Salem, noted in those days for its trade with the East, was soon to export a new cargo—missionaries. The young pioneers set sail on the *Caravan* and the *Harmony* soon after their ordination. They brought the Gospel as America's gift to Asia, and in their hearts echoed Watts' hymn which they had sung together at that memorable haystack prayer-meeting:

> Let all the heathen writers join
>   To form one perfect book;
>   Great God, if once compared to Thine,
>   How mean their writings look!

During the weary months at sea there was ample opportunity of searching the Scriptures. One result was unforeseen. Adoniran Judson and Luther Rice, sailing on different ships, came to the same conclusion by the time they reached Calcutta—that Baptist principles were among the foundation-truths of the New Testament. Both men were immersed, with their wives, in the Baptist church at Calcutta. Having secured the support of their own denomination with some difficulty, they had committed themselves to the care of another denomination by a simple act of faith. Would the American Baptists underwrite their hazardous venture ? Rice returned to the United States to appeal for support: Judson, not allowed (as a missionary) to settle in the domains of the East India Company, went on heroic adventure in Burma.

Fortunately for these pioneers of faith, Luther Rice found support among the Baptists of the eastern states. The " American

Board " found other Congregationalists to take the place of the seceders. An embarrassing conversion thus spread enthusiasm for the extension of God's kingdom to two denominations; another door of opportunity was opened. If, however, Judson and Rice had looked to the Baptists of the South West, they would have found little encouragement. It is surprising to learn that the frontier farmer-preachers, till some years after 1812, had little sympathy with Missions. For instance, the Apple Creek Baptist Association of Illinois passed the following resolution in 1830: " We as an association do not hesitate to say that we declare an unfellowship with foreign and domestic missions and bible societies, sunday schools and tract societies, and all other missionary institutions." This resolution was not exceptional but typical. As late as 1846 there were 46,000 anti-Missionary Baptists in the United States, mostly in the West. Alexander Campbell, afterwards founder of the growing Disciples denomination, was once among the arch-opponents of Missions. These critics were unreasonably suspicious of organisations and paid officials as sapping the simple spontaneity of Bible religion. Some of them were hyper-Calvinists, who could not see the good of preaching to the non-elect, " the devil's bona-fide children ". They were little men, not big enough to understand God's purpose for the world and the glory of His kingdom.

Samuel Mills said to his friends before they left for India: " You and I, brother, are little men, but before we die, our influence must be felt on the other side of the world." Mills devoted himself to Home Missions, making laborious journeys across the wilderness to New Orleans and founding the American Bible Society in 1816. He found " a famine not of bread, but of the word of God " (*Amos* 8.11). He saw the curse of slavery with his own eyes. His last venture was a voyage to West Africa (1816) in search of a site for a negro settlement (see below, p. 289). Before his death Mills had fostered sympathy for another coloured race. One day he found a Hawaiian youth, Henry Obookiah, weeping on the steps of Yale; he was hungering for the Word. This moving incident led to the formation of a training school for missionaries in the village of Cornwall, Connecticut. By 1823 it numbered 36 students, including 9 Sandwich Islanders, a Malay, a Maori, 3 Chinamen, a Portuguese, 2 Greeks and 15 American Indians of different tribes.

The " American Board " completed the conversion of Hawaii by 1863; degrading paganism was abolished, though at the cost of a rigid Puritanism hardly suited to the isles of the Pacific. Splendid schools and colleges were built in Asia Minor and Syria. New England transmitted the missionary impulse to other sections of the United States. So when Japanese ports were open to Americans in 1853, Episcopalian and Presbyterian missionaries entered a sphere untouched by the Gospel since the Jesuit heroes of the seventeenth century. Guido Verbeck, of the Dutch Reformed Church in America, became " Apostle of Japan ". Space restrictions unfortunately prohibit any exploration of American Missions overseas.

CHAPTER V

NORTH AND SOUTH

Once to every man and nation comes the moment to decide
In the strife of Truth with Falsehood, for the good or evil side.

LOWELL

EARLY in the nineteenth century the "Mason and Dixon line" dividing North and South became as cardinal as the moving frontier separating East and West. Economic interests tended to determine the prevalent religious attitude as well as the contours of social life. Estrangement hardened into hostility and the Civil War of 1861 ruined the South. The Slavery issue, which was at the root of the conflict, can only be understood in the light of its history. The negro was the only immigrant "invited" to come to America, as Booker Washington put it, with withering irony.

Slavery was imposed by the Spanish conquerors as early as 1517, at the suggestion of the saintly Las Casas. Seeing the sufferings of natives from the West Indies in the mines, he implored Charles V to import negroes, as more physically fit. The agony of one coloured race was relieved by bringing another into servitude. Later in the century the slave trade was systematised. Sir Francis Drake undertook to supply the Spaniards with negroes, and the "African Company" continued the business, British traders being assured a monopoly by the Treaty of Utrecht (1713). A Dutch ship sold the first lot of "black ivory" at Jamestown, Virginia, in 1619. White "indentured labour", semi-servile, was the basis of Virginian economy during the seventeenth century. By 1689 only 8% of the Virginian population was negro, compared to 12% in New York; by 1700 there were 18,000 slaves in British America, of which one-third belonged to the North Colonies.

In view of the assertions of nineteenth-century "Abolitionists", we must note that the Puritan conscience of the seventeenth century did not revolt at the idea of holding negroes as chattels. The Indian wars had familiarised the New Englanders with the expedient of slavery; were not subject races divinely predestined to be " hewers of wood and drawers of water " to the elect ? There was the obvious precedent of the Amalekites in Canaan. Nevertheless, prophetic warnings disturbed saintly slave-owners. In 1675 John Eliot, Apostle of the Indians, remonstrated against the sale of red men captured during " King Philip's War "; he also lamented " the abject condition of the enslaved Africans "; " to sell souls seemeth to me a dangerous merchandise." A quarter of a century later that convinced Puritan, Judge Sewall, declared that there could be " no progress in gospelling " till slavery should be abolished. Cotton Mather, " Puritan Priest ", agreed, but these eminent men were voices crying in the wilderness. By 1776 there were 6,000 slaves in Massachusetts alone, and among the slave owners were respected divines such as President Stiles of Yale and the morbidly conscientious Jonathan Edwards. The blacks were much in demand in households, for even then it was proverbially difficult " to get a Yankee girl to answer a bell ". The following is a typical advertisement in a Boston newspaper: " To be sold . . . the very best Negro Woman in town, who has had the smallpox and measels; is as hearty as a horse, as brisk as a bird, and will work like a beaver " (1742). Samuel Hopkins, the leading " Edwardian " divine, created genuine surprise when he brought his impassioned logic to bear against this " domestic institution " from his pulpit in Newport, R.I. He freed his own slaves and expected his fellow-citizens to do the same. Mrs. Stowe, in *The Minister's Wooing*, represents him arguing with his wealthiest parishioner, who is theoretically interested in Calvinism, but practically interested in the slave traffic.

Rhode Island, most tolerant and progressive of the New England colonies, was the headquarters of the slave traffic. Respectable householders invested as a matter of course in slavers like the *Jolly Bachelor*, which exported rum to Africa and returned with a cargo of slaves. Who can forget the advice of Peter Potter, privateer: " Make ye Cheafe Trade with the Blacks and Little or none with the White people. Worter ye Rum as much as possible and sell as much by the short measure as you can." Such fraud seems petty, however, compared to the horror of the " middle passage ", made more hideous by the odious piety of Bible-reading

Yankee skippers. The American Revolution stirred the New England conscience, but one has the uncomfortable conviction that slavery was given up in the " land of the Pilgrim's pride " mainly because it ceased to be profitable in a northern climate.

Among the Episcopalians, the Society for the Propagation of the Gospel did much to promote the Christian instruction of slaves, although they did not question the legitimacy of the institution. They persuaded a number of householders to encourage their negroes to become Christians, after reassuring them that baptism did not impair property rights. In the quaint little church at Goose Creek, South Carolina, we find that in 1705 there were 30 white and 20 coloured communicants. Mention should be made of Elias Meau, a Huguenot who joined Trinity Church, New York, in 1703. Meau held religious meetings for slaves in the steeple. During the negro rebellion of 1712 he was accused of fomenting disaffection; he was exonerated and his Christian work was officially approved. A later slave insurrection in New York evoked hysteria and iron repression (1741).

The Scots-Irish Presbyterians, the Baptists and other denominations were often too poor to own bondmen during the earlier eighteenth century, but the Quakers were prosperous and their pioneering against slavery is therefore significant. The Charter of Pennsylvania allowed slavery, with certain provisions for release after fourteen years of servitude. After 1711 the Friends' Quarterly Associations were unanimous in protesting against the slave trade.[1]

Parallel to this religious impulse was the political idealism that produced the Declaration of Independence. The Fathers of the Republic were well aware of the dangers of slavery. A slave-owner himself, Jefferson the Democrat declared that it menaced the whole future of American liberty. Washington sought its abolition " by slow, sure and imperceptible degrees ". Unfortunately these ideals were allowed to remain on the heights of rhetoric; they were not brought down to the dark valley of practical politics. Even Andrew Jackson, hero of the poor farmer and mechanic, did little to alleviate the black bondage; indeed he amassed " a goodly number of slaves ", as Beard reminds us.

If statesmen did little to advance gradual emancipation, anti-slavery societies flourished in the border states and spread north-

[1] For the work of Woolman and other Quakers, see p. 34 f.

wards. As early as 1784 the Methodist Episcopal Conference forbade their members to buy and sell slaves (their decision to excommunicate obdurate slave-owners, however, had to be relaxed within six months). In 1818 the General Assembly of the still undivided Presbyterian Church issued a monumental document calling for " unwearied endeavours . . . as speedily as possible to efface this blot on our holy religion ". Even in the South preachers and public men bewailed " our heaviest calamity ". In 1832 the Virginian Legislature failed by one vote to pass a Colonisation Bill, that would have ended slavery by instalments.

In 1816 an American Society was established with the object of founding in West Africa a colony for " free people " of colour. A beginning was made by a white American, Jehudi Ashmun, and by 1847 Liberia was recognised as a republic by most powers— except the United States. This " land of the free " never fulfilled the expectations of its supporters who visualised a steady flow of emancipated slaves to the Dark Continent. Indeed the project diverted much of the public sympathy that had hitherto fed the various Abolition Societies.[1]

About 1830 the whole question of slavery entered a new phase. Hitherto, the institution was seldom defended in the abstract save by those engaged in the trade; it was generally agreed that it ought to be gradually modified. But now the economic situation had changed and outweighed religious and humanitarian values. There was an urgent demand for cotton in England, which had the machinery for spinning. The United States had the raw material, which could be processed more profitably since the invention of Whitney's cotton gin. It became obvious that only slave labour could provide Manchester with adequate cotton. If Cotton was to be King, the plantations of the South must be exploited on purely commercial lines, which meant that the supply of black hands must expand considerably.[2]

When it appeared that slavery was reviving, a more aggressive agitation was launched by the New England Anti-slavery Society, which in 1837 called for the excommunication and ostracism of slave-holders. Lloyd Garrison and Wendell Phillips were the

---

[1] For an incisive criticism of Abolitionist behaviour see Maynard's *Story of American Catholicism* (Chs. 17-19, 1943).

[2] For the ordeal of the Lancashire operatives when the cotton supply was cut off (1861-5) and their anti-slavery idealism which Lincoln honoured as " sublime Christian heroism ", see T. Armstrong's novel, *King Cotton* (London, 1947).

spearheads of " Abolition "; Theodore Parker was its prophet and Whittier its poet. For a time public opinion in the North regarded Abolitionists as cranky extremists. Most of the rank and file were Methodists and Baptists, somewhat despised by those who belonged to the more " respectable " denominations.

When, however, the politicians of the South made it clear that it was their aim to extend slavery westwards into new territories, the issue was sharpened. The institution that had done so much harm was in danger of spreading with the expanding frontier. When the question was raised in Congress (1854) whether Kansas should be a slave-state or a free-state, the North responded to the challenge with alacrity. Thousands of New Englanders set out for Kansas, determined that the cause of freedom must obtain a majority. Christian faith had not been demonstrated by such concerted zeal, since the distant days of the Pilgrims. In many an historic New England parish the Kansas Crusaders were sped on their way with prayer, as they sang Whittier's inspiring hymn:

> We cross the prairies as of old
> Our fathers crossed the sea,
> To make the West, as they the East,
> The Empire of the free.

Dr. H. R. Niebuhr, however, considers that anti-slavery agitation was " probably less effective in influencing the social psychology of the North than in consolidating the pro-slavery feelings of the South ".[1] Slavery ceased to be a matter of debate when one crossed the Potomac. The " solid South " proceeded to glorify as their peculiar institution what they had questioned seriously a generation earlier on economic, political and religious grounds. Statesmen rationalised, preachers idealised. The Governor of South Carolina announced: " Domestic slavery is the cornerstone of our republican edifice " (1835). Presbyterian and Episcopal clergy dwelt on the beauty of the " patriarchal attitude " in the light of the Bible.[2] Dr. Thornwell, of South Carolina, preaching in 1860 at the dedication of a negro church, defined slavery as " an obligation to labor for another, determined by the providence of God ". Though founded on a curse (like class distinctions)

---

[1] *The Social Sources of Denominationalism*, p. 190 (New York, 1929).
[2] Propaganda was carried on in the North, cp. R. Fuller's *Domestic Slavery a Scriptural Institution* (New York, 1847); S. B. Howe, *Slave-holding not sinful* (New York, 1855). Bishop Hopkins of Vermont was pro-slavery.

slavery might operate in a fallen world under a dispensation of grace. The Christian should regard the slave, not as a tool, but as an immortal spirit assigned to a peculiar position in this world of sin. In 1849 the " Old School " Presbyterians (to which Dr. Thornwell belonged) resolved that it was " improper and inexpedient " for the Church to interfere. Their General Assembly resolved in 1854 that it was " the peculiar mission of the Southern Church to conserve slavery, and to make it a blessing to both master and slave ". The " New School " Presbyterians, who were strongest in the North, with a leaning to Abolitionism, lost 15,000 members in the South when a memorial from the Presbytery of Lexington, Kentucky, was ill received (showing that many of its ministers kept slaves " from principle as well as choice ".)

The Baptists and Methodists of the South, who used to protest against slavery, now veered round to the dominant view. Drawn from poor whites, some of them had prospered and were anxious to accommodate themselves to fashionable standards. They had become sensitive about their association with subversive movements (Nat Turner, who headed a negro insurrection in Virginia in 1831, had been a coloured Baptist preacher). Southern Baptists were so hurt by the anti-slavery activities of their Northern brethren that they separated from them in 1845. The same year the Methodists also split, following a test case. Bishop Andrews of Georgia had become the owner of a few house-slaves by marriage. The General Conference debated for eleven days, finally suspending him by 111 votes to 60, till he had ceased to be a slave-owner. The result was schism and the creation of " The Methodist Episcopal Church South ". A lawsuit over property followed, and the Southern Methodists secured a favourable verdict from the Supreme Court of the United States. In the words of the South Carolina statesman, J. C. Calhoun, the most vital cord that held the States together, Religion, was ominously snapping.

When the Civil War broke out in 1861 churches that had hitherto managed to hold together over slavery, split on the political issue. Many of the Episcopalians were ardent Confederates (Bishop Leonidas Polk of Louisiana fell in action as a major-general). After the defeat of the South, the Episcopalians of the North welcomed their Southern brethren back to fellowship, having tactfully overlooked their absence during the War. This irenic attitude was a contrast to the belligerent bearing of other denominations towards " the rebels ". The Southern Methodists stood aside till 1939. The Southern Presbyterians and Baptists were confirmed in their isolationist spirit after the War and still cherish ultra-conservative principles and " ethos ".

Reverting to the slavery issue, we must not forget the effective Abolitionist propaganda of Mrs. Harriet Beecher Stowe and her brother Henry Ward Beecher. *Uncle Tom's Cabin* (1852) was one of those books that are " great enough to be badly written ". Dramatised versions have had " the longest run in history ", culminating in the phenomenal success of the Players' Club (New York, 1933). An elaborate film would have been made in 1944, but for the protest of the Negro press against " Uncle Tom-ism "; the humility and patience of the humble hero irritated reformers who were battling to bring the coloured man abreast of his white brother in education and status.

Uncle Tom's Cabin originated when the " Crusader in Crinoline " was attending a Communion service in the First Parish Church (a New England meeting-house) at Brunswick, Maine. She had a vision of a negro saint being mercilessly flogged, and this suggested the martyrdom of his race. The story would doubtless have been better had Mrs. Stowe lived in the South, but she had seen something of slavery across the great river at Cincinnati. She cheerfully admitted the milder patriarchal aspects of the " peculiar institution ", and puzzled Southern critics by making her slave-driver, Simon Legree, a Vermonter. Against a realistic background, picturesquely and even humorously conceived, rose stark horror—the separation of husbands and wives, parents and children; the deliberate breeding of plantation hands for the " deep South ", and the unlimited power entrusted to sadistic masters. A fully documented *Key to Uncle Tom's Cabin* followed, and the unassuming little woman found herself world-famous.

From the pulpit of Plymouth Church, Brooklyn, her brother roused the feelings of thousands to fever-pitch with all the resources of an orator.[1] He even " auctioned " slave-girls at Sunday services to raise the price of their freedom; Mrs. Hunt recalled this experience as she stood in Plymouth pulpit sixty-seven years later with the pastor, Dr. Durkee. When the Civil War broke out (1861) Henry Ward Beecher toured England and faced hostile

---

[1] Ian Hay's play, *Hattie Stowe*, is a convincing one in the understanding of Christian motives and background, but he does not do justice to Henry Ward.

audiences. Cotton was cut off, millions were out of work; the governing classes sympathised with the Southern gentry, and middle-class individualism was inclined to sympathise with "State Rights ", as opposed to centralisation. It was the opinion of General Lee and his staff that " had it not been for *Uncle Tom's Cabin* and Beecher's speeches in the British Isles, the Confederacy could have secured the recognition of Britain and France ", with all that this involved in moral and material aid.[1] In England, Dr. Newman Hall, an eminent Congregational minister, turned the tide of public opinion in favour of the North. He awoke by humanitarian appeal what was afterwards called the " Nonconformist Conscience ". Dr. Hall crossed the Atlantic and received an ovation wherever he spoke; his sermon to Congress made a deep impression.[2]

During the Civil War, or " the War between the States " (as they still prefer to call it in the South) religion was much to the fore on both sides. The Confederates were as sure of the righteousness of their cause as the Union men. " Stonewall " Jackson (a Presbyterian) and Robert E. Lee (an Episcopalian) were fervent Evangelicals. At night the camps resounded with hymns. A typical entry in a Confederate chaplain's diary reads: " May 17, 1863. At three o'clock I preached in Bates' brigade: a very good time; revival. . . May 19, Johnson's brigade: 30-40 mourners; glorious work in this command." When President Jefferson Davis received the fatal news that Grant had broken through the lines and that the Capital must be evacuated, he was quietly worshipping in St. Paul's, Richmond,[3] one of the noblest shrines of Virginia.

The War was nearly over, but the horrors of " peace " were to follow. For ten years the South lay prostrate under military dictatorship supported by northern " carpet-baggers " (Republicans by trade), Southern " scalawags " and demoralised negroes. Most British people had no idea of what " Reconstruction " meant till they saw one of the first great historic films, " The Birth of a Nation". The courage, patience and resourcefulness of the

[1] Lyman Beecher Stowe, *Saints, Sinners and Beechers*, p. 293 (London, 1935).
[2] His American friends contributed towards the " Lincoln Tower " of Christ Church, Westminster Bridge Road. This spire (damaged in the *Blitz*) represented the Stars and Stripes in coloured stonework.
[3] Incidentally, one of the finest Greek Revival churches (1845) in the U.S. It is typical of the Episcopal tradition in Virginia, retaining the central pulpit (as in Christ Church, Alexandria, where Washington worshipped).

U

Confederacy live again for us in "Gone with the Wind," and the picture presented by fiction has been confirmed by historians.[1]

During the Civil War the Union Army was kept well supplied with comforts, tracts and books by a civilian organisation known as "The Christian Commission". The "Freedman's Relief Association" did its best to meet the needs of elated but distracted negroes, streaming aimlessly from the plantations into the towns. Little of this Christian spirit of helpfulness was shown towards the defeated white men of the South. They were simply "the rebels" and destined to be humiliated, as their country was occupied, state by state. In response to the call by Union chaplains, vacant churches of all denominations, which were numerous, were often placed under the provost-martial. These pulpits were filled with "loyal ministers, white and coloured". The general in command of Missouri deposed a well-known St. Louis minister, Dr. Samuel B. McPheeters, for his Confederate sympathies, and ordered him to leave the state within ten days. Dr. McPheeters protested to the Federal Attorney-General, who received a letter from Lincoln: "The United States government must not . . . undertake to run the churches. When an individual, in a church or out of it, becomes dangerous, he must be checked, but let the churches, as such, take care of themselves. It will not do for the United States to appoint Trustees, Supervisors, etc., for the churches" (January 1863).

After the assassination of Lincoln, popular hysteria in the North called for stern repression against the conquered South. President Johnson was impeached because he finally decided to be just to the defeated people. During his trial the General Conference of the Methodist Episcopal Church, then meeting in Chicago (May 1868) actually set aside an hour of prayer that his conviction might not be thwarted by "corrupt influences". Corrupt influences were not unknown among northern Methodists themselves, for political bosses and business interests were at work behind the scenes. Bishop Matthew Simpson, the denominational "spellbinder" used his oratory to keep up feeling against the South. "Parson Brownlow",[2] appointed Governor of Tennessee, announced: "The Devil is in the people of the South and in the

[1] C. Bower, *The Tragic Era* (Cambridge, Mass., 1929); cp. W. A. Dunning, *Essays on the Civil War and Reconstruction* (New York, 1931).
[2] *Parson Brownlow's Book* (1862), his wartime adventures, was a best-seller.

man at the White House in particular. If we are to have another war, I want a finger in that pie. I want your army to come in three divisions, the first to kill, the second to burn, and the third to survey the land into small parcels and give it those to who are loyal in the North " (*New York Herald*, 11th September 1866). The Baptists of the North did not have the advantage of a bureaucratic machine, but they too pressed for the retention of Union troops to hold the South in continued subjection. All this is a telling illustration of Dean Inge's aphorism: " The Church never goes in for politics without coming out badly smirched." One of the few outstanding Christians who withstood the hysterical demand for vengeance was a young Congregational minister named Washington Gladden, a pioneer in the application of the Gospel to economic and social questions. His sincere pity for the South and his manly appeal for reconciliation comes home to the heart of all who read his *Recollections*.

The type of missionary sent down from the North varied. Sometimes he was little more than a " carpet-bagger " wearing a white tie, who kissed negro babies, agitated for negro suffrage and told coloured folk that Jesus was a Republican. Sometimes he was a sincere Christian, who had no intention of setting the ex-slave against his former master. The Congregationalists (hitherto strangers in the South) were foremost in founding schools and colleges to train competent negro leaders. They realised the importance of handicrafts as well as literacy as a means of uplifting a backward race. They also stressed the importance of Christian ethics; it was not enough to " get religion ". The coloured man would have a stronger case if he proved by his behaviour that he was a moral and economic asset to the country, not a liability. Institutes like Hampton and Tuskegee have done much to foster self-respect and a sane Christian attitude on the racial question. If the " solid South " to-day exercises what is practically one-party government in the interests of white supremacy, the politicians of the North must share the blame; for ten years after the War they maintained military government, while " carpet-baggers " looted State treasuries and " crackpots " practised their theories of negro equality. " Reconstruction " on these lines, aided and abetted by Northern radicals and religionists,[1] gave the reactionaries of the

---

[1] Henry Ward Beecher, the slave's friend, evoked bitter animosity in Northern " Christian " circles when he persisted in advocating reconciliation in the South after Lincoln's assassination.

South a stock argument against any amelioration of the negro's lot (since 1946 there has been a fresh outbreak of lynching outrages). The tragedy is that Lincoln, the very man who wanted to befriend the defeated South,[1] became a bogy. Only a few years ago a man named Lynchfield circulated a petition in South Caroline urging the legislature to make the public display of Lincoln's portrait an offence punishable by $50 or 30 days imprisonment. " You wouldn't hang a picture of Hitler or Tojo in a public building, would you ? " asked the *Anderson Independent*. " Any such person would be tarred and feathered; but neither has done as much damage to the South as Abe Lincoln did " (*Nation*, 5th December 1942).

One of the most interesting problems of American Church History is the religion of the negro in genesis and development. By the nineteenth century white suspicion of their conversion to Christianity died down. Harriet Martineau about 1830 noticed advertisements of " pious negroes " as specially good bargains. An increasing number of slave-owners encouraged religion in the slave quarters. In 1847 Bishop Elliott of Georgia urged Episcopal planters to worship together with their workers; " there would be less danger of inhumanity and insubordination between parties who knelt around the same table." The patriarchal ideal was, however, seldom attained. The coloured folk were relegated to a gallery. It has been said that this is the origin of the term " nigger heaven ", but in Episcopal and Presbyterian churches they seldom felt at home; the ritual was too formal and the preaching was too doctrinal. When the negro " got religion " he felt more at ease in Methodist and Baptist churches, where there was more warmth and less inequality. Up till 1830 the Baptists had a number of " mixed " congregations. Just before the outbreak of the Civil War the Southern Methodists had 207,000 coloured communicants —one quarter of their membership.

The defeat of the Confederacy produced an exodus of negroes from the churches; race consciousness ran high and raised the cry, " Come ye out and be separate! " The whites accepted the inevitable implication of emancipation, and were quite ready to " let my people go " (in the words of the negro " spiritual "). In

---

[1] Lincoln's parents were " Predestinarian Baptists ". He had seen so much of sectarianism that he would join no church until it adopted as its sole qualification for membership Christ's condensed statement that true religion is love to man and God.

some places they even helped the ex-slaves to build their own churches, or gave them the use of ones they no longer required. Negroes from the North, who had experience of running their own congregations, were able to lend a hand. There was a nucleus for Methodists in the " African Methodist Episcopal Church ", founded in 1816 by Richard Allen, their first bishop, at Philadelphia. This originated in a secession from the historic St. George's, a " mixed " congregation, where the negroes had the worst seats and had to wait till the whites had communicated. The new body had only 20,000 members in 1856, but spread rapidly throughout the South after the Civil War, claiming 212,000 communicants in 1876 and 850,000 in 1907. In doctrine, polity and usage the African M.E. Church closely followed the body from which it sprang. In practice, it was naturally more illiterate, providing plenty of emotional outlet for ex-slaves. Another large body, similar to the above, but allowing the laity more power, is the " African Methodist Episcopal Zion " Church (Zion simply commemorating the name of the New York congregation where the new sect originated in 1820).

The Baptists, however, have won the heart of the negro. The first African Baptist congregation was founded at Savannah, Georgia, in 1788; but it was not till after the Civil War that the sect made phenomenal strides. The rite of immersion in sluggish Southern rivers was as popular among the coloured folk as operas among the white. Whole communities went Baptist. Lack of the " overhead " organisation so typical of Methodism has not prevented the Baptists from attaining a membership of about four million (nearly one-third of the total negro population of the United States, and two-thirds of the coloured communicant roll). The disadvantages of each congregation being a separate unit are offset by the pride felt by the average negro in the fact that his church property is held by the local church, not denominational headquarters.

There are still some 600,000 negroes who attend white churches. The Episcopal Church provides suffragan bishops for coloured people without segregation. In some places mulatto congregations of superior education (e.g. Charleston, S.C.) have aligned themselves with the "Reformed Episcopal Church" (see above, p. 226). Roman Catholicism has made little appeal to the negro, save in the Latin atmosphere of Louisiana, in spite of their love of pageantry and action. Rome, to be sure, was less race-conscious than Protestantism, but lost heavily after the Civil War owing to failure to organise special congregations for coloured folk.

The census of 1936 revealed a negro church membership of well over five and a half millions, accounting for 10.1% of all communicants in the United States. A considerable majority of coloured people belong to denominations that correspond to the major white Churches; a minority only belong to the weirder varieties of ecstatic experience—" Apostolic Overcoming Church of God ", " the Fire Baptized Holiness Church of God ", and " the Church of the Living God " (which claims Christ as a negro). Considering the degree of illiteracy and suggestibility that still prevails, it is surprising that a comparatively small number of flamboyant adventurers have flourished like " Father Divine ", self-deified and " combusted on the Earth plane ", keeping Court in New York, riding in a Rolls Royce, and protected by a uniformed bodyguard! The negro churches since the Civil War have shown a touching, naïve eagerness to do everything as in Bible times—immersion, love-feasts, speaking in tongues, faith-healing. Their preachers have only won popularity when they have followed coloured folkways in traditional " corybantic " style. Those who boast that they have " never rubbed their heads against a college wall " win a much larger following than those who have sought to train for the ministry as thoroughly as negro doctors, professors and lawyers. Since 1920 there has been an increase in the number of congregations that closely imitate cultivated standards of preaching and worship, but these will be a small minority till the general level slowly improves (only about 10% of school taxes is spent on negro children, compared to white).[1]

The white churches of the South, with honourable exceptions, have little to teach the coloured churches in enlightenment and culture. There is zeal, to be sure, evidenced by well-attended places of worship, but vision and breadth are conspicuously lacking. The Methodists and Baptists are almost as dominant in religion as the Democratic party in politics. Fundamentalist theology and ethics mould public opinion in rural areas and the smaller towns.[2]

---

[1] Nevertheless negro literacy has increased from 5% after the Civil War to 69% in 1910.

[2] See eight chapters on " The South: Problem Child of the Nation " in John Gunther's *Inside U.S.A.* (Hamish Hamilton, 1947).

Dr. Truslow Adams wonders what would have happened to the Puritans, had they settled (as they might have done) in Virginia rather than in New England. The irony is, that the South, in origin predominantly un-Puritanical, has become the headquarters of American Puritanism, while Puritanism in New England is almost extinct. This is a curious reversal of human tradition, as Mr. William Power has pointed out in a suggestive essay, *The World Unvisited*. One would imagine that the warm climate of the South would prove inhospitable to religion of a rigorous, austere type, and that in a generation or so ardour would cool to laxity; it would be interesting to pursue this historic enquiry along psychological and sociological lines.

Southern Puritanism has little of the New England respect for scholarship, the fear of " an illiterate ministry " that inspired the founding of Harvard College, while Boston was only a frontier village. Indeed, certain large denominations in the South have shown an unwholesome fear of learning.[1] Among the Baptists (so representative of the South) only 15% of the ministers have had a full professional education. Biblical literalism is invoked as a defence-mechanism to justify illiteracy. Even among the Presbyterians fanatical Fundamentalism forms a hard core. " Mr Moody honestly used all the grammar he had for God," remarks Dean Sperry, " and everyone honoured him for so doing. But the deliberate cult of ungrammatical speech and an uninformed mind is not necessarily an assured means of access to the world of the Spirit " (*Religion in America*, p. 179).

There are upland and inland areas of the South where the " old-time religion " of frontier revivalism still survives in its most primitive form.[2] Early in the twentieth century an Englishman, Cecil Sharp, explored the remote mountain districts of Kentucky and astonished his fellow-countrymen by the announcement that Elizabethan English was still spoken there and old folk-songs still

---

[1] Frankly expressed by the authentic prayer of a rural preacher: " O Lord, I thank Thee that I am ignorunt. Make me ignorunter! Make me ignorunt as a mule."

[2] In the Kentucky Mountains the " ole-time religion " has taken on thoroughly morbid characteristics that might be expected in Hayti or the Congo. Men of degenerate Anglo-Saxon stock have added to the tradition of orgiastic revivalism the practice of fondling poisonous snakes as a test of faith in their shanty chapels. H. Preece and C. Kraft explore " wild religions " in *Dew on Jordan* (Dutton, 1947). W. Berney and H. Richardson in *Dark of the Moon* dramatise witchcraft and revivalism among the Great Smoky Mountains—a powerful, imaginative play.

sung by the " hill-billies " More recently " folk-hymns " have
been discovered. At camp-meetings easily-remembered words
would be sung to traditional melodies, and " cautionary tales "
set to ballad measures with lilting choruses. Thus a once-gay
girl tells how before her conversion,

> I often times to church did go
> My beauty and fine clothes to show.

It was quite the thing to argue doctrinal points in folk-hymns.
The case against infant-baptism was invincible.

> Thus we have marched the ark around
>   And find no infants there:
> If there are any to be found,
>   We wish to ask you, where?

There were old favourites like the " Appletree hymn "—

> The tree of life my soul hath seen
> Laden with fruit and always green;
> The trees of nature fruitless be
> Compared with Christ the appletree.

The " folk-hymns " of half-educated whites cannot, however,
be compared for sheer beauty, power and poignancy with the
" negro spirituals ". Song leaders on the plantations would para-
phrase Scripture in language that illiterate slaves could understand, and create a melody that their hearers could take up.
Instruction was oral, hence the variations of familiar themes.
During the Civil War white officers of negro regiments who had
fought their way into the South took down the words of these
" Spirituals ", without realising the service that they were ren-
dering. It was some years before young coloured people who had
got education appreciated the songs of their fathers. It was only
gradually, from the 'seventies onward, that the American (and
British) public were introduced to these negro spirituals by
singers from Fiske, Tuskegee and other coloured colleges. A certain type of modern negro of left-wing politics, " emancipated "
from religion, has no use for songs emanating from slavery; the
Good Time A-Coming he interprets in terms of Socialism. Such
negroes are to be found in large numbers in Northern cities. But
educated negroes of Christian convictions realise that their race
has made a unique contribution to American Protestantism in
emphasising what Americans are only too ready to forget—suf-

fering is a way by which God often leads His children; death must
be faced with radiant faith, not evaded; patience despite persecution is a New Testament virtue.

> Deep river, my home is over Jordan;
> Deep river, Lord, I want to cross over into camp-ground.

· · ·

> Steal away, steal away, steal away to Jesus!
>   Steal away, steal away home,
>   I ain't got long to stay here.

· · ·

> Were you there when they crucified my Lord?
>   Were you there?
> They crucified my Lord,
> An' He never said a mumblin' word. . .

BOOK V

MODERN AMERICAN RELIGION
1865-1940

CHAPTER I

SOCIAL PROBLEMS AND THE GOSPEL

" Now that God has smitten slavery unto death, he has opened the way for the redemption of our whole social system."

EDWARD BEECHER (*brother of Henry Ward Beecher*)

IF " Reconstruction " after the Civil War was a tragedy in the South, in the North it was anything but a success from a spiritual and moral point of view. " When Johnny comes marching home," said a contemporary journalist, " he is a very demoralised member of society. . . You cannot take a man from his work in life and set him to fight for five years without turning his ideas and himself topsy-turvy. The older men fall back into the grooves more readily than the lads." Much had been done for the soldiers by the " Christian Commission ", but in spite of welfare work and Evangelism many of them kicked over the traces of Puritan upbringing. Drink, sex and gambling enslaved many a young man who had served his country. The liquor trade flourished as it had never done for forty years. Even before the war was over the Superintendent of Police in New York admitted that there were 599 brothels in the metropolis and 72 concert halls of equivocal character. In 1866 Bishop Simpson declared that there were " more prostitutes in New York than members of the Methodist Church ". The average ex-serviceman asked for " a religion of bread and butter "; he wanted a constructive policy that would help him to get a fair start in civil life. Unfortunately, individualism was rampant in politics and industry: the Churches, as yet, had nothing to offer besides individualistic ethics that stressed personal sin but had no real sense of social sin, save for slavery, recently abolished. " Things are in the saddle," said Emerson, " and ride mankind."

The United States emerged from the Civil War a changed nation. Not only was the old order overthrown in the South. The East was being rapidly industrialised. Active New Englanders moved West and a tide of immigrants from Europe flowed into their place and submerged old landmarks. A polyglot population, largely Roman Catholic, swarmed in the former strongholds of the Puritans. New York, Philadelphia and Baltimore were burdened with the pressing problems of a foreign-born proletariat. Between 1865 and 1884 seven million immigrants poured into the Atlantic ports. The melting pot was unable to assimilate so many aliens and no serious attempt was made to limit the influx in the interests of American civilisation. Large cities were rising in the agricultural Middle West. The frontier was pushing West relentlessly and its end was foreshadowed by the junction of the Central Pacific and Union Pacific Railroads at Ogden, Utah (10th May 1869). California had been opened up since the " Gold Rush " of 1849, and the cession by Mexico of the South West had brought into the Union an extensive, if arid, region.

Material civilisation developed rapidly. The first oil-pipe line was laid in 1865, the trans-Atlantic cable in 1866. Pullman cars made trans-continental travel less exhausting (1867). The New York " Elevated " took trains above the streets with characteristic disregard of amenity (1870). During the 'seventies there followed various inventions whereby America outstripped European progress—lifts, telephones, typewriters, refrigerators, gramophones. Cholera epidemics frightened city authorities into schemes of overdue urban sanitation.[1] The use of concrete produced tentative skyscrapers in the 'eighties that varied the monotony of a four-storey skyline; by the end of the century the church spires of New York were being dwarfed by " cathedrals of commerce ". Opulence produced pretentious public buildings and mansions. " Brown-stone fronts " with mansard roofs concealed gloomy interiors furnished in sombre splendour with heavy curtains, plush, walnut and horsehair. The " American spring " of Colonial and Greek Revival Architecture had been " nipped by an untimely frost " (Lewis Mumford).

The commercial era that followed the Civil War deserves Mark Twain's title, " The Gilded Age ". It was an epoch of unparalleled opportunity and optimism. Many a village lad " made good ", mounting from the office-boy's stool to the business executive's chair—the industrial equivalent to the older political romance,

[1] Before the Civil War pigs rooted for garbage in the streets of New York. Advt. in *Chicago Times*: " Strayed—a dark red cow from Quincy Street " (1st July 1865).

" from log-cabin to White House ". Tough, unscrupulous men made their way up from the lower strata of industry, and at the cost of cut-throat competition, carved out fortunes for themselves. A " new feudalism " emerged. Conspicuous was the Scots immigrant, Carnegie, political advocate of " triumphant democracy " but economic " lord of the steel demesne ". Other magnates were Rockefeller of the " oil estate ", Cyrus McCormick of the " pork-packing appanage ", Jay Cooke and Pierpont Morgan of the " financial seigneury ", and Vanderbilt of the " Railroad Kingdom ". The tendency to consolidation and monopoly became marked as the century drew to its close. Big corporations laid hold on such industries as steel, tobacco and oil. The successful business man became the symbol of modern America. There were only three millionaires in 1861, 3,800 by 1897—and 43,184 in 1929. By this time one-tenth of the population controlled nine-tenths of the nation's resources, whereas in the 1830's J. J. Astor's fortune of $2,000,000 was unparalleled. Glaring inequality has resulted from a century's cult of " the Almighty Dollar, that great object of universal devotion throughout our land " (Washington Irving, 1836).

Industrial feudalism produced a remarkable efflorescence of display among the new rich, whose taste was usually as bad as their business ethics.[1] They tried to outdo the dignified mansions of the old families by Renaissance palaces on Fifth Avenue, French châteaux on the Hudson, and Riviera villas at Newport. Plutocratic luxury did not mean that the standard of living improved for the working classes. Skilled workmen were paid $2 for a ten-hour day in 1866; shop girls worked from 9 a.m. till 9 p.m. for $5 a week. It was not a " gilded age " for them.

Ideals of personal behaviour were often quite strict among the well-to-do, but their standards of integrity in politics and business were certainly loose. Particularly demoralising was the financing of railways by political pressure; that sinister figure, " the corporation lawyer ", appeared on the scene. Federal and State politics were invaded by corrupt influences, as never before. Gangs of interested politicians got control of municipal affairs in the big cities. In Philadelphia the Republican party was involved in the

[1] Dogs wore diamond-studded collars, women who once did their own laundry wore ropes of pearls, chorus girls at " celebrations " took the place of blackbirds in a pie. The Martin-Bradleys gave a ball which brought a replica of Versailles to a New York hotel, while hunger stalked the streets.

" Gas Ring " scandal, being dependent on a " boss " and his henchmen; public funds were embezzled on a large scale, and it was not till 1885 that the worst elements in " the system " were eradicated by public opinion, at last aroused. In New York the Tweed Ring got municipal control (1868) and in three years made away with a sum ranging from $50,000,000 to $200,000,000. Here, the Democratic party were responsible for the wholesale bribery of immigrants, who obediently voted the " Tammany ticket ". The Irish Catholic politician was in his element, ready with promises of jobs. On the other hand, Tammany also had relations with " the saloon " and commercialised vice. Dr. C. H. Parkhurst, meteoric minister of Madison Avenue Presbyterian Church, drew attention to this unsavoury scandal. A Grand Jury investigated his charges, which they dismissed as based on newspaper reports, without any foundation in fact. Whereupon Parkhurst in-disguise and accompanied by detectives made a midnight round of Bowery haunts and proved to the satisfaction of the public that his charges were true.[1] Here was a minister of the Gospel who took social problems seriously. In 1931 a journalist named Lincoln Steffens published his *Autobiography*, describing how in his younger days he lifted the lid off the cesspool of vice and graft that made American municipal administration notorious. Theodore Roosevelt has well described that period as " the muck-raking era ". The other side of the " Gilded Age " was revealed in 1921 by *The Americanization of Edward Bok*—a " go-getter " who proclaimed the Gospel of Samuel Smiles with inimitable gusto.

The best-known autobiography describing this period is *The Education of Henry Adams* (1906). It is a complete contrast to the other two records of experience. A New England patrician, instead of finding inspiration in the ethical and humanitarian activity of his Unitarian family, drifts into urbane scepticism, finds the reality of contemporary America intolerable, and seeks refuge in his dream of *Mont Saint-Michel and Chartres: A Study of Thirteenth-Century Unity*. Henry James, cosmopolite and Anglophile, fled to Europe, feeling that the United States was " impossible ". Henry was a complete contrast to his brother William, who was temperamentally rooted in the American environment (see below, p. 328 f.). In varying degrees, cultured New Englanders were inclined to escape

[1] C. W. Gardner, *The Doctor and the Devil, or the Midnight Adventures of Dr. Parkhurst* (New York, 1894, 1931).

into the past. Boston Society reverted to its earlier colonial attitude of excessive deference to English traditions. Even a Jacobite
Movement was started. The " Order of the White Rose " corresponded with descendants of the Stuarts and offered expiation
on the Feast of St. Charles the Martyr. Tory traditions mingled
with imported Anglo-Catholicism. On Good Friday the fashionable Mrs. Gardner ostentatiously scrubbed the steps of the Church
of the Advent (" she wore religion as the best gem upon her
zone "). Young men of ability and rigid High Church views
(often ex-Baptists and Unitarians!) founded with fervour " The
Medieval Academy of America ".[1] One of them, Ralph Adams
Cram, treated the last four centuries as a mere interlude : salvation
could only come if we picked up the thread of Gothic and followed
it through the maze of a mechanistic age. He dreamed dreams
and saw visions of a new Scholasticism in stone, American
Cathedrals. Some of his dreams were realised in the twentieth
century.

Returning from this airy medieval vista to the crude realities of
the " Gilded Age ", we are faced with the question : Did these
merchant princes not devote a goodly portion of their wealth to
building up a Christian civilisation ? Most of the millionaires had
a Church connexion.[2] Pierpont Morgan and W. H. Vanderbilt
were Episcopalians, Rockefeller was a Baptist, Cyrus McCormick
a Presbyterian; John Wanamaker associated himself with the
Y.M.C.A. and Philip D. Armour with Home Missions. Higher
education benefited by lavish benefactions. Hitherto it had been
crippled for want of money. Up till 1870 most American colleges
offered the student little save the elements of the Classics. Even
at Columbia University one professor taught Philosophy, Moral
Philosophy, English Literature, History and Political Economy.
Of the 321 High Schools in the United States (1860) one half were
in Massachusetts. The State stepped in tardily, but a lead was
given by tobacco lords, oil barons and railroad kings. New
institutions of learning sprang into life, bearing the names of the
men who founded and endowed them—Stanford University, Duke
University, Vassar College, Cornell University. Matthew Vassar,
founder of a fashionable Women's College, was a poor English

---

[1] Van Wyck Brooks, *New England : Indian Summer*, 1865-1915 (New York,
1940).
[2] Mark Twain sneered at " The Church of the Holy Speculators ". He had
no objection, however, to their company.

x

immigrant who started an " ale and oyster saloon " in the days
when Baptists might also be brewers. Ezra Cornell, one of the
founders of the Western Union Telegraph Company, belonged to
a Quaker family; he had seen so much sectarian bitterness that
he resolved to make his University strictly un-sectarian. Most of
these new foundations were equipped with ornate chapels which
were filled by the traditional method of compulsory attendance
(in the twentieth century benefactors switched over to colossal
stadiums and swimming-pools).

Many a struggling denominational college found a business
potentate a veritable *deus ex machina*, ready to oil the creaking
academic wheels by sweeping away mean buildings from the
campus and providing the professors with a living wage. The
authorities were not too particular about the way in which prospective donors had built up their fortunes. One conscientious
churchman protested against his Foreign Mission Board's acceptance of a " princely gift " that involved " partnership with plun-
derers ". More characteristic than any shrinking from tainted
money was the cynical retort of a denominational college treasurer:
" The only tainted money I know is—'tain't enough !" Public
opinion was tolerant of millionaires who lavished their funds on
religion and philanthropy. Rockefeller had no qualms of conscience. He neither drank nor gambled; he lived a simple life
and taught a Sunday School class. Therefore he concluded,
" God gave me money " (J. T. Flyn, *God's Gold*, 1932). The
social conscience of to-day sees Daniel Drew as a stock-market
pirate and a railroad wrecker, but his contemporaries saw him in a
more favourable light. " He was founding a theological seminary
[Drew University, Methodist] and attending prayer meetings,"
says the Church historian, Dr. W. E. Garrison, " when he was
not printing bogus shares or devising the technique of watering
stock."[1] That nineteenth-century buccaneer, Commodore Vanderbilt, saw no inconsistency in roaring " The public be damned! "
and founding Vanderbilt University.

The historically-minded might be impressed by the parallel
between modern business men and the merchant founders of
great medieval colleges. Who could deny that Andrew Carnegie,
the immigrant who made good, opened a new cultural chapter

[1] Literally, as well as metaphorically. He fed cattle large quantities of salt
to make them drink more, and so increase their weight.

for his native Dunfermline, the ancient city of Queen Margaret ?[1] In the United States struggling colleges effloresced into universities, but the endowments of rich men often involved economic control. Business men replaced ministers as presidents and trustees; there was a danger of education and religion being commercialised. Even a progressive paper like Henry Ward Beecher's *Independent* failed to read the signs of the times in the economic sphere. This Christian paper thundered against slavery, but had no scruples about the patronage of men who used politics to promote their own ends. "We need all the Jay Cookes we have and a thousand more. We want them because they are a help to the present age; because they use their money for patriotic, benevolent and Christian purposes" (*Independent*, 5th November, 1868).

Jay Cooke belonged to the Episcopal Church—which became a stylish ecclesiastical setting for the promenaders of "Peacock Alley". After the Civil War this denomination enhanced its prestige by building Gothic Revival churches, richly sombre with walnut and stained glass, mosaics and murals. Exclusiveness was secured by augmenting pew-rents and omitting galleries, which used to be available for strangers. The American custom of letting, selling and bequeathing pews culminated in open auction at Beecher's church. As far back as the 1830's Presbyterians and Episcopalians erected special "free churches" for the poor. The "Open and Institutional Church Movement" (1894) was one of the inter-denominational activities that led to the American Federal Council of Churches (see below, p. 401 f.).

The "Institutional Church" was an adaptation of the "East End Settlement" scheme which in England offered the advantages of a club to the unprivileged classes. The rich men of the United States might worship in churches whose fashionable preachers "seldom alluded to modern ways of sinning and living" (to quote a contemporary journalist). Their social conscience, however, impelled them to do something for the slums that were already beginning to fester in the great cities. The Vanderbilts provided a palatial "Parish House" at St. Bartholomew's, New York, covering three and a half acres and costing $11,000,000 (1891-1901). Pierpont Morgan did likewise at St. George's. The

---

[1] His donations to Scots congregations who wanted organs (the Kirk anathematised the kist o' whistles till c. 1870) were characteristically conditioned by local self-help. "I will deliver thee 2,000 horses, if thou be able on thy part to set riders upon them" (2 Kings 18.23).

mansions of Sturtevant Square had become tenements. What could be done for the unsympathetic immigrants who were displacing the " first families " ? They should be afforded facilities for an ampler life—educational, recreational and spiritual. The scheme owed its success to a young rector, D. W. S. Rainsford, who came from England about 1880. He was Irish, evangelical and the very incarnation of Kingsley's " muscular Christianity ". He was appointed to St. George's on the understanding that he should have a free hand to " build up a truly democratic church ". His conception of this ideal varied from his patron's. Wealth built the Parish House, but only the magnetic personality of Rainsford could increase the congregation from 200 to 4,000 communicants (many of them Germans). " He brought the Church close to the working life of a great city ", said Theodore Roosevelt.

The pioneer of the Institutional Church was Thomas K. Beecher (brother of Henry Ward), a Congregational minister at Elmira, N.Y. When he rebuilt the Park Church there, he was fortunate enough to find a surplus of $80,000, which he used to cover the cost of a " Church Home ". He designed it himself— gymnasium, library, theatre, children's " romp-room ". It contained everything save statues of Use and Wont.[1] This was novel for 1873, also his practice of keeping his vestry open for callers at certain hours during the week (" Ye servants of the Lord, each in his *office* wait "). The clergy denounced his innovations, but eventually followed his example, "hustled out of their spirituality".

T. K. Beecher was exceptionally independent of Mammon. The churches as a whole were too deferential to the Golden Calf. They were too inclined to estimate spiritual influence in terms of dollars. The Baptists and Methodists, once proud of belonging to the poor, now talked of " The Sanctification of Wealth ", and paid attention to the prosperous.

Middle-class opinion was well expressed by a Mid-West theologian: " Men should make money according to the laws of business and spend it according to the laws of God." It all sounded so simple. This prescription was all right when America was a land of small farmers, tradesmen and mechanics. It no longer worked now that the Industrial Revolution was fast dividing the United States into two rival camps, employers and employees.

[1] In 1910 Dr. Stelzle started the New York " Labor Temple " in a disused Presbyterian Church. The name was a red rag to the rich, but it was simply a " settlement " with accent on adult education and family welfare.

It was easy to obey the Commandments to the letter, and yet
utterly miss their spirit. Some employers did their utmost to
exploit ignorant immigrants who were slow in learning English.
Arthur Clough (who had visited America) put the problem in a
nutshell, " The Latest Decalogue ":

> No graven images may be
> Worship'd, except the currency
> Thou shalt not steal; an empty feat
> Where 'tis so lucrative to cheat:
> Thou shalt not covet, but tradition
> Approves all forms of competition.

Those who had been brought up on the gospel of self-help
could not understand industrial strife. They were exasperated
when strikes led to riots. Even the most progressive Christian
paper asserted: " Whenever a riot appears . . . the club of the
policeman, bullets and bayonets, canister and grape, constitute
the one remedy " (*Independent*, 2nd August 1877). Not many
people in the Churches sympathised with " The Knights of
Labor " (1869) save Cardinal Gibbons, who resembled Cardinal
Manning in England in being friendly to the reasonable claims
of the working man. The American Federation of Labour had a
hard task in persuading the public to see the justice of their cause
in reducing long hours, increasing wages and improving working
conditions. There were serious strikes at the Carnegie Steel
Works at Homestead, Pa. (1892) and at the Pullman Palace Car
Company in Chicago (1894). Cheap foreign labour had been
introduced in the industrial centres. There was little of the practical idealism that had provided comfortable boarding-houses and
community life in the manufacturing villages of New England
before the Civil War. Visitors from Europe used to be told of
Lynn, Mass., where the shoe-operatives were " fit to be U.S.
Senators ", and of Lowell, where the mill-girls produced their
own magazine, *The Lowell Offering*. These idyllic conditions
passed. Business booms were followed by depression, with consequent unemployment. Cut-throat competition, unregulated immigration, high rents and land speculation produced congested
tenements; the slum appeared in America. Philanthropists like
Philip D. Armour built " model tenements " at reasonable rents
in Chicago, but the public failed to realise that city degradation
far exceeded the pace of municipal reform. As late as 1908 C. E.

Russell revealed the fact that the richest congregation in New York, the historic Trinity Parish, drew a large part of its income from slum property (*Everybody's Magazine*, 1908).

During the " Gilded Age " there was slight sense of corporate Christianity, few signs of a social conscience awakened by unbridled individualism. There were crusaders, to be sure—Temperance orators like J. B. Gough,[1] sleuth-hounds on the track of obscene literature like Anthony Comstock,[2] " Ward and Watch " committees to safeguard public morals, Sabbath Observance Societies to protest against Sunday trains and German beergardens. These reformers were often cranks, at best they were uplifters with a one-track mind. They saw everything in black and white, with no realisation of the relevance of environment and the complexity of social problems. Wage-earners, consequently, were being increasingly alienated from the Christian Church, finding little sympathy for their problems and often wholesale discrimination against " labor agitators ".

At the middle of the century there was nothing in the United States corresponding to the " Christian Socialism " of Maurice and Kingsley. A number of Utopian communities had been established on a religious basis, but these scattered groups were the expression of an escapist ideal; there was little attempt to apply Christian principles to economic problems, so that society might be gradually leavened. Among pioneers of social idealism a high place should be given to the Rev. Theodore Parker of Boston (1810-60), who expanded the principles of Channing. Parker was unlike most reformers of his time in being comprehensive. His was no one-track mind obsessed with the Abolition of Slavery. Parker was a universal reformer, with some inkling of the interlocking of social evils. Instead of attacking vice after the manner of Comstock, he pointed out that prostitutes were largely recruited from the ranks of underpaid women workers. The whole problem of sex was treated by the American public according to the Pharisaic principles rather than the spirit of Jesus (" What a deal of prudery there is here in New England "). Drunkenness was caused partly by extreme poverty, partly by the blindness of the " Puritan " tradition in branding innocent recreation as " carnal ". The penal system was vindictive, not reformative, worked in

[1] H. W. Morrow, *Tiger! Tiger!* (New York, 1930).
[2] *Life*, with contemporary cartoons, by H. Broun and M. Leech (New York, 1927); Arthur Train, *Puritan's Progress* (New York, 1931).

the interests of the rich against the unprivileged (prisons *ought* to be " moral hospitals ", not " schools of crime "). The real enemies of society were men who paid low wages and extracted high rents. When the walls of the Pemberton mills caved in and killed hundreds of workers, this was an " Act of God " only in the sense that it arraigned jerry-builders and exploiters. There was something far wrong when the factories at Lowell cut wages 10% and paid extra dividends of 12%. Theodore Parker was not a Socialist, but he did realise that social problems were interlocked. When he talked of " socialising Christianity ", he was a truer Christian than his orthodox opponents. The supporters of vested interests found his unbalanced radicalism in theology a useful means of discrediting his economic and social idealism.

By the end of the century the ordinary citizen was less sure that unlimited competition was an unmixed blessing. In 1902 the President of the Reading Railroad, George F. Baer, announced: " The rights of the laboring man will be protected, not by labor agitators, but by the Christian man to whom God in His infinite wisdom has given the control of the property interests of this country." This pontifical declaration opened the eyes of the people. They realised that they were passing from democracy to economic feudalism, directed by potentates like " Divine Right Baer ". A later generation asked: " Should we now reckon time by the year of our Ford rather than by the year of our Lord ? "

Prophets of social righteousness had already arisen. As far back as 1879 Henry George, reared an Evangelical Episcopalian in Philadelphia, won an international reputation by his *Progress and Poverty*—an attempt to base all taxation on " land values ". The growing urbanisation of the United States soon " dated " this theory. In 1884 James Russell Lowell surprised the public by explaining that Socialism means " the practical application of Christianity to life and has in it the secret of an orderly and benign reconstruction ". This interpretation was new to American citizens accustomed to think of continental Socialists as atheists. In 1887 came Edward Bellamy's novel, *Looking Backward*, 2000-1887. The author glorified applied science; " he naturalised Socialism and baptised it anew in the name of business efficiency " (Beard). Some of his readers formed an abortive political party to realise his ideals; others wondered if religion might not furnish the dynamic of a new order.

The serious study of Christian sociology in America has its roots in the constructive civics of Horace Bushnell, nurtured by British influences—Dr. Chalmers, F. D. Maurice, Kingsley and Seeley's " enthusiasm for humanity ". The Socialist activities of the Christian Social Union in England were copied in the United States by a similar society in the Protestant Episcopal Church, associated with the names of Professors R. T. Ely and Vida D. Scudder (1892). More moderate in tone was a Congregationalist group—Dr. Newman Smyth, of the First Church, New Haven; Professor Herron of Grinnell College, Iowa; and Dr. Washington Gladden, of Columbus, Ohio. Dr. Gladden approached the social problem, not from the platform or the study, but through his own experience as a pastor.[1] In his *Recollections* (1909) he has given an illuminating account of his crusade to capture the imagination and conscience of churchmen, not for doctrinaire Socialism but for social justice. Was human personality a mere commodity to be bought and sold on the labour market ? Were the " laws " of Political Economy so rigid as to exclude the protection of the poor man from inadequate wages, bad working conditions and unemployment ? Gladden's books answered these questions in clear language and concrete form, e.g. *Working Men and their Employers* (1876), *Applied Christianity* (1887).

In the 'nineties Chicago became the clearing-house of " applied Christianity ". Charles R. Henderson, who had acted as arbitrator in a major strike, was appointed to a Chair of " Ecclesiastical Sociology " in the University. His aim was to " orient " students, showing the relevance of this new study to their vocation as future pastors. Graham Taylor co-related thought and action by introducing them to " settlements " somewhat on the lines of those founded in the East End of London by Oxford men. Harry F. Ward took them to the Stockyards district where " labor feeling " ran high, and initiated them into the problems that confront the Christian conscience in a highly industrialised environment.[2]

It is interesting to note that the academic atmosphere of Harvard saw the production of a book on the " Social Gospel " that has

[1] Hence the enduring value of his *Christian Pastor* (International Theological Library, 1901). When sorely vexed by controversy, he wrote a hymn now familiar in Britain, " O Master, let me walk with Thee."

[2] It need hardly be said that the lot of the Christian Socialist is a hard one in America. There is a small, undenominational " Fellowship of Socialist Christians " (1938).

outlived nearly all its contemporaries in comprehensive scholarliness and realism. *Jesus Christ and the Social Question* (1900), a book with an international reputation, has had an immense influence on young men. That is not so surprising when we consider that the author was Professor Francis G. Peabody, whose published addresses on personal religion, given in Harvard College chapel, have reached such a wide circle.

Walter Rauschenbusch, like Dr. Peabody, was a convinced believer in personal Christianity; he never became entangled in 'isms like some of the later advocates of the " Social Gospel ".[1] Nor did he overrate environment and minimise sin. Like Henderson and Shailer Mathews, his contemporaries in social progress, he belonged to that most individualistic of denominations, the Baptists. He realised that sin is transmitted through institutions as well as through individuals. " It is not a private transaction between the sinner and God. Humanity always crowds the audience-room where God holds court."[2] The " kingdom of Evil " was a vast network, as he discovered in his first pastorate in the " Hell's Kitchen " area of New York. The son of a German Lutheran minister, born in America, Rauschenbusch aligned himself with a thoroughly American Church, yet he never forgot the struggles of the immigrants. He himself was a product of the " melting-pot ". No native American has had quite the same influence in advocating Christian responsibility for the Social Order. His *Prayers of the Social Awakening* (1910) will endure. These devotions blend two strains of religion seldom closely linked—deep personal piety and concern for the community. Rauschenbusch recalled prayer from confession of easy un-itemised sins and personal petitions of an egocentric narrowness to active sympathy with the sorrows of suffering humanity.

This reorientation became general enough for the Federal Council of the American Churches to formulate a " Social Creed ", issued in 1908 and revised from time to time.[3] It is heartening to know that Frank Mason North, who formulated this affirmation,

---

[1] Norman Thomas, an ex-Presbyterian minister, stood for the U.S. Presidency on several occasions.
[2] His *Theology for the Social Gospel* (1917) was a landmark in Christian thinking.
[3] Dean Sperry says of these resolutions: " They are probably to be interpreted as outposts held by more advanced persons rather than as . . . the opinion of the majority. They have an educational value . . . probably little direct effect upon legislation or public policy " (*Religion in America*, p. 64).

expressed his ideals in a hymn that has become justly popular in
the United States:

> Where cross the crowded ways of life,
>   Where sound the cries of race and clan,
> Above the noise of selfish strife,
>   We hear Thy voice, O Son of Man.
> O Master, from the mountain side,
>   Make haste to heal these beds of pain;
> Among these restless throngs abide,
>   O tread the city's streets again.

The Social Gospel also found effective voice in fiction. A striking instance is *In His Steps*, by Charles M. Sheldon (1896). Dr.
Sheldon, minister of the First Congregational Church, Topeka,
Kansas, was anxious to restore confidence in the Christian faith
among multitudes who had lost confidence in timid, time-serving,
individualistic " Churchianity ". What would happen if Jesus
actually visited a Mid-West city ? On successive Sunday evenings
the story was unfolded to crowded congregations. Dr. Sheldon
had some difficulty in obtaining a publisher for his earnest and
artless tale. No one was more surprised than he to find that his
fictionised tract became a best-seller, translated into nearly every
language, with a sale of at least 5,000,000 copies. Dr. Sheldon
rather over-simplified the issues of a complex civilisation, as he
discovered, when asked to edit the daily paper of Topeka for a
week as an experiment in applied Christianity. Nevertheless, *In
His Steps* proved that millions were interested in Christianity as
a way of life, purged from excessive dogma, ritual and cant.
Would a novelist of ability arise to proclaim the Social Gospel
with persuasiveness, insight and power ?[1]

Mrs. Humphrey Ward's *Robert Elsmere* (1887) had a large circulation in the United States, but public opinion was hardly prepared for it. The opinion was expressed that there was room for
a novel about a minister who did not leave the church when
persecuted by reactionaries, but remained at his post. In 1913
an American novelist depicted a church reformer as hero rather
than as exile. Winston Churchill had written a sequence of
popular novels dealing with aspects of American history and contemporary life. His *Inside of the Cup* presents a picture of a

---

[1] F. L. Mott, in *Golden Multitudes* (1947), a study of " Best Sellers " in
U.S.A., traces 15% to parsons. The pietistic, theme-ridden novels of Harold
B. Wright, a poorly-educated Disciples pastor, sold by the million. His success
was partly due to association with an enterprising mail-order bookseller.

complacent Episcopal congregation in a Mid-West city. Externally, the fabric is as impressive as Gothic art, ritual and social position can make it; but the " inside of the cup " is scandalous. The Gores and Goodriches, Atterburys, Plimptons and Larrabees were nearly all involved in fraudulent business concerns, cutthroat competition, unscrupulous finance and corrupt municipal politics. The opulent pillars of the church enjoyed public esteem for religion and philanthropy while they got other people to do their dirty work. Nelson Langmaid, the astute corporation lawyer, is mistaken for once in thinking that the young rector he " handpicked " will fall into step with St. John's. The Rev. John Hodder is at first hoodwinked, but has his eyes opened and makes a thorough examination of the " inside of the cup ". Neither the congeniality of Gordon Atterbury, his " ecclesiastically minded " treasurer, nor the social blandishments of office-bearers who had a genuine admiration for him, could deter him from the hard task of saving St. John's from the exploiters who controlled its affairs. Not even the philanthropy of Eldon Parr, the banker (who offered to build a palatial parish house for the poor immigrants who made their homes near the church) could divert him from his inflexible purpose. Eventually his enemies, in control of the vestry, stop his salary and lay charges of heresy before the bishop (he is a " Modernist " as well as a " Socialist "). Hodder, fighting manfully in the glare of publicity, secures the support of genuine Christians who fill the empty pews vacated by the wealthy. Financial sacrifices are shared by minister and people, and the congregation becomes a free and purified Christian fellowship, no longer dependent on the patronage of the rich. The author makes his clergyman a Broad Churchman in his attitude to dogma and ritual. Unlike Robert Elsmere, he remains a minister of the church, although preaching the good news of emancipation and brotherhood to all classes. He passes from a religion of the letter to a religion of the spirit without losing touch with Christian fundamentals. The *Inside of the Cup* illustrates the blending of theological liberalism and the Social Gospel, typical of progressive Protestantism in general in America.

.   .   .   .

After the Civil War immigrants swarmed over the broken ramparts of Anglo-Saxon tradition. They substituted the " continental

Sunday " for the Puritan Sabbath and forced the defenders of the Lord's Day to retreat by a series of compromises, e.g. the Chicago Exhibition of 1893 was to be open on Sundays, but the machinery must not run. The foreign vote was heavily on the side of liquor interests. " The future is ours ", asserted a brewers' journal in 1873. " The enormous influx of immigration will in a few years overreach the Puritanical element in every state in the Union."[1] Much ground was lost by Temperance. Of the twelve states that prohibited the manufacture and sale of alcohol before the Civil War, only Maine, New Hampshire and Vermont retained it. A " Prohibition Party " took the field in 1869 against the liquor interests and their political henchmen. The " corner saloon " went into action against the Anti-saloon League. The Women's Christian Temperance Union, led by Miss Francis Willard, organised a campaign whereby the ladies assembled at their churches, marched to saloons and held prayer meetings till the publicans capitulated and gave up business![2] In many cases these feminine crusaders won initial successes, particularly in the Middle West, but they were up against a machine. Their propaganda was apt to be whimsical when it was not hysterical: " Young ladies should never consent to lock arms with a walking jug-handle or throw their arms about the neck of . . . a filthy brandy bottle."

The churches were by no means of one mind as to the remedy of intemperance. The Roman Catholic and Lutheran attitude was that of the continental; wine was the gift of God, its abuse was no argument against its use. The Episcopalian outlook was similar. Presbyterians were divided; men like Dr. Henry Van Dyke had no sympathy with the legalist attitude that attempted to impose " sumptuary legislation ". The Methodists and Baptists were 100% prohibitionists. They claimed to be non-political, but utilised " pressure politics " as much as their opponents. In the North they were solidly Republican; they fulminated against the Democrats as the party of " Rome, Rum and Rebellion ". From

[1] New England was the first region to be overrun. In many districts the meeting-houses with their white steeples became mere monuments of the past. See W. T. Whitley's article in the (English) *Congregational Quarterly* (Jan. 1937).

[2] Women took an increasing part in church work, leaving politics to men. Even so, they had to struggle against traditional opposition. J. M. Buckley, Methodist historian, quoted Evangelist Finney with approval: " Desire to hear women preachers is an aberration of amativeness!" Not till 1904 were women admitted to General Conferences of his Church: they now are allowed partial ordination. In Newark Presbytery, N.J., a minister was censured in 1877 for allowing two ladies to speak in his church.

1907 onwards a series of " Dry " successes were registered. When Prohibition was written into the Federal constitution in 1919, it had already been adopted by 33 States. It was one thing to enact legislation, another to enforce it. The " Eighteenth Amendment " ignored the fact that the population of the United States was too heterogeneous to submit to a decree that represented the conscience of only a section of the population. Respectable citizens broke the law and the " boot-legger " became a characteristic figure of the 1920's. So serious was the disrespect shown for law that a number of total abstainers (including Rockefeller) voted against Prohibition, which was repealed in 1933. The " Great Experiment " broke down on a federal scale, though certain States remained " dry ". The Methodist " Board of Temperance, Prohibition and Public Morals " took itself too seriously as keeper of the nation's conscience.[1] " Tee-totalitarianism " failed like dictatorial regimes that override liberty.[2]

The Methodists and Baptists were not content to rage against strong drink. They were determined to impose their ideals and *mores* on the rest of the community. They went further than historic New England Puritanism. They banned dancing, smoking and games like billiards as well as card-playing and theatregoing.[3] The Methodist *Discipline* listed forbidden amusements in 1872, and other denominations had their unwritten laws (even Henry Ward Beecher, it was said, never entered a playhouse in his life). The Episcopal Church was much more sensible in its attitude to recreation than other Anglo-Saxon denominations. Instead of abusing the playhouse they founded a " Church Actors' Alliance ". After the Civil War most denominations insisted on the strictest standards in young people's organisations. The

[1] Methodism was apt to be a bureaucratic machine, organised from the top. R. J. Graves, a Baptist, attacked this bureaucracy in *The Great Iron Wheel* (1853, 30th ed. 1860). Later critics have appeared from within Methodism, e.g. Dan Brummit, a prominent religious journalist, an English Wesleyan by birth, whose novel, *Shoddy*, is illuminating. Harzell Spence, in a recent life of his father, a Methodist minister, gives an unfavourable view of this denomination (*One Foot in Heaven*). T. W. Lamont is sympathetic in his autobiography, *My Boyhood in a Parsonage* (London, 1948).

[2] In the newly-industrialised South, e.g. Gaston Co., N. Carolina, dictatorial employers have deliberately fostered obscurantist pietism to complete their economic control of poorly-educated employees. See L. Pope, *Millhands and Preachers* (Yale, 1943).

[3] Howells gives an instance of evasion in *An Open-Eyed Conspiracy*. Mrs. March had no objection to her guests going to the races, but not directly from the door, in deference to her clerical boarders. " She insisted that the appearance of not going to the races was something we owed to the cloth ".

Y.M.C.A., founded in England (1844) and successfully transplanted to America, spent much time at its eleventh annual convention in discussing recreation; might dancing and billiards be
allowed with certain restrictions ? The proposal was voted down,
though in compensation for this self-denying ordinance the delegates were regaled with a " sumptuous collation " (1866). Ten
years later the Rev. Thomas K. Beecher was expelled from the
Ministerial Union of Elmira, N.Y., for allowing dancing and
billiards in his new parish house. Only gradually and reluctantly
did the Y.M.C.A. admit such innocuous games as backgammon
and chess. In the twentieth century this cautious " Puritanism "
was entirely reversed. The " Y " became a well-equipped Youth
club with standards that satisfied the upper middle class. British
service men in World War II were particularly impressed with
the amenities of the American Y.M.C.A. in Jerusalem, whose
luxury surpassed their wildest dreams.

Parallel to the Y.M.C.A. and Y.W.C.A. was the Christian
Endeavour Movement, which started in Dr. F. E. Clarke's church
at Portland, Maine, and spread rapidly throughout the States
during the 'eighties till 1900. Edward Everett Hale, short-story
writer, gave a practical stimulus to young people's guilds by his
motto: " Look up and not down, look forward and not back, look
out and not in—and lend a hand!"[1] These inter-denominational
activities prompted the churches to build their own organisations.
In advance of the times was the Episcopal Brotherhood of St.
Andrew. Young men pledged themselves to the two-fold rule of
daily prayer and active service. The Brothers, who belonged to
all occupations, were grouped in 1,400 regional Chapters. A feature of this Brotherhood, badly needed in America, was the cultivation of the devotional life through " Quiet Days ", spent in
retreat—Communion, corporate prayer and silent fellowship. The
" Epworth League " (1889) was on a larger scale. It was organised
throughout the Methodist Church for young men and women
and soon had a membership of half a million. It was imitated by
the " Luther League ", etc. If a certain amount of mawkish
religiosity has characterised some of these groups, it must be
remembered that they grew out of a " Revival atmosphere ",
heavily charged with unction.

[1] Unfortunately he popularised the minimising of theology.

CHAPTER II

EVANGELISED AMERICA: MEN AND METHODS

" The American character, like their climate, has great decision about it. . . When it is cold it freezes, and when it is hot it burns."

DRS. REED AND MATHESON: *Visit to the American Churches*

REVIVALISM had been the dominant pattern of American Protestantism since the middle of the eighteenth century, when Whitefield the Awakener crossed the Atlantic and joined hands with Jonathan Edwards. From the Awakening of 1800 onwards Revival beat upon American life in a series of gigantic waves. In the middle of the century wild religious excitement was stirred by Finney and other peripatetic evangelists. Evangelism culminated in the campaign of Moody and his imitators after the Civil War; by the end of the nineteenth century it had subsided, and has now ceased to be one of the major characteristics of American Protestantism, though it still counts for much in backward sections and backward sects.

In 1857 a notable spiritual awakening took place in New York during a business crisis. It started quietly and owed its inception to the custodian of the North Reformed Church. Jeremiah Lamphier opened the " consistory room " at the lunch-hour so that business men might " with one accord make their common supplications ". In a few days other rooms in the building were opened in response to the demand. The movement was spontaneous, and the walls rang with prayer and praise.[1] Burton's Theatre was taken, well-known men spoke straightforwardly about their religious experience, and the press gave full publicity to this revival. It was largely a layman's movement, not directed by professional evangelists, and fortunately free from the hysterical extravagances that had hitherto marred most revivals. The prayer-

[1] The " prayer-meeting ", which grew out of the Puritan " mid-week lecture ", was a genuine power-house of revivalism. It has fallen on evil days except in the Fundamentalist sects. As anyone could rise and pray, loquacious religiosity was the peril.

meeting as a " thermometer of the church " registered a rising temperature. Enthusiasm spread to other parts of the United States and added, it is estimated, a million members to the Churches. The Revival of 1857-8 did much to nerve Evangelism for the ordeal of the Civil War and the Reconstruction period that followed.

Dwight L. Moody, herald of the New Evangelism, grew up in this revival atmosphere. A poor New Englander, he had to work at an early age to support his widowed mother and her big family. In his seventeenth year he started working in a shoe shop at Boston. " I have seen few persons whose minds were spiritually darker," said his minister, " or who seemed more unlikely ever to become a Christian of clear, decided views of gospel truth." Several years later Moody was in Chicago, doing well in the shoe business and encouraging young men to accompany him to church. He did not feel he was much good at giving an address or teaching a class, but he could tell a story well and hold the attention of the rowdiest audience. When he gave up business in 1860 to devote himself entirely to religion, he had little capital on which to live, and he was too modest to enter the Ministry. Yet he had courage and consecration, and these qualities made his evangelistic services a success. He discouraged the morbid manifestations that had hitherto discredited revivalism. When a woman cried out in his meetings, he would announce: " We will sing a hymn, while the stewards help our sister out. She has hysterics." Feeling was not the foundation of his faith but the Word of God. The kindling flame was spread by his associate, Ira D. Sankey, whose *Sacred Songs and Solos*[1] brought home to the hearts of thousands the strong, practical Gospel message of his comrade. Moody was impressed by his singing at the International Y.M.C.A. Convention, Chicago; they collaborated on Gospel tours, 1872-1899. Sankey confessed: " I am no musician; I was never taught to sing." J. S. Curwen (the church music authority) wrote: "A singing-master would find faults in every measure that he sings. His style is recitative . . . jerky, intermittent, disconnected. It is speaking with a sustained voice. But his eagerness is so transparent that it covers a multitude of thoughts . . ."

Sankey and Moody were an ideal combination for America, but they were ill-fitted by education and outlook to capture the

[1] See *My Life and the Story of the Gospel Hymns* (1906).

British public. Yet they went ahead full of faith. At Newcastle-on-Tyne they published a brochure of popular hymns, which they used with much success at their meetings; ballad-like measures, with lilting swing and flow, were irresistible in their appeal to mass-emotion. They even won the hearts of people as reserved as the Scots,[1] accustomed only to grave psalmody; indeed, one effect of their campaign in Scotland was to kill the immemorial Presbyterian prejudice against organs (for Sankey took his portable harmonium everywhere). But for the interest and sympathy of one man, the two evangelists might never have penetrated other circles than mission halls in back streets. Henry Drummond, man of culture, scientist and popular student leader, sponsored Moody's campaigns and gave him valuable introductions, with the result that his tours in Great Britain (1873-5 and 1881) made a tremendous impact on nearly all classes and denominations. Complete consecration overcame the defects of a neglected education and a crude working theology. Oxford undergraduates who came to ridicule the speaker's accent, remained to pray. Thousands of men and women in every walk of life (and children too) owed their souls to Moody.

Evangelism had called in the New World to redress the balance of the Old. Henry Drummond in turn crossed the Atlantic, addressed vast gatherings and toured the American Colleges (1887). Here was an evangelist of an unusual kind—a gentleman, a scientist and a man of liberal views. It says much for Moody's big-heartedness that he never resented Drummond's culture and proved a most loyal friend and fellow-worker. Well aware of his own defective education, Moody was always ready to learn from others. Drummond introduced him to leading British scholars of progressive outlook, like George Adam Smith, who blended Evangelicalism with modern views of the Bible and re-discovered the relevance of the Old Testament prophets to contemporary social problems. It could hardly be expected that a simple evangelist like Moody would feel at home among all these new and complex ideas. Yet Drummond taught him the value of linking the Gospel with education and social service. Not merely conferences but orphanages and homes for the aged were visualised as products of Evangelism. Notable were the High Schools in Moody's native

---

[1] Sankey extemporised the music of " There were ninety and nine " at a great meeting in the Free Church Assembly Hall, Edinburgh (he was a native of Edinburgh, Pennsylvania).

Y

village of Northfield, Massachusetts, which became the Mecca of the countryside for people of all ages. These experiments reflected his matured judgment that the era of revivalism was approaching its natural term, and that religious education was due to take its place. This statement calls for qualification, but his recent biographers are inclined to support it.

The imitators of Moody and Sankey had little of their big heartedness and willingness to co-operate with men of different views. It was no wonder that their trans-Atlantic success was not repeated by Torrey and Alexander in 1905. Thirty years had passed since the great campaigns. Popular education in Britain had spread and religious ideas were undergoing enlargement. The new crusaders were the last to exemplify Paul's principle that "the spiritual man is alive to all true values" (I Cor. 2.15, Goodspeed's trans.). Torrey and Alexander preached a harsh and intolerant revivalism, with emphasis on the fear of hell and Puritanical asceticism. "Would you like to have Christ find you at the theatre . . . the dance-hall . . . or the card-table?" Never had the egocentric note been struck so emphatically by evangelists. Salvation was presented in an utterly individualistic manner, and audiences were asked to respond in the chorus, "That will be glory, glory for me!" Torrey and Alexander, by reducing evangelism to the illiterate level of the back-street mission-hall lost a great opportunity, for 1905 was the year of the great Welsh Revival, with repercussions in England.

In the United States Moody's imitators, ultra-conservative in theology, adopted sensational methods of popular approach. High-pressure salesmanship heralded their campaigns. Vast timber "tabernacles" were erected, complete with "mourner's bench", "enquiry rooms" and "sawdust trail". When the evangelists arrived they exploited popular psychology by sentimental tricks; they were apt to reduce the Gospel to professional patter, with invariable denunciations of "worldly" amusements and "unbelieving" ministers. They lowered still further the none-too-high level of "Gospel Songs" by such refrains as "When the roll is called up yonder, I'll be there!"

The eccentric streak in revivalism persisted. Promoters undertook colossal campaigns to "Reduce the Population of Hell by One Million Souls". One read of "Evangelist Barnes" converting 33 convicts at Frankfurt, Kentucky, duly marched to the river under armed guard and soundly immersed. One also read of women and girls whose nerves had been wrecked by the ordeal of revival hysteria.

Logan Pearsall Smith recalls, in *Unforgettable Years* (1937) his first visit to Europe with his evangelistic parents, who were prosperous Philadelphia Quakers. The Pearsall Smiths toured England under the aristocratic wings of Lord and Lady Mount Temple; they addressed fashionable audiences in Oxford, Brighton and London. In Berlin they received personal favours from the Kaiser; pietistic cliques, even professors, responded warmly to their prophetic orations (interpreted in German). Unfortunately the party from Philadelphia indulged in " The Higher Life "; they obeyed the apostolic injunction, " Salute one another with an holy kiss ".[1] So shocked were their English supporters that the campaign was suspended *sine die*, and the Pearsall Smiths went home in sackcloth and ashes—" off to Philadelphia in the morning!"

Professional American evangelists have been providentially provided with significant names, e.g. Dr. Pentecost and Dr. Sunday. Some of the questionable features of revivalism were carried into the twentieth century by " Billy Sunday ", who added " the church acrobatic " to " the church militant ". He would prance round the platform in his shirt-sleeves, hurling the furniture about, to demonstrate his intention to " soak it into Satan ".[2] Like politicians of a certain type, he would descend to personalities in the vernacular. Dr. Washington Gladden, the progressive, who criticised his methods, he dismissed as " a bald old mutt ".[3] As late as 1932, at Memphis, Tennessee, he denounced liberal ministers as " a lot of pussy-footed, white-livered, yellow softies ". Dr. Sunday (some Bible Institute honoured him with a D.D.) addressed during his stupendous mission at Philadelphia 2,330,000 persons in eight weeks. His version of Christianity was sincere enough, but distorted and vulgarised. He had no sense of reverence, no conception of the Church as the body of Christ, no idea of the complexity of modern life. " If the churches would teach

---

[1] See Professor Warfield's *Perfectionism* (Oxford, 1931).
[2] For a mordant exposure of the worst type of revivalist, see Carl Sandburg's verses, " To a Contemporary Bunkshooter " (*World's Great Religious Poetry*, Macmillan, 1926). The best type Vachell Lindsay honours in " General Booth enters Heaven ".
[3] The prophets have always made enemies. " Go up, thou bald head!" shouted rude lads at Elisha (2 Kings 2.23).

the virgin birth, the literal resurrection and the second coming, the evangelistic fires would burn once more, and do more good in this Christ-blaspheming world than all the disarmament conferences and leagues of nations."

Another twentieth-century exponent of religious vaudeville was Aimee Semple McPherson, prophetess of " The Four Square Gospel ". Her " Angelus Temple " ("largest fire-proof auditorium in the world ") was the embodiment of high-pressure salesmanship. Her adroit use of pageantry, drama and music exploited " Hollywood " mentality. Her matrimonial adventures and kidnapping were front-page news. Almost every feature of her " Full Gospel Revival " is reproduced by Sinclair Lewis in his chapters on " Sharon Falconer " in *Elmer Gantry*. Here we find blatant Evangelism set to jazz, gaudy with coloured lights.

Earlier phases of Revivalism made possible one of America's religious classics, *The Varieties of Religious Experience* (1902). William James inherited from his remarkable father Swedenborgian tendencies. Professor James worshipped regularly in Harvard University Chapel; his real interest, however, was not in the churches but in persons " so mystically aware of the Divine that religion burned in them as an acute fever "·. Pathological aspects of sin and conversion attracted attention; science had at last entered the most inaccessible and complex domain, religion. Educationalists like Starbuck and Coe passed from the " Second Birth " to more normal aspects of the Christian life. It was largely owing to the investigations of psychologists that educated opinion in America gradually realised that too much emphasis had been laid on conversion, too little on Christian nurture. Youth, sex, sectarianism, heredity and environment were now taken into account. Dr. Stanley Hall even wrote two big volumes on *Jesus Christ in the Light of Psychology* (1917). Those who approached religion from the psychological point of view were usually laymen, interested in philosophy as well as psychology. Professor Hocking, of Harvard, produced a classic, *The Meaning of God in Human Experience* (1912). Another Professor of Philosophy, Dr. J. B. Pratt, broke new ground in his *Religious Consciousness* (1920) by stressing the importance of the objective element in religion, as a corrective to humanistic theories. Many European theologians resent any attempt to penetrate their domain, but the experimental attitude is characteristic of American thinkers, e.g. Walter M.

Horton's *Psychological Approach to Theology*. British scholars who have studied the question will be disposed to agree that the most valuable American contribution to the study of religion is its " psychological approach ".

Few brothers have been more dissimilar than Henry and William James. Henry shrank from emotional expression and dwelt on the formal aspects of religion, desiderating the " old ecclesiastical arrogance " of Europe; in the *American Scene* he compared the English cathedrals to bullion, and the American churches to " small change "—plentiful but common. William, on the other hand, had a naturalist's curiosity and was attracted by the very peculiarities of queer sects. About the time he wrote his *Varieties of Religious Experience,* a popular naturalist penned *Wild Animals I have known.* James, it was submitted, should have called his book, *Wild Religions I have known.* Dean Sperry of Harvard exhibits the United States as a happy hunting-ground for the church historian. " There is no other land in Christendom where the fauna is as diverse and as grotesque." America has attracted the big-game hunter and the curious naturalist—so much so that even educated people in England are apt to picture its religions as a kind of extended Barnum museum of freaks. In the " hinterland " strange sights may be found by those who take the trouble to explore patiently. It is the object of this study, however, to survey the normal religious scene. We have time for the merest peep into the zoo, where curious specimens are assembled. Competent guides are available (see Bibliography).

California is the home of freak religions, but in other sections of the United States less favoured by nature the climate seems to stimulate energy and nervous tension to an extent unknown in Britain. There are cults appropriately described by Dr. Winfred Garrison in his *March of Faith* as " Unassimilable Varieties of Religious Expression ". He classifies them as *metaphysical*, e.g. Christian Science, New Thought and Unity; *oriental and occult*, e.g. Theosophy and Baha'ism; *religious communities*, e.g. " House of David ", " Zion City ", Mormons; *non-religious groups*, e.g. Ethical Society, " Humanism " and anti-religious leagues. We have already noted that the *metaphysical* group had its roots in the teaching of Emerson (p. 197). The era of expansion after 1865 produced wealth, optimism and the increase of minor nervous disorders that multiply when ladies have too much money and leisure. Therapeutic psychology was the mainspring of Christian Science (Mrs. Eddy's *Science and Health* appeared in 1875).[1] " New Thought " and " Unity ", while not denying the reality of suffering, concentrate on " right thinking ". The key-note was set by Ralph Waldo Trine's popular book, *In Tune with the Infinite*. These " correspondence schools of the soul " promise Health, Happiness, Harmony, Personal Magnetism, Success. " Unity " resembles " New Thought " in emphasising meditation; it has also points of contact with the occult (Madame Blavatsky founded " The Esoteric School of Philosophy ", 1887).

How far have the Christian Churches tried to meet needs that are stimulated but not satisfied by these cults ? Two Broad Church Episcopalian clergymen, Samuel McComb and Elwood Worcester, have tried to understand the mentality that is attracted by Christian Science. They have adapted therapeutic elements consistent with Christianity in the light of Gospel healing. Dr. Worcester has told the story of this " Emmanuel Movement " in his autobiography, *Life's Adventure* (New York, 1932). More recently Psychiatry has engaged the attention of pastors. Mount Pleasant Congregational Church, Washington, D.C., pioneered in sponsoring clinics, under the direction of the Revs. R. Clinchy and M. Lovell. A staff of volunteer doctors, lawyers and psychiatrists dealt with all sorts of maladjustments, fears and unshared burdens; it was recognised that " the cure of souls " in Protestantism has been ineffective through failure to substitute some alternative for priestly confession in the case of " sick souls ". Throughout the country enlightened ministers have learned from " Unity " and " New Thought " to lay more emphasis on meditation, thought-control, the identification of " holiness " with " wholeness ", and the resolute facing of life with happy confidence.

Eccentric sects still make their conquests when headed by men of hypnotic power, self-assurance and business ability. The heresiarch starts in a small way, using the familiar language of revivalism; in due time he claims to be the mouthpiece of a special " Revelation from the Lord ". A crank may turn the world.

" Pastor " Russell started his " Watch Tower Bible and Tract

----

[1] A good modern Life of Mrs. Eddy, with emphasis on heredity and environment, by Lyman P. Powell (London, 1933). It is interesting to compare Christian Science with Mormonism—the most distinctively American cults. The former has appealed to the elite, etherealising religion: the latter has attracted the masses by its apotheosis of the flesh

Society " in 1884. High-pressure propaganda successfully transmitted throughout the land a parody of Christianity, which cle-
verly exploited latent fanaticism. Russell was as successful among
the poor as Mrs. Eddy among the rich. The rich wanted a mind
at ease so as to derive more satisfaction from life: the desperately
poor, having nothing more to expect from life, looked for a cosmic
cataclysm that would make them masters of the world in the
millenial reign of Christ. Here again, familiar Biblical language
is churned into a queer farrago of irreverent nonsense, effectively
" put across " through radio, loud-speaker vans and cheap literature. Hatred of all Christian Churches is fomented (one wonders
why they drop belief in hell). " Judge " Rutherford, successor to
" Pastor " Russell, coined a sensational slogan. " Millions Now
Living Will Never Die " has been proclaimed in many a free
lecture throughout Britain, and " Jehovah's Witnesses " have had
their opportunity of martyrdom on two continents as conscientious
objectors in time of war.

Popular education has done much to reduce the margin of suggestibility and hysteria that afforded such combustible material
for the old-time revivalism. Self-control and common sense act as
bulwarks against fanaticism except in the backward sections of the
South and West, where obscurantism applies modern business
methods and popular psychology to delude the credulous.[1]

Even in the nineteenth century revivalism did not touch the
upper classes except in isolated instances. A retarded wave of
evangelism reached them after World War I, when Frank Buchman started operations in fellowship with a few friends. Under
the Rev. Sam Shoemaker, Calvary Episcopal Church, New York,
became a regular " rescue mission for the Four Hundred ". Young
people whose religious background had been purely formal and
institutional developed a great hunger for personal religion. Buchman had originally been a Lutheran minister; he had not sprung
from the typical American denomination with a revivalist background. His conversion dated from a visit to England where a
chance visit to a small chapel in Cumberland gave him a " vibrant
feeling up and down the spine "; the exhortation of a simple
woman reoriented his life. This dapper, well-manicured surgeon
of the soul was very different from the popular evangelist. He

[1] It is surprising that the Salvation Army originated in England. Its spectacular appeal and demands for immediate results would waken a response in
the U.S., but American individualism does not like regimentation.

dealt incisively with sin in personal interviews. His assertion that
" 90% of ultimate sin " is based on sexual irregularities did not
make him popular with college Presidents, and the amateur psychiatry of unskilled practitioners at " house-parties ", etc., was
often crude. Sometimes Buchmanite " leadings " from God remind one of " New Thought " in a this-worldly response. Thus,
one woman testified that she was " led " to buy a $1,000 coat for
$300; a business man declared that he was enabled " not only to
find God but to meet the Queen of Rumania and make a better
impression on customers "! The key-words for soul-winning
were " Confidence, Confession, Conviction, Conversion, Conser-
vation ". Evangelism was provided with a new vocabulary (e.g.
as " life-changing "), new emphasis on the necessity of silence,
meditation and group devotion. They claimed to be a " First
Century Christian Fellowship ", spontaneously " sharing experiences ". Harold Begbie, an English journalist well-known as " A
Gentleman with a Duster ", introduced F.B. and his circle to the
British in such books as *Twice Born Men* and *Life Changers*. This
resulted in Buchman crossing the Atlantic, like Moody, and becoming almost a household name, winning converts in all walks
of life, and returning home with a new name for his fellowship,
the " Oxford Group ". Whatever the historian of the future may
say of this un-denominational and predominantly layman's movement, there can be no doubt that in the evolution of Evangelism
it has marked a decisive swing from the whirlwind meeting to the
group, from the mass-gathering to the " cell " leavening the mass.

A word about non-religious propaganda. The Society for Ethical Culture was founded in 1876 by Professor Felix Adler, who
had imbibed rationalism at German Universities and felt unable
to succeed his father as Rabbi in the Reformed synagogue, Fifth
Avenue. " Human personality is the only holy thing we can know,"
affirms the Society; " man's religious duty is wholly definable in
ethical terms." Stanton Coit, whose social idealism attracted
attention in England, was inspired by the achievement of Toynbee
Hall to start the Neighbourhood Guild in New York (1886).
Jews who could no longer accept their ancestral faith even in
liberal dress gravitated towards Ethical Culture, while others
joined a " Liberal Christian Science Church ", whose " Christianity " is reduced to vanishing-point. As Ethical Culture grew
out of Reformed Judaism in the nineteenth century, " Humanism "

grew out of attenuated Unitarianism in the twentieth. God was replaced by Humanity after the analogy of Comte's Positivism, with emphasis on the Brotherhood of Man and the Revelations of Science. " Humanism " seems to have flourished mainly in the academic circles of the Middle West; whether its belief in Man will prove equal to the strain of post-war crisis, remains to be seen. The movement is organised in societies with meetings and " open forums " on Sundays. Like Ethical Culture, its motto might well be " Deed, not creed ".

As early as 1829 Robert Owen, the Socialist, held public debate with Alexander Campbell, founder of the " Disciples ", maintaining that religion was an obstacle to human happiness. After the Civil War, Colonel Ingersoll, lawyer and politician (1833-99) took the field as apostle of Unbelief. " Bob " Ingersoll was a characteristic figure of the " Gilded Age "—the personification of confident atheism, just as Moody was the embodiment of revivalism, and Barnum of showmanship. He was full of elemental energy, touring the country with ready rhetoric, and like Tom Paine lecturing on " The Mistakes of Moses ". It is doubtful whether he made any converts. He probably drove many a timid soul back to naïve supernaturalism, and unlike his opposite number in England, Charles Bradlaugh, he was rejected by the people as a legislator owing to his atheism. At a freethinkers' convention Ingersoll asserted that " Churches were dying out all over the land ". Chaplain C. C. McCabe, Methodist Church Extension leader, read this item in the newspaper on one of his incessant railway journeys to the West. At the next station he sent the following telegram to the oracle of unbelief: " Dear Robert—All hail the power of Jesus name—we are building more than one Methodist church for every day in the year, and propose to make it two a day." The Colonel was unable to compete with this constructive energy. Triumphant Methodism caught the refrain and swept West, singing: " All hail the power of Jesus' name! We're building two a day!"

Not till 1925 was " The American Association for the Advancement of Atheism " chartered. The executive announced, " We are going to undermine the churches of America as certain as time ". Slogans were adopted such as " Fight with the 4A, Kill the Beast!—Religion must go. It poisons life. If you would free mankind of its frightful curse, fight with the 4A. Kill the Beast!"

So Messrs. Hopgood and Smith decided to " put across " atheism, and translate into the American vernacular the imperative of Voltaire, " Écrasez l'Infâme!" They collected anthologies of atrocious passages from Holy Writ, sent martyrs to their doom among the Bible-loving fanatics of Arkansas, established a branch opposite the fundamentalist tabernacle of Dr. John Roach Straton in New York, sent foreign missionaries to Canada, Mexico and Sweden, organised student societies under such titles as " Damned Souls ", and set up machinery to wean the young from " Big-Man-up-in-the-Sky stuff ". All this sounds as silly as the undergraduate infidelity that was scotched by President Dwight at Yale. Twentieth-century American atheism, advanced by revivalist methods, has become, paradoxically enough, a new religion!

Scepticism in the United States has owed something to the German element in the nineteenth century who imported various brands of unbelief from the Fatherland, largely motivated by truculent anti-clericalism. Anglo-Saxon opposition to organised religion has seldom crystallised except when Christianity has been presented by the churches in a repressive or obscurantist manner.

During the period of phenomenal prosperity that followed the First World War a group of ultra-radicals felt so optimistic that they thought that they could now afford to bow God out of the universe, trusting in man's own will-to-goodness and ability to advance to unlimited progress by ethics, science and education. They appropriated Bob Ingersoll's axiom: "There is no God except Humanity." These bland advocates of " ourselves alone " appropriated the name of " Humanism ".[1] Not many of them dwelt on the historic association of the word with Renascence culture. They were more interested in the present than the past, with emphasis on the possibilities of scientific advance and the improvement of human nature. Some doubtless considered that they had minted a new word by dropping out the middle syllables of an old one, but " Humanism " fell as far short of " Humanitarianism " as " gent " falls short of " gentleman ". These optimists expected the fruits of unselfishness after cutting off its roots, ignoring the fact that humanitarian causes have owed most to those whose faith has drawn its power from belief in Jesus Christ as the Saviour of the world.

[1] Apologetic literature: C. F. Potter, *Humanism* (1930); Eustace Haydon, *The Quest of the Ages* (1929).

The new " Humanists " did not find that the world took their claims seriously. Scientists, impersonal in outlook, had their reservations as to lyric enthusiasm about the possibilities of Man as " lord of all being ". Men who wrestled in the world of business could not share their naïve belief in the ability of human nature to get along without God and Christ. Even thinkers whose hold on the Christian verities had relaxed, lamented the " acids of modernity " that had eaten into religion, which had gradually relinquished the lordship of one " lost province " after another— business, the family, art, etc. Walter Lippmann wrote his important book, *A Preface to Morals* (1929) in nostalgic mood. To the three Parts of his thesis he prefixed significant mottos: " Whirl is King, having driven out Zeus " (Aristophanes), " The stone which the builders rejected . . . is become the head of the corner " (Luke), and " Where is the way where light dwelleth ?" (Job). It is clear that Lippmann did not share the illusions of the " Humanists ". He said, in effect: " I come to bury ' Progress ', not to praise it."

.   .   .   .

One of the liberalising factors in American Protestantism has been " Religious Education ". Dr. Nicholas Murray Butler " named the beast " in 1900. This new movement was the fusion of the scientific attitude and the spirit of humanistic idealism, tinged with the after-glow of evangelical ardour. On the practical side, it can be traced back to improved methods of teaching religion. Even sects cradled in revivalism found it necessary to pay more attention to their Sunday Schools. Among the pioneers of efficiency was a Methodist, Bishop Vincent. He was responsible for the emergence of the Sunday School from the church base-ment—the " dark age " was to give way to light. His " Akron plan " consisted of a large hall furnished for " preliminary exer-cises ", with movable partitions for the separate classes. The whole auditorium was so arranged that, by means of sliding doors or a mysterious portcullis, it might on occasion be thrown open into the church. This curious experiment was first tried out at Akron, Ohio. It was crude enough, but marked the beginning of a serious attempt to house the Sunday School worthily.

In 1872 Bishop Vincent was instrumental in persuading most of the denominations to adopt a uniform series of S.S. Lessons

devised by the International Sunday School Convention. " Every-
one from a four-year-old beginner to the oldest member of the
Men's Bible Class studied the same portions of Scripture every
Sunday, working through the entire Bible every seven years (in
the South and West, adults' classes are often integrated with the
Sunday School, as in Wales).

It is characteristic of the conservative mentality of many teachers that this modest reform held back " Graded Lessons " till
1908. Diehards were obsessed by the big idea of " the whole
Christian world keeping step " by studying the same lesson at
the same time. They ignored the obvious advantage of adapting
the lessons to the age of the pupils. The change of emphasis
from " material-centred " teaching to the " unfolding of personality " registered a significant expansion of Sunday Schools and
increase of 36% between 1906 and 1916.[1]

Child-Study conditioned the reorientation of Religious Education. Since Bushnell published his epoch-making *Christian
Nurture* in 1847 a growing number of ministers had been turning
their attention to " the child in the midst ". Were the revivalists
always right in stressing Conquest rather than Growth ? At the
close of the century William James, Starbuck and other pioneers
made a special study of conversion. The new " Psychology of
Religion " made it clear that Revivalism had been too readily
taken for granted as the dominant pattern of American religion;
stereotyped evangelistic methods had done harm as well as good.
Complaints about the decay of family life and juvenile delinquency
led welfare workers to provide constructive social activities for
neglected city children. Stanley Hall studied genetically the characteristics of various age-groups and published his important
Adolescence in 1904. G. A. Coe's *Social Theory of Religious Education* (1917) registered the change of emphasis wrought since the
beginning of the century. He defined Christian Education as " the
growth of the young towards and into mature and efficient devotion
to the democracy of God and a happy self-realisation therein ".
The aim was not primarily to teach the Bible, but to guide the
development of body, mind and soul, through Christ, in relation
to the changing circumstances of life.

By 1922 the modest beginnings of 1903 had been consoli-

---

[1] In 1936 14,000,000 children attended American Sunday Schools—
20,000,000 if teachers and adult members be included.

dated into the " International Council for Religious Education ".
In response to the demand for specialised vocational leadership,
congregations were beginning to appoint full-time Directors of
Religious Education. During the week they were busy using the
" released time " allowed in many States since 1913 for religious
teaching on church premises.[1] During the summer they organised
summer vacation courses for juveniles, blending recreation and
study, lasting from ten days to six weeks.[2]

In churches of a " Fundamentalist " outlook, modern equipment was sometimes used, but ungraded lessons persisted for
children of all ages. The teaching continued to be " material-
centred " rather than " child-centred ". The object was still to
impart dogma through Bible text and catechism (the latter particularly favoured by Presbyterians and Lutherans), " bending the
will and stirring the emotions ". The Religious Education Movement, on the other hand, seeks rather to develop the child's
personality by expansion towards God, in fellowship with his
fellow-men, with a view to promoting a civilisation embodying
ever more fully the ideals of Jesus. The movement emphasises
wholesome nurture rather than " revival ", shared experiences
rather than pietistic individualism, " discovery " rather than formal instruction. Drama, so long anathema to the dominant pattern
of American religion, became a fresh means of grace. The sense
of wonder, so long suppressed, was released. " Man's chief end "
was apprehended as the enjoyment of God through the appreciation of the beautiful, the creation of things lovely, and the attainment of harmonious living.

Sometimes Religious Educationalists have over-driven their
principles, criticising preaching as " authoritarian " and treating
" indoctrination " as an educational crime.[3] As regards the left
wing the danger is that the reaction from " a revealed metaphysic
which needs no further thought " may lead to a " behaviouristic
pragmatism " in which " Society takes the place of God and

[1] R.C. abuse of such privileges has hardened Protestant insistence on
keeping American schools completely secular. See Johnson and Yost, *Separation of Church and State in the U.S.* (Minneapolis, 1948).
[2] Started in 1900, these " Vacation Church Schools " now enrol about
1,500,000 children, distributed in 15,000 groups.
[3] During the depression (1930) the machinery of Religious Education was
crippled. This was salutary in breaking the complacency of specialists and in
reminding pastors that the care of the young is an integral part of their Christian
ministry. Some congregations were relieved of the obvious rivalry of " rectors
and di-rectors ".

socialised behaviour the place of worship " (Professor E. S. Brightman). Apart from extremists, religious education has done much good in bringing men and women of various denominations together in the service of God. One instance of their principle of " the revaluation of prejudice " is a reversal of the Puritan attitude to colour and candles, pageantry and drama, which outlived the Puritan theology. " Holiness " conceived in terms of " wholeness " has resulted in the appreciation of many " worldly amusements " formerly banned but now hallowed for higher service. (Bushnell's *Work and Play*, 1864, pointed the way.)

Even in the Age of Revivals the camp-meeting had been " a glorious combination of piety and picnic ". Moody's campus at Northfield was white with tents every summer, when an annual conference met to hear the most eminent Bible expositors and preachers of America and Britain (not even George Adam Smith's bold theory of the " two Isaiahs " barred him from the Northfield Convention). In England, " Keswick " was attuned to the most rigid traditions of verbal inspiration. " Northfield ", however, offered people who were perplexed about the Bible the opportunity of hearing how the new scholarship might be reconciled with evangelical experience.

Bishop Vincent, the Methodist pioneer of " Religious Education ", conceived the happy idea of transforming the disused site of a " camp-meeting " into the *venue* for a fortnight's conference for S.S. teachers every summer. This experiment at Lake Chautauqua, N.Y. (1874) was such a success that it developed into a kind of " people's university ", with lectures on a wide range of subjects. Permanent buildings were erected in beautiful surroundings, and visitors stimulated to study were offered miscellaneous correspondence courses (including Hebrew). The remnants of the popular " lyceums " of Emerson's era have thus been gathered together, under Christian auspices. A varied programme of adult education, conceived on broad, inspirational lines, has been successfully maintained in an atmosphere of cheerful fellowship. Two hymns by Mary Lathbury for her Chautauqua friends have proved particularly popular with American Youth. One of these, " Break Thou the bread of life, dear Lord, to me ", is fairly familiar in Britain. The other deserves to be better known. No one who has heard it sung in the open air by thousands at sunset can deny its " inspirational " appeal, set to Sherwin's swinging melody, though few would go so far as the English hymnologist, Garrett Horder, who ranked it with " Lead, kindly light ".

> Day is dying in the west:
> Heaven is touching earth with rest;
> Wait and worship while the night
> Sets her evening lamps alight
>   Through all the sky.
> Holy, Holy, Holy Lord God of Hosts!
> Heaven and earth are full of Thee!
> Heaven and earth are praising Thee,
>   O Lord most high.

CHAPTER III

THEOLOGICAL EMANCIPATION AND RE-STATEMENT

" In 1890 the ' liberal' was debating whether there were two Isaiahs: in 1930 the extreme ' modernist' was debating whether there was a personal God."—G. G. ATKINS

AMERICAN Protestantism was overwhelmingly conservative in theological orientation when the Civil War closed in 1865. The Presbyterians might be Calvinists and the Methodists Arminians, but both were united by a common belief in a literally-inspired Bible, and, like the Baptists, feared lest any presumptuous hand touch the ark of the Covenant. Theology moved within denominational grooves, and when it moved out of them, got no further than the closed circle of stereotyped Revivalism. The Unitarian departure had stiffened conservatism without raising up any theologian who was big enough to re-state orthodoxy in its relation to changing thought. There was Bushnell, to be sure, but the leaven of his stimulating ideas was slow to penetrate the heavy dough of traditional ways of thinking. If English theology was insular in the middle of the nineteenth century, assimilating little from the various schools of German thought (and denouncing everything unfamiliar as " neology "), American theology was even more densely provincial.

When Darwin's *Origin of Species* fell like a bomb in England (1859) the complacent " religious world ", from Lord Bishops to Nonconformist preachers, was shocked and reacted violently. It made little impact on the United States, however. Not till the 'seventies and 'eighties did Evolution come to the fore in America. John Fiske, scientist and man of letters, familiarised the educated classes with this new idea in books, lectures and magazines. In lucid exposition he reconciled Evolution with Theism; " It is God's way of doing things," he would remark (with an eye on the clergy).

" The future is lighted for us with the radiant colors of hope,"
he predicted in *The Destiny of Man* (1890). " Strife and sorrow
shall disappear. Peace and love shall reign supreme. The dream
of poets, the lesson of priest and prophet, the inspiration of the
great musician, is confirmed in the light of modern knowledge."

This optimistic interpretation of Evolution was readily lapped
up by progressives. Dr. Charles Hodge[1] of Princeton thought
differently: "A more incredible thing was never propounded!" he
exclaimed. Such a verdict was to be expected from a theologian who
gloried in the fact that " Princeton has never originated a new
idea ". Professor McCosh, who came to Princeton from Belfast,
surprised conservatives by announcing: " Supernatural design
produces natural selection." The widest publicity was given to
Darwin's epoch-making ideas by Henry Ward Beecher, who explained Evolution in simple terms by press and pulpit. His
successor in Plymouth Church, Brooklyn, Dr. Lyman Abbott,
popularised current scientific ideas in his persuasive *Faith of an
Evolutionist* (1898). Quoting the familiar words of the *New England Primer*, " In Adam's fall, we sinned all," he retorted; "Adam
did not represent me—I never voted for him." This was rank
blasphemy to the journalist-preacher's contemporaries in Brooklyn, Theodore Cuyler and De Witt Talmage.

In spite of misgivings, the convictions of educated men were
inevitably modified by the new scientific outlook. The visit of
Henry Drummond (1887) was a triumphant vindication of the
compatibility of Evolution and Evangelism. Here was an Edinburgh professor, fresh from Scotland (home of sound theology).
A literary man, a gentleman and a winning public speaker, he
could write *Natural Law in the Spiritual World*, and also appear
on revival platforms with Moody. Nevertheless the more belligerent conservatives opened fire on Moody for associating with
such a heretic. Drs. Charles Eliot of Harvard and A. D. White
of Cornell, as presidents of the only universities where Evolution
could get a fair hearing, became targets for heated controver-
sialists. It is not surprising that the latter wrote a rather biassed
History of the Warfare of Science with Theology (1897). Some
years later, however, W. H. Carruth found his convictions widely
accepted in the churches:

[1] His *Systematic Theology* (3 vols., 1873) remains the ablest modern exposition of Calvinism. Cp. C. A. Salmond, *Charles and A. A. Hodge* (New
York, 1888).

z

> A fire-mist and a plant—
> A crystal and a cell—
> A jellyfish and a saurian,
>   And caves where cave-men dwell;
> Then a sense of law and beauty,
>   And a face turned from the clod,
> Some call it Evolution,
>   And others call it God.

In 1865 the National Congregational Council gave " profound attention " to a sermon lasting over two hours from the text, " Ask for the old paths ". The same year a local " Ecclesiastical Council " in Maine refused to ordain a minister who was orthodox enough to declare *ex animo* that all who died impenitent in Christian lands would be hopelessly and permanently damned: he was " advanced " in holding (privately) that the " offer of salvation " might be available in the next world for " heathen and others " who did not have the opportunity of hearing it on earth. In 1877 an Ecclesiastical Council at Indian Orchard, Mass., declined to install the Rev. J. F. Merriam because he rejected " everlasting punishment "; in this instance the congregation proceeded with the induction on their own.

Congregationalists claimed to be the most " advanced " denomination in America.[1] Their progress was certainly slow,[2] but they had this advantage over highly organised sects—the people *could* protect their pastor from heresy-hunters. Thus when Bushnell was harried in Hartford by the local " Consociation ", his congregation separated from a body that was consultative, not judicial. Henry Ward Beecher resigned from the " Congregational Association " of New York in 1882 after stating his beliefs. To his surprise these brethren indicated " the propriety of his membership on this or any other Congregational Association ".[3] Never-

---

[1] In the shadow of Yale stand two historic churches, Center and United Outstanding men ministered in both. Dr. Munger wrote *The Freedom of the Faith*, and Dr. Newman Smyth *The Orthodox Theology*. Queen Victoria read " those wonderful books ", given her by Bishop Boyd Carpenter. They helped to revive her faith in years of doubt after Prince Albert's death.

[2] Even at the end of the century, the American delegates to the International Congregational Council in London were so strong on hell that Dr. Parker announced he would have to get the pulpit of the City Temple fumigated from sulphur fumes!

[3] By 1913 liberalism triumphed in finding a " creed " for " general use ". This formula, adopted by the National Council at Kansas City, was about the same length as the Nicene Creed, but its emphasis is quite different. Christian belief is summarised in six lines, while the manward task is stressed—" laboring for the progress of knowledge, the promotion of justice, the reign of peace, and the realisation of human brotherhood."

theless he persisted in maintaining his isolation.[1] The Baptists enjoyed the same autonomy as the Congregationalists, but had few thinkers of a forward-looking outlook, save in their Divinity Schools at Newton, Mass., and Chicago.

It was in the Presbyterian Church that the conflict between " Old and New " was fiercest. The Conservatives' fastness was Pennsylvania and the mantle of Charles Hodge had fallen on Dr. F. L. Patton, afterwards President of Princeton University. Dr. Patton determined to prosecute in the Church Courts men who denied the Plenary Inspiration of the Bible. " Princeton is a fortress!" declared this champion of the Church militant. David Swing of Chicago, acquitted of heresy by his presbytery, feared that his opponents might take the case to the General Assembly. He withdrew from Presbyterianism, and Dr. Preserved Smith resigned his Chair at Lane Seminary, Cincinnati (1893). Union Seminary, New York, became a centre of light and leading for Liberals. It was confidently hoped that freedom of thought, within reasonable limits, might be won in the United States, as in Scotland, despite the removal of Professor Robertson Smith from his Aberdeen Chair. Surely the spirit would prevail over the letter.

Popular interest in the Bible had been stirred up in 1870 when the Convocation of Canterbury voted " to invite the co-operation of some American divines " in their task of revising the King James Bible. Dr. Joseph Angus landed in New York in August and conferred with Dr. Philip Schaff of Union Seminary. A leader of the Reformed Church, Schaff was Swiss by birth, German by education and American by adoption. An all-round scholar of distinction, known in Europe as a Church historian, he was well equipped to head the American committee. He succeeded in harmonising those denominational jealousies that are apt to hold up progress in a land where there is no National Church to initiate joint enterprises. The American revisers, representing nine churches, kept in touch with their English colleagues by correspondence. When the New Testament was finished, a telegram (180,000 words) brought the Good News from New York to Chicago (20th May, 1881). The leading newspapers

[1] When Dr. G. A. Gordon was installed in the " Old South ", Boston (1884), the " Ecclesiastical Council " of neighbouring ministers, etc., met at 5.30 and only decided at 9 p.m., by 48 votes to 18, to proceed with the induction. They were punished for their contentious spirit, for the congregation had already dined and " heard " distinguished visitors like Phillips Brooks; the " Council " had to put up with a cold collation! For many years Gordon was isolated as a liberal.

printed the four Gospels next day. Within twenty-four hours of publication 33,000 copies of the Revised Version were sold in New York.

In 1911 President Taft sent the following message at the Tercentenary of the King James Bible: " The Book of books has not only reigned supreme in England for three hundred years, but has bound together, as nothing else could, two great Anglo-Saxon nations—one in blood, in speech, and in a common religion. Our laws, our literature and our social life owe whatever excellence they possess, largely to the influence of this our chief classic—acknowledged as such equally on both sides of the sea." The supremacy of the Authorised Version was generally admitted in England where traditional liturgical associations hallowed old-world phraseology. In the United States informed public opinion was not altogether satisfied; too much tenderness was shown by the Revised Version of 1881 to archaic diction which was becoming increasingly unintelligible to the ordinary Bible reader. The American Revisers therefore continued their labours independently and inserted in the text of their recension many readings relegated by their English colleagues to the margin, e.g. " very religious " for " somewhat superstitious " (Acts 17.22). They also discarded usages sanctioned by hoary tradition but not by the text, e.g. " Saint " in the title of the four Gospels. They substituted for " Holy Ghost ", " Holy Spirit ". Following ancient MSS. they omitted Paul's name from the Epistle to the Hebrews. These changes were embodied in *The American Standard Version*, which appeared in 1901 and has been used to a much greater extent than the Revised Version of 1881 in Britain.

In this connexion, we may note the prophetic words of President Ezra Stiles of Yale College, dating from the middle of the eighteenth century: " I do not wish to see another English Translation till the English dialect shall have become altogether obsolete and unintelligible to posterity. But this will not be till English America is fully settled . . . when the English of the present idiom may be spoken by one hundred million." In 1932 it was felt that the time was ripe to " translate the original Greek text into the every-day language of Americans of to-day ". A commission representing many Protestant denominations set to work under the chairmanship of Professor Luther A. Weigle of Yale Divinity School; most of the leading members belonged to Anglo-Saxon denominations, with the notable exception of the Lutheran scholar,

Dr. Abdel R. Wentz. They produced in 1946 *The Revised Standard Version of the New Testament*. This is not a translation into everyday American speech, like Professor Goodspeed's version (Chicago, 1923), but rather a recension of the revision of 1901.[1] The atmosphere of the King James Version is skilfully preserved, in spite of a rigorous excision of archaisms. The 1946 New Testament has been criticised as " a modernised antique ", but has been well received on both sides of the Atlantic.

The revision of the English Bible opened the eyes of many ministers, teachers and church workers to the difficulties of " plenary inspiration ", which had hitherto been almost unchallenged. During the 'eighties the " Higher Criticism " gradually trickled into the Divinity Schools. Most of the " accredited scholars " of the new order returned to the United States with German visas on their intellectual passports. They had learned how to prosecute research work intensively in *seminars*; they spoke much of Ritschl's " judgments of fact " and " judgments of value ". Engrossed in the task of taking the Bible to pieces and putting it together again, they did not always have the imagination to put themselves in the place of the layman who was confused by hearing the authority of German scholars cited, in place of the authority of God. Sometimes crude attempts were made to popularise the Higher Criticism before the people were prepared. As D. L. Moody used to say, " What's the good of talking about two Isaiahs when most people don't know there is one ? "

Allowing for a certain cocksureness and lack of perspective on the part of some scholars, America was well served by men who broke new ground, like Robertson Smith at Aberdeen and Cheyne at Oxford. Chicago had her Harper, and Yale her Bacon. A Baptist and a Congregationalist might do with impunity, however, what a Presbyterian at that time could only attempt at considerable risk.

In 1883 Professor Charles A. Briggs of Union Seminary, New York, issued a balanced handbook on *Biblical Study: Its Principles and History*. This landmark of advancing scholarship[2] did little

---

[1] Weigle, *An Introduction to the Revised Standard Version of the New Testament* (International Council of Religious Education, 1946).

[2] Anglo-American scholarship, progressive yet balanced, produced monumental series, sponsored by famous publishers on both sides of the Atlantic. On the technical side, there was the *International Critical Commentary*; more popular was the *Expositor's Bible* that included George Adam Smith's epoch-making volumes on the Prophets. Men like A. B. Davidson contributed to the Biblical side of the *International Theological Library*.

to modify the perspective of his opponents in the Presbyterian Church. They were too preoccupied with the Evolution controversy to molest him at the time. Ten years later the storm broke. The General Assembly was still committed to " the Inerrancy of the Original Texts of the Bible ", while admitting that these were lost! The venerable Court were not, however, restrained by this significant admission. Nor had they learned anything from the Robertson Smith case in Scotland. Professor Briggs was not merely suspended but charged with the violation of his ordination vows. He took refuge in the Episcopal Church, for he had considerable sympathy with Catholic Churchmanship, provided it allowed reasonable liberty of thought.

Not all Episcopalians had the same idea of legitimate latitude. In 1905 a middle-aged rector of Rochester, N.Y., roused considerable controversy by advanced views expressed in the pulpit. The Rev. Algernon S. Crapsey was an excellent public speaker, a clear if not profound thinker and a fearless advocate of " social justice ". He was not the kind of clergyman likely to balance himself by cautious equilibrium between inherited orthodoxy and dangerous inquiry. The worst that could be said against Crapsey was that he was unduly sensitised to the rationalistic atmosphere of his era. When he publicly rejected the Virgin Birth, he was inevitably summoned by his bishop before an ecclesiastical court at Batavia, N.Y. He appealed to the Scriptures against the Creeds and the Prayer Book. After a long trial, in which he was ably defended by two prominent Broad Churchmen, Samuel McComb and Elwood Worcester, he was suspended from the Holy Ministry and resigned in 1906.[1] Some years later Mr. Crapsey wrote his autobiography, *The Last of the Heretics* (New York, 1924). The title was hardly justified, as Dr. Percy S. Grant, of St.-Mark's-in-the-Bowery got into trouble about that time with the Bishop of New York for much the same kind of heresy.[2] The climate of the Episcopal Church, however, was no longer favourable to heresy hunts *á l'outrance* and Dr. Grant was not removed. It was many years before the Presbyterian Church became as tolerant.

[1] The influential laity were more concerned with Crapsey's economic heresies. This was the case with Winston Churchill's parson hero (*The Inside of the Cup*, 1906. See above, p. 319).

[2] Dr. Grant's heresy may be summed up in his bland statement: " Very few clergymen educated in the larger Universities, where science is taught, accept the idea that Jesus had the power of God." His original use of pageantry and drama in worship offended the conventional mind of Bishop Manning.

The narrowness of Presbyterian orthodoxy was to be found at its worst in Pennsylvania among the Scots-Irish, who were dominated by the stereotyped dogmas of Princeton. Never has rebellion against theological bigotry been more effectively voiced than by Margaret Deland in her novel, *John Ward, Preacher* (1887). Alleghany, her birthplace, was the seat of three rival Seminaries (Presbyterian, United Presbyterian and Reformed Presbyterian) differing only in the extremes to which they carried Calvinist tenets; all had Chairs of " Didactic and Polemical Theology ". John Ward was an able and earnest young minister who had just married Helen Jeffrey, niece of a kindly, easy-going Episcopal rector. John's rigidity drove Helen into good-natured agnosticism. " Perhaps we all sin in original ways," she said with a smile, " but I don't believe in original sin . . . I can't think of any greater heresy than to deny the love of God." John objected, " But the Bible says . . ." She interrupted him: " The Bible was the history, and poetry, and politics of the Jews, as well as their liturgy; so that, unless we are prepared to believe in its verbal inspiration, I don't see how we can argue, ' The Bible says '." " And do you not believe in its verbal inspiration ?" he asked slowly. " No," she replied, " I could not." She found little comfort in the dour Presbyterian flock at Lockhaven who took a sadistic pleasure in singing Watts' gloomiest hymn:

> My thoughts on awful subjects roll,
>   Damnation and the dead. . .
> There endless crowds of sinners lie,
>   And darkness makes their chains,
> Tortured with keen despair they cry,
>   Yet wait for fiercer pains![1]

Helen refused to attend prayer meetings whilst such hymns were sung. " Why, dearest!" exclaimed John, " *I* believe in hell." " I know it," she replied; " Never mind. I mean, it does not make any difference to me what you believe. . . One man is born a Roman Catholic, though his parents may be the sternest Protestants. He cannot help it; it is his nature! And you—you were born a Presbyterian, dear; you can't help it. Perhaps you need the sternness and horror of some of the doctrines as a balance for your gentleness." John Ward, failing to lead his beloved wife to " the truth ", made the supreme sacrifice of separating from her,

[1] E. M. Geldart, a distinguished English Law professor, " used to gloat on this hymn as a child ".

so that he might haply " save her soul ". Dr. Howe, in a stormy but futile interview with Mr. Ward, exclaimed: " She shall never return to a man who reads such books as these!" (pointing to the *Works* of Jonathan Edwards, Calvin Redivivus).

It is interesting to note that *John Ward* was published about the same time as *Robert Elsmere*. Mrs. Deland and Mrs. Humphrey Ward were both at home in theology and social problems. They wrote on different sides of the Atlantic, one making her clergyman a tenacious conservative and his wife an agnostic, the other reversing the rôle! *Robert Elsmere* created an immense sensation in the United States; *John Ward* did not have the same enormous circulation, but was widely read. These were the days when Robert Ingersoll, Apostle of Unbelief, was tilting at orthodoxy, equipped with the panoply of Huxley, much as Paine armed himself with Voltaire's arguments a century earlier. In the *North American Review* the redoubtable Colonel engaged in tournament with such proved champions of orthodoxy as Gladstone and Cardinal Manning (1887-8). Nine years later he was still testifying to his militant unbelief in *Why I am an Agnostic* (1896). Ingersoll was a minister's son, who reacted violently against the unreasonable and grim exaggerations of dogma as he had experienced them. Only gradually did the churches realise that there were faults on both sides. They were slow to admit the truth of Edward Markham's lines:

> He drew a circle which shut me out,
> Heretic, rebel, one to flout:
> But love and I had the sense to win,
> We drew a circle and took him in.

The Presbyterians were backward pupils in the art of drawing inclusive circles. They lost needlessly a number of whole-hearted but thoughtful Christians, who joined the Congregationalists or Episcopalians. But for the opportune secession of the Southern Church owing to the slavery issue, American Presbyterianism might never have escaped from the bondage of the letter. In 1889 the General Assembly proceeded in a cautious manner to consult Presbyteries as to the advisability of modifying the venerable Westminster Confession ; 134 Presbyteries favoured revision, but 68 were opposed to any change. Whereupon, it was moved that a footnote be appended to the effect that reprobation must not be understood so as to exclude the love of God. Then rose Dr.

Howard Crosby, with uplifted hands: " Brethren, has it come to this, that the Presbyterian Church proposes to relegate the love of God to a footnote ?" Not till 1902 was a timid supplement to the Confession drawn up, offering concessions to those who preferred the spirit of the Gospel to the letter of a scholastic seventeenth-century document.

Among those who yearned and toiled for a " comprehensive church " was Dr. Henry Van Dyke of New York. He " freely subscribed to the Presbyterian doctrines, without being slavishly subject to them " (to quote the apt phrase of Harvard, on the occasion of his D.D. in 1894). " This great city wants the bread of life," pleaded Dr. Van Dyke. "Don't let us give it the stone of controversy instead." In the Brick Church, in the Press and the Presbytery, he spoke manfully and persuasively, undeterred by his opponents (aided and abetted by the *New York Sun*). " Without liberty there is no true orthodoxy. A man cannot be taught to believe and think right without liberty. Orthodoxy must flourish in an air of freedom; and the best way to defend the Bible is in the open air, and in the light of facts. . . That is the position of a conservative."[1] This fine, magnanimous appeal made a great impression, especially among younger men. ·The church that had cast out Professor Briggs was recalled to the spirit of Christ by Dr. Van Dyke. In his own words, it had—

> Something to learn and something to forget:
> Hold fast the good, and seek the better yet:
> Press on, and prove the pilgrim-hope of youth—
> That creeds are milestones on the path to truth.

The cause of freedom was vindicated, but the liberals did not feel at ease in Zion. Their stronghold, Union Seminary, New York,[2] dissociated itself from the Presbyterian Church in 1905, the Faculty ceasing to subscribe to the Westminster Confession. Like the Divinity School of Chicago University (originally Baptist) " Union " numbered professors and students of all denominations in a free academic fellowship; impressive Gothic buildings were erected; distinguished scholars like James Moffatt and Foakes-Jackson were called from Great Britain. In New York and other academic centres, groups of colleges pooled their intellectual re-

---

[1] Tertius Van Dyke, *Henry Van Dyke, A Biography*, p. 129 (New York, 1935).
[2] Title referring to the Presbyterian-Congregational " Plan of Union ", which the former abrogated a year after the founding of the seminary (1836).

sources, pointing to the ideal of a " University of Religion " providing adequate facilities for research, with vocational training for
the minister, missionary, Christian educationalist and church
musician. Eager students were attracted even from the more
backward denominations, which they leavened with liberalism.
The University Divinity Schools at Yale (Congregational) and
Harvard (Unitarian) gradually lost their sectarian tinge. The former became " Liberal Evangelical ", drawing many students from
the conservative South: the latter might be labelled "Modernist"[1]
and laid special emphasis on research (Kirsopp Lake, the brilliant
New Testament scholar, was among their English acquisitions).
When Dr. Willard L. Sperry, now Dean of the Harvard Divinity
School, returned to the States in 1907 after three years at Oxford
as a Rhodes Scholar, a leading American theologian asked why
he had wasted his time in England, when he might have gone to
Germany. Men who had studied at Berlin, Marburg or Leipzig
brought home reverence for exact scholarship, the " seminar "
method for group-research, and veneration for Ritschl, Harnack
and other luminaries.

William Adams Brown, appointed Roosevelt Professor of Systematic Theology at Union, New York, in 1898, quoted with
approval Kaftan's depreciation of professors who took an active
interest in church work: " We theologians have something more
important to do. *Wir schmieden Formeln.* Our business is to
hammer out formulae." Adams Brown, however, outgrew this
Teutonic one-sidedness.[2] He realised that rationalism can be quite
as dry as dogmatism; marginal criticism must yield to constructive
convictions (*Beliefs that Matter*, London, 1928). Theology could
only be alive if Christ was its " vitalising principle " in the process
of keeping contact with ordinary life. In his later books he was
so eager to reach the educated layman, that he dispensed with the
minister as " middleman " and trajected his thought over the
pulpit straight to the pews. He reversed the process of most
theologians by starting with man instead of God.

Dr. Brown's *Christian Theology in Outline* (1906) is still one of
the most thorough and balanced of " Introductions ". It was

[1] In 1922 a " Modern Churchmen's Union " was formed in the Episcopal
Church, after the English model; High Churchmen and Evangelicals were also
organised on party lines.
[2] *The Church through Half a Century: Essays in Honor of William Adams
Brown* (ed. Van Dusen, New York, 1936).

preceded in 1898 by Dr. W. Newton Clarke's *Outline of Christian Theology*. This book exercised a widespread influence in reassuring his generation that the acceptance of the Higher Criticism in no respect loosened the foundations of historic Christianity. A devout Biblicism irradiated Dr. Clarke's personal experiences of the painful transition from uncritical acceptance of Scripture to mature, discriminating conviction (*Sixty Years with the Bible*, 1912).

Dr. Kirsopp Lake has divided theologians into " fundamentalists, institutionalists and experimentalists ".[1] Thinking Americans tend to be experimentalists. Such was Dr. Borden P. Bowne, professor at Boston University (Methodist Episcopal). Bowne had studied at Paris, Halle and Göttingen in 1873-5 where Lotze greeted him as a student of great promise. He was a caustic critic of Spencer's agnosticism—assigning to science all that was knowable and to religion all that was unknowable. He used Spencer's *First Principles* as a " cadaver " for his students to acquire practice in dissecting. No system-builder, Bowne avoided the faults of the German doctrinaire, while he learned from the Germans to estimate a University by its scholarship rather than by material equipment. A staunch Theist and a warm-hearted Methodist[2] (in spite of Philosophy and Psychology) he was a living example of " truth through personality ". Indeed, he found personality, not abstract theory, the best approach to God as supreme reality (*Personalism*, 1908). Strangely enough, Bowne had been teaching for eighteen years in Boston University before he was charged with " heresy " in 1904. He was heretical only from the point of view of those who rejected freedom of thought and the findings of mature scholarship. He was unanimously acquitted by the New York East Conference, and that was the end of heresy-hunting in the (Northern) Methodist Church, the largest Protestant body. In most denominations culprits were merely admonished with a verdict that amounted to this: " Not guilty, but don't do it again."

It appeared as if American theology had found its balance in " Liberal Evangelicalism ". Unfortunately, it did not. There were hide-bound conservatives who wanted to be evangelical

---

[1] *The Religion of Yesterday and To-day*, p. 56 ff. (Boston, 1926).
[2] The first significant Methodist thinker. Methodists and Baptists are still backward in theological productivity. Episcopalians, despite their culture, are apt merely to reflect English Church thought. The Presbyterian contribution is more weighty, but Congregationalists still lead.

without the slightest toleration for liberals, and there were liberals who seemed incapable of realising that there *was* an evangelical core in the Gospel. Cocksure radicals and prejudiced conservatives were often at loggerheads through sheer ignorance of the real issues. Just when more education was sorely needed, there was a marked decline in the intellectual status of the clergy. Of all United States college graduates in 1870, 19.8% entered the Ministry, in 1928 only 2%.[1] Even in the larger denominations at least two-fifths had taken neither a B.A. nor studied at a theological seminary. Among the Methodists, Baptists, Disciples, etc., educational short-cuts admitted an appalling proportion of ill-educated pastors. The ministry naturally lost caste, and often gave good cause for the gibes of Sinclair Lewis and H. L. Mencken. Without adequate leadership from the clergy, it is not surprising that many earnest laymen were influenced by the shallow but fanatical ultraorthodox propaganda.

In 1909 twelve booklets appeared, entitled *The Fundamentals*. No reader could fail to grasp their meaning. To be a Christian, one must accept without reservation five points—the Inerrancy of Scripture, the Virgin Birth of Christ, His physical Resurrection, Substitutionary Atonement and Imminent Second Coming. This movement was " backed by the ample resources of Lyman and Milton Stewart, Californian oil millionaires " (W. E. Garrison). Nearly 3,000,000 copies of *The Fundamentals* were published, pastors and divinity students receiving them gratis. Here was clear-cut authoritarianism. The trumpet was blown on the bastions of Zion. The alarum evoked an immediate response from the " hard-shell " Baptists of the South, the survivors of " old time Methodism ", and Presbyterians of the rigid type; in the front rank were the " Bible Institutes " of Chicago and Los Angeles, who claimed to be the standard-bearers of the Moody tradition. Hot little souls raised the cry, " To your tents, O Israel!" The outbreak of World War I supplied " Fundamentalism " with apocalyptic fervour. The " signs of the times " pointed to Armageddon. It was the bounden duty of the true Church militant to capture denominational machinery so that the Truth might prevail. In 1919 the " World's Bible Conference " drew 6,000 delegates to Philadelphia. " Fundamentalism " was reactionary in its

---

[1] From 1700 till 1725 almost 100% of New England ministers (including the western frontier) were college graduates. See W. Adams Brown, *The Education of American Ministers* (4 vols., 1934).

effects as well as its creed. It was the kind of religion that inspired the revival of Klu Klux Klan—hatred for Catholics, negroes, modernists, socialists—indeed, for all kinds of new ideas ill-understood. It was the kind of religion that the more unscrupulous section of " Big Business " sought to promote, as a means of keeping the workers content by the offer of " pie in the sky ". In the backward parts of the South and West agitators had no difficulty in stirring up racial and sectarian feeling by exploiting religious emotionalism.

It was a Fundamentalist victory to secure as an apostle that whirlwind orator, W. J. Bryan, Presbyterian elder and Democratic candidate for the Presidency.[1] Bryan combined zeal for the common man with zeal for Biblical literalism. " The modernists have taken away my Lord, and I know not where they have laid Him." This old campaigner knew how to arouse popular passion, whether he was declaiming in a political speech against financial interests (" America crucified on a cross of gold ") or pleading for the " old time religion " of a literally-interpreted, cover-to-cover inspired Bible. Here was a modern Peter the Hermit crusading to recover the Holy Place from the infidel.[2]

The issue was focussed with dramatic intensity on the humble stage of Dayton, Tennessee (1922). A young science-master, John T. Scopes, had contravened the State law prohibiting the teaching of Evolution in the schools. He must be prosecuted for denying the Word of God. Dayton, typical small town of the South, was buzzing with excitement, as the Courthouse filled to overflowing with men in their shirt-sleeves. In spite of the heat, there was no apathy. Banners and posters were conspicuous. Young girls displayed the legend, "YOU CAN'T MAKE A MONKEY OUT OF ME!" Revivalists held meetings at night by the light of flares and denounced Evolution as one of the Devil's cutest snares. On the other hand, tough newspapermen and motion picture operators treated the whole matter from a merely professional point of view. They were mainly interested in Bryan's speech and its effect. Everyone was waiting for Bryan, who was to prosecute. Amidst great excitement, the statesman arrived and fulminated against

[1] Both Bryan and Woodrow Wilson were ardent Democrats and Presbyterians, but they lived in a different world of mind and soul.
[2] American Fundamentalism was organised internationally by Griffith-Thomas (an Anglican rector). It received external support from Professor Orr (Glasgow), Dr. Campbell Morgan (till 1928) and a famous detective from Scotland Yard, Sir Robert Anderson.

heretics who " believed in the ages of rocks rather than in the Rock of Ages ". Scopes was defended by Clarence Darrow, known throughout the United States as an advocate of " advanced " causes, a successful criminal lawyer, and an " atheist ". The issues were thus simplified to suit the mentality of " the Bible belt ".[1] Twelve unlettered hill-men constituted the jury to decide this momentous question. In spite of local prejudice against Darrow's views, his logic and sense of fairness steadily altered the atmosphere; and though Scopes was condemned, the fine was nominal.

W. J. Bryan died shortly afterwards from the effect of a shock. In what country save the United States could a famous statesman have behaved as Bryan did? He simply made sport for the Philistines. Fortunately the trial shocked educated Americans as a singular display of poor taste, provincialism and bigotry. Bibliolatrists made the most of the Scopes verdict. " Flying Fundamentalist " columns carried the issue as far north as Minnesota. Mississippi, Arkansas and Texas passed anti-Evolution laws. No wonder the Civil Liberties Union was concerned about impending restrictions on the freedom of thought. The stars in their courses, however, did not fight against the cause of science. Dr. Gaius Glenn Atkins has made this incisive comment on the aftermath of the Dayton trial: " On 22nd July a British wireless phone had called a United States warship 8,000 miles away—science was still sovereign, the epoch of embattled moral idealism was over. America was getting ready to revise its liturgy: the Scopes trial marked the end of the age of *Amen* and the beginning of the age of *Oh yeah!*"

By 1922 Dr. Harry Emerson Fosdick of New York had become the bugbear of the Bible belt. His published sermon, " Shall the Fundamentalists win ? " created a sensation. They were determined to compass his downfall. Legally, he had put himself in a weak position by acting as " stated supply " of the First Presbyterian Church, New York, although he was a liberal Baptist who objected to creed subscription. Requested by the General Assembly to enter the Presbyterian Ministry, or quit preaching indefinitely in her pulpits he chose the latter alternative. In 1930

[1] H. L. Mencken on " Troubles of the learned in the Bible Belt. . . C. S. Fothergill, instructor in History in Baylor University, Texas, resigned to-day because he did not believe that Noah's ark with the dimensions mentioned in the Bible was capable of accommodating a pair of all animals extant in the world in Noah's time, and because he had been criticised for expressing that belief " (*Americana*, 1925).

Fosdick's supporters built for him the splendidly-equipped River-side Church, near Columbia University. Thereafter his influence spread rapidly by lecture, book and radio. His *Modern Use of the Bible* (1924) made a profound impression; his spiritual and ethical view of Scripture made headway even in circles where he was once suspect.

At Princeton, Professor Gresham Machen and his friends, failing to capture the Theological Seminary for Fundamentalism, withdrew and founded the Westminster Seminary, Philadelphia; in 1930 they seceded from the Presbyterian Church and formed a small sect of their own. Princeton still remained conservative, for even the " positive " divine, Emil Brunner, called from Zurich, did not stay long in America. After 1930, however, the wave of aggressive Fundamentalism spent its power. Despite the " high pressure " campaign of A. C. Dixon and W. B. Riley it ceased to menace the freedom of thoughts, except in the more backward sections of the South and West.

One reason for the progress of Fundamentalism was the emergence of a liberalism that went far further than just vindicating the modern view of the Bible. Some " Modernists " were inclined to discard the supernatural element in Christianity and even the unique inspiration of the Bible (as distinguished from other great religious books);[1] by emphasising the " Man of Galilee " rather than the Risen Christ, they might be classified as " Jesusites " rather than " Christians ". Other " Modernists ", not content with Borden P. Bowne's definition of faith as " personal companionship with the personal God, who is the immanent upholder of the cosmic order ", found themselves in the company of Professor Wieman of the Chicago Divinity School, whose view of religion was distinctly abstract.[2] Wieman's meagre Theism saw in God little more than " the integrating purpose of the universe ". This approach appealed to men trained in scientific method, but led to no inner shrine where God could be seen in the face of Jesus. Devotion to truth, deference to science, accommodation to

[1] Dr. D. H. Betts produced a questionnaire-digest, covering 20 denominations around Chicago, *The Beliefs of 700 Ministers* (New York, 1929). One third of these ministers believed that the Bible had no unique inspiration. Unanimity was only reached on one point out of 56: God exists.

[2] Religious leaders who in their youth had " greeted Evolution with a cheer " were chilled in middle age by negative winds blowing from the " unsunned spaces of the mysterious universe ". Their lyric enthusiasm for science as an ally of the faith had been premature.

modern culture satisfied few save the " Ph.D.-ified " (to use the expression coined by my old professor, Sir Patrick Geddes).

Karl Barth had his American interpreters (Lehman, Pauck, Horton) but not many 100% disciples; what could the average American congregation have made of Barthianism, anyhow? It was widely felt, however, that a small quantity of the Theology of Crisis, well diluted with common sense, would serve as a valuable astringent tonic. Edward Lewis, the most prominent Methodist theologian, called for a more " positive " expression of Christianity in his *Christian Manifesto* (1936). Even Dr. Fosdick, arch-Modernist, declared that the Gospel did not exist to be " harmonised " with modern civilisation, but to challenge it. Reinhold Niebuhr, nurtured in a small denomination of German immigrants, came into the foreground as a prophet of judgment. Not since the days of the " New England theology " had sin been so unsparingly denounced; Niebuhr's conception of sin was social as well as individual, but he struck at the roots of the community instead of merely piercing the surface, like the optimistic exponents of the " Social Gospel ". He moved to the left politically, but to the right theologically. Soon he was an international figure —one of the few Americans to receive an Oxford D.D.

Two constructive developments deserve mention. Theology must be " realistic ", i.e. certain of God's power to meet the needs of our times,[1] ready to acknowledge the wilfulness of man, prepared to consider drastic methods in dealing with men and nations, inclined to treat as illusions too-rosy visions of a warless world and a Christianised social order. Dr. W. M. Horton has delineated *Realistic Theology* (London, 1935). It is an answer to the question, " After Liberalism—what ? " It is based upon a frank facing of eternal issues in relation to the contemporary situation in the United States. In the best sense of the word " Realistic Theology " is opportunist. While recognising that America has much to teach the world in organising religion, she has much to learn from Europe where " the imponderables " are concerned. There is an eager desire to share in the tested certainties of Christendom as these have flowed down the " River of God ". Readiness to

---

[1] Canon Streeter's *Reality* (1926) was widely read in the U.S.A. Interest in psychology, evangelical passion tempered with a certain pragmatic attitude, a touch of liberalism and an incisive literary style—made many Americans feel more akin to Streeter than other English theologians, whose writing was voted " dull ".

enter into the " Catholic heritage " of theology[1] and devotion are qualified by the requirement that " abiding experiences must be expressed in changing categories ", i.e. the straightforward language of the present day.

Two World Wars have deflated the over-confident belief of " Social Gospellers " that the Kingdom of God would steadily go on from strength to strength.[2] Pessimistic theology has blown across from Europe, proclaiming that the Victory of God is achieved " not in history but beyond history ", for the world is bound " to go to pot ". It is strange that ignorant frontier Baptists over a century ago commonly used such phrases as the Barthians: " If God wants a better world He will bring it about in His own time and way." Even in the confused and groping America of to-day this kind of quietism is unlikely to oust an activism that courses through the very blood of the people. Dr. W. W. Sweet, the doyen of American Church historians, rejects this " do-nothing theology " as nonsense.[3] " And," he concludes, " God pity us and the world if the time ever comes when we shall throw all the burden on the Lord and fold the hands and acquiesce."

[1] Consider specialist studies (e.g. Dr. Lowrie's on Kierkegaard) and more popular " Introductions " (e.g. Dr. W. M. Horton's *Contemporary Continental* and *Contemporary English Theology*).

[2] Thorough theological grounding would have acted as a corrective. The depreciation of theology in the U.S. went too far. Beecher seems to have been partly responsible. When a youth told him he was studying Divinity, he replied: " No harm in that—if you don't believe it."

[3] *The American Churches*, p. 74 (Epworth Press, 1947). Lectures given in England.

CHAPTER IV

THE AMERICAN PULPIT

" The types of American preaching of the past will not be wholly lost, but modified by each other . . . and will be harmonised into a single institution, the American Pulpit."

A. S. HOYT: *The Pulpit and American Life*

T HE close of the Civil War witnessed the supremacy of the sermon, the priority of the pulpit (1865). Oratory was one of the few outlets permitted by dominant Puritanism for the expression of the dramatising instinct. The great cities were illuminated by " stars ". If New York catered for the flesh and the devil, the neighbouring city of Brooklyn assumed responsibility for the cultivation of mind and soul. Theodore Cuyler, T. de Witt Talmage and Heny Ward Beecher were its leading luminaries.

Talmage's popularity was phenomenal from the War till his death in 1901. He could count on a congregation of 5,000 each Sunday, and hundreds were usually turned away. His supporters thrice rebuilt his vast " tabernacle ". An educated man, he attracted the uneducated by lush rhetoric, lurid illustrations and bizarre texts. He had no conception of the complexity of modern life and the new demands it made for reinterpretation. Yet he was not content to denounce sin in the abstract and visited New York's haunts of vice to collect evidence for his fulminations.[1] He did not reason; he declaimed. His florid style was the very antithesis of Spurgeon's Anglo-Saxon simplicity, but it undoubtedly appealed to the taste of " the Gilded Age ", and even found favour in the Church of England. A famous London canon actually preached (and published as his own) Talmage's sermon on the wickedness of cities, merely substituting lists of English places

---

[1] A characteristic sermon was on the Drink Menace, " A Bloody Monster " (Gen. 37.33). This and other discourses of American " major prophets " will be found in *The World's Great Sermons,* ed. G. Kleiser (London, 1909).

for American ones![1] This was certainly high tribute to an American preacher, whom some of his own countrymen disparaged as a mountebank. When Talmage preached in London (1879) excited crowds gathered; there had been nothing like it since the days of Edward Irving.[2] Talmage was unconcerned with modern thought, as a preacher. He preached " the old Gospel "; he preached for conversion; and he preached to help folk who fought a hard battle.[3] His printed sermons had an immense circulation; they appeared regularly in 600 newspapers and are said to have reached 25,000,000 readers at home and abroad. A journalist himself, he edited the *Christian Herald*, which still survives as a popular conservative monthly. His pulpit topics resembled screaming headlines, and he certainly stimulated the appetite of the public for sensational preaching. During the 'eighties, *Puck* (the American *Punch*) satirised the unseemly competition of " rampageous preachers " whose rival posters invited the public to hear them on this murder and that divorce (a trait by no means extinct in American religious advertising).

The full glare of publicity flood-lit a featureless preaching-place known as Plymouth Church, Brooklyn, founded by a small group of New Englanders who named it after the historic port of the Pilgrims (1847). Within a comparatively short time Henry Ward Beecher had made it an " American institution ". It was a Mecca of sightseers and sermon-tasters. Maybe Dr. Joseph Parker built the City Temple in 1874 in order that it might be the English equivalent of Plymouth Church; he was spoken of as a probable successor to Henry Ward Beecher,[4] and certainly drew visiting Americans; indeed Dr. Cuyler of Brooklyn used to say that the back galleries of the City Temple were in the Rocky Mountains!

To find Plymouth Church, you had only to follow the crowds that streamed off the Fulton Street Ferry from New York twice every Sunday. It was essentially an " auditorium ", built with the

[1] See A. G. Gardiner's essays, *Leaves in the Wind*.
[2] John Lobb, of the *Christian World*, edited a popular life of Talmage for British readers; 3,000 copies were sold within three hours of publication.
[3] He declared: " The human heart is essentially the same in all ages, and the same keys that drew music from it in the days of our fathers will strike responsive chords still."
[4] A magnetic young Englishman, Dr. Berry, actually declined an unanimous " call ". His preaching at Washington (1897) did much to improve Anglo-American relations, then strained by the Venezuela dispute. English Nonconformists understood Americans as the C. of E. never has. See J. S. Drummond, *Charles A. Berry* (London, 1899).

one aim of accommodating a maximum number of hearers; the acoustics were perfect. Within these utilitarian limits the edifice was admirable, as Thackeray experienced when he lectured there on " The Four Georges ".

Henry Ward Beecher will rank high in the apostolic succession of orators for God. His own countrymen called him the " Shakespeare of the American Pulpit " because he was such a marvellous blend of contradictions and opposites. Profound melancholy and boyish humour, keen sympathy for human frailty and a glowing belief in man's spiritual destiny fused to produce an affluent, genial and creative personality. Here was a new phenomenon in American Protestantism—a man of God who was emancipated from the old, repressive dogmas which reduced Christianity to a soul-numbing chain of demonstrated doctrines . . . emancipated, but ardent in evangelical enthusiasm for the Lordship of Christ and the conversion of souls. In any country Beecher would have been a prince of the pulpit. He was in touch with the most advanced thought of his era, as few preachers were, yet he never lost touch with the ordinary men busy at their task. He studied life more than books; he got his sermons from shops and streets, ferries and factories; like Walt Whitman, he knew his New York. One of his favourite illustrations was a visit to an organ workshop, where he was deafened by the din of various processes, but followed with zest their development, till they finally combined in producing sublime strains, with a master-organist playing the finished instrument; here was a parable of life—harmony eventually emerging out of discord. Such glowing word-pictures were unforgettable. His exuberant mind teemed with subjects and illustrations all week. He seldom sketched his sermon outlines till Sunday—after breakfast, and again after tea. He did not, however, recommend this method to budding sermonisers! Few great preachers have had his ability to transmit pulpit-power. His *Lectures on Preaching* (London, 1872) are still amazingly vital, sparkling with wisdom and wit.

" This country is inhabited by saints, sinners and Beechers," said Dr. Leonard Bacon, an intimate friend of the family. We have already met Lyman Beecher, " father of more brains than any man in America ".[1] A New Englander, he responded to the

[1] His children included Catherine (educational pioneer), Edward (scholar), Isabella (suffragette) and, of course, Harriet of *Uncle Tom's Cabin*. See Lyman Beecher Stowe, *Saints, Sinners and Beechers* (London, 1935).

Call of the West, as did many of his sons and daughters. Henry
Ward Beecher derived his immense vitality from environment as
well as heredity. In his frontier pastorate (Indiana) he had to act
as sexton; he would have rung the bell (had there been one); he
" did everything but hear himself preach!" He pushed scholastic
theology aside and preached plainly in language that the people
understood.[1] He was called to Indianapolis and in 1847 to the new
congregation of Plymouth Church, Brooklyn. He could never
have captured New York but for robust, western humour and
the gift of telling a story that always appeals in the East,[2] when the
author is a genius. Would Mark Twain ever have achieved celebrity but for youthful experiences in the West ?

Till the close of the Civil War, Henry Ward Beecher was a
spearhead of the Anti-Slavery movement (see p. 292). He was
ill-fitted, however, for the corrupt, demoralising " Gilded Age "
that followed. He stormed at social evils, as he had stormed against
black bondage. In consequence there lined up against him an
unholy alliance of the ultra-orthodox, the politically conservative,
an " advanced " clique, and those financially interested in drink
and vice. His unsophisticated confidence in human nature made
him the victim of unprincipled adventurers like Virginia Woodhull, Tennessee Claflin[3] and Theodore Tilton. Tilton accused
him of having improper relations with his wife—a preposterous
charge from which he was cleared by the most representative
Congregational Council ever called in the United States (1876).
Time has justified that vote of confidence, but has also taken note
that the great preacher's indiscretion delivered him into the hands
of the Philistines. " Never did anyone know man so well and men
so ill." When his lawyer apologised for calling on him one Sunday
on business, he referred him to the Biblical precedent of drawing

[1] On a missionary journey, his horse threw him into a river. " Well, Brother
Beecher," said a Baptist preacher, " I've heard of your immersion—I thought
you would adopt our custom in the end." " Haven't adopted it," rapped out
H.W.B.; " I was immersed by a horse—not an ass. "

[2] New York lacked metropolitan sophistication, In the 'fifties its leaders
were—" a wandering showman, a backwoods preacher, and a rural printer,
transformed in scale, unchanged in nature " (Barnum, Beecher and Greeley).
Beecher won the masses, not the elite. Walt Whitman, at Grace Church, had
to wait for an hour till the rich were seated (Van Wyck Brooks, *Whitman and
Melville*, 1947).

[3] *Woodhull & Claflin's Weekly* was sensational. The glamorous editors were
the first " lady-brokers " on Wall Street, pioneers of woman suffrage, advocates
of spiritualism and " free love ".

up an ass out of a pit on the Sabbath: " there was never a bigger ass nor a deeper pit. . ."

In spite of the cloud that darkened his later years, Henry Ward Beecher had still huge congregations and a host of loyal friends. He was still active when struck down by apoplexy in 1887, after forty mighty years in Brooklyn. He had " the greatness of the childlike spirit." After his last sermon, he lingered in church listening to the organ. Noticing two homeless newsboys who had been in the habit of stealing into the church for shelter, he walked down the aisle for the last time, arm-in-arm with them. At a memorial service in 1928 the scene was described by a minister who had been one of these boys forty-one years before.

Beecher's successor, Lyman Abbott, wrote his biography (1903) but was a complete contrast in personality. A venerable-looking, bearded New Englander, Abbott was a religious journalist of progressive outlook, whose preaching experience was limited to " supply " duty in a small Presbyterian church at Cornwall-on-the-Hudson. He admitted that for seventeen years he had not written a single sermon. He knew that he could not preach as eloquently as his magnetic predecessor, but he could preach for 25-35 minutes instead of an hour or more. This metropolitan precedent was welcomed in the country generally. A contemporary cartoon pictures a rural preacher droning on, while his hearers are glancing anxiously at the gallery clock behind them— " The Long Sermon and the Waiting Christmas Dinner ". Even in academic circles it was not long till the college president's advice to the visiting preacher ceased to cause surprise: " Preach as long as you like, but remember no souls are saved after the first twenty minutes."

Lyman Abbott was instrumental in popularising a conversational style, instead of the " pulpit eloquence " so highly prized by the previous generation. Sermons were no longer to be projected like fireworks or exhibited as show-pieces; they were to be shared in a spirit of humility, the breaking of the Bread of Life. Dr. Abbott's aim was to go slow and take his hearers with him, applying " the psychology of persuasion ". He followed Beecher's example of avoiding the technical terms of theology, on the grounds that controversy had thriven in the past by magnifying definitions and watchwords, which were approximations (at best) to divine truth. Abbott had given up a lucrative legal career in the family firm to enter the Ministry, and he used his lawyer's experience to good purpose. Gritty realism was the groundwork of his idealistic superstructure. As a public speaker, he was adroit and resourceful, adapting himself to novel situations. He excelled even Beecher in applying the lecture-method to the evening service, differentiating its treatment and atmosphere from morning worship; he was at his best in the pulpit explaining the " Higher Criticism ", the inspiration of good literature, or the spiritual relevance of new scientific theories. Lyman Abbott was a lucid, persuasive interpreter of life. His successor, Newell Dwight Hillis, also maintained the high-toned literary note, but by the time of the First World War the great days of the Plymouth pulpit were over. Dr. Hillis, gentle scholar though he was, thundered against Germany[1] as Beecher proclaimed his *delenda* against the slave power.

Lyman Abbott resembled Henry Ward Beecher as a promoter of religious journalism, but his associations with the press were unclouded by unhappy memories. Abbott was fortunate enough to come into his kingdom as a great editor at a propitious time. The way had been prepared by considerable journalistic activity connected with church news. As early as 1837 no less than 37 religious weeklies flourished in the United States, the *Christian Advocate* leading with a circulation of 15,000. Even on the frontier papers of a " family " type exercised a wide influence; they not only carried the " weekly Sunday School lesson ", but hints for housewives, agricultural news, articles on education and temperance. The success of these periodicals led to the experiment of the " Christian daily ". This proved, however, too ambitious; the New York *World* (1860), issued at two cents, only lasted thirteen months; the New York *Sun* was " Christian " only in the negative sense, in excluding theatre advertisements.[2] Beecher's *Independent* (1848) was a pioneer in religious journalism; it was undenominational, enterprising, and militant in fighting slavery. Beecher, disagreeing after the Civil War with his radical and cranky protégé, Theodore Tilton, over " reconstruction " in the South, founded the *Christian Union* (1866), which was progressive

[1] A reaction occurred in 1919 against " pulpit patriotism "; but " Pearl Harbor " shattered Pacifism, except among sects where it was traditional, e.g. the Quakers. Among the clergy, the Methodists were foremost in anti-war propaganda, being influenced by the " Social Gospel ".

[2] Of religious dailies, the brilliant (and objective) *Christian Science Monitor* (1908) still flourishes.

in policy. It carried his sermons—and much else. Every member of a typical American family could find their human interest met. Beecher awoke latent intellectual interest, expounded new theories in relation to the unfolding spirit of Christianity, and claimed for the Kingdom of God everything that stood for truth, beauty and righteousness.

Lyman Abbott succeeded Henry Ward Beecher as editor-in-chief as well as Plymouth preacher. He re-named *The Christian Union*; *The Outlook* (1893) became an American institution, " likely to be found ", says Dr. G. G. Atkins in reminiscent mood, " on the ' center table ' of the parlor, flanked by the *Ladies' Home Journal*, R. L. Stevenson's *Essays* and a novel by Edith Wharton." It was much read and quoted, exercising a national influence comparable to the *British Weekly*. Religious journalism was never more brilliantly served than by two contemporary editors, Robertson Nicoll in London and Lyman Abbott in New York. The " twilight afterglow of Victorian idealism " was eventually destined to end. Dr. Abbott's successor did not inherit his genius, and after the first World War *The Outlook* became significantly secular.

As *The Outlook* diminished, the *Christian Century* increased. This paper grew out of an obscure mid-western Disciples' background. The title was prophetically chosen in 1900, and the destinies of the paper guided for many years at Chicago by one of the most creative of religious editors, Dr. Charles Clayton Morrison. Denominational lines were ignored and vested interests castigated. Liberal theology went hand in hand with the " social gospel ". Idealism was given an incisive, practical Mid-West edge. Never has a religious editor sustained such a pungent and provocative policy for so many years, moulding the minds of ministers and educationalists on such themes as " The Crime of War " and " Our Pagan Idea of Property ". The *Christian Century* is now the nearest equivalent to the *British Weekly*, with a nation-wide circulation.

Religious journalism in the United States has fallen on evil days, partly through the competition of bright secular magazines, the pressure of radio, and the cost of production. Old-established weeklies have survived only by becoming monthlies, e.g. *The Advance* (Congregational). Among denominational papers, *The Living Church* continues, as the " opposite number " of the

English *Church Times*, while liberal Episcopalianism is ably repre-sented by *The Churchman*.[1] The only denominational paper with a really big circulation is the Methodist *Christian Advocate*, which is managed on decentralised lines according to the sectional re-quirements of widely separated areas.

Religious journalism at its best carried to the family circle a love of good literature. The evening sermon was often attuned to a literary note. Newell Dwight Hillis set the fashion in this respect and his *Great Books as Life-Teachers* (1900) had a wide circulation in Britain as well as the States. These were golden days for the pulpit when the pew responded to an enlightened " inspirational " stimulus,[2] emancipated from the grimmer dog-mas, and not yet caught up in the current of secular thought or obliged to show that religion had an immediate answer to all kinds of pressing problems. In these spacious days preachers loved to quote Browning and Tennyson. Indeed Dr. Gaius Glenn Atkins has said that *In Memoriam* dated two epochs: one when preachers began to quote it, the other when they stopped.

The tide turned about 1928 when Dr. Lynn Harold Hough, a distinguished preacher and an alert scholar, arrested the imagina-tion of thoughtful ministers by his attractive books and published lectures advocating the renewed study of literature in its relations with life and religion.[3] He drew attention to the spiritual rele-vance of Literary Criticism, and his zest for the subject secured a host of new readers for Irving Babbitt's *Rousseau and Roman-ticism*, and the *Shelburne Essays* of Paul Elmer More, " the American Ste.-Beuve ". Through P. E. More and T. S. Eliot, a stream of Platonism refreshed the American pulpit. " Professors of Biography " arose, like Dr. Ambrose Vernon. At Chicago Pro-fessor Fred Eastman discussed, wrote and produced plays with a Christian significance. Religion made a fructifying friendship with literature.[4]

Returning to the pulpit, it is a moot point whether the influence

[1] The Episcopal *Southern Churchmen* (Richmond, Virginia) changed hands in 1927 and became aggressively Evangelical, fulminating against Modernist and Catholic alike.

[2] Preachers discovered De Quincey's distinction between " the literature of knowledge " (to instruct) and " the literature of power " (to move).

[3] His books range from *Synthetic Christianity* and *Productive Beliefs* to *The Artist and the Critic* and *Adventures in the Minds of Men*.

[4] Dr. Richard Roberts, *The Preacher as Man of Letters* (Dent, 1931); Dr. S. Parkes Cadman, *Imagination and Religion* (Macmillan, 1926).

of Henry Ward Beecher or Phillips Brooks was greatest. Brooks was born in 1835, the same year as Abbott. He was directly descended from John Cotton, the Founding Father of New England. His mother was an " introvert "—her one passion the soul: his father was an " extrovert "—a man of affairs in sympathy with human idealism. His mother was a Congregationalist, an earnest Calvinist: his father was a Unitarian. The parents compromised by joining the Episcopal Church, which in Boston tended to be Evangelical. It has been said that Phillips Brooks recognised the facts of life with his father's eyes, but he saw the possibilities of life through the eyes of his mother. After graduating at Harvard he tried schoolmastering and proved a failure. He then turned to the Ministry. After a depressing experience of the (Low Church) Theological Seminary at Alexandria, Virginia, he was appointed rector at the Church of the Advent, Philadelphia. Here he took a firm stand for the Union against the timid and compromising conservatism of parishioners who were secretly in sympathy with the slave power. It was in 1869 that he began to exercise his unique ministry at Trinity Church, Boston. Never till the time of " Dick " Sheppard did a parson kindle such warm affection in the ordinary folk. " It was a dull, rainy day . . . but Phillips Brooks came down Newspaper Row and all was bright." He radiated the sheer joy of Christian experience.

What was the secret of his popularity ? Lord Bryce, comparing his preaching with that of Liddon and Spurgeon, was impressed by the absence of studied effect. " What amount of preparation he may have given to his discourses I do not know. But there was no sign of art about them, no touch of self-consciousness. He spoke to his audience as a man might speak to his friend, pouring forth with swift yet quiet and seldom impassioned earnestness the thoughts and feelings of a singularly pure and lofty spirit. The listeners never thought of style and manner, but only of the substance of his thoughts."[1] When Brooks crossed the Atlantic, Westminster and St. Paul's were crowded. English congregations found his delivery too rapid (he was the despair of reporters), yet his printed sermons had a wide circulation and he was acclaimed as " the American F. W. Robertson ". He used illustrations

---

[1] Prof. Ambrose W. Vernon rates highly Brooks' permanent influence on " later theology ", although he did not discuss current issues in the pulpit, like Dr. Abbott (*Cambridge History of American Literature*, Vol. III, 1931).

sparingly, but his style was pictorial, musical and mystical. One of his characteristic texts was " The sea of glass mingled with fire " (The Permanent Value of Trial). In his own country he attracted Unitarians by his breadth and Evangelicals by his passionate love of Christ. The fact that so great a preacher was an Episcopalian caused surprise in certain circles. Well aware of the dangers of formal ecclesiasticism, he preached " Christianity only for Christ, the doctrine only for the Person!" Here was a generous manly soul, using a wide range of gifts. His definition of preaching, struck out in his famous Yale Lectures, was " truth through personality ". Phillips Brooks by the radiance of his Christ-inspired character made Christianity attractive in the best sense to the younger generation.

Even in Brooks' lifetime the old homiletic tradition of viewing everything through four or five dominant doctrines, died hard. " The themes were great," said Dr. Munger, biographer of Bushnell, " but the assumptions and the method predetermined what was to be said. . . There was no such thing as a *direct look.*" Since the beginning of the twentieth century, American as well as British preachers have taken increasingly that direct look at religion and life. The conversational tone has definitely displaced high-pitched oratory. A terse, clear vocabulary has generally ousted a theological " dialect of Canaan ", though equally unintelligible psychological jargon has sometimes been introduced (even in prayers!). Just before World War I, Dr. Harry Emerson Fosdick began to appeal to the younger generation by starting his sermons with a concrete " life-situation ", instead of with a text, which was aptly introduced once he had captured the interest of his hearers. Many a British and American student was helped by his *Meaning of Prayer* series. Fosdick was a master of the psychology of persuasion both of the written and the spoken word; he delighted young and old by graphic " picture-thinking " in vivid metaphor and illustration—a modern application of teaching by parable. When wireless services commenced, Fosdick shared with Parkes Cadman (an Englishman by birth) the reputation of being " a prince of the air ". Religious people found a new meaning in the old text, " The Word of God is not bound " (2 Tim. 2.9), but it took the clergy some time to work out a broadcasting technique, recognising that the radio preacher is stripped of gesture, " presence ", etc., and reduced to a Voice (*vox et praeterea nihil*). Gradually, however, the " commentary " (new style) affected the make-up and tone of the ordinary Sunday sermon.

A few years ago in a certain college chapel a preacher was charming his older hearers with a richly-textured Scriptural sermon of the Scottish type, when an undergraduate left his pew, retired to the outside steps and proceeded to read the Sunday paper! Questioned as to his motives, he said that he would not listen to a preacher who did not know the language of the younger generation (he was doubtless unaware of the rapidity with which college fashions and slang become " dated "). Few preachers in any country find it easy to address students. A generation ago in the United States the Presidents of Universities were usually distinguished clergymen. They " led compulsory chapel " in the cold grey dawn of winter mornings, they preached on Sunday, lectured on ethics and philosophy, they wrote books, e.g. Hyde's *Five Great Philosophies of Life.* In recent years Presidents have been selected mainly for administrative ability, without reference to religion; " compulsory chapel " has been generally abandoned, following the example of Harvard (1886); and the student body lacks the homogeneity once produced by the standardised discipline of Evangelical homes. Even in America's two hundred " denominational colleges " the orthodox urge is weakening (save in the case of the Lutherans); inadequate endowments make these institutions a burden, and enrolments have fallen off generally. On the other hand, the new State Universities (co-educational), mainly in the Middle West, with their enormous student membership (often ranging from 15,000 to 20,000) are strictly secular; there is no chapel on the campus, and the neighbouring churches have to provide chaplains and premises for the youth of their own denomination. In the older Universities and Colleges of the East (where men and women are educated separately) the chapel, often denominational in origin,[1] is usually neutral ground, under the care of a chaplain and an advisory committee. Visiting preachers of all denominations, including liberal rabbis,[2] occupy the pulpit during term, and the students have the opportunity of hearing a cross-section of America's preaching power. At its best the chapel

[1] Yale was Congregational, Harvard became Unitarian, Princeton was Presbyterian; the Prayer Book is still used in St. Paul's Chapel, Columbia University.
[2] e.g. R. Joshua Liebman, Boston. Besides lecturing on Judaism to Christian Divinity students at Newton-Andover, he is heard as radio preacher by a million New Englanders weekly.

is an " Interpreter's House " where the values of life are examined *sub specie eternitatis*, and preaching is presented in a setting of simple but dignified ritual that reflects the sharing of the best ideals in common worship.

Among leaders of youth who have endeavoured to restore the Bible to its proper place in the affection of modern Christians, Dr. Henry Sloane Coffin, of Union Seminary, New York, is pre-eminent. Might not Christian doctrine, he asked, be presented in an attractive light by a more imaginative use of Biblical material ? President Coffin convinced a considerable number of his fellow-ministers that American preaching had been impoverished by the lure of superficial " topics ", too often suggested by newspaper headlines. His Yale Lectures, *What to Preach* (1926), provided a mine of matter for students embarking on the venture of winning men for God. Dr. Coffin owed much of his enthusiasm for " expository preaching " to his own experience as a post-graduate student in Edinburgh. Scottish influence was also reflected by Dr. H. T. Kerr of Philadelphia, who introduced a " children's address " into the morning service (*Children's Story-Sermons*, 1911). American preachers set a good example in letting the children out of church before proceeding with the adult sermon. In recent years, however, there has been a tendency to hold special services for the children, if possible in a Youth Chapel. Educationalists as well as liturgiologists have been aware of the danger of crowding too much into morning worship and over-emphasising the hortatory element by providing what often amounts to two sermons.

" Great is the company of the preachers " (Ps. 68.11, Prayer Book Version). In the Revised Version of 1881, this reads: " The women that publish the tidings are a mighty host." The United States have produced no lady preacher of the brilliance of Maud Royden, but a much larger proportion of girl students take up theology than in Britain. Women are, of course, barred from the Episcopal priesthood, and the Presbyterian General Assembly refused them ordination in 1947, " as likely to mean scandal in the church " (cp. p. 320 n.). They are allowed ordination by the Congregationalists and other denominations, but are seldom in full charge, save in the smaller rural congregations. Usually they serve on the staff of city churches as ministers' assistants, but a considerable number preach. Indeed, Dr. Fosdick has admitted (judging from his experience of them in a Homiletics class) that they are sounder sermonisers, on the whole, than men!

The *Christian Century* has formulated a resounding phrase, " Peers of the American Pulpit ". A good many editions of a homiletic Debrett would be required to take account of changes in this preachers' peerage, but the names of the following would be emblazoned without serious challenge. Dr. Charles E. Jefferson filled Broadway Tabernacle, New York, by solid and searching Biblical preaching, set in a framework of reverent worship; this he continued to do throughout a long ministry; miracles will never cease. Dr. Russell Bowie, an Episcopalian from Virginia, persuasively proclaimed a " liberal Evangelical " message in historic Grace Church, near the southern tip of Manhattan. Dr. Leighton Parks, of the same communion, interpreted " the sacramental quality of common life " in St. Bartholomew's, now one of the most beautiful churches in the Empire City.

In Baltimore Dr. Harris E. Kirk, a Presbyterian, has maintained a high reputation for many years as an expository preacher on conservative lines. Dr. Kirk's name has been long familiar as a summer preacher in British pulpits. Dr. G. Campbell Morgan, prince of expositors, throughout a long ministry, felt equally at home in pastorates on both sides of the Atlantic. We must not forget Dr. J. Fort Newton, of New York, a Universalist, whose ministry during World War I at the City Temple,[1] made such a deep impression on London. While no outstanding American preacher seems to have assumed a permanent pastorate in the United Kingdom, a number of British subjects have risen to eminence in American pulpits. Dr. S. Parkes Cadman of Brooklyn and Dr. G. A. Buttrick of New York crossed the Atlantic as poor youths, and rose to fame. Some of the leading Presbyterian churches in the United States have " called " eminent British preachers. Thus, Fifth Avenue, New York, looked to England on one occasion and selected Dr. J. H. Jowett of Birmingham, a Congregationalist; on the other, the choice rested on Dr. Kelman, of Free St. George's, Edinburgh. In both cases, the pace of American city life was too exhausting. Adaptation in such an environment has been proved successful only in the case of men transplanted from the old country in their youth. Such was Dr.

[1] It is a curious coincidence that Fort Newton, like R. J. Campbell, went Anglican.

George A. Gordon, an Aberdeenshire lad who studied in America at the cost of much hardship and eventually rose to the height of the historic Old South Church, Boston. Cautiously liberal in outlook and well trained in philosophy, Dr. Gordon would have distinguished himself in any country and in any walk of life. The title of his book of collected sermons, *Through Man to God*, set the keynote of enlightened Evangelicalism for many a preacher seeking inspiration and suggestion.

During the prosperous decades of the twentieth century the American pulpit tended to be swayed by a fair-weather theology, and guided overmuch by the insights of pragmatism and humanism. World catastrophe discomfited the opportunist prophets who had prophesied smooth things. Reinhold Niebuhr recalled his countrymen to a deep-founded faith in the eternal Christ, whose Kingdom is " not of this world ". His volume of sermons, *Beyond Tragedy*, was reprinted thrice in Britain between 1938 and 1944.

American preaching has doubtless benefited by the iron tonic of neo-orthodoxy, but is not likely to lose touch with human interests and human needs. It would require many volumes to assess its practical effects on business and public life.[1] Let one instance suffice. In 1888 Dr. Henry Van Dyke of the Brick Presbyterian Church, New York, preached on " The National Sin of Literary Piracy ". How many British authors had suffered loss through their works being reprinted in the United States by unscrupulous " pirates "! Is it likely that Dickens would ever have written *Martin Chuzzlewit* and *American Notes* in a bitter, controversial spirit, unless he smarted under a sense of injustice that no lavish hospitality could offset? Dr. Van Dyke had his sermon printed and distributed throughout the Union, and reprinted at Washington, D.C. Three years later a Bill was passed by Congress that offered protection to foreign authors. Here is a modern parallel to Lyman Beecher's sermon against duelling and historic discourses later in the nineteenth century that contributed to the rousing of public opinion against slavery.

As late as 1900 the American pulpit occupied a strategic position in national life. The Sabbath was still well observed, save in certain cities where Catholic immigration had succeeded in knock-

[1] See the succession of Lyman Beecher Lectures on Preaching delivered at Yale by eminent preachers, including Britishers, e.g. Silvester Horne, Hensley Henson and J. R. P. Sclater.

ing down traditional battlements. There were no engrossing alternatives to church-going. On Sunday evenings few lights attracted the passer-by on Main Street, and these were subdued lights of stained glass. The Puritan ideal of a " godly, righteous and sober life " was still generally accepted by public opinion for one day in the week. The Monday newspapers in town and country devoted a column to " Yesterday's Sermons "; otherwise there was little press publicity. American churches often rejoiced in anonymity, as Dr. Gaius Glenn Atkins has remarked in kindly irony.

" A Latin cross meant a Catholic church, a Greek cross and ivy an Episcopal church, spacious and solid hewn stone was likely Presbyterian, Corinthian columns Congregational. Their communicants knew when and what they were, the rest of the world could find out by asking. In time a modest sign—likely to be lost in ivy—announced the name of the church, its hours of service and the minister's name. . . The sexton's name and address were also sometimes added for the convenience of the living who wanted to enter the church during secular hours and of the dead if the sexton offered the services of an undertaker " (ibid. p. 258).

This halcyon era of modesty could not survive the speeding-up of American life that became pronounced after the First World War. The Sunday papers and trains, which the godly used to deplore, were but harbingers of the automobile, the cinema and the radio. The big city congregations found themselves compelled to advertise widely. Sermon " topics " resembled newspaper headlines, and the contemporary interest was apt to oust the eternal, though Dr. I. M. Haldeman, a Baptist pulpiteer of New York, offered to answer the question: " Is there a city as real as New York in Heaven?" In Ashville, a North Carolina spa, a prominent preacher discussed the absorbing problem:

How do Sons-in-Law get along with Mothers-in-Law in Heaven ?

Pastor Owen is original. He gives you thoughts no other preacher ever suggested—you never read them in a book, either.[1]

In Detroit a magnetic Methodist, Dr. William L. Stidger, offered counter-attractions to his nearest competitor, " one of the most blatant, blazing amusement parks " of the Middle West. He announced that " for 26 consecutive nights people have been turned away from St. Mark's for want of room ". Stidger had an

[1] Sinclair Lewis found church publicity a perfect mine of unconscious humour, with which he spiced his *American Mercury*, e.g., " Change your wife through Prayer! "

engaging, dynamic personality. His severest critics admitted that he had a remarkable flair for understanding the mind of the restless crowds that parade the city streets. He provided drama sermons, " echo singing ", hymn whistling, symphonic preaching and much else. His was " The BIG Church with the BIG Heart and the BIG Crowds. . . The revolving cross outside indicates that there are IDEAS inside." The fire marshall of Detroit warned St. Mark's that Stidger-bound cars were obstructing traffic. In his next advertisement the pastor proclaimed to the public his gratification that his activities had attracted the attention of the fire and police departments. This " enfant terrible " (hardly popular, surely, among his fellow clergy ?) ended up in an unlikely spot, the institution known in America as " B.U." (Boston University). Extravagant advertising had overreached the limits of good taste and common sense. One of the most successful Detroit preachers, Merton S. Rice of the Metropolitan Church, did much less advertising than his contemporaries. Nevertheless, publicity is much more necessary in American cities than in Britain. The notice board with movable type sets forth in illuminated letters the preacher's theme, that he who runs may read; the tower may be crowned with a flashing electric cross, or the whole church may be flood-lit after dark. " Let your light so shine before men!"

It is difficult to generalise about the power of the American pulpit in recent years, in its fight to adjust itself to new ideas and new ways of living.[1] The evening service, except in the more Evangelical sections of the South and Middle West, may be safely numbered among " the lost causes and impossible loyalties ", though there are always a few outstanding metropolitan magnets who will doubtless continue to attract crowds. Americans will probably always respond to a preacher who can get his message across and offer a convincing solution to the problems of human pain, unrest and sorrow—the theme of " life adjustment ". Attendance is much more uneven than fifty years ago, but in certain places it is so large that services have to be duplicated, e.g. in Florida and California. On the other hand, in sections where the Roman Catholic immigrant is triumphant, e.g. New England, the Protestant community has to a large extent lost heart and interest in public worship. Taking the United States as a whole, it can be

[1] The need for mobility was recognised by a *fin-de-siècle* cartoon. A flock of cyclists are followed by a horse-drawn " float " accommodating portable pulpit, surpliced parson and organist.

2B

safely said that preaching attracts a larger proportion of the population than in Britain, nor has the slump in church-going gone so far. The faithful can sing with confidence:

> O God, above the drifting years
>   The shrines our fathers founded, stand;
> And where the higher gain appears,
>   We trace the working of Thy hand.

CHAPTER V

THE RENASCENCE OF WORSHIP

" A generation ago the outstanding question was: ' What have you been preaching recently ?' Later another question forged to the front : ' What are you doing with your young people now ?' In these days a third is heard with increasing frequency: ' What changes are you making . . . in worship ?' "—PROFESSOR BYINGTON

WHEN Thomas K. Beecher preached on one occasion at Plymouth Church there was an unseemly rush for the doors, on the part of sightseers, as he entered the pulpit instead of the popular idol. Raising his hand he announced: " All those who came here to worship Henry Ward Beecher may now withdraw—all who came to worship God may remain!" This nineteenth-century Thomas was not content, like Andrew, to be " Simon Peter's brother ". Indeed he once remarked: " Being a son of Lyman Beecher and a brother of Henry Ward Beecher has been the greatest misfortune of my life."

The era of Henry Ward Beecher was the age of the orator. The dignified pulpit gave way to the rostrum—an open platform where he could walk up and down, plead, gesticulate and fulminate.[1] Beecher was impatient with decorous convention. " The man that merely comes to administer ordinances on Sundays or Saints Days, who goes through a regular routine, is nothing but an engineer who runs a machine."[2] The great Brooklyn preacher went to the opposite extreme. He would enter inconspicuously with the congregation, and take off his hat, coat (and " rubbers ") on the rostrum. The decorum of colonial days had entirely gone. The house of worship became an " auditorium ", where a " spell-binder " held sway. Eloquence, wit and pathos evoked applause,

[1] " Time makes ancient good uncouth." The problem of making Plymouth Church worshipful enough for modern standards and yet preserving it as a shrine of Beecher has been adroitly solved by building around his spindly " sacred desk " an enclosed pulpit of the historic type.

[2] Despite his unconventional ways, Beecher was attracted by the Prayer Book. He even urged: " Should our own children find their religious wants better met in the services of the Protestant Episcopal Church, we should take them by the hand and lead them to its altars " (Lyman Abbott, *Henry Ward Beecher*, p. 123, London, 1903).

laughter and tears in church. Preacher and people made themselves very much " at ease in Zion ". Lyman Abbott's style was much quieter than Beecher's; he could see the value of liturgy as well as extempore prayer; but like his mighty predecessor, he had an instinctive distaste for anything " clerical ". When asked to preach at Harvard, he looked askance at the Geneva gown in the vestry. " Have I to wear that ? Because if I've got to, I won't." This was the minister's robe which his ancestors had worn and hallowed.

Provincial preachers imitated the metropolitan stars by removing " mahogany tub " and " swallow's nest " pulpits. They copied the mannerisms of the " top-notchers ", but missed their magnetism. They lowered the level of the pulpit and thought that they had increased its power; they stooped—but did not always conquer. They waxed oratorical even in the " long prayer " which prefaced preaching. In the sermon-centred service everything before the discourse constituted (as in Scotland) " the preliminary exercises ". The leading preachers of the United States, instead of setting an example to their humbler brethren, pursued an egocentric policy that held up progress and helped to perpetuate the popular tradition that still refers to the American minister as " the preacher ".

The twentieth century had run into its second decade before there emerged any widespread movement in favour of viewing the sermon as a devotional act in a liturgical setting, rather than as the dominating feature. The " recovery of worship " (to quote the title of a significant volume by G. W. Fiske, 1931) has been a slow process. It may be traced back to the middle of the nineteenth century. Dr. Nevin, in the obscure German Reformed Church, endeavoured to restore the Lord's Supper as the central rite of Christendom, replacing lax Zwinglian views by Calvinist convictions. His *Mystical Presence* (1846) heralded the " Mercersburg Movement " which was inspired to a considerable extent by the Oxford Movement (see above, p. 222 n.). In 1855 St. Peter's Presbyterian Church, Rochester, N.Y., issued its *Church Book* containing prayers and " responsive readings " from the Psalter. The same year, the Rev. C. W. Baird published *Eutaxia*, a skilful sketch of Reformed worship, which had a considerable circulation in England. It was a surprise to most Presbyterians to hear that they were committed to a Liturgy by their earliest traditions!

Professor C. W. Shields of Princeton followed by re-issuing the almost forgotten alternative Prayer Book, submitted by the English Presbyterians at the Restoration (1662). He intended this volume to serve both as a memorial and a source-book. In an essay appended, Dr. Shields deplored the abuse of extempore prayer in the United States. He rightly criticised " a depraved taste for the impressive, rather than the expressive ", prayers— " interesting, solemn and touching ". Instead of building " imitation Parthenons and Westminsters ", it would be " safer, wiser and more economical, to pay more attention to the form and materials of the service ". Conservative Presbyterians like Dr. A. A. Hodge of Princeton were in favour of restoring the *Te Deum*, *Apostles' Creed* and other liturgical elements, within the framework of the traditional Puritan service. The rank and file of the " non-liturgical " churches were, however, slow to realise that the abuse of extempore prayer was a serious matter. The " most eloquent prayer offered to a Boston audience " was no fiction.[1] An eminent Evangelical preacher of the Episcopal Church, the Rev. D. W. S. Rainsford, remarked: " If all men prayed always as some men pray sometimes, then we could do away with the Liturgy; but they do not."[2] Even at the end of the century Dr. Henry Van Dyke, of the Brick Presbyterian Church, New York, could only persuade his cultured congregation to join in the Lord's Prayer by allowing objectors to remain silent!

Lewis Tappan, patron of Finney the evangelist, used to quote Oliver Cromwell's order regarding twelve silver statues of the Apostles at York Minster: " Take them down, coin them, and let them go about doing good." Tappan considered that Christian beneficence would be better invested in Evangelism than in " superfluous architecture " which merely ministered to human pride. That was in 1835 when American Architecture had passed from its tentative " Colonial " stage, through the conscious classicism of the early Republic, to its culminating phase, the Greek revival. This fine tradition of building churches, houses and schools in clean, austere symmetry petered out by the time of the Civil War. The " Gilded Age " that followed witnessed the final disintegration of sound craftsmanship. The " superfluous architecture " deplored by Tappan now sprouted in superabundant growth.

[1] It was declaimed by the Rev. Horace Holley, who was complimented on his eloquence by the *Columbian Sentinel*.
[2] *A Preacher's Story of His Work*, p. 146.

Mass production catered for a parvenu taste that exhausted the historic styles in search of novelty, perpetrating such monstrosities as " Hudson River Bracketted ". In their churches, as well as their homes, Americans now demanded the flamboyant, the picturesque and the quaint. Jerry-builders presented plausible plans and " tasty " designs in cheap materials. Timber, which had been well managed by carpenters trained in the classic tradition, was crudely adapted to " Gothick " form. Episcopalians made medieval architecture fashionable. Spires, turrets, prickly pinnacles and high-pitched roofs (usually covered with multi-patterned slates) rapidly displaced classic colonnades and cupolas.

The basement of the average church was now generally utilised for housing the Sunday School, the prayer meeting, and the " Ladies' Aid ", which had hitherto operated in a detached building of painful plainness known as " the chapel ". To transfer social fellowship to dim subterranean regions was a downward step in more than one sense, though possibly a few historically-minded persons may have felt that the Early Christian precedent of the catacombs was being followed at a respectful distance! From the street-level, winding stairs, sometimes enclosed in turrets, conducted the worshipper to the church vestibule. The Gothic Revival interior was even less successful than the exterior for Christian symbolism was feared. Non-liturgical churches, as yet, avoided the chancel. High galleries on cast-iron posts were the dominating feature, the walls were covered with dingy housepainter's decoration and light of a sickly greenish-yellow hue was admitted by tinted leaded glass; walnut was deemed the most suitable wood for ecclesiastical furnishing, owing to its sad, unworldly colour.

In the 'eighties the Romanesque Revival captured the imagination of America. H. H. Richardson's masterpiece, Trinity Church, Boston, was hailed as the harbinger of a new era. The bold central tower, suggested by Southern French Romanesque, dominated the structure, the four arms of the Greek Cross plan being short and equal. Here was an auditorium that was also a sanctuary, rich in symbolism. Trinity Church became a household name in the United States, associated with the magnetic preaching of Phillips Brooks (p. 366 f.). Why not reproduce this type of church all over the country ? Richardson was right in believing that the largeness and simplicity of round-headed arches could express the

American genius more adequately than Victorian Gothic, with its complicated detail. Unfortunately, like Ruskin, he was indirectly responsible for the hatching of an innumerable brood of ugly ducklings. Other architects discovered that Romanesque was easier to manipulate than Gothic in two respects. It facilitated the seating of the people in a semi-circle: it rescued the Sunday School from its subterranean retreat under the church and placed it on the same level as "the auditorium", separated only by sliding doors (see p. 335).

These churches still remain the despair of "renovating" architects. The stencilled ornament can be removed from the walls, but large memorial windows are a perpetual eyesore—Biblical scenes executed with startling realism in "opalescent glass". It was a favourite Baptist motif to depict a river that started overhead, meandered down the walls and eventually emptied into the place of immersion (the symbolism would have been more effective but for the fact that the baptistry was a tank concealed beneath the pulpit). In most denominations the arrangement of the sanctuary was stereotyped. Instead of a pulpit you would find a shallow platform, with highly varnished furniture—the "sacred desk", "occasional tables", and three stiff chairs or a sofa. The minister generally wore a long "Prince Albert" coat. Behind him, in a balcony, the lady choristers provided a background of colour, with a battery of gilded organ pipes dominating the setting.

President Coffin has described the atmosphere of these "auditoriums" as "formal informality". The semi-circular pewing suggested fellowship. Notices of meetings were intimated with repeated appeals for attendance. Hymns stressed "sunshine in the soul". They were announced, "Shall we sing No. — ?" America was becoming a land of wealth as well as opportunity; the old Puritan sense of sin was declining with the growth of unbounded faith in the destiny of man. The humanity of God was so stressed at the close of the nineteenth century that worshippers often lost sight of the fact that worship calls for reverence.[1] Prayers tended

[1] Winston Churchill, in *The Dwelling-Place of Light* (1917), describes a typical Congregational church vainly attempting to keep up with the times. It was a shapeless mélange of "rounded knob-like towers covered with mulberry-stained shingles. The minister was sensational and dramatic". Decadent, bewildered Puritanism was no match for the Roman Church round the corner—"brazen, prosperous, serene". There was, to be sure, a dignified church of his own denomination which Edward Bumpus passed daily; he admired its terraced steeple and classic façade, "but hesitated to join the decorous and dwindling congregation, the remains of a social strata from which he had been pried loose".

to address the people rather than the Most High; they were ram-
bling and subjective. There was only one brief Lesson, generally
from the New Testament. The " Responsive Reading " of the
Psalter by minister and people in alternate verses was often impaired by the use of faulty " Selections "—a mere medley of texts.
Solos, anthems and choral responses took up a disproportionate
amount of time and were apt to be irrelevant. The Benediction
once pronounced, the preacher would rush to the vestibule under
cover of a seven-fold choral *Amen* to shake hands with the retiring
worshippers (a gesture of " formal informality " that is still practically universal in America).

The term " auditorium " was appropriate, for these churches
were mere " listening-posts ". There was little of the hearty congregational singing that enlivened English Nonconformist services.
The only remedy (applied by Methodists and Baptists) was the
introduction of revival songs, which the people had learned to sing
in Sunday School. These two sects have not hesitated to sacrifice
reverence in getting religion across. Public worship has been
reduced to religious vaudeville by " echo singing ", cinema illu-
mination, and other " snappy, fascinating features " advocated by
Dr. W. L. Stidger in *Standing Room Only!* H. L. Mencken for
years exposed strange instances of religious eccentricity in the
" Americana " column of *The American Mercury*. The following
Californian instance comes to us from the 1920's :

" In tribute to the ' greatest of all carpenters ', the Rev. Arthur L.
Pratt, St. Stephen's Methodist Church, Oakland, preached yesterday
from behind a carpenter's bench instead of a pulpit. Honor guests were
the members of . . . the Building Trades Council. A man's choir, garbed
in white overalls, replaced the customary choir. Their selections were
supplemented by a special musical programme, played on saws and nail
kegs."

Since the First World War there has been a remarkable recovery
of reverence in the non-liturgical churches. This movement expressed itself particularly in church architecture. In 1900 such
religious art as existed could be found (by careful scrutiny) in the
Episcopal Church alone. Conditions were unpromising and it
looked as though the last shreds of churchliness had been abandoned. Twenty years later a miracle occurred. America was now
producing good church architecture that roused the surprise and
delight of Europeans. Much was due to Dr. Ralph Adams Cram

a learned and enthusiastic medievalist, who stabbed the spirit of complacency wide awake by his rhetoric, wit and sarcasm. A minster-building campaign was inaugurated by the Episcopal Church, and Cram was chosen to complete (in Gothic) and on a colossal scale St. John the Divine in New York. Cathedrals were planned for Washington and other cities, thus supplying something of " the old ecclesiastical arrogance " thàt Henry James found wanting in America. These costly temples intimidated " the quiet in the land " who felt more at home in simple surroundings (*Procul, O procul este, profani*). On the other hand, they aroused the competitive instinct among other denominations, who, ashamed of their shoddy utilitarianism, turned to men like Dr. Cram in sackcloth and ashes. He prescribed the cruciform plan, with a chancel[1] instead of a platform backed by an organ-loft, though he sometimes built noble churches which made concessions to the non-liturgical tradition, e.g. the First Baptist Church, Pittsburgh. Cram's conservative treatment of Gothic is well illustrated by the Princeton University Chapel, which is an interesting contrast to the Chicago University Chapel, designed by his colleague, Bertram G. Goodhue. Both structures are cathedral-like in dimensions, and intended for undenominational worship, yet genuine Gothic. But whereas Cram was content to be a traditionalist, Goodhue sought by massive simplicity and clear outline to blend the eternal spirit of Gothic with the rational clarity of twentieth-century America.

In response to a demand for a " free cathedral " in New York, Mr. John D. Rockefeller supplied the funds for Riverside Church, where the magnetic and vital Dr. Fosdick aimed at integrating the major strains of worship—liturgical, evangelical, and meditative. Riverside Church was designed by Messrs. Allen and Collens in 1930. What appears outwardly as a French Gothic tower is inwardly a steel skeleton framework 400 feet high, the elevator shaft rising from bowling alleys in the basement, past innumerable floors housing Sunday School and administration, to the 72-bell carillon (" the largest in the world "), 24 stories up.[2]

[1] The first non-liturgical church designed with a chancel was the Central Congregational, Boston (1867).

[2] Some " skyscraper churches " have actually been built—often ingenious devices for serving God *and* Mammon, many of the stories being let as offices. The Prospectus of Broadway Methodist Temple, New York, called for an " income-producing plant ", combining " salvation and 5% ", based on ethical grounds, also gilt-edged real estate mortgage ". This new Tower of Babel was to be crowned by a gigantic illumined cross, guaranteed to change Manhattan's skyline.

The acoustical engineer, the welfare-worker and the Religious Education expert have presided over the destinies of Riverside, but the interior is as medieval as wealth[1] and taste can make it, though the figures in stained glass and statuary include scientists, humanitarians and reformers; behind the marble altar is a baptistry for immersion, reminding us that this is the usage of Riverside Church, though the title " Baptist " is not used. Whatever may be said by way of architectural criticism, Riverside is of special interest to the British observer as an illustration of the present American tendency to combine old and new, prophetic and priestly, sacred and secular.[2]

Throughout the United States there has been a general desire to build sanctuaries worthy of God's worship and designed to minister to body, mind and soul. The Episcopal, Presbyterian, Congregational and Unitarian Churches were foremost; the Methodists, hitherto very backward, organised a bureau of Church Architecture that " stepped down " the best ideals to the limitations of small churches.[3] Even denominations that were formerly hostile to beauty in form and shape, gradually came under the influence of this nation-wide movement, though the South and West inevitably lagged behind. Dr. Cram, once a stern Crusader for Gothic (like the men of the Oxford Movement) mellowed in his stiff opinions and cheerfully acquiesced in the use of other styles—Romanesque, Byzantine, " Spanish Mission " and the regional varieties of Anglo-Saxon " Colonial ", in addition to German, Dutch and Scandinavian contributions to American architecture.

Religious education, which in the nineteenth century had lowered none-too-high standards of church architecture, now proved an ally of good building. The modern American church was multi-cellular, involving extensive accommodation for separate class-rooms, recreation, devotional chapel and assembly hall. Was there not an analogy between the modern church with its ancillary buildings and the medieval monastery, the sanctuary organically related to library, refectory, garden and cloister?

[1] Advocates of the " Social Gospel " are inclined to criticise expensive churches as an expression of class pride or as " an escape " from the harder task of rebuilding an ugly industrial order.
[2] See illustrated description in *Riverside Church Monthly* (Dec. 1930).
[3] The pioneer, Elbert M. Conover, was successful in federating denominational boards; ideals (and achievements) are reflected in his *Building the House of God* (New York, 1928).

Gothic had its homelike as well as its churchly aspects. A well-known and much-loved pastor, Dr. Gaius Glenn Atkins, remembers a panelled room graciously furnished and candle-lit, where the people gathered from a scattered parish to sit around a welcome fire, share in a common meal and an intimate act of worship, thus becoming one family. " Some may have come for the food—but they stayed for the prayers. I still think it was not far from the sacramental breaking of bread in a long-vanished room."

Symbolism has commended itself to the " Religious Education Movement " as a means of embodying the Beautiful, the True and the Good. This has been confirmed by Hocking among the philosophers, Pratt among the psychologists, and Sperry among the theologians. Dean Sperry refused to have worship reduced to a utility—even the laudable purpose of making better men and a better society.[1] He maintained the high definition of the Shorter Catechism that man's chief end is " to glorify God and to enjoy Him for ever ". Aesthetic and social effects could be obtained only as by-products, when God is worshipped for what He is (*Reality In Worship*, 1925). The revolution in the setting for worship (1919-39) seems, on the whole, to have been motivated by *subjective* rather than *objective* ideas. Most influential in this connexion has been the work of Dr. Von Ogden Vogt, a Unitarian Congregational minister serving in a Unitarian pulpit. Dr. Vogt, like Schleiermacher, defined worship as " the celebration of life ". For him, it flowered in processionals, responses, litanies and altars. Ministers and choirs were now robed. Colour and rhythm set new patterns of worship a-dancing in the imagination. The sacramental " view of life " became real to many young people.

The defect of the " Worship Movement " is the fact that it originated with " liberal Protestants " who had gone far to the left in theology. Evangelicals were slow to realise the need of expressing their objective views in appropriate form. Too long content with featureless preaching-halls and shapeless services, they had no alternative to offer to the vogue of elaborate chancels and furnishings completely at variance with Reformed doctrine and tradition. Instead of clarifying their order of service, they vested their choirs. There is something incongruous in the spectacle of a Congregational minister dispensing the Lord's Supper

[1] This is precisely what Dr. C. C. Morrison, the well-known editor of the *Christian Century* wanted to do. In *The Social Gospel and the Christian Cultus* (1933) he proposed to gear public worship to " social Gospel " propaganda.

with " individual cups " at an elaborate altar adorned with cross and candlesticks.[1] What is to be said liturgically for the custom (almost universal) of adorning the pulpit or chancel with conspicuous Stars-and-Stripes ? " These be thy gods, O Israel!" Hitherto American services have been " enriched "; they have still to be unified by consistent symbolism.

In the Protestant Episcopal Church the influence of the mother Church of England has been felt in two directions—the infusion of warmth and variety into chilly decorum by means of supplementary manuals like Suter's *Devotional Offices* (1928) and the latest imported fashions in ecclesiastical millinery. The church's worship is found at its simplest in Virginia, where the Evangelical tradition still lingers. At Chicago " Anglo-Catholic " ritual prevails. Bishop Manning of New York (an Englishman) did his utmost to level up ceremonial to standard " C. of E." level. The Prayer Book appears to be more closely followed than is now customary in England, but with less chanting and intoning. The Episcopal clergy are the only non-Roman ministers in the United States who insist on the clerical collar so common among all British denominations, but in some of the leading New York churches the " laic " tradition of Phillips Brooks has persisted.

The Prayer Book came into use in the American Army and Navy during the nineteenth century for want of any other manual of devotion; that partly accounts for the Episcopal service being used at West Point and other Military Academies.[2] In spite of a strong Puritan tradition in the non-liturgical churches, the Prayer Book is often used for marriages, funerals, etc., without any tendency towards Episcopal ideas of Church Order. The influence of the Methodist Episcopal Church has doubtless been potent, for their *Ritual* carries the Anglican services for the sacraments with slight modifications. Now that the Methodist Church is passing from its primitive frontier stage to maturity, the transition from " sect type " to " church type " has brought back " John Wesley's Sunday Service " to some of the city churches. Far beyond Methodism the classic prayers of the church (e.g. the *General Thanksgiving*)

---

[1] One recalls *Punch's* cartoon of Archbishop Tait admonishing a group of English clergy holding flower-vases, crosses and candles: " You must not bring your playthings into Church, little men!" (1858).

[2] Chaplains to the Forces are classified as Catholic, Protestant and Jewish. No Episcopalian padre, however " High ", would be allowed to refuse Communion to, say, a Baptist or a Presbyterian.

have become familiar to worshippers. Enlightened ministers have had a hard struggle to oust unwholesome traditions. In rural districts custom has usually prescribed a funeral sermon, extolling the virtues of the deceased (however slight); then the mourners pass on to peer at the corpse in its open " casket ". In the cities burials have been commercialised by too enterprising " morticians ". In some parts of the country sensational settings for weddings have had to be tactfully discouraged. The aim of the clergy has been to restore reverence to funerals and marriages[1] by having them solemnised in church, if possible, or in private houses rather than in hired premises.

In spite of the conservatism of the Scots-Irish element in the Presbyterian Church, the General Assembly appointed a Committee to prepare a *Book of Common Worship* in 1895. Dr. Henry Van Dyke, the church's most eminent literary man, was mainly responsible. The object was to provide a standard of worship that should express the noblest ideals of the Reformed Church, serving as a guide without being in any sense a compulsory liturgy. So strong was the fear of " canned prayers " that it did not appear till 1905. A new edition was published in 1932, with Dr. Van Dyke as editor again.[2] Its austerity was a much-needed corrective to the lush rhetoric still too common in trans-Atlantic pulpit prayers. The influence of the mother-Church of Scotland may be noted in this connexion, also the work of a famous Scottish preacher, John Hunter, whose *Devotional Services* had a wide circulation in America. Dr. Hunter was a Congregationalist and his communion in the United States has done much to make the Worship Movement really creative and corporate by retreats and conferences, and the issue of devotional literature. It is significant that this work is done by the " Commission on Evangelism " (a few years earlier Evangelism and ordered worship were strangers).

The Lutheran Churches, numerically strong though divided into rival groups by language and tradition, were forced by circumstances to adopt the English language to a large extent. This led to the publication of a *Common Service Book* in 1917, which yielded sifted treasure to the common store. In early days the Lutherans tended to " accommodate " themselves to American

---

[1] In 1949 U.S. judges debated the legality of a sailor's marriage in California. The " officiating minister ", aged five, was ordained by the " Old-Time Faith Church "; he was assisted by his brother, aged two.

[2] Recast in 1948 to satisfy more exacting liturgical standards.

ways. Now they have repaid the debt with interest by rich contributions from chorale and liturgy.

The desire to understand other churches and to borrow freely what may be assimilated can be traced to *The Quest for Experience in Worship* (to quote the title of a characteristic book by Professor E. H. Byington (New York, 1929). In spite of denominational barriers there is a remarkable uniformity in the average American service—Congregational, Presbyterian, Methodist and Baptist. The differences are " horizontal " rather than " vertical ". In rural districts you will find greater informality, modified by the use of liturgical material at the end of the hymnary (or mimeographed orders of service placed in the pews each Sunday, in imitation of the printed weekly folders of large churches). In the cities extempore prayer is less exclusively used. The Silent Worship of the Friends has stemmed to some extent the unmitigated flow of words. Ancient collects and litanies have been used alongside of modern equivalents, linked by responses. Experiments have been made to fuse the heritage of the ages with worship-material that will satisfy the needs of modern America. There is an unofficial *Book of Common Worship, for use in the several Communions of the Church of Christ* (New York, 1932), edited by a Methodist bishop and a Congregational minister. Among its interesting features is a collection of alternatives to the historic creeds. One of these comes from the American mission-field, the Church of Christ in Korea :

" We believe in one God, Maker and Ruler of all things, Father of all men; the source of all goodness and beauty, all truth and love.

We believe in Jesus Christ, God manifest in the flesh—our Teacher, Example and Redeemer, the Saviour of the world.

We believe in the Holy Spirit, God present with us for guidance, for comfort and for strength.

We believe in the forgiveness of sins, in the life of love and prayer, and in grace equal to every need.

We believe in the Word of God contained in the Old and New Testaments as the sufficient rule both of faith and practice.

We believe in the Church as the fellowship for worship and for service of all who are united to the living Lord.

We believe in the final triumph of righteousness, and in the life everlasting. AMEN."

For many years America's contribution to hymnology was slight. Even to-day, of the 200 hymns in general use in the average congregation, a large number are British (according to questionnaires). The tunes are not always the same, but Heber's " Holy, Holy, Holy " is permanently wedded to Dykes' *Nicaea* and Perronet's " All hail the power of Jesus' Name " to *Coronation*. Two of the most popular hymns are eighteenth century—" Come, Thou Almighty King (*c.* 1757, anon., tune by Giardini) and Watts' " Joy to the world! " (*Antioch*, arranged from *The Messiah* by Lowell Mason).[1] In Britain we still use Mason's *Heber* for " Greenland's icy mountains " and his *Olivet* for " My faith looks up to Thee ". In the 1830's the turbid tide of sentimental music was flowing through revival meetings even into the sanctuary. Lowell Mason in Boston and Thomas Hastings in New York did their best to reject the intrusion of " the vulgar melodies of the street, of the midnight reveller, of the circus and the ballroom ". They had to compromise to some extent, but their work as pioneers of *good* popular praise is generally recognised. " Rocking-chair rhythm " they did not despise, and the typical American hymn-tune enjoyed by plain people owes much to them. After the Civil War came a spate of " Gospel Songs " far worse than the " folk hymns " of the early nineteenth century. For a time it seemed as if the barriers of taste and reverence would be swept away.[2] The process of purifying church hymnals from flotsam and jetsam was protracted, but only the better type are still retained, such as Gilmore's " He leadeth me ", and Hawkes' " I need Thee every hour ".

By the middle of the nineteenth century very few " classic " hymns had been composed by Americans. Ray Palmer, a Congregational minister, wrote " My faith looks up to Thee " in 1830. C. W. Everest, a young Connecticut rector, was the author of " Take up thy cross " (one of the first American inclusions in *Hymns Ancient and Modern*). Two bishops contributed fine missionary hymns—Doane's " Fling out the banner! " and Coxe's " Saviour, sprinkle many nations ". Samuel Wolcott, a Presbyterian, composed a hymn that deserves to be better known in Britain, " Christ for the world we sing ". And that is about all. One reason for the lack of good American hymns is the fact

---

[1] Some old-fashioned hymns and tunes still retain a place in popular affection, e.g. " How firm a foundation, ye saints of the Lord " ('K' in Rippon's *Selection*, 1787).

[2] A publishing firm contracted with Fanny Crosby, the blind author, to supply three hymns a week for many years (" I have often composed six in one day "). Her output amounted to over 8,000 Gospel Songs.

that most congregations preferred to offer their praise by proxy. The Episcopalians set the fashion of replacing the choir by a professional quartette who " rendered " languishing " selections " from such tune-books as *The Shawm, The Dulcimer,* and *The Grace Church Collection.* Mute worshippers listened to " parlor music ". It was said to be " one of Mr. Beecher's oddities " that he encouraged the people to sing in his Brooklyn church. The *Plymouth Collection* (1855) was helpful in this respect, for it printed the tunes above the words (a welcome innovation). This unwieldy hymnary (1,374 numbers) was edited by John Zundel, Beecher's organist. One of the few original hymns in it was composed by his sister, Mrs. Stowe, who brought a new romantic note into her nature hymn: " Still, still with Thee, when purple morning breaketh."

It was the Unitarians, however, who opened a new epoch by the freshness and originality of their contribution. When Theodore Parker received *A Book of Hymns* (1848) he is said to have remarked, " I see we have a new book of Sams!" The editors were Samuel Longfellow (brother of the poet) and Samuel Johnson, his fellow-student at the Harvard Divinity School. They were the first to introduce Newman's " Lead, kindly Light " to America (they had found it printed anonymously in a newspaper). While the " two Sams " altered a good many classic hymns to suit their own theology, they did unique service to Christendom by making hymnic use of Whittier's poems—" Dear Lord and Father of Mankind ", " Immortal Love, forever full ", " O brother man ", etc. It was a providential paradox that the Quaker advocate of Silent Worship should have thus become vocal in many " a nest of singing birds ".

These young men published *Hymns of the Spirit* in 1864. They were more than editors, however; they were creative poets of the free spirit, who imparted to New England a final lyrical genius that had already flowered in philosophy and literature. When Liverpool Cathedral was opened in 1924, " the massed choirs burst forth with the following hymn at the climax of the service ":

> City of God, how broad and far,
> Outspread thy walls sublime ?
> The true thy chartered freemen are,
> Of every age and clime.[1]

[1] Curiously enough, it does not appear at all in the *Inter-Church Hymnal* 1 930), compiled on a basis of proved popularity in American Churches.

Probably most of the congregation attributed the authorship to Samuel Johnson, lexicographer, and not to an obscure Unitarian minister in Lynn, Mass.! Samuel Longfellow has five hymns in the Scottish *Revised Church Hymnary* of 1927, but it was half a century before the editors of standard British collections took note. As Percy Dearmer has remarked, while English compilers were ransacking the Dark Ages and the Counter-Reformation for material, the best hymns, voicing modern idealism, were being written in the United States. Sound Anglicans neglected Dr. Holmes' magnificent nature hymn, " Lord of all being ", though it was not unnatural that they should jib at

> Our Father! while our hearts unlearn
> The creeds that wrong thy name,
> Still let our hallowed altars burn
> With faith's undying flame.

Oliver Wendell Holmes, Unitarian as he was, in later years numbered himself among " those who believed more " rather than " those who believed less ". E. H. Sears (d. 1876), author of " It came upon the midnight clear ", was also a Unitarian but all his life preached the absolute divinity of Christ. Such men were unwilling exiles from Christendom, repelled by a grim orthodoxy that denied " the humanity of God ". F. L. Hosmer carried into the twentieth century the yearning for brotherhood, rooted in the conviction that religion is something larger and richer than Christianity; nevertheless, orthodox Christians on both sides of the Atlantic can join with " the passing ages " in singing " Thy Kingdom come!"

In recent years the Trinitarian hymn-writers of America have followed the Unitarians in their enthusiasm for the " Social Gospel ", world friendship, and a preference for " the goodly company of the prophets " over against " the Holy Catholic Church ". One of the best missionary hymns with a modern note has been written by Professor H. H. Tweedy of Yale, " Eternal God, Whose power upholds both flower and flaming star ". Each verse voices a different approach: " O God of Love, whose spirit wakes in every human breast " . . . " O God of Truth, whom Science seeks " . . . " O God of Beauty, oft revealed in dreams of human art ", all culminating in " O God of Righteousness and grace, seen in the Christ, Thy Son ". One is glad to note that George Matheson's missionary hymn has appeared in many American hymnaries.

2C

though not contained in the Scottish collection: " Gather us in, Thou Love that fillest all " (each verse expressing an aspiration felt by other religions, but satisfied only by Christ). It is safe to say that not many modern American hymns of the Social Gospel will live, apart from those that have already become classics. They are too touched with Tennysonian " wishful thinking " about the " parliament of Man, the federation of the world ", to meet the desperate needs of the present day. The ecumenical note also is often struck in an amateurish style. Dr. Tweedy includes Vachel Lindsay's lines in the hymnary, *Christian Worship and Praise* (1939):

> And endless line of splendor,
> These troops with heaven for home,
> With creeds they go from Scotland,
> With incense go from Rome.

The last fifty years have seen the denominational stamp growing fainter and fainter in American hymnody (the Episcopalians, Methodists and Baptists have produced little that is creative). It is interesting to note that a Baptist, S. F. Smith, wrote " My country, 'tis of Thee " while he was still a student at Andover (1832). Lowell Mason, not knowing German, sent Smith some chorale books in the hope that he would find something worth translating. Smith was fascinated by a tune set to some patriotic verses, to which he wrote his own words. He did not know until later that the music was the same as that of " God save the king "! Francis Scott Key, a devout Episcopalian of Baltimore, had already written " The Star-spangled Banner "—" O say can you see ? "— during the war with Britain in 1814. Smith sang, not of " rockets' red flare and bombs bursting in air ", but of " rocks and rills and templed hills ".[1] That was the utterance of a good New Englander, but it was not so easy for the men of the South or West to associate liberty with " land of the Pilgrims' pride ". Other sections of the country were included in " America the Beautiful " by Katherine Lee Bates of Wellesley College (1899). It has found its way into most hymnaries, sung to the fine swinging tune *Materna*:

> O beautiful for spacious skies,
> For amber fields of grain,
> For purple mountain majesties
> Above the fruited plain!

---

[1] In times of crisis, the militant note stirs, e.g. Lowell's " Once to every man and nation ". Julia Ward Howe's " Battle Hymn of the Republic ", written during the Civil War, was popular in Britain as well as in America during World War I.

America, America!
God shed his grace on thee
And crown thy good with brotherhood
From sea to shining sea!

Modern American hymns for young people strike a very different note from the doleful lays of the early nineteenth century
(" Remember sinful youth, you must die, you must die . . . ") or
the sentimental refrains of the Gospel Song (e.g. Lowry's " Shall
we gather at the river ?"). Turning to Professor H. Augustine
Smith's *New Hymnal for American Youth* (1930) we find expressed
a radiant joy in life, a stirring call to the service of God and man
in faith, fortitude and hope. There are very few hymns about
heaven for children, which are still popular in Britain. Among
hymns popular for some years among young people have been:
Howard Walter's " I would be true, for there are those who trust
me ", Maltbie Babcock's " This is my Father's world " and " Be
strong! We are not here to play, to dream, to drift ". The call to
action is characteristic of modern American hymns. W. P. Merrill's
" Rise up, ye men of God " is expressive of what Continentals
call " American activism ". The Bishop of Ripon told Dr. Merrill
a few years ago that he used this hymn at every Confirmation in
his diocese.

The popularity of " Fairest Lord Jesus ", translated from a German hymn of 1678 and set to a Silesian Folk Song in 1850, reminds
us of the eclectic character of modern American hymnaries. America is more backward than Great Britain in this respect, but the
Presbyterian *Hymnal* (1933) compared with its predecessors of
1895 and 1911, discloses a revival of interest in old psalm tunes,
chorales and folk melodies—English, Irish, Scandinavian, Welsh
and Czech. America has produced church musicians like *The
Hymnal* editor, Dr. Clarence Dickinson, and hymnologists like
Dr. Louis F. Benson, but few composers of first-class hymn tunes.
There is a marked tendency to set new hymns to old tunes of
acknowledged excellence and emotional association.

Considering the traditions of the denominations, we find that
the Episcopal *Church Hymnal* of 1892 was a pale imitation of
Hymns Ancient and Modern, the difference being the fact that the
former was officially sponsored. Its editors took little account of
hymns written outside the sacred " Catholic " ring (Roman, Anglican and Greek). Its successor, the *New Hymnal* (1918), was the

first Episcopal book with set tunes. Timid and compromising, it looked askance at the right, represented by the epoch-making but Anglo-Catholic *English Hymnal* (1906), and also at the left, represented by the free spirit of liberal Protestantism.

The *New Hymnal* belied its name for it was heavily laden with Victorian " cathedral music ", which the English had left behind. A striking contrast was the Harvard *University Hymn Book* (1926) which almost outdid *Songs of Praise* in banishing Dykes and Sullivan and setting " Onwards Christian Soldiers " to a German chorale! The editor of this Harvard book, Professor A. T. Davidson, criticised the vogue of the boy-choir, which had spread from the Episcopalians to other churches, on the grounds that a mature mixed choir was more capable of " singing with the understanding "; the singers, instead of being " on review ", split into two sections on each side of the chancel, would be better " heard and not seen " (*Protestant Church Music in America*, 1933). Union Theological Seminary, Princeton and other schools now provide adequate courses for the training of church musicians. What the British visitor in America misses is hearty congregational singing; the " professional minstrel " tradition dies hard. The Hymn Society of America (1922), working in harmony with a similar British movement, is the modern successor of " The Society for Promoting Regular and Good Singing, and for reforming the Depravations and Debasements our Psalmody labours under ", which was inaugurated by the Rev. Thomas Walter in Boston (1722).

From a musical point of view, one of the best American books is the new Unitarian *Hymns of the Spirit* (named after Johnson and Longfellow's famous compilation of 1864). Its value is necessarily impaired owing to its doctrinal orientation. The best known Congregational book, *The Pilgrim Hymnal* (1904) was " markedly undogmatic, non-ecclesiastical and humanitarian in tone ", 115 out of 547 hymns being ascribed to Unitarians; this evoked criticism and some modification in subsequent editions (1913, 1931). In its revised form the *Pilgrim Hymnal* has tended to oust other collections. Among its rivals is the more " Catholic " *Hymns of the Church* (1913). Like most modern Protestant collections, this reveals Episcopal influence running back to *Hymns Ancient and Modern* in arranging the contents according to the Christian Year, rather than " topics " devised to suit preachers (the nineteenth-

century hymnaries were essentially " preachers' aids ", with copi-
ous indices showing what hymns to choose in keeping with one's
text).[1] It was largely through the hymn books that the Christian
Year has come to be observed so generally by the non-liturgical
churches. In 1935 American Methodists agreed on a common
Methodist Hymnal, which marks a considerable advance to cultivated and churchly standards, with only limited concessions to
those who still demanded " Gospel Songs ".

[1] Homiletic misuse involved mutilation by verse omission. Dr. Lyman
Abbott remembered a ludicrous instance:

> " When Thou, my righteous Judge, shall come,
> To take my righteous people home,
> Shall I among them stand?
>
> .   .   .   .   .
>
> O Lord, forbid it by Thy grace "!

CHAPTER VI

TOWARDS UNITY

"America is God's crucible, the great Melting-pot, where all are melting and reforming."—ISRAEL ZANGWILL (1908)

IT is difficult to tabulate the hold of religion on any nation, but it is significant that the nineteenth century, the era of "manifest destiny" and material enrichment, witnessed a more rapid increase in the churches than the previous periods, commonly supposed to be "God-fearing and church-going". At the time of American Independence only one out of every twenty-five citizens was a communicant. Between 1800 and 1850 church membership increased twelve-fold, while the population multiplied by only four-and-a-half. Between 1850 and 1870 church membership increased 84%, mounting from six to eleven millions;[1] while ecclesiastical property rose in value by 65% (due partly to unearned increment on urban real estate, partly to the building of more churches, better equipped). Progress in Evangelism and outward organisation outran spiritual maturity. Santayana has remarked that one half of the American mind is driving away at inventions and industry, "leaping down a sort of Niagara", while the other half floats gently in a backwater of timid acceptance. Progress is swiftly registered by anything material that can be organised or built: the "Activist" is apt to oversimplify issues too complacently when he invades the domain of thought where immaterial standards prevail. Hence the poor quality of cultural life in many a "Zenith" of the Middle West, where business permeates religion to saturation point.

It would be instructive to compare the effects of "Prosperity Unlimited" (1919-29) and the subsequent Depression on the church. It is certainly a big field of enquiry, but this much can be said. A few figures taken from the book of commerce reveal

[1] The proportion of persons who are church members in the U.S. ranges between 62% on the Atlantic coast to 35% on the Pacific (Rockies, 44%).

staggering gains. In 1924 2% of the population owned 60% of the nation's wealth: on the other hand the average income of every person " gainfully employed " rose from $1,500 (£300) in 1921 to $2,000 in 1926. The churches built elaborate " plants ", for ecclesiastical display as well as for recreational activities. Ministers were now required to be primarily " promoters " rather than preachers or pastors, leaders capable of raising money for church budgets and special enterprises. Their stipends were not increased to anything like the same degree as the profits, wages and salaries of their parishioners;[1] probably they were worse off than in the 'eighties, when Lord Bryce considered that their position compared favourably with that of British and German Protestant clergy.[2]

" Prosperity Unlimited " was an era of getting and spending. It was an age of salesmanship. The " hire-purchase system " was carried to its limits, in Dr. Henry Van Dyke's phrase, " to buy things we did not need with money we did not have ". In the less sophisticated sects evangelists even spoke of " selling religion ". There was certainly " money enough to buy everything " said a New York preacher in 1927—" everything except the peace that passeth all understanding". Yet there was no proportionate increase in happiness. There was an increase in divorce, an epidemic of suicide among those in comfortable circumstances, an eruption of dissolute living among " flaming youth ". An American who had wrecked mind and body by the ceaseless scramble for money went to see a great nerve specialist. He asked: " How much does your religion mean to you ?" The patient was so surprised that he was unable to reply. The famous doctor then explained that there was one class whom he scarcely ever saw in his consulting room—" the people who believe and practise the Christian religion".

In 1927 there were 35,000 millionaires in the United States.

[1] In 1918 the average pastor's salary in the U.S.A. amounted to $937, and the average contribution per church member $4 p.a. Making allowance for the fact that this includes negro preachers and white ministers of small obscure sects (many of whom are practically " lay preachers " according to English standards) clerical remuneration was generally inadequate, especially in the South and West. In some states clergy are worse remunerated than elementary school teachers, who are notoriously ill-paid.

[2] Lord Bryce stated that in 1889 a few city ministers received $10,000 upwards. In the smaller cities the average among Presbyterians, Congregationalists, Episcopalians, was about $3,000 p.a. (£600) and in rural districts seldom below $1,000. Remuneration was on a lower level generally among Methodists and Baptists (*The American Commonwealth*, 1889, Vol. II, p. 581).

In 1928 there were 511 men with *incomes* exceeding $1,000,000 a year: in 1932 there were only 20 in such a position. In 1928 there were 43,200 incomes exceeding $50,000 per annum, in 1932 only 7,430. People with fortunes found themselves reduced to comparative poverty: people with good salaries found themselves standing in the bread-line; the promoter of New York's pioneer skyscraper, the Flatiron Building, was given a pauper's funeral.

Cynics predicted that the churches, which had over-built and over-spent in prosperous times, would topple over into moral as well as financial bankruptcy. In 1932 the United States spent 72% less on recreation than in 1929, 61% less on comforts and luxuries; the national income fell by 54%, but church incomes fell only by 40%. One out of every 22 business concerns went bankrupt; one of every six banks failed; but only one out of every 2,344 churches dissolved (which was probably a blessing in an over-churched country). The aggregate debt on church fabrics amounted to no more than 10%. The membership of the Protestant Churches in 1932 was nearly 1,000,000 over the increase in 1931. Indeed, it was the largest gain recorded since national records were first kept; 6.8% of the population were church members in 1800, 40.1% in 1932. The general drift of statistics clearly indicates that the churches had strengthened their hold on the affections of the people during the Depression period.

American publicists have often drawn attention to the fact that the countryside is being steadily depopulated. In 1880 there were 26 cities with over 100,000 inhabitants: in 1936 this figure had mounted to 93, covering half the total population. For many years the city churches had been largely recruited, in ministry and membership, from the rural areas, but this " exportable surplus " is no longer abundant. It is instructive to compare the geographical distribution of the various denominations in Britain and America. Anglicanism is much in evidence in the English countryside, symbolised by the towers and spires of numerous parish churches: in the United States this feature is missing from the landscape, for less than 50% of the Episcopalians live on the land. The Methodists, Baptists and Disciples, on the other hand, are predominantly rural—traditionally inclined to be suspicious of big cities as " sinks of iniquity " and unbelief; in 1906 no less than 86% of the Baptists lived outside big industrial areas. Except in New England, the Congregationalists tend to be urban—and suburban.[1] The Presbyterians are to be found in town and country, but register the urbanising trend. In 1945 five-sixths of the Roman Catholics lived in the cities.

As regards the social distribution of denominations, class stratification (under the euphemism of " income groups ") counts for more than the British public supposes, though democracy is a reality as you go west. It is a safe generalisation to state that Methodists, Baptists and Disciples are predominantly of the working class, allowing for rich, even cultured minorities, in their city churches. Episcopalians, conversely, are characteristically upper class, giving their church an influence out of all proportion to its numerical size[2] (it has also expanded as a result of Home Mission work). Congregationalism tends to be a kind of religious club of the upper middle class.[3] In spite of a high level of education, these circles have completely lost their old interest in theology, which has given place to Christian ethics. " It would be a mistake to suppose that a Congregational Church to-day is a body of deeply religious people ", admits a representative minister; " there are many who are quite uncertain what their religious convictions are, though quite willing that their clergy should believe more than they do themselves."[4] Shades of Increase and Cotton Mather!

The Second World War undoubtedly shook the sandy foundations of churches that stood for little more than human fellowship organised for good will. Divine worship was appreciated as something more than the Sunday section of a weekday programme that embraced bridge and basket-ball, dramatics, concerts and dancing. City congregations had to cut down expenditure on paid staff (some churches employed over a dozen paid persons). Institutions of marginal significance from a spiritual point of view were shaken, " as of things that are made, that those things which cannot be shaken may remain " (Hebrews 12.27). Adversity convinced countless Christians living on a superficial level of good fellowship

---

[1] In prosperous residential areas the Congregational Church is usually the nucleus of an undenominational " Community Church ", in which clubs for young married couples and other social activities flourish.

[2] One of the advantages of the Episcopal Church is the fact that whether you worship in Boston, Charleston, Indianapolis or San Francisco, you can count on the same liturgical service, the modifications being relatively slight; whereas in the " non-liturgical " churches there is likely to be considerable diversity even in the same denomination.

[3] Not " lower middle class " as in England. The Congregational ministers of city churches are usually outstanding men; it surprises no one in America to know their personal friends are Bishops and Deans.

[4] W. B. Thorpe, D.D., in the (English) *Congregational Quarterly* (Jan. 1939).

that the Gospel is " optimism whose foundations are laid in pessimism ". In 1946 the Methodist Church added one million communicants to her roll. An English observer, Bishop Stephen Neill, has singled out America as " the one part of the Western world where the church, so far from being on the decline, is increasing in strength and opportunity.[1] That seems to me to be by far the most important single fact in the world Christian situation at the present time " (1947).

In view of the American process of " the melting pot ", it may be asked: have heterogeneous sects, mostly of European origin, shown any tendency to fuse ? Has there been any diminution of sectarian divisions, any urge to form larger units ? We have seen that the American Revolution inaugurated an " era of good feeling ", followed by an era of sectional selfishness from about 1830 onwards; this corresponded to the revival of aggressive sectarianism.

When the denominational current was at its height in 1838, Dr. Samuel S. Schmucker, a broad-minded Lutheran, took the first step towards conciliation by publishing a noble " Overture ", pleading for Christian Unity.[2] Contemporary idolatry of Luther, Calvin and Knox reminded him of made party-cries of " Paul, Cephas and Apollos ". His own church, unfortunately, had already turned its back on his leadership, in its quest for isolation. Schmucker's ideals, however, were better appreciated by the other American Churches in the more spacious era that followed the Civil War. In 1866 Dr. James McCosh, of Belfast (afterwards President of Princeton), interested the United States in the " Evangelical Alliance ", which had been started twenty years earlier in England, to bind British and Continental Protestantism in a crusade against " Popery, Puseyism and Rationalism ". Its theological basis was too narrow for the younger generation, whose ecumenical ideals were better expressed by Professor Philip Schaff, a scholar of international reputation who had come from Switzerland to New York.

Strangely enough, it was the Episcopal Church (isolationist in

[1] The " trade journal ", *Church Management*, edited for many years at Cleveland, Ohio, by W. H. Leach, will give the British reader a good idea of a whole apparatus of publicity unfamiliar to him. Despite somewhat undue reliance on " business methods ", we may be grateful for American concern for the " outward business of the house of God " (Neh. 11.16).

[2] The " Apostolic Protestant Church " was to consist of Lutheran, Episcopal and Presbyterian " Branches ", with a common Confession of Faith and considerable autonomy for the constituent groups (cp. *Life and Times of S. S. Schmucker*, 1896).

trend since the Oxford Movement) that took the first step of pro-
posing a basis of Christian reunion. Their " Quadrilateral " of
1886 anticipated Lambeth in making definite suggestions. Agreement might be reached on four minimum points—acceptance of
the Bible, the Nicene Creed, the two Sacraments, and the historic
Episcopate " locally adapted ". As the dominant party in the
Episcopal Church stood fast by the High Anglican interpretation
of " Catholicism " and other Protestant Churches tended to under-
estimate the importance of " Faith and Order ", the " Quadrilateral " was somewhat premature. It served as a useful basis of
discussion and re-emerged as a live issue at the Lausanne Conference (1927), the most notable ecumenical gathering since the
Reformation. On this occasion two representative American
Churchmen sponsored the cause of Christian Unity, Bishop Brent
and Professor Adams Brown, a loyal Episcopalian and a loyal
Presbyterian.

American Christians became conscious of their part in Christendom partly through co-operation in Foreign Missions. In 1886
the Student Volunteer Missionary Movement was founded " for
the evangelisation of the world in this generation ". Missionary
enthusiasts at that time were usually Evangelical in a narrow,
individualistic sense. Then came Dr. John R. Mott, whose journey
round the world (1895-7) was marked by the planting of the
Student Christian Movement, which has fruitfully linked Missions
with the ideals of a World Church and World Peace. Since the
First World War the more liberal section of American Missionary
planners have applied the " Social Gospel " in an " activist "
sense. The " Laymen's Commission of Inquiry ", headed by Professor W. E. Hocking, the Harvard philosopher, considered that
the " failure of Christianity to dominate our economic and political
life " had " brought about widespread scepticism regarding the
value of our religious profession " (*Re-Thinking Missions*, 1932).
Critics of the Commission complained that undue emphasis had
been laid on the need for better social conditions and the means
of amelioration—with too little regard for the redemption of the
soul; the wheel had turned right round from other-worldly pietism
to sheer secularism.[1] This drastic change of emphasis can be
understood only in the light of American " dual " psychology.

[1] Some progressives were almost " honorary members " of non-Christian
religions.

The co-operation of different American Churches also held good in Home Missions. A striking instance of the team-spirit was the " Men and Religion Movement ". Its herald was a Wall Street banker, James G. Cannon—a very different kind of prophet from Peter the Hermit. Cannon called for a modern crusade—" a swift and ferocious attack on the Devil ", which he proceeded to organise " in ninety cities ". *Collier's Weekly* announced on 23rd December 1914 that religion was now " Going After Souls on a Business Basis ". The " Men and Religion Movement " was on the move, as the nations in Europe grappled in deadly conflict. The plan was to enlist all denominations and religious organisations in a gigantic network from the Atlantic to the Pacific—an all-out campaign to win people to the Christian message and the Christian way of life. One of the objectives, in particular, was " to find 3,000,000 men missing in participation in church life ". The movement was successful in showing millions that Jesus was relevant to their personal problems and aspirations. It registered an increased attendance in churches. A social, humanitarian note was sounded (hardly heard in the older evangelistic campaigns). " It went far toward creating a camaraderie between fathers and sons which has since been one of the more assuring aspects of American home life ". In this crusade, liberal and conservative, sacramentarian and Quaker marched side by side.

Then came America's participation in the First World War. Vast sums of money had been raised by War Loan and War Charity drives. The pugnacious instinct had won the support of Mammon. Croesus and Mars became comrades-in-arms. What about a Christian super-Crusade to rehabilitate the land when the War was won ? The " Inter-Church World Movement " was launched in the firm belief that the millions of ecclesiastically unattached citizens who had supported " war drives " could be counted on to rally to the holiest of causes. The promoters persuaded the bankers to underwrite their venture. Unfortunately they miscalculated the attitude of the public, who failed to respond to high-pressure salesmanship in the service of religion. Even in America publicity can be carried too far. The Inter-Church World Movement collapsed before it had got going, leaving a vast debt, due to the expense of preliminary " surveys " and office elaboration. The churches shouldered the debt, but gave no further encouragement to colossal crusades of this kind.

As far back as 1908 Dr. Charles F. Aked saw in a movement to
federate the Protestant Churches of the land " the greatest effort
of the Spirit of God poured out upon the peoples since the day of
Pentecost ". His hopes were realised to a much greater extent
than is usual with such spectacular pronouncements. As an English pastor who had thoroughly identified himself with the United
States since accepting a " call " to a large Baptist church, he had
known the value of " federation " at home; the " Free Church
Council " had given to English Nonconformity a common platform, on which to hold its own against the power and prestige of
the Established Church, as well as to issue programmes of social
reform. " United we stand, divided we fall." That was the moral.

In the United States a number of inter-denominational societies
had been formed during the nineteenth century—for the dissemi-
nation of the Bible, for Religious Education, Temperance, Missions
and other Christian causes. Many of these associations overlapped.
Would it not be possible to integrate their activities ? Negotiations
culminated in the foundation of " The Federal Council of the
Churches of Christ in America ". This new body reflected a
growing recognition of Theodore Roosevelt's[1] observation that
" there are plenty of targets to hit without firing into each other ".
Targets were accordingly set up—no less than " Fourteen Points "
—the number anticipating President Wilson's Peace programme.
The whole field of economic and social life was scheduled for
Christianisation. With American good sense, it was agreed that
theological differences must not be allowed to hold up the traffic.
As might be expected, the extreme right and left wings held aloof,
contenting themselves with a balcony view of the experiment.
The Roman Catholic Church, of course, abstained from participation. The Episcopalians did not accept full membership till 1940.[2]
The Lutherans, although not Episcopal in polity, demonstrated
their isolationist convictions by standing aside, but their most
progressive group has now contact with the Council. On the extreme left, Universalists and Unitarians were excluded. Nevertheless, twenty-eight denominations were affiliated to the Council.
One of the strong points of this Federal principle was its de-

[1] Theodore Roosevelt belonged to the Dutch Reformed Church (Franklin
D. Roosevelt was an Episcopalian).
[2] " Wishful thinking " underlies Theodore Wedel's *The Coming Great
Church* (1947). Converted from the Mennonite to the Episcopal Church, he
visualises an American Church on an Anglican basis.

centralisation. It was not simply an overhead, with pretentious offices and resolution-passing conferences. It was built up from below. It was represented by Councils of Churches in the cities, which were " going concerns " by 1920. Their activities ranged from bringing Christian influence to bear on municipal officials to softening racial tensions. They would persuade rabbis and priests to co-operate with them in public work; they would arrange united Lenten services, and negotiate the closing of shops on Good Friday. Annual " Go-to-Church " Sundays aimed at increasing the public appetite for religion through harnessing the gregarious instinct to the highest end. The Federal Council has taught the churches that " diversity need not mean divisiveness ", but the problem of Christian reunion it has not yet solved.

Sectionalism and sectarianism were the ruling passions in the United States during the nineteenth century. The devout practised " the perseverance of the saints "—which in sinners is called obstinacy. The domination of sectarian isolationism was maintained till the twentieth century. It yielded to a new " era of good feeling ". Two World Wars quickened the tendency towards integration. Dr. Schmucker, the ecumenical idealist born out of season, in an era of consequential sectarianism, would have rejoiced in quite a few marriages among the descendants of once-hostile denominations. These unions, however, have only been achieved after years of patient courtship. To quote Lowell's " Hosea Biglow ":

> Theory thinks Fact a pretty thing,
> An' wants the banns read right ensuin';
> But Fact wont nowise wear the ring
> 'Thout years o' settin' up and wooin'.

The outstanding unions have been marriages within the limits of what we may call the ecclesiastical clan or tribe. No set of people were so contentious and divisive as the Lutherans in America by the middle of the nineteenth century (see p. 218). At the slightest provocation they parted company. Even the oldest and largest Lutheran body, that avoided extremes, split in 1867 into " General Synod " and " General Council ", the latter breaking away in fear for their ark of the covenant, the Augsburg Confession. By 1918, however, hair-splitting distinctions no longer loomed so large, and these two bodies, along with a Southern Synod, merged to form " The United Lutheran Church ". It was an impressive way of celebrating the four-hundredth anniversary of the Reformation. The product was a compact denomination, organised on practically Presbyterian lines.

This union did not embrace the more orthodox Lutherans who had immigrated from Germany to the Middle West during the nineteenth century (the separate Synods of Buffalo, Ohio and Iowa). These more conservative groups, however, combined to form " The American Lutheran Conference " in 1930. Their membership is half a million, compared to the United Lutheran total of 1,709,000; it is distributed over a wider area in a decentralised administration. The " American Lutherans " did not succeed in persuading the " Missouri Synod " to join them. The latter is no longer confined to Missouri, but has spread all over the Middle and South West; indeed, it has churches in all but three States. Missouri is rigidly confessional in doctrine, emphatically congregational in polity and isolationist in policy. The paradoxical fact is, hard-shell exclusiveness and legalism have not prevented this sect from developing a most enterprising spirit. Their Concordia Publishing House is one of the best equipped in the United States; their theological seminary at St. Louis is the second largest of any denomination, and their membership has risen to over 1,320,000.

It will be seen that German Lutheranism is conservative on the right centre (United Lutherans Church); more conservative on the right (American Lutheran Church); and ultra-conservative on the extreme right (Missouri Synod). Is there no left wing? There is, but it is pitiably small compared to the strength of the right. The " Evangelical Church " represents the Prussian Union, Frederick William III's " merger " of 1817. Not many Prussian immigrants were drawn to this body, which found itself cold-shouldered by simon-pure Lutherans. " Evangelicals" have found that their affinities were with the German Reformed. They formed " The Evangelical and Reformed Church ", with a synodical constitution, a Liturgy and Hymnbook, and a membership of 660,000 (1934).[1] In the Prussian Union of 1817 the Reformed were swamped by the Lutherans: in America the Reformed element prevailed, but the " Evangelical Church " was numerically small.

Scandinavian Lutheranism, stiffly conservative in doctrine, mus-

[1] They now merge with a purely Anglo-Saxon body, the " Congregational-Christians ", to form " The United Church of Christ " (hardly that, surely!).

ters over a million members, and is organised as a federation of Swedish, Danish and Norwegian branches. In 1918 an over-all " National Council of Lutherans " was established to represent some five million communicants in relation to the State and to other Churches. The conservative contribution of Lutheranism to modern American Protestantism cannot be neglected. Its membership, equal to that of all the Presbyterians and Episcopalians combined, is not explained merely in terms of immigration waves;[1] orderly administration, reverent worship without sensationalism, emphasis on doctrinal instruction, from the Sunday School to the Ministry, and a definite, theological note in every pulpit—have all contributed to its widespread influence. It cannot continue to stand aloof indefinitely.

Among the Anglo-Saxon denominations unions have recently been achieved mainly among small groups such as the Unitarians and Universalists, the Congregationalists and the " Christians ". Local attempts to improvise " community churches " and " federated churches " in over-churched and under-populated rural districts have not been altogether successful; in cities they have even threatened to produce a new denomination, " leftish " in orientation and colouring (such as Dr. John Haynes Holmes' well-known Community Church, New York). The Methodist Episcopal Churches, North and South, separated for nearly a century by the long-settled slavery issue, blended in 1939 to form " The Methodist Church " (doubtless many Anglicans are relieved to note that they have dropped the " Episcopal " claim!). The Southern Baptists and Presbyterians, mostly militant " Fundamentalists ", show no signs of seeking to re-join their more liberal co-religionists in the North.

The formation in 1925 of the United Church of Canada out of Presbyterian, Methodist and Congregationalist elements, has given a fresh impetus to projects for merging Churches of divergent polity and tradition. The Congregationalists were foremost in making overtures to other denominations.[2] Recent negotiations in the United States propose to unite the Presbyterian and Episcopal Churches, the former to accept diocesan Episcopacy

---

[1] Only 7% of the Danes, 20% of the Swedes and under 30% of the Norwegians joined any church. See p. 269 f.

[2] The marriage of a German body in Pennsylvania to " New England " is a sign of the times. The Dutch Reformed are also negotiating with the " U.P.'s " (very orthodox, much smaller than the main Presbyterian Church). These unions, however delightful ecumenically, will not do much to reduce overlapping.

and the latter to adopt the eldership—a method of grafting illustrative of the pragmatic American mind. It is difficult to imagine how this could be accomplished except at the cost of a secession on each side—High Church Anglicans and conservative Presbyterians. Moving from the historic centralised churches to the more loosely organised denominations, we find that even here tradition has held up progress. In 1928 the Disciples of Christ, acting in accordance with the ideal of their founder, Alexander Campbell, held out an olive-branch to their Baptist cousins. In reply to this overture the Baptist Northern Convention demanded that they give up " Baptismal Regeneration " (an interpretation of believers' baptism by immersion that the Disciples certainly never held).

Denominationalism, with its vested interests and ancestral traditions, may hold up these plans of union for many years to come. Yet the United States, as a new country, looks to the future rather than to the past. Americans are out to create traditions as well as to inherit them.[1] They are less bound by precedent than Europeans. They gratefully accept the liturgies, the architecture, the devotional classics and the hymns of Christendom. They are increasingly conscious of their own limitations; in the spiritual sphere it is indeed hard to create even in a new world. Old World quietism must correct New World activism. At the same time the American Churches rightly cherish strong convictions as to the spiritual independence of the Church from State and hierarchy, the supreme value of the individual soul and the function of the layman as a Christian priest. " Depending, as did our fathers, upon the continued guidance of the Holy Spirit to lead us into all truth, we work and pray for the transformation of the world into the kingdom of God; and we look with faith for the triumph of righteousness and the life everlasting."[2]

> God of the prophets, bless the prophets' sons;
> Elijah's mantle o'er Elisha cast:
> Each age its solemn task may claim but once,
> Make each one nobler, stronger than the last.[3]

[1] The large number of students who receive practically undenominational religion in many colleges form a large nucleus for non-sectarian Christianity. They are allowed credit for Courses on English Bible, Church History etc.

[2] From the Affirmation adopted for general use by the Congregational Churches in the United States (1913).

[3] Rev. Denis Wortman's hymn composed for the Centenary of the Dutch Reformed Theological Seminary, New Brunswick, N.J.

BIBLIOGRAPHY

(Place of publication is London, if not otherwise stated)

SOCIAL BACKGROUND

The Pageant of America (Yale, *c.* 1926). A dozen volumes of illustrations, annotated by experts, inclusive in scope. L. A. Weigle's *American Idealism* covers religion, education and philanthropy.

Billington, R. A., and others, *The United States: American Democracy in World Perspective*, 1492-1947. Fully illustrated (New York, Reinhart, 1947).

A History of American Life (New York, Macmillan, *c.* 1930). Twelve volumes on Social History, some excellent, e.g. T. J. Wertenbaker's *The First Americans.*

Beard, C. and M., *The Rise of American Civilisation* (Cape, 1930).

Nevins, A. (ed.), *America through British Eyes* (Oxford, 1949). Travel Anthology.

Benét, S. V., *Western Star* (Oxford, 1944). A poet's interpretation.

Lord Bryce, *The American Commonwealth* (Macmillan, 1888, new ed. 1910). Vol. II covers social life and religion.

Cambridge History of American Literature (Cambridge, Eng., 1917-21).

Dictionary of American Biography, 21 vols. (Oxford, 1928-44).

Short reliable Histories of U.S.A. by C. Chesterton (Everyman), D. C. Somervell, D. W. Brogan, André Maurois.

GENERAL CHURCH HISTORY OF THE UNITED STATES

Sweet, W. W., *The Story of Religion in America* (New York, Harper, 1939); *Makers of Religion from John Cotton to Lyman Abbott* (New York, Holt, 1937).

Bacon, L. W., *A History of American Christianity* (Jas. Clarke, 1899).

Dorchester, *Christianity in the United States* (New York, Hunt & Eaton, 1889). History for the statistically-minded, replete with graphs and maps.

Mode, P. G., *Source-Book and Bibliographical Guide for American Church History* (Menasha, Wisconsin, 1921). Unfortunately out of print.

The New Schaff-Herzog Cyclopedia of Religious Knowledge (New York, Funk & Wagnalls, 1908-14).

DENOMINATIONAL HISTORIES

The " American Church History " series (New York, 1894-8) gives balanced treatment to all the Churches. Williston Walker's *Congregationalists* still important. Time has cast its shadow on this series, but A. H. Newman's *Baptist Churches* was revised (Philadelphia, 1915), also A. C. Thomas' *Friends in America* (5th ed., Boston, 1919).

OTHER STANDARD HISTORIES:

Perry, W. S., *The American Episcopal Church*, 1587-1883, 2 vols., (Boston, Houghton, Mifflin, 1885).

McConnell, S. D., *The American Episcopal Church* (New York, 1890; 10th ed., Mowbray, 1916).

Wentz, A. R., *The Lutheran Church in American History* (2nd ed., Philadelphia, United Lutheran Publications, 1933).

Atkins, G. G., & Fagley, F. L. *American Congregationalism* (Boston, Pilgrim Press, 1942).

Garrison, W. E., *Religion follows the Frontier . . . The Disciples of Christ* (New York, Harper, 1931).

Maynard, T., *The Story of American Catholicism* (Macmillan, 1941). An excellent R.C. History.

Many American Churches lack up-to-date histories. Popular books fill the gap; e.g. Luccock and Hutchinson, *Methodism in America* (Abingdon Press, 1926); Zenos, *Presbyterianism in America* (Nelson. 1937).

BOOKS I-IV

THE COLONIAL PERIOD

Doyle, J. A., *The English Colonies in America*. Standard survey by an impartial English scholar. Five vols. (Longmans, 1882-1907).

Wertenbaker, T. J., *The Old South* (New York, Scribners, 1942).

Sweet, W. W., *Religion in Colonial America* (New York, Scribners, 1942).

Weis, F. L., *Churches and Clergy of the Middle and Southern Colonies*, 1607-1776 (Lancaster, Mass., 1938).

Jones, Rufus M., *The Quakers in the American Colonies* (Macmillan, 1911).

Comfort, W. W., *William Penn, a Tercentenary Estimate* (Oxford, 1944). *Lives* of Penn, by J. W. Graham (1917), B. Dobree (1932), and C. E. Vulliamy (1933).

Brooks, G. S., *Friend Anthony Benezet* (Univ. of Pennsylvania Press, 1937).

Shore, W. T., *Life and Times of John Woolman* (Macmillan, 1913).

Baird, C. W., *The Huguenot Emigration to America* (New York, 1895).

Briggs, C. A., *American Presbyterianism: Its Origin, etc.* (T. & T. Clark, 1885).

Ford, H. J., *The Scotch-Irish in America* (New York, Princeton, 1915).

Thompson, E. T., article " Makemie ", *Dictionary of American Biography*.

Mann, W. J., *Life and Times of H. M. Muhlenberg* (Philadelphia, United Lutheran Publications, 1887-1911).

Sachse, J. F., *The German Pietists of Provincial Pennsylvania* (Philadelphia, 1895); *The German Sectarians of Pennsylvania* (Philadelphia 1899).

Faÿ, B., *Franklin, the Apostle of Modern Times* (Sampson Low, 1929).

Belden, A. D., *George Whitefield, the Awakener* (Sampson Low, *c.* 1930).

Maxson, C. H., *The Great Awakening in the Middle Colonies* (Chicago, 1920).

Gewehr, W. M., *The Great Awakening in Virginia*, 1740-90 (Duke University Press, 1930).

Ettinger, A. A., *General Oglethorpe* (Oxford, 1936).

Cobb, S. H., *The Rise of Religious Liberty in America* (Macmillan, 1902). Steps marking separation of Church and State.

McConnell, F. J., *Evangelicals, Revolutionists and Idealists* (Abingdon Press, 1942). Including Oglethorpe, Whitefield, Berkeley, Paine and other English contributors to American thought and action.

COLONIAL NEW ENGLAND

The Religious History of New England (Oxford, 1917). " King's Chapel Lectures " by authorities belonging to different denominations.

Fiske, J., *The Beginnings of New England* (Houghton, Mifflin, 1892).

Willison, G. F., *Saints and Strangers* (Heinemann, 1946). Best modern account of Pilgrim Fathers, by an American.

Chronicles of Pilgrim Fathers (Everyman); further source-material, ed. by E. Arber; *Story of Pilgrim Fathers* (1897).

Bradford, John, *Of Plimouth Plantation*, ed. W. C. Ford (1912); a modern tr. by V. Paget (Alston Rivers, 1909).

Winthrop, John, *History of New England* (1630-49), ed. J. K. Hosmer (New York, 1908).

Morison, S. E., *Builders of the Bay Colony* (Houghton, Mifflin, 1930).

Miller, Perry, *The New England Mind: The Seventeenth Century* (New York, Macmillan, 1939).

Earle, A. M., *The Sabbath in Puritan New England* (Hodder & Stoughton, 1892).

Scholes, P., *The Puritans and Music in England and New England* (Oxford, 1934).

Walker, Williston, *Ten New England Leaders* (New York, Silver, Burdett Co., 1901).

Burgess, W. H., *Life of John Robinson* (Williams & Norgate, 1920).
The "Makers of America" series (1891) includes reliable lives of
Higginson, Winthrop, Hooker and Cotton Mather; the last, by
Barrett Wendell, reprinted (Harvard and Oxford, 1926). A more criti-
cal life of Cotton Mather by R. P. and L. Boas (Harper, 1928). K. B.
Murdoch has portrayed *Increase Mather, the Foremost Puritan* (Cam-
bridge, Mass., Oxford, 1925). Recent lives of Roger Williams by
Easton (1930) and J. Ernst (1932); of Anne Hutchison, by H. Augur,
An American Jezebel (1930). Judith Welles' fine study of Cotton
awaits publication (Edinburgh, Ph.D. thesis). Ola E. Winslow's
Jonathan Edwards (Macmillan, 1940) is his best biography.

FROM INDEPENDENCE TO CIVIL WAR

Baldwin, M., *The New England Clergy and the American Revolution*
(Duke University Press, 1928).
Collins, V. L., *President Witherspoon: a Biography* (Princeton, 1925).
Lewis, J., *Francis Asbury, Bishop of the Methodist Episcopal Church*
(Epworth Press, 1927).
Beardsley, E. E., *Bishop Seabury* (Hodges, 1884).
Cuningham, C. E., *Timothy Dwight*, 1752-1817 (Macmillan & Co., 1942).
Beecher, Lyman, *Autobiography*, 2 vols. (London, 1865).
Lives of *Channing*, by J. W. Chadwick (Houghton, Mifflin, 1903);
Theodore Parker, by H. S. Commager (Boston, 1936); *Emerson*, by
Van W. Brooks (Dent 1934); *Bushnell*, by T. Munger (Jas. Clarke,
1899); *Leonard Bacon*, by T. D. Bacon (Yale, Oxford, 1931); *Bishop
Meade*, by P. Slaighter (3rd ed., Boston, 1885).
Biographies may be supplemented by studies of movements, e.g. J. F.
King's Ph.D. thesis on "Origins of American Unitarianism" (Edin-
burgh University); E. R. Hardie's essay on the High Church Revival
(*N. Catholicism*, ed. Harris, London, 1933); and W. E. Garrison's
Catholicism and the American Mind (Chicago, 1928).

THE FRONTIER, WEST AND SOUTH

Mode, P. G., *The Frontier Spirit in American Christianity* (Macmillan,
New York, 1923).
Sweet, W. W., *Religion on the Frontier* (New York, 1931-9). A monu-
mental collection of source-material on the Baptists, Methodists and
Presbyterians, etc., 1783-1850.
Latourette, K. S., *The Expansion of Christianity*, Vols. IV, V, VII.
Eggleston, E., *The Circuit Rider* (New York, 1874) and other Novels
for the flavour of the Frontier; also H. Garland's *A Son of the Middle
Border* (1917).
Wissler, C., *The American Indian* (3rd ed., New York, 1938).

Chase, Bishop Philander, *Reminiscences* (3rd ed., Boston, 1848).

Lives of *Judson*, by E. Judson (1883); *Mills*, by R. C. Richards (Boston, 1906); *Marcus Whitman*, by C. M. Drury (Caldwell, Idaho, 1937); *Sheldon Jackson* (New York, Revell, 1908).

McNally, J. H., *Religion and Slavery: A Vindication of the Southern Churches* (Nashville, Tenn., 1911).

Benét, S. V., *John Brown's Body* (Oxford, 1945). A stirring epic of the Civil War.

Wilson, Forrest, *Crusader in Crinoline: Harriet Beecher Stowe* (Hutchinson, 1942).

Washington, Booker, *Up from Slavery: an Autobiography* (1901).

Mays, B. E. and Nicholson, J. W., *The Negro's Church* (Institute of Social and Religious Research, 1933).

Mays, B. E., *The Negro's God* (Boston, Chapman & Grimes, 1939).

BOOK V

GENERAL

Garrison, W. E., *The March of Faith: Religion in America since 1865.* (New York, Harper, 1933).

Van Dusen, H. (ed.), *The Church through Half a Century* (New York, Scribners, 1936).

Smith, G. B. (ed.), *Religious Thought in the Last Quarter-Century* (Chicago Univ. Press, 1927).

Atkins, G. G., *Religion in our Times* (New York, Round Table Press, 1932).

Sperry, W. L., *Religion in America* (Cambridge, 1945). A contemporary guide for British readers.

THE " SOCIAL GOSPEL "

Parrington, V. L., Jr., *American Dreams ... Utopias* (Providence, 1948).

Hopkins, C. H., *The Rise of the Social Gospel in American Protestantism, 1865-1915* (Yale, 1940).

Hughley, J. N., *Trends in Protestant Social Idealism* (New York, King's Crown Press, 1948). Social Gospel and Neo-orthodoxy Conflict.

Abell, A. I., *The Urban Impact on American Protestantism, 1865-1900* (Harvard, 1943).

For the " Gilded Age ", see Mark Twain's *Innocents Abroad*, Howells' *Silas Lapham*, etc.; also Lewis Mumford's interpretations, *The Golden Age*, etc.

FROM REVIVALISM TO "RELIGIOUS EDUCATION"

Sweet, W. W., *Revivalism in America: Its Origin, Growth and Decline* (New York, Scribners, 1944).

Lives of *D. L. Moody* by Gamaliel Bradford (New York, 1927) and W. R. Moody (New York, 1930); Sir G. A. Smith's *Henry Drummond* (1899).

Clark, E. T., *The Small Sect in America* (Cokesbury Press, 1937).

Atkins, G. G., *Modern Religious Cults* (New York, Revell, 1923).

Ferguson, C. W., *The Confusion of Tongues* (Heinemann, 1929). Noted by Foakes-Jackson as a fascinating introduction to " Wild Religions " of U.S.A.

Ferguson, E. M., *Historic Chapters in Christian Education in America* (New York, Revell, 1935).

Soares, Theodore, *Religious Education* (Chicago Univ. Press, 1928). Classic exposition of a movement characteristically American.

RELIGION IN HUMAN EXPERIENCE

Schneider, H. W., *A History of American Philosophy* (New York, Columbia Univ. Press, 1946). Views American theology in perspective.

Buckham, J. W., *Progressive Religious Thought in America* (Boston, Pilgrim Press, 1919). Biographical treatment, New England in foreground.

Cole, S. G., *History of Fundamentalism* (New York, Richard R. Smith, 1931). Essentially fair. On the conservative side, F. L. Patton fulminated *Fundamental Christianity*, following Gresham Machen in *Christianity and Liberalism* (1923). This provoked modernist rejoinders from Leighton Parks, Episcopalian (1924); Shailer Mathews, Baptist (1924); and W. P. Merrill, Presbyterian (1925).

An interesting by-product of theological strife is autobiography. Thus, H. Preserved Smith, unfrocked by the Presbyterians in 1894, penned *The Heretic's Defence* (Scribners, 1926). Prof. H. G. T. Mitchell, who had antagonised Methodist orthodoxy, recalled his experiences *For the Benefit of my Creditors* (Boston, Beacon Press, 1922). Dr. G. A. Gordon traced the advance of liberalism in *My Education and Religion* (Allen & Unwin, 1920). Dr. Lyman Abbott published his *Reminiscences* (Houghton, Mifflin, 1915), and Bishop Lawrence looked back *Fifty Years* (S.C.M., 1924).

Bishop McConnell was biographer of Borden P. Bowne, one of the few philosopher-theologians (1929). In Britain D. R. Davies has hailed *Reinhold Niebuhr, Prophet from America* (1945). Lyman Abbott chronicled the life of his colleague in Plymouth Pulpit, *Henry Ward*

Beecher (1903). Lyman Beecher Stowe surveyed his own numerous tribe of preachers in *Saints, Sinners and Beechers* (Nicholson & Watson, 1935). The greatest preacher's biography is surely A. V. G. Allen's *Phillips Brooks* (New York, Dutton, 1907, 1923). A. S. Hoyte sketched *The Pulpit and American Life* (1921) in historic perspective. E. T. Thompson noted *Changing Emphases in American Preaching* (Philadelphia, Presbyterian Publications, 1945)—from Bushnell till to-day.

WORSHIP AND ITS SETTING

Rines, E. F., *Old Historic Churches of America* (New York, Macmillan, 1934). Reliable survey of " historic shrines " of all denominations·

Drummond, A. L., *The Church Architecture of Protestantism* (T. & T. Clark, Scribners, 1934). Deals largely with America, from Colonial era to neo-Gothic. Full bibliography, including worship.

Coffin, H. S., *The Public Worship of God* (Philadelphia, Westminster Press, 1947; Independent Press, London). Good American bibliography.

Benson, L. F., *The English Hymn* (New York, 1912). Full account of American Praise in evolution from metrical psalmody.

Foote, H. W., *Three Centuries of American Hymnody* (Harvard, 1940).

FINAL ESTIMATE

Zollman, C., *American Church Law* (St. Paul, Minn., 1933).

Bass, A. B., *Protestantism in the United States* (New York, 1929).

Fry, C. L., *The United States looks at its Churches* (Institute of Social and Religious Research, 1930).

Douglas, H. P., *Church Unity Movements in the United States* (I.S.R.R., 1934).

McNeill, J. T., *Unitive Protestantism* (Chicago, Abingdon Press, 1930).

INDEX

Abbott, Lyman, 341, 362 ff., 376
Adventism, Second, 259 ff.
American Constitution and religion, 158 ff.
Andros, Governor, 10, 94 f.
Arianism, 46, 184 f.
Arminianism, 46, 128, 151, 184 f., 236, 250
Asbury, Bishop, 134 f., 150 ff., 237 f., 240
Atheism, 91, 158 f., 172 f., 332 ff.

Baptism, 3, 67, 84, 100, 107, 167, 208, 241, 243, 245, 263, 326 f., 405
Baptists, 66-70, 73, 122 f., 128 f., 131, 136, 140, 143 f., 147 f., 236, 241, 243 f., 268 f., 283 f., 292 f., 297 ff., 381 f., 396 f.
Beecher, Henry Ward, 205, 249 n., 292 f., 295 n., 311, 359-63, 388
Beecher, Lyman, 201-5, 214, 371
Beecher, Thomas K., 312, 322, 375
Berkeley, Bishop, 129 f., 137 n., 274
Bible Translation, 245, 277, 343 ff.
Biblical Criticism, 173, 198, 213, 245 f. 254, 342-6, 349 ff.
Bishops and the American Colonies, 6, 8 f., 15 f., 22, 43, 49 f., 102 f., 137 f., 149-57
Blair, "Commissary" James, 8-11, 15, 132
Bradford, Governor John, 49-52, 90
Brainerd, David, 278 f.
Brewster, Elder William, 5, 48-52
Brooks, Phillips, 227, 366 f., 378
Bryan, W. J., 353 f.
Bryce, Lord, 159 f., 366, 395
Buchman, Frank, 331 f.
Bushnell, Horace, 129, 207-10, 235, 336 ff.
Business and Religion, 4, 9 f., 13 f., 18 f., 22 f., 25, 27 ff., 34 f., 39 f., 44 f., 49-54, 79 f., 90 ff., 100 ff., 116 f., 263-6, 269, 277, 280 f., 286-93, 306-19, 394 ff.

Calvinism, 46, 58, 61, 75 ff., 81, 108 ff., 123-7, 142 n., 173 ff., 179-86, 236, 250 ff., 343, 347 ff.
Cambridge, England, 59, 79, 146 n., 183
"Cambridge Platform", 63, 104 n.
Campbell, Alexander, 242-7, 284
Cartwright, Peter, 238-41
Catholics, Roman, 13-16, 136 f., 143, 148, 153, 228-32, 275 f., 297 f.
"Cavalier" Party, 7 f., 10 f., 90-3, 156 n., 309
Channing, W. E., 190-3
Charles I, 7, 13
Charles II, 8, 17, 26, 69, 93 f.
Christian Year, 77, 90, 93, 159, 164, 362, 392 f.
Church Architecture, 3, 10, 12, 19, 29, 52, 82 f., 167-71, 222 f., 375-83
Church Halls, 311 f., 319, 322, 335, 378, 381 ff., 395
Church Music, 88 ff., 161-5, 223, 245, 324 f., 379 f., 384, 386-93
Church of England, 3-20, 23, 30 f., 42 ff., 55 ff., 90-5, 102 f., 106, 118, 129, 131 f., 136-41
Church of Scotland, 44 ff., 124, 127, 149 250
Church Unity, 211-6, 218, 226 ff., 231, 243 f., 248-56, 398-405
Coke, D. Thomas, 149 ff. 279
Communion rites, The, 3, 12, 83, 85, 100, 139, 151, 166, 194, 218, 223 ff., 242, 246 f., 292, 376, 383 f.,
Contacts with America, *Continental*, see Lutheranism, Mennonites, Reformed Church.
Contacts with America, *English*, 49 f., 70, 80 f., 115-22, 125 ff., 129 f., 137 f., 149-55, 185, 220 f., 257, 267 f., 279, 292 f., 299 f., 320 n., 321 n, 325 ff., 331 f., 340, 342 n., 343 f., 358 f., 366, 370
Contacts with America, *Irish*, 44 ff., 118, 130, 133 f, 141, 143, 229 f., 242-5, 248, 347.